ANCIENT WOMEN PHILOSOPHERS

Despite the common misconception that ancient philosophy was the domain of male thinkers, sources confirm that women engaged in philosophical activity in antiquity. Bringing together a collection of essays on ancient women thinkers, with special focus on their ideas and contributions to the history of philosophy, this volume is about the earliest women philosophers, their breakthroughs, and the methods we can use to excavate them. The essays survey the methodological strategies to approach the surviving evidence, retrieve the largely unresearched thought and the original ideas of ancient women philosophers, and carve out a space for them in the canon. The broad focus includes women thinkers in ancient Indian, Chinese, and Arabic philosophy as well as in the Greek and Roman philosophical traditions. The volume will be valuable for a wide range of researchers, teachers, and students of ancient philosophy.

KATHARINE R. O'REILLY is Assistant Professor of Philosophy at Toronto Metropolitan University. Her research areas include moral psychology in the Ancient Greek and Roman traditions and ancient women philosophers, particularly in the Hellenistic schools.

CATERINA PELLÒ is a Research Fellow at the University of Geneva (SNSF Ambizione). She has published *Pythagorean Women* (2022) in the series Cambridge Elements on Women in the History of Philosophy.

ANCIENT WOMEN PHILOSOPHERS

Recovered Ideas and New Perspectives

EDITED BY

KATHARINE R. O'REILLY
Toronto Metropolitan University

CATERINA PELLÒ
University of Geneva

Shaftesbury Road, Cambridge CB2 8EA, United Kingdom

One Liberty Plaza, 20th Floor, New York, NY 10006, USA

477 Williamstown Road, Port Melbourne, VIC 3207, Australia

314–321, 3rd Floor, Plot 3, Splendor Forum, Jasola District Centre, New Delhi – 110025, India

103 Penang Road, #05–06/07, Visioncrest Commercial, Singapore 238467

Cambridge University Press is part of Cambridge University Press & Assessment,
a department of the University of Cambridge.

We share the University's mission to contribute to society through the pursuit of
education, learning and research at the highest international levels of excellence.

www.cambridge.org
Information on this title: www.cambridge.org/9781009013895

DOI: 10.1017/981009028769

© Cambridge University Press & Assessment 2023

This publication is in copyright. Subject to statutory exception and to the provisions
of relevant collective licensing agreements, no reproduction of any part may take
place without the written permission of Cambridge University Press & Assessment.

First published 2023
First paperback edition 2025

A catalogue record for this publication is available from the British Library

ISBN 978-1-316-51618-8 Hardback
ISBN 978-1-009-01389-5 Paperback

Cambridge University Press & Assessment has no responsibility for the persistence
or accuracy of URLs for external or third-party internet websites referred to in this
publication and does not guarantee that any content on such websites is, or will
remain, accurate or appropriate.

For our sons, Filippo and Jack.

Contents

List of Contributors		*page* ix
Acknowledgements		xi
List of Abbreviations		xii

	Introduction: The Value of Women Philosophers for the History of Philosophy Caterina Pellò and Katharine R. O'Reilly	1
1	Beyond Gender: The Voice of Diotima Frisbee C. C. Sheffield	21
2	Sulabhā and Indian Philosophy: Rhetoric, Gender, and Freedom in the *Mahābhārata* Brian Black	38
3	Women's Medical Knowledge in Antiquity: Beyond Midwifery Sophia M. Connell	57
4	Ancient Women Epicureans and Their Anti-Hedonist Critics Kelly Arenson	77
5	Arete of Cyrene and the Role of Women in Philosophical Lineage Katharine R. O'Reilly	96
6	Women at the Crossroads: Life and Death for the Stoic Wife Kate Meng Brassel	114
7	Pythagorean Women and the Domestic as a Philosophical Topic Rosemary Twomey	134

8 Perictione, Mother of Metaphysics: A New Philosophical
   Reading of *On Wisdom*   152
   Giulia De Cesaris and Caterina Pellò

9 Not Veiled in Silence: The Case for Macrina   170
   Anna B. Christensen

10 Women Philosophers and Ideals of Being a Woman
   in Neoplatonic Schools of Late Antiquity: The Examples
   of Sosipatra of Ephesus and Hypatia of Alexandria   190
   Jana Schultz

11 Reappraising Ban Zhao: The Advent of Chinese
   Women Philosophers   209
   Ann A. Pang-White

12 The Reception of Plato on Women: Proclus,
   Averroes, Marinella   228
   Peter Adamson

References   247
Index   269

Contributors

PETER ADAMSON, Professor of Late Ancient and Arabic Philosophy, the Ludwig Maximilian University of Munich

KELLY ARENSON, Associate Professor of Philosophy, Duquesne University

BRIAN BLACK, Senior Lecturer in Politics, Philosophy and Religion, Lancaster University

KATE MENG BRASSEL, Visiting Assistant Professor of Classical Studies, University of Pennsylvania

GIULIA DE CESARIS, FWO Postdoctoral Fellow, KU Leuven, De Wulf-Mansion Centre for Ancient, Medieval and Renaissance Philosophy

ANNA B. CHRISTENSEN, Assistant Professor of Philosophy, Central College

SOPHIA M. CONNELL, Senior Lecturer in Philosophy, Birkbeck College, University of London

KATHARINE R. O'REILLY, Assistant Professor of Philosophy, Toronto Metropolitan University, and Visiting Research Fellow in Philosophy, King's College London

ANN A. PANG-WHITE, Professor of Philosophy and Director of Asian Studies, University of Scranton

CATERINA PELLÒ, Research Fellow at the University of Geneva (SNSF Ambizione)

JANA SCHULTZ, Postdoctoral Researcher, Humboldt University Berlin

FRISBEE C. C. SHEFFIELD, Associate Professor of Classics, University of Cambridge

ROSEMARY TWOMEY, Assistant Professor of Philosophy, Queens College, City University of New York

Acknowledgements

We are grateful for the support of the Footnotes Writing Circle, Lea Cantor, Alesia Preite, Joachim Aufderheide, Gábor Betegh, Brian Black, Sophia Connell, Voula Tsouna, M. M. McCabe, Ursula Coope, Charis Jo, Diane Enns and the Society for Women of Ideas, Robert Murray, Hilary Gaskin at Cambridge University Press, and Louise Chapman at Lex Academic. We would also like to thank Thornton Lockwood, Sandra Wawrytko, Laura Viidebaum, Nonnie Suso, the participants at the Women Intellectuals in Antiquity Symposium, and the contributors to this volume. We are especially grateful to Peter Adamson for his encouragement of this project from its inception. The project was supported by the British Society for the History of Philosophy, King's College London, the University of St Andrews, the Office of the Dean of Arts at Toronto Metropolitan University, University College London, the University of Nottingham, and the Harvard Center for Hellenic Studies.

Abbreviations

Aristotle (Ar.)
Apo.	Posterior Analytics
Apr.	Prior Analytics
Cael.	On the Heavens
EE	Eudemian Ethics
EN	Nicomachean Ethics
GA	Generation of Animals
HA	History of Animals
MA	On the Motion of Animals
Met	Metaphysics
Mete.	Meteorology
PA	Parts of Animals
Phys.	Physics
Protr.	Protrepticus
Resp.	On Respiration
Sens.	On Sense and Sensibles
Top.	Topics

Damascius
In Parm.	On Plato's Parmenides
In Phd.	On Plato's Phaedrus
Isid.	Life of Isidorus
Procl.	Life of Proclus

Epicurus
Ad Men.	Letter to Menoeceus
Diss.	Diatribes
VS	Vatican Sayings

Gregory of Nyssa
De An. et Res.	*On Soul and Resurrection*
Ep. 19	*Letter 19*
VSM	*Life of Saint Macrina*

Hippocrates (Hp.)
Carn.	*On Fleshes*
Decent.	*On Good Manners*
Dieb. Judic.	*On Critical Days*
Ep.	*Epidemics*
Foet. Exsect.	*On the Excision of the Foetus*
Genit.	*On Generation*
Loc. Hom.	*On the Places in Man*
Mul.	*On the Diseases of Women*
Nat. Mul.	*On the Nature of Women*
Nat. Puer.	*On the Nature of the Child*
Oct.	*On the Eight-Month Child*
Praec.	*On Preconceptions*
Steril.	*On Sterile Women*
Superf.	*On Superfetation*
VM	*On Ancient Medicine*

Iamblichus (Iamb.)
DCMS	*On the Common Mathematical Science*
De Myst.	*On the Mysteries*
Protr.	*Exhortation to Philosophy*
Theolog. Arithm.	*Theological Principles of Arithmetic*
VP	*Life of Pythagoras*

Plato (Pl.)
Grg.	*Gorgias*
Leges	*Laws*
Men.	*Meno*
Parm.	*Parmenides*
Phd.	*Phaedo*
Phdr.	*Phaedrus*
Phil.	*Philebus*

Pol.	Statesman
Prt.	Protagoras
Rep.	Republic
Symp.	Symposium
Th.	Theaetetus
Tim.	Timaeus

Plutarch (Plu.)

Mor.	Moralia
Non Posse	That Epicurus Actually Makes a Pleasant Life Impossible

Porphyry (Porph.)

Marc.	Letter to Marcella
VP	Life of Pythagoras

Proclus (Procl.)

In Alc.	On Plato's Alcibiades
In Cra.	On Plato's Cratylus
In Phil.	On Plato's Philebus
In Rep.	On Plato's Republic
In Tim.	On Plato's Timaeus
Inst.	Elements of Theology
Theol. Plat.	Platonic Theology

Ps-Archytas (Ps-Arch.)

De Vir. Bon.	On the Good and Happy Man
Intell.	On the Intellect and Sense Perception
Univ. Log.	On the Universal Logos
Wisdom	On Wisdom

Seneca

Aga.	Agamemnon
Ben.	On Benefits
Const.	On the Firmness of the Wise Person
Ep.	Moral Epistles
Helv.	On Consolation to Helvia
HF	The Mad Hercules

Ira	*On Anger*
Marc.	*On Consolation to Marcia*
Tro.	*The Trojan Women*

Synesius
Ad Pae.	*On an Astrolabe*
Ep.	*Epistles*

Other authors
Alcin. *Didask.*	Alcinous, *The Handbook of Plato*
Cic. *Off.*	Cicero, *On Obligations*
Clem. *Strom.*	Clement of Alexandria, *Stromata*
Cod. Vat. Gr.	The Codex Vaticanus
D.L.	Diogenes Laertius, *Lives of Eminent Philosophers*
Ecph. *De Regn.*	Ecphantus, *On Kingship*
Eur. *Her.*	Euripides, *Heracles*
Euryph. *Life*	Euryphamus, *Concerning Human Life*
Eus. *PE*	Eusebius, *Preparation for the Gospel*
Gnom. Vat.	Gnomologium Vaticanum e Codice Vaticano Graeco 743
Hippol. *Ref.*	Hippolytus, *Refutation of All Heresies*
Jer. *Adv. Iovin*	Jerome, *Against Iovianus*
Liv. *AUC*	Livy, *Ab Urbe Condita*
Olymp. *In Alcib.*	Olympiodorus, *On Plato's First Alcibiades*
Origen *Cels.*	*Against Celsus*
Perict. *Harm. Wom.*	Perictione, *On the Harmonious Woman*
Phint. *Moderation*	Phintys, *On the Moderation of Women*
Phot. *Bibl.*	Photius, *Bibliotheca*
Plin. *Ep.*	Pliny, *Epistles*
Plotinus, *Enn.*	*Ennead*
S.E. *PH*	Sextus Empiricus, *Outlines of Pyrrhonism*
SSR	*Socratis et Socraticorum Reliquiae*
Stob. *Flor.*	Stobaeus, *Florilegium*
Strab. *Geog.*	Strabo, *Geography*
SVF	*Stoicorum Veterum Fragmenta*
Tac. *Ann.*	Tacitus, *Annals*
Theag. *Virt.*	Theages, *On the Virtues*
Xen. *Mem.*	Xenophon, *Memorabilia*

Introduction
The Value of Women Philosophers for the History of Philosophy*

Caterina Pellò and Katharine R. O'Reilly

Including Women in the Picture

Thales of Miletus is commonly taken to be the first philosopher to write in Greek: Aristotle, for example, introduces him as the first ancient thinker to dedicate himself to natural philosophy (*Met.* 983b18).[1] Rarely is it acknowledged that Thales was a close acquaintance of Cleobulina, herself a philosopher, known for authoring riddles.[2] Cleobulina is one of the figures who prompted us to work on this volume: ancient female thinkers whose breakthroughs and contributions have long been left out of the history of philosophy.

Our sources suggest that in antiquity there were women engaging in philosophical activity alongside men. However, with the only – and very contested – exceptions of the Pythagorean women from the first century BCE and the Confucian writer Ban Zhao in the second century CE, almost no direct evidence and no writings by these thinkers have survived. We are left with a list of names and sparse information about these women's lives and intellectual activities, all of which has been written by men. As a result, the ideas of female ancient philosophers remain unrecorded and untaught.

This book is about ancient women philosophers, their ideas and contributions to the history of philosophy, and the methods we use to retrieve and re-evaluate them. In what follows, we outline the objectives and key questions of the volume. We devote a substantial section to the specific challenges in the study of ancient women philosophers, with special focus on source issues. We also discuss the methods our contributors have

---

* Our title is an homage to Antognazza (2015). We dedicate this chapter to her memory.
[1] See Cantor (2022) for an important troubling of the assumption that the Ancient Greeks shared this view.
[2] D.L. 1.22. Diogenes writes that Cleobulina was given an education (1.91). Plutarch lists her among the most prominent women thinkers of antiquity (*Mor.* 145e – see also Clem. *Strom.* 4.19.122–23) and writes that Thales admired her wisdom (*Mor.* 148d). For recent work on Cleobulina's riddles, see Plant (2004: 29–32), Hueso (chapter 3) and Potamiti (chapter 4) in Chouinard et al. (2021: 31–60).

adopted to face the challenges and approach these thinkers philosophically. We argue that the study of ancient women philosophers has a special value for our understanding of the history of philosophy. While at first a daunting enterprise, work on this unique set of thinkers and the available evidence both enriches our insight into the methodology of the history of philosophy and re-introduces philosophical contributions that would otherwise be lost.

This Book: Rationale, Scope, and Objectives

We start by asking three questions to problematise the very title of this volume. The book is about a broad range of thinkers, who lived at different times and in different places, and discussed a wide variety of topics. They share three features: they are women, philosophers, from antiquity. Each of these features, however, raises further questions.

The first question is whether it matters that these thinkers are women and, if so, why. Should we be interested in these figures *insofar as they are women*? Do we ever think of Plato and Aristotle as *men* doing philosophy? Our answer is yes, it matters, to some extent. Our aim is not to argue that in ancient philosophy we come across female-specific ways of thinking, sets of issues, or approaches and solutions to puzzles. This book makes no essentialist claims about women's ways of reasoning and doing philosophy. On the one hand, then, the answer to the question of whether it matters that these philosophers are women is no. While some women philosophers, such as the authors of the Pythagorean letters and Ban Zhao, write about topics traditionally associated with the female gender, such as motherhood and married life, this book shows that ancient female thinkers discussed a much wider range of questions, from home economics to rhetoric; from ethical theories about pleasure, the self, and renunciation to theoretical doctrines about the structure of the cosmos and the knowledge of first principles; and from gynaecology to the fate of the soul at death.

There is, however, at least one reason why it *does*, and should, matter that these thinkers are women. One of the aims of this volume is 'reparatory': we redress a historical wrong and reclaim a place in the history of philosophy and the philosophical canon for those thinkers who have not received enough academic attention. The reasons for this exclusion range from the lack of primary sources to the fragmentary and dubious nature of the available evidence. Yet we suspect that at least part of the reason why women thinkers have been overlooked is because they were women. For example, insofar as in their own time women had a less direct access to philosophical practice or because some of them discussed female-coded topics, which modern scholars did not consider worthy of philosophical investigation. Since these figures were partly disregarded *because they were women*, it is partly *as women* that we now propose to reintroduce them in the scholarship.

That said, we are primarily interested in these female intellectuals *insofar as they are philosophers* and had philosophical ideas. This leads us to our second, more challenging, question: what does it mean for a woman, or for any ancient thinker, to be a philosopher?

Scholars have proposed various criteria to decide which ancient female intellectuals should be classified as philosophers: women are called philosophers (i) when they are referred to as such in the sources,[3] (ii) when they author philosophical texts,[4] (iii) when they live with and study under other (male) philosophers,[5] and (iv) when they have philosophical ideas.[6] For the purpose of this book, we are interested in *philosophical ideas*. Specifically, we focus on women philosophers either insofar as they contribute original arguments to ancient philosophical debates or because the study of these thinkers offers new perspectives to the understanding of our philosophical history. As detailed in the next section, most of the existing studies on women philosophers focus on their lives. In a sense, therefore, our volume aims to give a philosophical, rather than historical and biographical account of these figures and their intellectual contributions.[7]

---

[3] This criterion is discussed by Waithe (2015). For a recent overview of the criteria for women philosophers, See Bonelli (chapter 1) and O'Reilly (chapter 2) in Chouinard et al. (2021: 3–30).

[4] This criterion is especially strict, for male thinkers such as Pythagoras and Socrates are commonly referred to as philosophers and nonetheless did not leave any written works. The criterion is used by Waithe (1987b), who lists sixty-five women philosophers from Greece and Rome, and Snyder (1989), who lists only eight women writers.

[5] The first to divide women by philosophical schools is Gilles Ménage in his *Historia Mulierum Philosopharum* (1894).

[6] For a more inclusive list of criteria, see Warren (2009: 4). For a discussion of the issues each criterion raises, see Pellò in Bonelli (2020: 55–78).

[7] It should be noted that these approaches are not always at odds with each other, for certain traditions conceive of philosophy as a way of living. On how the historical milieu in which a philosopher lived sheds light on their arguments, see Hutton (2019). This is discussed further in the 'Biographical Focus' section. We also want to clarify that we do not view these other approaches as less valuable. While our focus is recovery of the philosophical ideas and novel contributions of women philosophers, we recognise that the importance of their place in the history of philosophy extends well beyond ideas and their novelty.

Finally, one may ask, which period counts as *ancient* in the history of philosophy?

Another limit of the existing literature on *ancient* women philosophers is that it is focused on *ancient Greek and Roman* women. As such, current scholarship risks promoting the narrative according to which philosophy was first invented by the Greeks in the sixth century BCE with thinkers like Thales. This raises several difficulties: first, there is evidence that philosophy was not an exclusively Greek phenomenon and that the Greeks themselves acknowledged the influence of other philosophical traditions.[8] Second, in the case of female thinkers, the argument that philosophy was invented by the Greeks seems less relevant, as most of these figures are not described as philosophers in the sources.[9] Third, it is unclear how one might draw boundaries between what counted as Greek or Western in antiquity and what did not, especially when we consider figures such as Hypatia of Alexandria, who lived in Egypt but wrote in Greek. Not all studies are as Eurocentric: Buxton and Whiting's recent book *Philosopher Queens* (2020) includes women thinkers like Ban Zhao and Lalla, and Waithe and Boos Dykeman are currently working on a volume on women philosophers outside the Greek, Roman, and Judaeo-Christian tradition. Finally, more work on non-Western women thinkers has been done by scholars of Indian and Chinese philosophy, but this work has been largely ignored in Hellenic studies.[10] By bringing women philosophers from the ancient philosophical traditions in India and China into dialogue with those of ancient Greece and Rome, our book aims to contribute to the ongoing work of decentring ancient philosophy.

As a result, the volume comprises women from various philosophical traditions. Different traditions, however, have different periodisation and different ways to date antiquity. We cover women who count as 'ancient' within their culture and consistent with the categories operative within those traditions. For example, ancient Greek and Roman philosophy is dated approximately between the Archaic Age in the sixth century BCE and the spread of Christianity in the fifth century CE. Yet Indian philosophy

---

[8] On the Eastern influence on Greek philosophy, see, for example, West (1971); Burkert (1992); and Whitmarsh and Thomson (2013). Challenging the Western philosophy narrative and the belief in the Greek invention of philosophy are Lloyd (2005); Park (2013); and Allais (2016), as well as a forthcoming volume by Lea Cantor and Josh Platzky Miller.

[9] It is not entirely irrelevant, of course, since Ancient Greeks had a concept of 'philosophy', and female thinkers were understood to occupy a position relative to this. But the disciplinary lines are blurred, in ways we discuss in the 'Job Title and Genre' section.

[10] On women in ancient Indian philosophy, see, for example, Brodbeck and Black (2007). For Confucianism, see Mann and Cheng (2001) and Lui et al. (2013).

begins around the eighth century BCE with the composition of some of the earliest philosophical texts from antiquity – namely, the Upanishads – and Chinese philosophy extends into the fifth century CE.[11]

Status Quaestionis: Previous Scholarship from Ménage to the Philosopher Queens

The attempt to include women thinkers in the history of philosophy is not unprecedented. In recent years, the scholarship on women philosophers has been expanding and attracting growing academic attention. The initial trend has been to recount the lives of women philosophers – to *name, date,* and *place* ancient female thinkers. This was an essential first step, which laid the foundations for current work on women philosophers and enabled researchers to go beyond biography and engage with these thinkers' philosophical ideas. We should then start by recognising our debt of gratitude to those scholars who first raised the questions of what role women played in the history of philosophy and why their voices had mostly been silenced, and by so doing, put ancient women philosophers on the academic agenda.

In Europe, modern engagement with ancient women philosophers starts in 1690s France with the publication of *Historia Mulierum Philosopharum* by Ménage. After reading Diogenes Laertius' *Lives of Eminent Philosophers*, Ménage compiled his own philosophical history focused on women philosophers to challenge the assumption that there had been none up to the early modern period. The result is a list of sixty-five names, divided by schools: Platonists, Academics, Cyrenaics, Cynics, Peripatetics, Stoics, and Pythagoreans. The focus is exclusively on women philosophers from Greece and Rome.

Recent scholarship on ancient women philosophers can be grouped according to two trends: scholars interested in what philosophers said about women and scholars who focus on ancient women who were themselves philosophers, but who primarily give biographical accounts of these thinkers.

More attention has been given to ancient philosophical theories *about*, rather than *by*, women, and concerning gender, family life, and the female role in society: notable examples are Tuana's *Feminist Interpretations of Plato* (1994), Freeland's *Feminist Interpretations of Aristotle* (1998), Pang-White's *Handbook of Chinese Philosophy and Gender* (2016), and Howard's

---

[11] For a timeline of ancient Indian and Chinese philosophy, see Harrison (2012: Appendix 1).

Handbook of Indian Philosophy and Gender (2019).[12] The advantage of these studies is showing that ancient thinkers considered women and other topics traditionally linked to the female gender, such as home economics, to be philosophically valuable. Yet this approach leaves the canon itself unaltered. Our aim is to include women philosophers in the philosophical canon *alongside* Plato, Aristotle, Buddha, and Confucius.

In 1987, Waithe published her *History of Women Philosophers*. The first volume of this anthology, *Ancient Women Philosophers 600 BC–500 AD*, focuses on Greek and Roman philosophers. Waithe's approach is optimistic and charitable. Despite the several and challenging source issues we discuss in the next section, she argues that the available evidence shows that through history there have always been women doing philosophy. After Waithe's epoch-making anthology, scholars turned their attention to women philosophers. Further examples are Kersey's *Women Philosophers* (1989) and Warren's *Unconventional History of Western Philosophy* (2009).[13] The former is a biographical dictionary of women thinkers. The latter puts women philosophers in conversation with better-known male philosophers by comparing their theories and arguments. Both strategies succeed in including women in the existing canon. Yet they risk conveying the idea that either we cannot engage with these women's ideas or that women are philosophically interesting only when in dialogue with men. Our aim is to show that women are philosophers *in their own right*.

Subsequent to Ménage and Waithe, only a few article-length works engaged with the ideas of ancient Greek and Roman women: for example, Wider's 'Women Philosophers in the Ancient World' (1986), Hawley's 'The Problem of Women Philosophers in Greece' (1994), and Deslauriers' 'Women, Education, and Philosophy' (2012). More work has been done on Indian and Chinese women philosophers, both historical and fictionalised, such as Blackstone's *Women in the Footsteps of the Buddha* (1998), Wang's *Images of Women in Chinese Thought and Culture* (2003), and Lindquist's 'Gender at Janaka's Court' (2008). Recent and forthcoming publications include studies of female thinkers throughout the history of philosophy, such as *Philosopher Queens* by Buxton and Whiting (2020), *Women's Perspectives on Ancient and Medieval Philosophy* by Chouinard et al. (2021), and a forthcoming book on teaching women philosophers by Hagengruber and Hutton. Others look at women both as authors and as

---

[12] On Plato, see also Blair (2012). On Aristotle, see Connell (2016) and Trott (2019). For feminist interpretations of ancient philosophy, see Bar On (1994); Ward (1996).
[13] See also Acker (2002).

subjects of philosophical investigations: for example, *Filosofe, Maestre e Imperatrici* by Bonelli (2020), and the new *Routledge Handbook on Women and Ancient Philosophy* by Brill and McKeen (forthcoming).

Our book complements and builds upon these works. The original contribution we hope to make to the ongoing conversation about ancient women philosophers is threefold. First, we introduce new figures to the academic discourse, such as the Cyrenaic Arete and the Pythagorean Perictione. Second, and related, we do not restrict antiquity to Graeco-Roman philosophy. Rather, we include chapters about the ancient Indian, Chinese, and Arabic philosophical traditions. Third, and most importantly, we pay special attention to these women's philosophical achievements, their novel arguments and, where extant, their writings. As argued in the next section, this enquiry takes different shapes in different schools and different stages of the history of philosophy, and ranges from close argument analyses of philosophical texts to studies of ancient philosophical communities that include women, as well as philosophical readings of ancient biographies, medical treatises, novels, and poems.

This leads us to our final remark: while this book aims at including a wide variety of figures, ideas, themes, and scholarly approaches, it is not exhaustive. The panorama of female intellectuals in antiquity is much wider, and there are more figures, traditions, and methodologies one could discuss. Our hope is that the chapters in this volume will encourage new scholarship in the field of ancient women thinkers, globally.

Challenges and Approaches

In this section, we discuss the methodological challenges we face when we attempt to learn more about the philosophical ideas of ancient women. These can be divided into two groupings: those that impact the recovery of women's ideas *where we have texts written by women,* and those that impact the recovery *where we have no texts*. We include women covered in the chapters of this volume, as well as some others (Figure 1).

We include in each discussion a defence of the approaches our contributors have taken to make use of the sources notwithstanding these issues. Looking across these case studies, we have found that engagement with ancient women philosophers raises questions that have wide-ranging implications for the methodology of the history of philosophy. We begin by describing the general state of the source material.

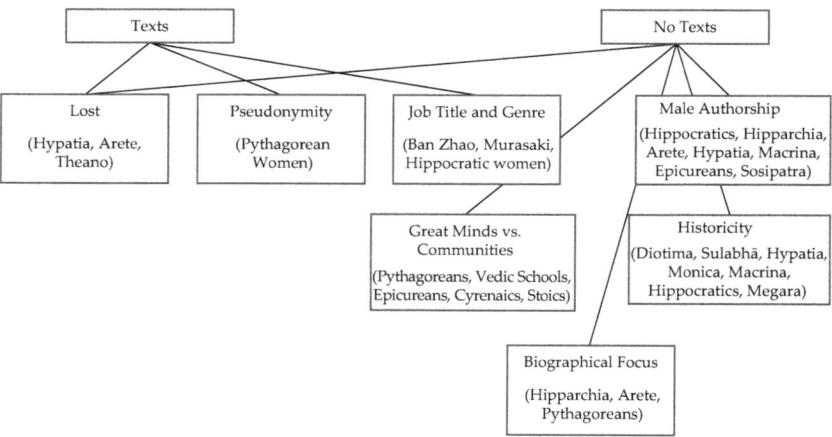

Figure 1   Methodological Challenges

The Source Issue

It is difficult to overstate the challenge we face regarding sources for the philosophical thought of ancient women. After all, in the Greek and Roman philosophical traditions, there is not a single surviving text incontestably ascribed to a woman philosopher. On the face of it, you might think that would, or *should*, sink a project like ours before it even gets started. We want to begin the discussion of challenges and approaches by facing up to the source issue and discuss how it is that there is material for a book on ancient women philosophers at all. We feel it crucial to be frank about the state of the evidence, the significant challenge it poses, and the ways we (and our contributors) have found to engage with the ideas of ancient women notwithstanding these.

There are a few different source categories. Outside of the Greek and Roman traditions, we find a comparatively rich set of sources. However limited, this is one of the many benefits of widening the scope of this volume to the degree that we have. We have direct evidence for Ban Zhao in the Confucian tradition, for instance. Though work on Ban Zhao faces other challenges (e.g., the Job Title section, below), her voluminous writing, across a number of genres, is well preserved.[14]

---

[14] See Chapter 11. Other examples might include Murasaki Shikibu, a Japanese philosopher and novelist of the (late ancient) Heian period. See Wawrytko (2019).

Some women left writings that are now lost. This includes Hypatia of Alexandria, Arete the Cyrenaic, and possibly Theano the Pythagorean.[15] Others, such as the group known as Pythagorean women, are credited with writing letters and treatises, but their philosophical status, authenticity, and dating is now contested.[16] We will discuss these rich yet challenging texts in the Pseudonymity section.

The bulk of our evidence of ancient women philosophers (e.g., the Hippocratic women, Hipparchia the Cynic, Arete, the Neoplatonists Hypatia and Sosipatra, Macrina, the sister of Gregory of Nyssa, the Epicurean women) is to be found in works authored by men.[17] These are more often accounts of their lives than their doctrines (e.g., Hipparchia, Arete, Hypatia). In some cases, it includes men's reflections on women's ability to practise philosophy (e.g., in Plato and Aristotle, but also Musonius Rufus in the Stoic tradition).[18] Within the group of women whose evidence is all via male-authored works, there is then a category of fictional or *fictionalised* women – where the latter are representations of historical women philosophers (e.g., the Hippocratic women, Hypatia, Macrina, as well as Augustine's mother Monica) or of those who may have been real (e.g., Diotima, Sulabhā).[19] Finally, there are depictions of fictional women in the works of men that are nonetheless evidence of the role of women in ancient philosophical communities (e.g., Megara in the Stoic tradition).[20]

The situation is complex, and there is a question of how to approach each of these types of evidence. We have found that doing so requires both specificity and generality: each case needs to be researched carefully and considered contextually. At the same time, it is helpful to look up from the specifics to the landscape of ancient women's philosophical engagement and the sources to draw some general methodological conclusions. In the rest of the introduction, we aim to provide some of this latter perspective.

Challenges with Texts

Lost Texts

Bridging our main groupings (Texts and No Texts, Figure 1) is the category of lost texts – that is, instances where we know of the work of

---

[15] On Arete and Hypatia, see Chapters 5 and 10. There is evidence in the *Suda* that Theano may have written books (*s.v.* Theano [*theta* 83]).
[16] See Chapters 7–8.   [17] See Chapters 2, 5–6, 9–10.   [18] See Chapters 6 and 12.
[19] See Chapters 1–2, 9.
[20] See Chapter 6. Macrina may also fit under this category, since she is historical, but her philosophical abilities are believed to be fictionalised and to be properly attributed to her brother. For a defence of Macrina's philosophical independence, see Chapter 9.

some ancient woman, usually only by title, but this has been lost. Sources like Diogenes Laertius are full of lists of lost works from male philosophers. Thus, we should perhaps not be surprised that so many works by ancient women failed to survive. Yet, when we look across the oeuvre of ancient women generally, we think it is – and should be – shocking how little direct evidence of their thought is available to us. To dismiss this worry too quickly by pointing out that many works by men are also missing too prevents us from enquiring further into the historical and cultural forces that have resulted in the current loss. We urge scholars not to shy away from this issue. In the chapters of this volume, many of our contributors find interesting ways of dealing with lost texts, including considerations of what information can be gleaned from a title, speculations regarding the content of lost works, and reflections on the reasons why certain works have failed to be preserved. We can also step back and consider the wider question of why so few texts by ancient women have reached us, which is a question worth asking in both research and teaching contexts.

Pseudonymity
The sole texts allegedly by women surviving within the ancient Greek tradition are the Pythagorean texts a collection of ten letters and five treatises ascribed to named Pythagorean women. The dating of these texts is debated, though the prevailing view places them between the first century BCE and the first century CE. These texts have not received the sustained scholarly attention one might expect of the only surviving works by ancient women philosophers in the Western tradition. This is, principally, for two reasons: their content and authorship.

The letters are written by women to other women, and many discuss female-coded topics such as female virtues, the married life of wives, childcare, household management, and the role of women in society. This has led to them being perceived as non-philosophical. In our volume, Twomey makes the case for reading them as philosophical, especially when considered against some of Aristotle's remarks about home economics (Chapter 7). Doing so demands a broadening of what is considered a properly philosophical topic, including re-thinking the philosophical concerns that can emerge in practical ethics in the domestic sphere. We consider this outcome a philosophically provocative one, whose impact goes beyond these specific texts. Furthermore, not all of the texts are concerned with female-coded issues. For instance, Aesara's *On Human Nature* concerns the make-up of the human soul. In Chapter 8, Pellò and De Cesaris discuss Perictione's *On Wisdom*, which concerns metaphysics, epistemology, and the value of wisdom. Even by the standards of the traditional canon, the questions these women raise would be considered philosophical.

The second reason why these letters and treatises have not been welcomed into the dominant philosophical discourse is controversy over their authorship. It is not clear whether they are written by the named authors (i.e., the women from ancient Pythagorean societies), by a group of Neopythagorean women using the names of their predecessors, or, most problematically, by men using female pseudonyms. There are contemporary arguments from scholars on either side, and there is, in our view, still doubt.[21] We will say more about the sense in which this doubt matters in discussing male authorship. Regarding pseudonymity, we find that the debate over authorial attribution has eclipsed philosophical engagement with the content of these texts. While we think it is important to take up the issue of the gender of the authors, we are also of the view that this should not be a barrier to our engagement with the philosophical significance of the writings ascribed to the Pythagorean women. These texts purport to express the views of ancient women on philosophical issues. Rather than starting from the pseudonymity debate, we condone our contributors' focus on the content and philosophical arguments of these writings.

Job Title and Genre

A further reason why women philosophers have been excluded from the historical narrative involves the question of who counts as a philosopher and what counts as a philosophical text. We have already discussed the shifting criteria for who counts as an ancient woman philosopher. In terms of disciplinary association, women philosophers have continually been branded, instead, as *hetairai*/courtesans (the Epicurean women); mystics, prophets, or Saints (Diotima, Macrina); or poets (Ban Zhao, Sappho). Alternatively, they have been excluded from the realm of the professional by being depicted primarily as daughter, mother (Arete, Perictione), sister (Macrina), wife (Hipparchia, Theano, Sosipatra) or similar, in relation to male thinkers. Sometimes both moves are made: for example, Macrina is both Saint and sister, to the exclusion of philosopher. This is, of course, not an issue for women alone. Not all ancient male philosophers, especially outside of the Greek tradition, are referred to as philosophers. Therefore, though this issue is especially prevalent with women, the approaches we

---

[21] See Chapter 8 for an overview of this debate.

take to circumvent it could be relevant to our recovery of other philosophers, too.

We approached this volume with an awareness of this issue, sometimes known as 'coat-tailing', in which women thinkers are situated not according to their ideas or even their philosophical allegiance but rather are subsumed under and identified by their association with some male relation or teacher.[22] One solution has been to refer to these women as the more generic 'thinker' or 'intellectual'. While this might be pragmatic in certain contexts, for this project we want to resist this move. We feel it is important that these women be recognised as philosophers. There are several reasons for this, one of which is that we would like them to be included in philosophy curricula. We want to restore them to the canon of philosophy, which better reflects their historical and intellectual status.

Our contributors resist this deflationary trend through their close consideration of these women, the assessment of their ideas, and a refusal to limit our description of them in this restrictive and gendered way. In many cases, they can show that, in their own time, these women were indisputably considered philosophers. Many figures resist rigid categorisation and prompt us to question attempts to create a dichotomy between, for example, sex worker and philosopher or mother and educator.[23] Though there are lingering issues with criteria, these are challenges that pertain to all genders. If we want to be stricter, we might sooner be excluding Milesian 'natural scientists', for example, than some of these women.

A related issue is genre. While some ancient women philosophers write philosophical treatises, others write letters, journals, poems, or communicate their commitments through lifestyle. While there are examples of male philosophers doing the same, it is particularly common in our evidence to see women using non-mainstream genres. And there is reluctance, then, to accept these works as philosophical. For example, Pang-White spends a stretch of her chapter on Ban Zhao defending her status as a philosopher despite a tradition of resistance to reading her works of fiction and advice to women as such (Chapter 11). Here again, our view is that we ought to first engage earnestly with the content of the work, then determine its philosophical merits, rather than seeing genre as a barrier to engagement. Our contributors confront this issue as it pertains both to

---

[22] On which see Hawley (1994); Waithe (2015); and Hutton (2019: 686–87). The latter identifies the same issue in early modern philosophy.
[23] See Chapters 4 and 5, respectively.

individuals and groups of women, and in doing so encourage greater general reflection on the issue of labelling and its justification.

Challenges without Texts

Male Authorship
How should we approach evidence of ancient women philosophers that exists only in male-authored works? This issue raises a dilemma, because, on the one hand, in an effort to recover and engage with the philosophical ideas of ancient women, our general approach involves an open-mindedness to different types of source. We would frankly cripple our ability to work on these figures at all if we were to exclude evidence of their thought that is written by men. In this volume, Adamson writes that 'there is no sharp contrast between studying ancient women philosophers and reading what ancient men said about women philosophers' (Chapter 12).

That said, there is a potential clash between this open-minded approach and our motivation. In addition to concerns about bias, distortion, misrepresentation, and invention, cases where our only evidence of an ancient woman's thought is in the writing of a man, or where a man writes in the guise of a woman, are particularly problematic if one of the principal reasons we are interested in this material is the gender of the author. We might seem to undermine the aims of the project by including – and indeed relying heavily upon – male-authored works. What if all these sources tell us is what a certain ancient audience would have accepted as being the philosophical perspective of a woman, without them accurately reflecting the work of any particular historical woman philosopher? Would we still consider them valuable?

Consider the parallel with Presocratic philosophy. McKirahan (1994: ix) summarises the state of our evidence as follows:

> Not a single work of any of the 'Presocratic' philosophers has been preserved from antiquity to the present . . . . We are confronted instead with a variety of quotations and paraphrases of their words, summaries of their theories, biographical information (much of it fabricated), in some cases adaptations and extensions of their views, and also parodies and criticisms. These materials come from a wide range of authors who write with different purposes and biases, and whose reliability and philosophical and historical acumen vary enormously. These circumstances have led some scholars to despair of the possibility of reaching the truth about the early philosophers.

But of course, scholars have not given up engaging with Presocratic philosophers, or Hellenistic philosophers, for that matter.

The parallel between the evidence for Presocratic and ancient women philosophers is not a perfect one. We have more instances of reports of Presocratic ideas, for instance, than we do for ancient women, even if these reports are problematic in their own ways. Like the Presocratics, however, much preliminary work goes into assessing the reliability of the sources and whether we have additional evidence to corroborate their claims. And like for the Presocratics, we have reasons, still, to engage with the available evidence, with all the caveats required to do so in a responsible way.

A different version of this question is raised in the Indian tradition, which includes important canonical texts that are not attributed to a single author but are rather the product of an intellectual community.[24] The natural result of this is less emphasis on individual authorial attribution in general, and more focus on the identity of particular characters or speakers. The inclusion in this volume of work from this tradition thus prompts a question: does the example of a communally authored text emphasise the 'male authorship' issue and make it *more* pressing, or does it provide a way of making it less urgent, via a focus on representation rather than authorial attribution?

Historicity
We mentioned the landscape of real vs. fictional vs. fictionalised women. This is a thorny issue for this kind of project because if one wants to exclude any fictional or fictionalised woman from the study of ancient women philosophers, we are down to very slim pickings. We also lose some of our most interesting examples, such as Diotima. This is the kind of loss which, if applied to male equivalents, would not be acceptable. If we were to exclude Socratic dialogues from our research and teaching because Plato fictionalises Socrates, for instance, or the *Analects* because they were composed by Confucius' disciples, the impoverishment that would result would be keenly felt.

And of course, when we teach Socrates, Plato, Cicero, and the Buddha, this is not what is done. We do not take the divide between fiction and history as a reason not to engage with their philosophy. This comparison helps justify our inclusion of fictionalised women. Yet it does not dissolve the issue of fictional women, where there is no historical basis. Moreover, there is the added burden of gender. The question therefore remains: to what extent are we entitled to use fictional or fictionalised figures as evidence of the thought of ancient women philosophers? Should the lack

---

[24] For the Upanishads, see Cohen (2008, 2018).

of historical evidence prompt us to reject these figures and sources as inauthentic?

To aid consideration of this question, we observe three interpretive trends in the scholarship and some advantages and disadvantages of each.

Artifact This view is developed by Dutsch in relation to the debate regarding the Pythagorean women (2020: 3). It contends that, given the impossibility of establishing historicity, a different approach is required. One such approach is to consider women as icons, to abandon hope of connecting specific women to texts, and to focus instead on texts as cultural artifacts. An advantage of this view is that we avoid what can be a distracting focus on the historicity debate, which can draw us away from the works and ideas themselves. It also encourages open-mindedness regarding the forms an intellectual legacy can take. The major disadvantage is that this view detaches too much from the importance of the fact that there existed women philosophers throughout antiquity.

Literary This is the kind of 'bite the bullet' view where we accept that the fictional and fictionalised is all we have and work within that frame.[25] The major advantages of this approach are that, like the Artifact view, it avoids being taken over by the historicity debate. It also facilitates the attribution of value to fictional accounts of women. The existence of literary women philosophers itself can be an argument for the existence of real women philosophers inspiring these characters. Minimally, it can tell us what a certain audience would accept as the view of an ancient woman philosopher. In addition, it raises the possibility that in novels, authors can do more with women philosophers and give them more argumentative strength.[26] The major disadvantage of this view is that, again, it can underestimate the importance of the connection to real, historical women: if part of our motivation is to engage with the philosophical ideas of ancient women philosophers, how can we be satisfied with evidence that has or may have no connection to these women? We must at least do more to articulate what information this evidence gives us about existing ancient women philosophers.

Strong Historicity This view argues that our default position should be to trust the evidence for ancient women philosophers and implicitly shifts the burden of proof to those who reject it.[27] Where other approaches require strong positive evidence that works originate with or provide evidence

---

[25] See Chapter 12, for example.   [26] See Chapter 6.   [27] See, for example, Waithe (1987b).

from historical women, this view says that this requirement is too strong in part because it would result in the elimination of ancient women from the canon. The advantage is that this forces us to reconsider what the threshold of evidence ought to be. The disadvantage is that it may seem unduly optimistic. We find it imperative to be honest about the source issues, and we consider some of the value of working on these figures to come from this transparency, where this view tends to suppress or downplay the challenges. We also feel the exclusively historical aim is too high. It undervalues the fictional and the role it plays in informing us of real women philosophers in antiquity.

We think of these approaches as on a continuum. Our position is not to force a generalisable choice on this spectrum. Rather, we recognise that each philosopher and source demands a nuanced approach, and encourage close consideration of the costs and benefits of the approach one takes to categorise the evidence.

Biographical Focus
One of the ways we distinguish our project from previous studies is our focus on the philosophical ideas of ancient women, as opposed to their lives. This distinction is a troubled one because, in some cases, all we have as evidence for some ancient women philosophers really is biographical. The question is whether, in some cases, it is possible to use the biographical as evidence for the philosophical. We are of the view that we can, and in fact that we ought to, especially in cases where ancient women are members of schools whose doctrines are best displayed in their lifestyles.

We have at least two examples of this in the book: the Pythagorean women and Arete the Cyrenaic. These schools are distinguished by their practical bent: they were insistent that their followers not only ascribe to certain core ideas but also live a certain lifestyle reflecting the shared values of the school. Other such examples may be the renunciate communities in ancient India, of which the character Sulabhā in the *Mahābhārata* is a spokesperson, the Epicureans, and the Cynic school, of which Hipparchia was a member. Learning about the lives of male and female adherents adds to the wider picture of these philosophical communities and the ideas behind the lifestyle, as well as to our understanding of what philosophically informed lives looked like within these traditions.

'Great Minds' vs. Communities
Several chapters in this volume urge us to reconsider what kind of unit we ascribe philosophical ideas to, both in ancient philosophy and, quite

possibly, more broadly. Some of our most direct evidence of ancient women philosophers reports them as members of philosophical communities without ascribing to them original or independent philosophical ideas. Yet we know a lot about the doctrines of these communities.

The general strategy in history of philosophy has been to focus on the great minds to whom we can more confidently ascribe particular philosophical ideas – for example, Pythagoras and Epicurus – and discuss philosophical communities as a kind of outgrowth of the thought and influence of these prominent figures. The focus (in both the ancient and contemporary scholarship) is often on student-teacher chains generating lines of individuals.[28] These trends suppress the role of philosophical communities and especially those members whose individual contributions are not independently recorded.

An alternative approach is to think more holistically about the development of philosophical theories and the role we can attribute to those of any gender identity. We could focus on school doctrines rather than individual authorship, like scholars already do, for example, with Stoicism. If women were active members of philosophical communities, we should resist the assumption that their presence was merely as passive followers. We should instead consider the evidence to the contrary – for example, in the Pythagorean, Cyrenaic, Vedic, and Epicurean traditions. Even where we lack the specifics, we have evidence that women contributed to forming and developing the ideas ascribed to these schools. What happens, then, when we reframe the unit of emphasis from individuals to communities and acknowledge the full membership of these communities? Why should we restrict our interest to those who create, rather than inspire or preserve, philosophical ideas? Once again, these are wide-ranging methodological questions that concern philosophers of any gender identity, tradition, and stage in the history of the discipline.

Philosophical Contribution from Sulabhā to Lucrezia Marinella

We now revisit our overarching proposal that there is a unique value to the study of ancient women philosophers that benefits our understanding and practice of the history of philosophy. In this final section, we want to

---

[28] Our dependence on biographers such as Diogenes Laertius, who is known to emphasise and even construct these familial and pedagogic chains, partly explains this. See Warren (2009). According to Bernasconi (1997: 218), the lack of identifiable teacher-pupil lineages was used to exclude non-Greek traditions from the philosophical canon. Once again, non-Greek traditions may make the Great Minds narrative less pressing.

support this thesis by highlighting some of the original philosophical contributions of ancient women philosophers that the chapters bring to light and some of the methodological questions the work on women raises.

Each chapter in this book revolves around an individual philosopher, or a group of thinkers, focusing on their ideas and novel contributions. Broadly, each chapter addresses three questions: (i) What is our evidence, and what methodological challenges do we face when learning about this figure's ideas? (ii) What strategies and approaches could one use to engage with this figure philosophically? (iii) What are the original philosophical takeaways from the study of these women thinkers?

The chapters are organised chronologically. The book opens with two studies on the general question of whether philosophical activity is gendered or genderless and whether women have their own distinctive way of doing philosophy. The first two chapters address this issue with examples from two different ancient philosophical traditions in Greece and India. Chapter 1 is about Diotima, the priestess from Mantinea and Socrates' teacher from Plato's *Symposium*. The scholarship has so far primarily focused on the question of whether Diotima is a historical figure and why Plato chose to ascribe his philosophical theories about love and beauty to a woman philosopher. Frisbee Sheffield, by contrast, leaves the question of Diotima's historicity aside and argues that this episode in the *Symposium* shows that according to Plato philosophical activity goes beyond gender. Similarly, Chapter 2 focuses on the Sanskrit epic *Mahābhārata* and, in particular, the episode featuring a debate between King Janaka and the woman philosopher Sulabhā concerning good speech and the ethics of renunciation. Once again, Brian Black does not focus on the question of whether Sulabhā was a historical figure. Rather, he considers the implications of gender identity on *mokṣa*, enlightenment. Like Diotima, Sulabhā's arguments show that philosophical activity is believed to lie beyond the dualities of gender distinctions.

Chapter 3 moves on to another group of female intellectuals from antiquity: women physicians. We previously mentioned that one should be broadminded as to what counted as philosophy in the ancient world and which genres should be considered as philosophical. Sophia Connell introduces a new source of evidence for Greek philosophy: the medical treatises from the Hippocratic school. Specifically, Connell shows that medical texts include references to women who both practised medicine and held theories about the human body and human health. Women's medical expertise included both topics related to the female gender such as fertility and gynaecology, and genderless discussions of the nature of disease and pharmacology.

The book then turns to the issue of philosophy as a way of life and the philosophical value of ancient biographies. The next three chapters focus on Hellenistic philosophy and the role of women in the Hellenistic schools: Epicureanism, the Cyrenaics, and Stoicism. Chapter 4 focuses on Epicurean women. As previously mentioned, most women thinkers from antiquity are not referred to as philosophers in our sources. Specifically, the Epicureans are portrayed by Epicurus' critics as *hetairai* and prostitutes. Kelly Arenson counters this narrow picture by focusing on what the available doxographical evidence can tell us about these women's intellectual achievements: for example, Leontion is reported to have written a book refuting Theophrastus. In Chapter 5, Katharine O'Reilly analyses the available evidence for Arete, who is the daughter of the founder of the Cyrenaic school Aristippus, and the mother and most importantly the teacher of Aristippus the Younger. There is limited evidence for Arete's life and no direct evidence of her philosophical activity. Nonetheless, her son Aristippus was oddly known as *mētrodidaktos*, mother-taught. This leads O'Reilly to consider what ancient biographies have to say about Arete's role in setting and continuing the Cyrenaic philosophical tradition. Finally, Chapter 6 looks at the position of women in Stoic theory and narrative. Kate Meng Brassel proposes to interpret the dramatisation of a woman's moral choice in a Senecan tragedy as a stand-in for the lost voices of historical women Stoics.

The next two chapters revolve around the Pythagorean women, the best-known and most debated case of female engagement with ancient Greek thought. The question is what makes the letters and treatises ascribed to Pythagorean women philosophical. We mentioned that, so far, the scholarship has primarily debated whether these texts were in fact authored by women rather than men writing under female pseudonyms. In contrast, these chapters focus on their content. In Chapter 7, Rosemary Twomey analyses the letters and treatises about female-coded topics, such as family life and home economics. Her argument is twofold: first, since these topics are also addressed by canonical philosophers and in canonical texts, such as Aristotle's *Politics* and Plato's *Republic*, we should not question that domestic life was considered worthy of philosophical investigation. Second, and more importantly, these texts add to Plato and Aristotle's social and political philosophy by considering how we are to apply these theories to the private sphere inside the household. In Chapter 8, Caterina Pellò and Giulia De Cesaris analyse a treatise titled *On Wisdom* and ascribed to the Pythagorean woman Perictione. In *On Wisdom*, Perictione distinguishes different kinds of things that are and three different sciences to study them. Wisdom is introduced as the highest form of human activity, for it enquires about universals. This shows how the texts of the Pythagorean women contribute novel arguments and original philosophical theories.

In Chapter 9, Anna Christensen analyses the arguments about the nature and immortality of the soul, which Gregory of Nyssa ascribes to his sister Macrina. Once again, the authorship of these doctrines is contested. Christensen argues for Macrina's intellectual independence from her brother and reclaims for her the title of philosopher. In Chapter 10, Jana Schultz gives an overview of the best-known Neoplatonist women, such as Hypatia and Sosipatra. The focus is again on the available evidence for their lives and intellectual activities. The challenge is to determine what our sources can tell us about both these women's ideas and the way in which they exemplify Neoplatonic philosophical ideals of womanhood and femaleness. In Chapter 11, Ann A. Pang-White analyses the philosophical ideas of Ban Zhao, a Confucian thinker who writes about pedagogy and women's education. While Ban Zhao is traditionally seen as a poet and historian, Pang-White shows that her numerous writings include philosophical theories about gender, women's roles in society, and the value of harmony in the household. We close with a synoptic study of the reception of women's philosophical potential. In Chapter 12, Peter Adamson investigates how Plato's theory about women being able to rule and philosophise in the *Republic* is received by the Neoplatonist Proclus, in the Islamic tradition by Ibn Rushd, and by the early modern feminist Lucrezia Marinella. While the fifth book of the *Republic* includes arguments written by a man about women doing philosophy, the way in which these theories are interpreted by Plato's successors is influenced by the historical evidence for real women philosophers.

This is far from the end of the study of ancient women philosophers. What we hope to show, nonetheless, is that philosophical traditions from the ancient world include a wide and diverse range of women thinkers, which is as diverse as the discipline itself.

CHAPTER I

Beyond Gender
The Voice of Diotima
Frisbee C. C. Sheffield

Introduction

In the *Symposium*, Plato's great work on *eros* (passionate love, or desire), the central insights are gleaned from a wise woman (201d5, 204d2, 207a5), from whom Socrates learnt the single thing to which he laid claim to expertise, *ta erotika* (*Symp.* 177d; *Phdr.* 257a; *Lysis* 204b; Xen. *Mem.* 2.6.28). Since there is a widespread view that Plato stands at the head of a tradition of philosophical thinking in which women are eclipsed, or marginalised, this fact has been seen as significant.[1] That Diotima's gender has been the subject of such scholarly interest speaks volumes about the assumptions we make about gender and its importance; it is not clear whether and how Diotima's gender is significant for the philosophy of the *Symposium*, however. Gender categories are an explicit feature of this text, but Plato's playful and provocative use of them is not just a dialectical ploy to provoke reflection on the social norms around sexuality and gender that held sway in his day; toying with them exposes both the contingency of gendered categories and, ultimately, their irrelevance to a philosophical account of *eros*. It is in fact doubtful whether any of the images, or vocabulary employed by Diotima, or even Diotima's status as a 'woman' itself are, properly speaking, 'gendered' in any straightforward way. One of Diotima's central insights is that *eros* is a mediator between binary oppositions; *eros* is a non-binary facilitator. This explains a number of features of the supposedly gender-polarised vocabulary and imagery in this text, which fluctuates between (Plato's) contemporary associations of the male

---

[1] Lovibond (2000: 11): 'The most influential theme during this period has been that of the masculinism of ancient thought – its assumption, explicit or otherwise, of the centrality and superiority of the male point of view.' The seminal paper on the significance of Diotima's gender is Halperin (1990). See also Saxonhouse (1984); Brown (1988); du Bois (1994); Nye (1990); Tuana and Cowling (1994).

and the female and the gender-muddled portrait of Diotima herself, fused with her 'feminised' Socratic counterpart. Platonic *eros* seems genderqueer insofar as it does not subscribe to conventional gender distinctions. One lesson learnt from Diotima is that human beings are needy, incomplete, and markedly *in*determinate creatures; any determination we may ultimately find is up to the individual and the work they are prepared to do, which, ideally here, takes them beyond gender. Plato challenges the gender categories of his day in a way that serves as a timely reminder of their contingency; in doing so, he 'de-center[s] the importance of gender' in philosophy. From that perspective, such interest in Diotima's gender reveals how far we are from that goal.[2]

The Question of Diotima's Gender

Determining whether Diotima's gender is significant is made difficult by the following features: (a) the difficulty of establishing whether Diotima is evidence for the thinking of any historical woman (the consensus has been negative, in which case she has little historical significance);[3] (b) the fact that Socrates speaks her truth so that her presence is eclipsed, or at least mediated, by a man (in which case she is thin evidence for a vindication of the female voice);[4] (c) the fact that Plato elsewhere attributes insights to certain 'men and women who are learned in divine matters' (*sophoi peri ta theia pragmata*, *Meno*, 81a–b) – which may make Diotima seem less unusual and minimise the significance of gender by making it parasitic on a relationship to the divine.[5] It is worth noting,

---

[2] I take the phrase 'de-center[s] the importance of gender' from Faucette (2014: 78) who outlines this as part of the work of non-binary activism and those who identify as 'genderqueer'. Faucette (2014: 75–76) argues that 'non-binary activism brings something valuable ... because it questions the logic behind rigid gender norms, hierarchies, and the state's use of gender as an unnecessary control mechanism. This questioning benefits people of all genders, not only non-binary people.' Compare Olson et al. (2019); Griffin (2020).

[3] For a historical reading of Diotima, see Waithe (1987a: 83–117) and D'Angour (2019: 202), who argues that Aspasia of Miletus stands behind the figure of Diotima; she was the 'intellectual midwife ... whose ideas helped to give birth to European philosophy'. Attempts at a historical grounding for Diotima go back to Rettig (1876: 262). For scholarship on Diotima's 'historical authenticity', see Halperin (1990: 119 n. 34).

[4] On the 'male embodiment of the voice of a woman', see Irigaray (1989: 32).

[5] Compare Aspasia in the *Menexenus*. We are told three things about Diotima: she is a foreigner, a priestess, and a woman. For an explanation of Diotima's gender in terms of 'prophetic temperament' see Bury (1932: 193). Compare Nye (1989: 53): 'In historical context ... it is neither surprising nor anomalous that Diotima would appear in the authoritative role as the teacher of Socrates. As prophetess/priestess she was part of a religious order that had maintained its authority from Minoan/Mycenaean times.' Evans (2006: 1) argues that: 'The dialogue, including Diotima's

though, that Diotima gives arguments and proposes a philosophical theory here and does not just supply a premise for an argument as those who are learned in divine matters do in the *Meno*. Diotima is one of the few named female interlocutors we witness engaged in philosophical thinking. So, despite the fact that this chapter will not approach Diotima as a historical woman philosopher, the dialogue nonetheless promises to show what female figures can tell us about gender dynamics, and their significance or lack thereof, in Platonic philosophy. The question is not whether Diotima the woman philosopher existed, who she was, and what she thought – but rather what this figure, the way Plato describes her, and the arguments ascribed to her, teach us about the significance of gender in Plato's philosophy.

Three features have lent urgency to the question of Diotima's gender: the context, the topic, and the imagery used to explore *eros*. I take each in turn. Diotima's 'presence' is situated in an all-male context (a symposium). This fact alone will not do much work because any female voice anywhere in the Platonic dialogues falls into that category (e.g., Sappho in the *Phaedrus*, Aspasia in the *Menexenus*). This need not be indicative of any deep-seated misogyny on Plato's part; the dialogues represent the cultural contexts of his day in dramatic form. Plato recognises the importance of embedding his philosophical thinking within 'socially articulated spaces', dominated by men though they were. This 'situatedness' allows for greater

---

speech, contains mystical language, some of which specifically evokes the female-centred celebrations of Demeter.' Further,

> just as the Demeter tradition celebrated at Eleusis allowed individuals to reconstruct their conception of the divine and its relation to the human social and political structures inherent in the polis, so Plato in Diotima's speech presents a different conception of human experience and its relative distance to and difference from the divine. Centred on the experience of the divine mother and daughter, the Eleusinian Mysteries allowed initiates, both male and female, to experience the divine immediately and with their own eyes during the night ritual in the Telesterion at Eleusis. Likewise, Diotima the mystagogue leads Socrates to realise that initiates into her rites of love will, in loving their beloved, see Being and thereby enter into a new, mutual relation with the divine and become *theophiles*, both loving the divine and beloved of the divine. (7)

For Evans, then, Diotima's gender is explained in terms of the Eleusinian mystery cult, which, though based on the female experience of birth and nurturing, bestowed blessings on all human beings 'regardless of gender and civil status' (16). It is this feature, rather than anything distinctively 'female' that is to the fore here. Halperin argues that focus on her role as a prophetess should not detract attention from her being a woman (1990: 129). It is the latter issue that forms the focus of this paper. Though religion was one of the few areas beyond the household in which women could hold roles of authority, I agree with Halperin that the gendered language and imagery used here bolsters the question of Diotima's gender, which makes it difficult to reduce her gender to her role as a priestess, rather than to features of the theory under discussion.

scrutiny of existing prejudices around class and gender, for example, by encouraging awareness of the extent to which knowing subjects are not 'innocent and waiting outside the violations of language and culture'.[6] The characters, along with their social status, gender, contextual situation, and the speech practices that are tethered to those, are brought to the fore in the *Symposium* and elsewhere, along with the social and political implications of this foregrounding.[7] Plato nowhere professes to speak from a position of supposed neutrality; such devices serve as reminders of the embeddedness of his thinking in a particular time and place and expose the extent to which the gender of the participants and the dominance of their voices arise from, and are perpetuated in, particular social structures, such as those that dominated at the symposium.[8] Whether Plato *endorsed* the kind of structures that are in evidence at this all-male gathering of the intellectual elite is another matter altogether. Diotima has been seen as one way in which Plato destabilises the gendered hierarchy of those structures, as he was to do elsewhere by providing a wholescale reform of society underpinned by argument for the equality of the sexes.[9]

---

[6] See Haraway (1991: 183–201) on 'situated knowledge' and the claim that knowing subjects cannot be treated as straightforward, pre-theoretical entities, 'innocent and waiting outside the violations of language and culture'. See also Fricker and Hornsby (2000: 7): 'The space of reasons is a socially articulated space, so that all conceptual activity is understood as activity within a setting in which people adopt attitudes towards each other.' A virtue of this position is taken to be that 'they speak of something ineluctably related to other such subjects', and 'when the knowing subject is treated as a social being, testimony assumes its place as a fundamental mode of knowledge acquisition, attention is given to epistemic practices, and relations between knowers are brought to the fore'. This gets past 'the neutralism of traditional philosophy' to 'acknowledge located-ness' (8).

[7] The latter of which is made vivid by the dramatic date of the work set in 416 BCE, just before the doomed Sicilian expedition, in which one of the participants played a central role, and the affair of the Mysteries in which three participants were implicated.

[8] Though notice that the depiction of the golden age symposium-style gathering in the city of pigs in *Republic* 2 is not gendered or hierarchical (372b–c).

[9] See Peter Adamson in this volume (Chapter 12). *Republic* 5.455d–e: 'There is no pursuit of the administrators of the city that belongs to women because she is a woman or to a man because he is a man. But the natural capacities are distributed alike among both creatures, and women naturally share in all pursuits and men in all.' Whether that is sufficient to make Plato a feminist depends in part on what his motivations are for postulating such an idea, on which see Annas (1976) with the riposte by Lesser (1979). See also Vlastos (1994). Though there are debates about how far the proposals go, the *Republic* seems to continue what there is good reason to believe is a Socratic tradition of thinking about virtue as gender neutral (*Meno* 73a–c). As El Murr (2020: 96) has argued, in the *Politics* (1.13.1260a20–24), Aristotle takes this to be the view of Socrates and 'it is safe to assume that the beginning of the *Meno* and this passage from Aristotle's *Politics* echo a debate whose Socratic background should not be overlooked'. El Murr cites further evidence in support of this view from Xenophon, Aeschines of Sphettus, and Antisthenes. It is also worth noting that the provision of state-run nurseries in the *Republic* to free women to engage in higher education and allow them to stand as Philosopher Queens shows sensitivity to the kinds of issues raised time and again in feminist political philosophy (e.g., Okin (1989)). Okin (1979: 31, 42) gives Plato his due as

One feature that differentiates Diotima's presence in the *Symposium* from other dialogues where Socrates takes a female voice (e.g., Sappho in the *Phaedrus*, Aspasia in the *Menexenus*) is that Socrates introduces Diotima after women have been explicitly excluded from the discussion by the symposiarch (Eryximachus, 176e). This is certainly a transgression of the rules of this particular symposium, as are the attempts at dialectic instead of rhetoric in discussion with Agathon (Phaedrus has to remind Socrates of the rules). Eryximachus' move, by dismissing the flute girl, marginalises physical *eros* from the gathering, to focus on 'theoretical' *eros*, which suggests that within this social circle women were not considered to be part of any such discussion; anything that is noble and valuable (i.e., educative) in *eros* belongs to *paiderastia*. Socrates' transgression does not consist just in introducing a woman (who usually did take part in male symposia, i.e., as prostitutes or flute girls) but both in giving a woman the role of a wise discussant, which was traditionally assigned to men, and in making her knowledgeable on this particular topic.[10]

This is the second feature that has been thought to give Diotima's gender prominence: Diotima is responsible for insights on *eros*. Would it be more or less surprising if the insights of a woman had informed the topic of, say, false statements in the *Sophist*?[11] The issue is not that 'love' as opposed to 'negation' is a topic particularly suited for women – certainly not in ancient Greece, where the erotic paradigm was homoerotic.[12] The issue is that a woman schools men in a topic for which the paradigm was homoerotic, *to orthos paiderastein* (211b5–6). The extent to which Plato was committed to that focus is not clear, however.[13] This is for two reasons. First, Plato's interest in homoerotic relationships takes us to the heart of his interest in moral education; relationships of the sort discussed

---

a pioneer with his argument for the equality of the sexes but argues that since this is tethered to the 'communism' of Book 5 it has limited appeal for a modern feminist).

[10] I thank Christian Keime for discussion of this paragraph.

[11] Though here one could find historical precedent. The Muses, after all, are female sources of wisdom and inspiration on various subjects. Athena is the patron god of the arts, skill, wisdom, etc. And, perhaps closer, Parmenides' poem has the *kouros* instructed by an explicitly female divinity. Pythagoras was reputed to have been educated by a priestess Themistoclea (D.L. 8.8, on the evidence of Aristoxenus), but the evidence for this is post-Platonic.

[12] No less is the issue that love is a marginal topic for Platonic philosophy and so a member of a marginalised group will do. The repeated characterisation of philosophy as itself a form of *eros* in a number of dialogues (*Symposium, Republic, Phaedrus*) is indicative of the kind of value wisdom is for Plato and the role he wants it to play in our lives. See Sheffield (2017).

[13] There are those who speculate on Plato's own sexual proclivities here, which seem impossible to substantiate (e.g., Wender (1973: 31); Plass (1978)). It remains to be shown whether such speculation reveals anything interesting about Plato's philosophical commitments.

here, *to orthos paiderastein*, which took place at symposia such as this one, were a central way in which virtue was transmitted to the young. At their best, they had an educational function.[14] The question, then, is whether there is evidence that Plato supposed moral education to be the preserve of men (i.e., one should not make the assumption that Plato had any deep investment in the institution of Greek pederasty for its own sake and take the significance of Diotima's gender from there). The fact that in the *Republic* Philosopher Queens, along with their male counterparts, have responsibility for civic education shows at least one context where moral education is *not* exclusively male. This is a context in which the moral education of men as well as women is not the exclusive concern of men. It would have been less unusual to think that women might be responsible for the moral education of other women.

Second, though in this context most speakers evidently do hold the view that such educational practices are male, the speech of Socrates-Diotima shows little investment in *to orthos paiderastein* as a male–male practice; this forms the *context* in which this discussion takes place (for reasons given above), but the *content* of the account of *eros* is not tethered to servicing this goal. The account of *eros*, with all of its educational aspirations, applies to *all* human beings (*pantes anthropoi*, 206c1–2), who are pregnant in both body and soul and enabled by *eros* in their creative endeavours as they strive to create a life worth living, be that as parents, educators, poets, lawmakers, or philosophers. The account applies to human beings regardless of gender (*anthropoi* 211e2, 212a1, b7; *thnetes*, 211e3), and it is nowhere stated or implied that women are less good than men at the higher cultural pursuits described in the Highest Mysteries (209e5–12a7).[15] The single line that could be so used is widely misunderstood.[16] This is where Socrates describes those (presumably men) who are pregnant in body and turn to women to produce children, supposing

---

[14] That pederasty was an important social institution in Classical Athens is now a commonplace of Classical scholarship, on which, see Dover (1978, 1980); Foucault (1985); Calame (1999). On the educative function of the symposium, see Bremmer (1990); Calame (1999).

[15] See Evans (2006: 20) and Nye (1990: 142): 'Diotima, as any good teacher, uses homosexual examples relative to her audience's experience and refers to her potential initiate, who is in fact Socrates as male. There is nothing, however, in the content of her teaching that makes a sexual distinction necessary. We are all pregnant, she says, both in body and in soul. The generality of this conception can only be discounted if one is determined to accommodate Diotima's teaching with the gynophobia of several of the preceding speakers. It is not comprehensible that Diotima, taking the authoritative tone that she does on the subject, would think her own sex incapable of practicing her advice.'

[16] E.g., Irigaray (1989: 41), who argues that love between men is superior to love between men and women.

that this will supply them with memory and *eudaimonia* for all time to come (208e5–6). The target is those who are pregnant in body and who suppose that producing physical offspring is sufficient for *eudaimonia*. This is a demand that we (all human beings) be culturally (particularly, philosophically) creative and not just biologically so. However much joy parents find in their children, Plato (along with many feminist thinkers) is surely persuasive in urging one to broaden aspirations beyond physical reproduction (leaving aside the obvious burden it brings to children to make them bearers of our *eudaimonia*). Nor is there anything here that tethers the female to being the beautiful 'object' that inspires creative work (unless one falls into the category of those who suppose that *eudaimonia* is had by the production of physical offspring). It is in the presence of another beautiful person (*anthropon*, 209b7) that one can give birth, and those who give birth to 'wisdom and the rest of virtue' (209b4) are also described by the inclusive 'humans' (*anthropoi*). The speech is consistent with the *Republic*'s proposal that 'there is no pursuit ... that belongs to women because she is a woman or to a man because he is a man' (455d), and it is consistent with other accounts of gender-neutral virtue (e.g., *Meno* 73a–c).

Such a reading might bolster the significance of Diotima's gender. If Plato's contemporaries thought that such educational practices were the preserve of men, then there is value in showing us the 'singularly fecund' association between Socrates and Diotima to exemplify the inclusive tone of the speech.[17] True education is revealed to be a form of reproduction, a point that suggests that the female voice needs to be incorporated – on the assumption that there is something distinctively female about this experience. From the perspective of the other symposiasts, the presence of a woman may well serve as a dialectical provocation, useful for the purposes of disrupting norms (e.g., those set by Eryximachus at 176e). So argues Halperin (1990: 129): 'By the very fact of being a woman, Diotima signals Plato's departure from certain aspects of the sexual *ethos* of his male contemporaries and thereby enables him to highlight some of the salient features of his own philosophy.'[18] Whether Diotima's gender moves beyond such provocation, what it provokes specifically, and whether it emphasises 'salient features' of Plato's own philosophy – which I take, for

---

[17] The phrase is taken from Wardy (2002: 41). For other scholars who argue that the introduction of a woman lessens the focus on the homoerotic in particular, see Nussbaum (1979: 145); Dover (1980: 137); Evans (2006: 20).

[18] Compare Saxonhouse (1985: 62): Plato 'has found in women – those who give birth, those who are different from the males, those who are closer to the private realm – a symbol that becomes useful for his critique of an Athenian society devoted to the political life of ambition, money, war'.

reasons I cannot defend here, to be best (albeit not exclusively) expressed in the speech of Socrates-Diotima – are further questions. In Halperin's view (1990: 117): 'Diotima underscores the specifically feminine character of her purchase on the subject of erotic desire by means of the emphatically gender-polarised vocabulary and conceptual apparatus she employs in discussing it.' This third feature, which is how the topic is treated here, has been seen as the most promising way to promote the significance of Diotima's gender. To that I now turn.

Mixing Things up

The seemingly gender-polarised vocabulary is included in the following account of *eros*. It is argued that the aim of *eros* is to secure the good things we suppose will bring us *eudaimonia* (205d). Since we are mortal, and subject to flux and change (207–8), we cannot secure anything without productive work; human beings have to be productive in a way that gods do not (207c–8b). This explains the productive work (*ergon*) of *eros*, which is giving birth in the beautiful (206b8), as the distinctively mortal way to secure those good things thought to be constitutive of *eudaimonia*. According to Halperin, the fact that the work of *eros* is *procreation* in the beautiful (206b–c) and that the text is rife with images of pregnancy, birth pangs, and nourishing offspring 'serves to thematize two of the most distinctive and original elements of Plato's erotic theory'. More specifically:

> In Plato's conception (male) *eros*, properly understood and expressed, is not hierarchical, but reciprocal; it is not acquisitive, but creative. Plato's model of successful erotic desire effectively incorporates and allocates to men, the positive dimension of each of these two Greek stereotypes of women, producing a new and distinctive paradigm that combines erotic responsiveness with (pro)creative aspiration. (Halperin 1990: 130)[19]

In this way, 'Diotima's gender ... is a condition of her discourse'. Evidently, here the 'feminine' (which Halperin makes clear refers to what is constructed by the social group or historical culture in question) is playing a central role.

The reading assumes two things: (a) that the female (however conceived) can be located and (b) that it is then positively deployed, appropriated, or incorporated, in the account of '(male) *eros*'. The first assumption is in fact fraught with difficulty. Consider the gender-polarised

---

[19] For the ancient Greek sexual norms for male desire that this picture disrupts, see Winkler (1990: 70).

vocabulary. A translation of the crucial passage by Robert Wardy brings out the ambiguities:

> Whenever the [neuter] pregnant [*kuo* = 'in pres. and impf., of females, conceive; in aor. act. *ekusa*, causal, of males, impregnate' (LSJ s.v.)] approaches what is beautiful,[20] it becomes gracious and in its enjoyment relaxes and produces [*tikto* = 'of the father, beget; of the mother, bring forth' (LSJ s.v.)] and generates [*gennao* = 'causal of *gignomai*, mostly of the father, beget' (LSJ s.v.)], but whenever it approaches what is ugly, it turns away and curls up and does not generate, but rather is in travail because it retains the embryo. That is why what is beautiful occasions much excitement in the pregnant and already swollen: *either* [taking *ton echonta* as subject and 'understanding' *to kalon*] because *he* who has beauty releases the pregnant from great pangs [*wdis* = 'pangs of the birth of childbirth' (LSJ, s. v.)]; *or* [taking *to kalon* as subject and *ton echonta* in one sense as object] because beauty releases *him* who has the embryo from great pangs; *or* [again taking *to kalon* as subject, but *ton echonta* in another sense as object] because beauty releases him who has great pangs from them. (206d3–e1; translation with notes taken from Wardy [2002: 45-6])

Many of the key terms in Greek do not have a meaning that is gender specific.[21] For example, *kueo* (209a1, a2, b1, b5, c3) can mean 'conceive' in the sense that a woman conceives a child and becomes pregnant; but with a male subject, it has a causal meaning, 'impregnate'. *Tikto* (209a3, b2, c3) can mean 'bring into the world' and 'engender'; used with a female subject, it means 'bear', and with a male subject, 'beget'. *Gennao* is used mostly with male subjects but can also be used with female. As Evans (2006: 14) argues: 'It becomes clear that these words in Greek cover semantic ground the corresponding English words do not. In English, beget and conceive are thought to be conceptually different, one used solely of the male, the other solely of the female; but in Greek, each single verb covers the role that both genders play in procreation. Verbs like *kueo* and *tikto* are, in a

---

[20] It should be noted that all the manuscripts have τὸ κυοῦν (i.e., the participle of κυέω), which never means 'impregnate' but always 'conceive' or 'be in travail' (Liddell et al. (1940) and other dictionaries). Only κύω (non-contract) can mean (very rarely) 'impregnate', but its participle would be τὸ κῦον: it is this verb (not κυέω) that we find in the example from Aeschylus' Fr. 44 ('ὄμβρος ... ἔκυσε γαῖαν'). The aorist of κυέω would be ἐκύησε. I thank Christain Keime for drawing attention to this.

[21] Noted by Dover (1980: 147); Halperin (1990: 117 and 139*ff.*); Wardy (2002: 45-7); and Evans (2006: 14–15, n. 12), who cite examples of *kueo* meaning 'conceive' or 'be pregnant' are found in Hesiod *Theogony* 405; *Iliad* 19.117, 23.266; Herodotus 5.92. The causal meaning 'impregnate' that applies to the male is attested in the aorist tense in Aeschylus' Fr. 44 (a fragment from the *Danaids*). In Homer, *tikto* is used of both men and women: of men, for example, *Iliad* 2.628, 6.155 of Phyleus and Glaucus; of women, for example, *Iliad* 16.180, 22.428 of Polymele and Hecuba. *Gennao* is the causal form of *gignomai*, become, be born. See, for example, Sophocles, *Electra* 1412.

sense, gender neutral.' Plato did not invent this male paradigm of procreation, which was well attested in early Greek mythology and thought.[22] From the perspective of a gender binary at least, the language seems muddled on the issue. The question is why that is.

Let us first note that there is *no* reason to take this language as metaphorical.[23] It is only if we are already assuming that pregnancy, birth, and procreation are exclusively female activities, and their salient expression is physical, that we *then* suppose that their application beyond the sphere of the female is metaphorical. There is no evidence that Plato made this assumption, however; on the contrary, the text is emphatic that *all* human beings are pregnant in body and soul – in which case 'it is no accident that the pregnant one is expressed by a neuter participle, *to kuoun*, to avoid a choice between masculine and feminine gender: the grammar is not casual'.[24] Pregnancy is categorised by *us* as female, but the philosophical point (supported by, and perhaps giving philosophical expression to, the use of *kuein* and cognate terms more inclusively by poets and philosophers who applied such terms to males) is that physical pregnancy is but one species of a much larger phenomenon, which covers human creativity of all kinds (205b7–c3). The same point, which is grounded in clarifying genus and species correctly, is made more explicitly about *eros* (205d1–8): there is no 'sublimation' in this account of sexual *eros* onto *eros* for knowledge and so on; nor is *eros* for the intelligible form a metaphor. 'The whole' of desire for good things and happiness is *eros* (205d1–2): 'But those who direct themselves to it in all sorts of other ways, in business, or in their love of physical exercise, or in philosophy are neither said to be in love nor to be lovers, while those who proceed to give themselves to just one kind of love have the name of the whole love' (205d4–8). This is a mistake; just as it is to suppose that pregnancy comes in just the one physical, female, form.

Now, if it is the case both that the language is muddled (from the perspective of a gender binary at least) and that this is not a metaphorical usage of terms that apply properly and exclusively to women, then we cannot make assumption (a) that the 'female' can be located; nor then can we suppose, as (b) urges upon us, that Plato is 'appropriating' or 'exploiting' the female for his own 'purely masculine philosophical and

---

[22] For example, consider Zeus pregnant with Athena and Dionysus. See Leitao (2012).
[23] Contra Evans (2006: 14): 'Diotima's phrase "birth ... in both body and soul" (206b7) clearly points to a metaphoric usage.' Rowe (1998: 178): 'All of human life is seen – for the moment – in terms of a metaphorical (or sometimes, where real sex is involved, actual) process of reproduction.' Rightly seen by Wardy (2002: 29): 'It is vital to realize that Diotima is not speaking metaphorically'.
[24] Wardy (2002: 46).

reproductive process'[25] or that he 'effectively incorporates and allocates to men, the positive dimension of each of these two Greek stereotypes of women'.[26] There is nothing distinctly female about procreation, or its accompanying reciprocity and nurture, at all. That, I submit, is the philosophical point exemplified by the ambiguous language. Those who insist that this is no more than male 'appropriation', or 'eclipsing', of the distinctively female reveal themselves either to be stuck in a retrograde essentialism (if this is a biological claim) or to be entrenched in a gender binary (even if socially and historically constructed) that Plato is evidently at pains to resist.

Beyond Binary Thinking

The picture is both more confusing and more promising. Consider Diotima herself. Though introduced as a woman (201d2), her portrayal is muddled by the fact that she exemplifies characteristics of *eros* that were previously associated with a male character. To appreciate this, we need to turn to the story of Eros' parentage, which describes the nature of *eros* (203b1–4a7). According to this story, the gods held a feast to celebrate the birth of Aphrodite. Penia (who becomes Eros' mother) is needy and lacking, uninvited to this feast and associated with the mortal. Being aware of this state, she seeks out the resourceful and divine Poros to fulfil her lack. As a result of this union, Eros was conceived. Though some of this story seems to exploit relatively conventional gender-associations, even here there is disruption: the apparently resourceless Penia schemes, showing the resourcefulness associated with Poros, to make up her lack with an active seduction, while Poros, drunk on nectar, passively sleeps while being taken advantage of by Penia. Such scheming, as it is inherited by Eros in the story, is owed to the father, Poros, and his 'resource'. This mixed parentage enables Eros to be 'a schemer after the beautiful and the good, courageous, impetuous and intense, a clever hunter, always weaving new devices, both passionate for wisdom and resourceful, philosophising throughout his life, a clever magician, sorcerer and sophist' (203d4–8). The central point, though, is that Diotima is described in terms of Eros' *father* Poros and Socrates in terms of Eros' *mother* Penia. Socrates sought out Diotima because he was aware of his need (207c1), just as the experience of need motivated Penia to find her Poros in the story; Diotima is presented as 'wise' (201d) and *sophistes* (208c1), like Poros

---

[25] As du Bois argues (1994: 169, 183).   [26] Halperin (1990: 130).

(203d6–7, d4), and her Mantinean origins suggests a relationship to the divine, which is the preserve of Poros, invited to dine with the gods. Diotima, in other words, embodies the euporetic aspect of *eros*, which is figured in the story, at least, as coming from the father, even though he falls short of any straightforwardly gendered characteristics by failing to perform the assigned attributes, which are exemplified better by *Penia*'s 'resource' and 'scheming'. If Diotima is a 'woman', and aligned with Poros, it is simply not clear what associations this brings.[27]

The story, which gives us the tools to appreciate the characteristics of Socrates and Diotima, takes us to the heart of Diotima's concern with the notion of the *metaxu*, from which it takes its lead (202e–3a) and to which it returns immediately after the tale is told (204a–b6). Consider the very first thing that Socrates learnt from Diotima, which was a lesson in how to move beyond binary thinking. Socrates, much like Agathon, had assumed that *eros* is beautiful and good. Diotima refutes this view, on the grounds that *eros* desires what it lacks, either now or in the future. Since *eros* desires what is beautiful and good, *eros* cannot be beautiful nor good (199d–201c). Socrates then wonders whether this commits him to supposing that *eros* is the opposite of these things. Once he has grasped the difference between contraries and contradictories, he sees that something can be not beautiful and good, without being ugly and base. Binary thinking is evidently not helpful when understanding the phenomenon of *eros*. What follows is an elaboration of this point with an account of *eros* as intermediate (*metaxu*) between opposites (201e8–2b5) – for example, beautiful and ugly, good and base, knowledge and ignorance, divine and mortal, which culminates in an account of *eros* as an intermediary *daimon* (202e5–3a8), and which is then given further expression in the story of Poros and Penia. Once the story is completed, Diotima returns to her central point about the *metaxu* with the example of those who philosophise (204b1–b5), explaining that it is due to the characteristics inherited from Poros and Penia that Eros is in this intermediate state (b6–7). Elaborating the *metaxu* structures this entire section.[28]

---

[27] On such grounds, Wardy concludes that: 'Despite appearances, Diotima is not a woman, and her towering presence in the depths of the interior of the dialogue is no vindication of the female' (2002: 44). He relays various characteristics that are more commonly associated with males that are ascribed to Diotima, as well as pointing out that it seems that Socrates has been 'impregnated' by her.

[28] For the importance of this see Irigaray (1989: 10); Frede (1993: 403–7), with Wardy (2002: 39), who argues that 'beyond her speech, intermediaries, intermediates, and liminal characters are salient in the dialogue.'

The notion of the *metaxu* requires unpacking. It could mean that *eros* is a combination of opposite qualities, or it could mean that *eros* oscillates between opposite qualities, such that a desiring agent is never properly determined by either.[29] In the story of Poros and Penia, the suggestion is that Eros is intermediate in a *dynamic* sense, which is to say that he fluctuates between a variety of opposite characteristics; *eros* mediates between opposites (201e8–2b5). For example, from his mother Eros has need as his constant companion, but in virtue of his father Eros is a resourceful schemer after the beautiful and the good. Eros' nature is *neither* that of a mortal nor an immortal; rather he lives and flourishes whenever he finds resources but then dies again because those resources are always slipping away from him (203e4–5), though he has the ability to 'come back to life again' (203e3). From this description, it seems that Eros at least temporarily manifests the properties of the one parent, then that of the other, and so on. The story of Eros is evidently designed to explicate human *eros*, and it suggests that *eros* is a dynamic experience. This coheres well with the description of mortal life in a constant state of flux and change (207b5–8c5). According to this, moral beings are indeterminate creatures, unlike the gods who have a fixed identity that persists through time (208a8). Described as the best helper for human nature (212b4–5), *eros* is the engine, or energy of self-constitution, which assists in the task of self-determination. This occurs through creative effort, which is geared towards reproducing the value seen in the world and to capturing it in a life of one's own, as a parent, poet, legislator, or philosopher, depending on how one conceives of value and the creative efforts one deploys to secure it. This explains the emphasis on stability and fixity at the apex of the ascent (211a1–b7). We are seeking a creative environment – a beauty – which inspires an act of self-creation that speaks not only to our aspiration for the good but for stable determination in a world of flux. This is the world in which *eros* not only operates but brings to our attention in the experience of desire, as we sense that lack and neediness, coupled with a forceful urge to overcome it.

---

[29] Allen argues as follows: 'Plato uses the term intermediate in at least two distinguishable senses. Sometimes intermediates are described as having a share of opposite qualities; if *eros* were intermediate in this sense, it would be both good and bad, ugly, and beautiful, mortal and immortal. In another sense, intermediates instead of possessing both opposites possess neither ... the intermediate character of *eros* is of this kind' (1991: 49). Compare *Gorgias* 467e3–5: 'Is there anything which is either good nor bad, or what is in between these, neither good nor bad?', which is later elaborated as 'such things partake of the good, sometimes of the bad, and sometimes of neither' (468a1). See also *Lysis* 216c; *Prt.* 351d.

Viewed against the backdrop of the notion of the *metaxu*, the interaction between Socrates and Diotima not only exemplifies the interaction between Poros and Penia but the complexity of *eros*' nature in the delivery of this speech. Any collapse of gendered polarities into a more fluid picture is very much to the point. The upshot is not that desiring agents exhibit a kind of psychic hermaphroditism in the experience of desire but rather that they dynamically fluctuate between any perceived binary, including that between genders.[30] Socrates is both the 'beautiful' student who allows Diotima to 'give birth' to wisdom (the speech of which Socrates is the recipient), and Socrates, in turn, due to encountering this 'beautiful' wisdom gives birth to wisdom of his own (dialectical enquiries of which Diotima's theory gives the inspiration). Are these gendered? Not any more than they were earlier, where attention to the language suggests it is decidedly genderqueer (e.g., 206d–e). The lesson from Diotima is that *eros* is a non-binary facilitator and we create ourselves anew as desiring beings who are 'self-determining and fully participate in the development of' whatever self-determination we suppose will deliver *eudaimonia*.[31] Though the discussion of the *metaxu* is general enough to accommodate gender binaries, notice that they are not explicitly included in this list of beautiful and ugly, good and base, knowledge and ignorance. Perhaps gender categories exist, just as knowledge and ignorance, or beauty and ugliness, but if so, how they are conceived remains an open question. Or it could be the case that they are not included in this list precisely because, unlike the good and the bad, or the mortal and the divine, gendered characteristics are not objective or relevant opposites. Or they might be objective (like 'tall, short') but not relevant, which is the important criterion here (cf. the *Republic* 5. 455d–e). Whatever the answer to that question, *eros*' relationship to (real or perceived) binaries is surely clear; desiring agents will never be determined by them. The genderqueer vocabulary and portrayal of Socrates and Diotima works beautifully to illustrate that point.

The determination eventually advocated in the ascent, where *eros* is envisaged to reach its *telos*, is markedly inclusive (*anthropoi* 211e2, 212a1, b7; *thnetes*, 211e3) and beyond gender. The cultural pursuits of the Highest Mysteries are neither shaped nor determined in any significant way by gender. Diotima is not sure whether Socrates can follow them, but

---

[30] The position of psychic hermaphroditism I once entertained, was taken up by Wardy (2002: 47), who rightly raises the question of whether the disparity between genders disappears in this mix.

[31] I adapt the phrase from Grant (1994: 183), whose humanist vision for feminism argues that 'the aim of feminist politics is the end of gender and the creation of new human beings who are self-determining and fully participate in the development of their own constantly evolving subjectivity'.

that is not because he is a man who has failed to grasp 'female' truths but because they are difficult, and it is not clear how far he has come at that point. The 'entry criteria' such as they are, concern whether one is willing and able to engage in the reflective activity characteristic of the ascent, which involves a turn away from the body (*kataphronein*, 210b5). Lest we suppose that the denigration of the body brings with it a denigration of the female,[32] it should be noted that there is *no* association of the female with the body here: all human beings are pregnant in both body and soul (*pantes anthropoi*, 206c1–2), where that means, on the psychic level, that women no less than men carry 'wisdom and the rest of virtue' (209c). Those (presumably men) who are pregnant in body and turn to women to produce children are denigrated not for turning to women but for doing so with the sole purpose of physical reproduction in mind, supposing that this will bring them memory and *eudaimonia* for all time to come (208e5–6). The privileged relationships are not gendered, entered into by gendered beings, on account of their gender difference. It may be true that the disdain for the body shown in Diotima's speech is indicative of *somatophobia*, as Spelman argues (1982), on the grounds that bodily identity is not indicative of who we are, but this is not (as Spelman argues) tethered to misogyny because there is no association of the female with the bodily here. As she rightly argues later, 'it doesn't make any difference, ultimately, whether we have a woman's body or a man's body'; or rather, it does not make any difference for these purposes, or for ethical evaluation more generally.[33] That is not to say that Plato was unaware of the disfiguring effects for society as a whole that existing categorisations place

---

[32] See, for example, Spelman (1982: 118): '[Plato's] misogyny is part of his *somatophobia*: the body is seen as the source of all the undesirable traits a human being could have, and women's lives are spent in manifesting those traits'; '[Plato] depicts women's lives as quintessentially body-directed' (19). Compare Saxonhouse (1991: 151) on the body in the *Republic*.

[33] Spelman (1982: 117–18):

> Plato insists, over and over again in a variety of ways, that our souls are the most important parts of us. Not only is it through our souls that we shall have access to knowledge, reality, goodness, beauty; but also, in effect, we are our souls ... our bodies are not essential to our identity ... if we are our souls, and our bodies are not essential to who we are, then it doesn't make any difference, ultimately, whether we have a woman's body or a man's body ... if the only difference between women and men is that they have different bodies, and if bodies are mere incidental attachments to what constitutes one's real identity, then there is no important difference between men and women.

It seems unlikely that Plato supposed immortal souls had a gender; in which case, Spelman is surely right that gender differentiation is a facet of embodiment. Notions of metempsychosis prior to Plato do not usually restrict souls to embodiments of just one gender. Empedocles claims to have lived various human and non-human lives and to have been individuals of different genders.

upon those who are physically capable of bearing children; *Republic* 5 is evidence to the contrary. It is to say that in this text at least, only those who are enslaved to the body have to take heed of gender difference (208e5–6). Those who suppose that *eudaimonia* is satisfied in physical reproduction have to adhere to a gender binary, for the simple fact that in this instance at least it is indeed the case that 'a woman bears and a man begets'; but if we move beyond the body then we are liberated from attaching such relevance to this simple fact; it becomes as relevant as the fact that some people have hair and some are bald (*Rep.* 454c). The body can be played with, along with whatever gender markers others may bring to that: Socrates can 'beautify' himself for Agathon (174a7); he can show endurance and hardiness through his body if he chooses (220a); he can use his body to pursue or to be pursued. Do we wish to gender that behaviour? And why? There is little value attached to the body or to any of the gender markers we (or the ancient Greeks) may apply to it. Since the body continues to invite the constraints of gendered categories, this is surely all to the good. If the question is not 'Does this text reflect female experience in the use of Diotima?', but 'Does Diotima assist not just the liberation of women (however conceived), but all those who question the relevance of gendered categories?' (of which the non-binary movement is now the stellar example), then Diotima is surely an ally.[34]

Conclusion

It is a curiosity of the age that we are being invited to reflect on whether we can identify with the authors we study. Perhaps this only seems curious from the vantage of a philosophy characterised by strangeness and provocation. If prompted to reflect as a woman (conceived by my culture and time), then I find that identifying with Plato's dialogues is not difficult. One can find recognition of the experiences our own age continues to gender as female (birth, pregnancy, midwifery). The drive to acknowledge a care-centred component of rationality associated with feminist thinkers (Gilligan [1982]; Kittay and Meyers [1987]) is not news to any reader of Plato, for whom caring interpersonal relationships form a crucial part of his

---

[34] Particularly those in the non-binary movement who identify as genderqueer, on which see, for example, Faucette (2014: 74): 'Non-binary activism is not about taking away others' gender identity; rather it's about questioning the unique pedestal on which gender stands as a system of classification and an identity marker, and especially the heavy use of a classification system that is based on assumptions rather than consent.'

ethical outlook.³⁵ And the 'morality of responsibility', associated with Gilligan (1982) is foreshadowed in the ethics of the *Republic*, in which philosophers have responsibilities to others they would otherwise not have had *because* they stand in a relationship of friendship and care for those others.³⁶ Membership of a community plays a constitutive role in self-identity.³⁷ While both Plato and Gilligan value an ethics of care and responsibility to others in our communities, unlike Gilligan, Plato does not take this trait to be gendered. For those who resist attaching such weight to the gendering of these laudable characteristics, it is the provocative Plato with whom one identifies, who provides a liberating dialogical space that recognises the social markers of his time, 'outs' them as mere contingent playthings of the age time, shows sensitivity to the political and philosophical dangers their associations can bring, and invites us to conceive new imaginative possibilities.³⁸ Perhaps this overlooks the casual sexism that litters certain dialogues.³⁹ Arguably, this is the price we pay for the acknowledgement that Plato meets interlocutors on their own terms in these 'situated' dialogical spaces (*Phdr.* 269d–74b); this means using the language and associations of his time and place. As for philosophical commitments, more persistent are accounts of virtue as gender neutral, a gender-neutral soul, and an inclusive appeal to all human beings to take up philosophy. From that perspective, why there continues to be so much investment in Diotima's gender is one question Plato invites us to entertain.⁴⁰

---

³⁵ Ruddick (1980); Gilligan (1982). Compare MacIntyre (1999: 3) who cites feminist thinkers as allies in acknowledging dependence and the importance of social relationships in human development.
³⁶ On this, see Sheffield (2021).   ³⁷ See Benhabib (1986/87).
³⁸ For resistance to the vindication of the 'female', see Simone de Beauvoir (1949/52: 123): women's demand is 'not that they be exalted in their femininity; they wish that in themselves, as in humanity in general, transcendence may prevail over immanence', cited in Spelman (1982).
³⁹ For the association of women with weakness and emotional incontinence, see *Rep.* 395d–e: 'A woman, young or old, wrangling with her husband, defying heaven, loudly boasting, fortunate in her own conceit, or involved in misfortune or possessed by grief and lamentation, still less a woman that is sick or in labour.' Compare *Rep.* 605c–d: 'When in our lives some affection comes to us you are aware that we pride ourselves ... on our ability to remain calm and endure, in the belief that this is the conduct of a man and giving in to grief that of a woman.' Compare the description of the tyrant, who 'must live for the most part cowering in the recesses of his house like a woman, envying among other citizens anyone who goes abroad and sees any good thing' (*Rep.* 597c). In the *Timaeus*, incarnation into a woman is a degeneration (*Tim.* 42b–c; 76e; 91a).
⁴⁰ Thanks to Christian Keime and James Warren for comments.

CHAPTER 2

Sulabhā and Indian Philosophy
Rhetoric, Gender, and Freedom in the Mahābhārata

Brian Black*

Introduction

In a well-known scene from the *Mahābhārata*, the female renunciate Sulabhā engages in a philosophical debate against King Janaka. This chapter will examine Sulabhā's arguments and method of articulating them, as well as show that she makes important contributions to philosophical discussions that are going on throughout the text. I will do this by focusing on three aspects of her argument in particular: (1) her formulation of what constitutes a good speech, (2) her articulation of *mokṣa-dharma* – the ethics of renunciation – which is a major innovation of the *Mahābhārata*, and (3) her characterisation of the highest knowledge as beyond the dualities of gender distinctions. In developing these arguments together, I will show that Sulabhā makes original contributions to ongoing debates about rhetoric, ethics, and ontology in Indian philosophy. This chapter will also address the thorny question of whether or not Sulabhā should be understood as a woman philosopher or as a literary character most likely constructed by male authors. As I will argue, despite the ultimate unanswerability of this question, Sulabhā articulates an understanding of enlightenment (*mokṣa*) that is as available for women as for men.

The *Mahābhārata* as a Philosophical Text

The *Mahābhārata*, composed in Sanskrit and most likely compiled in the first centuries of the Common Era, is a multi-genre text that defies categorisation.[1] The main story is about two sets of rival cousins – the

---

* I would like to thank Naomi Appleton and Emily West for reading a draft of this chapter and offering helpful feedback.
[1] For a discussion of scholarly debates about the composition of the *Mahābhārata*, and other textual issues, see Sullivan (2016).

Pāṇḍavas and the Kauravas – who both claim to be legitimate heirs to the throne. The narrative follows these two sets of cousins from their birth to their emerging rivalry as adolescents to their young adulthood, when a full-scale war breaks out between them. Because Western scholars have tended to approach the text as narrative, myth, and epic, its philosophical dimensions have been undervalued.[2]

As I have argued elsewhere, when reading the *Mahābhārata* philosophically, we need to pay particular attention to its use of the dialogue form (Black 2021a: 8–11). In addition to being framed by two conversations, at the very beginning of the text, many of the crucial scenes in the main narrative unfold as verbal exchanges, with the central characters discussing and debating among themselves about how they should act in a number of difficult and morally ambiguous circumstances. Many of these dialogues reflect upon the central ideas of Indian philosophical and religious traditions, such as morality (*dharma*), enlightenment (*mokṣa*), causality (*karma*), discipline (*yoga*), truth (*satya*), fate (*daiva*), human agency (*puruṣakāra*), non-violence (*ahiṃsā*), ultimate reality (*brahman*), the self (*ātman*), and devotion (*bhakti*).

Moreover, the dialogue form itself often contains embedded arguments, as characters articulate reasons in their attempts to persuade each other to think or act in particular ways. In addition to the specific arguments made by individual characters, there are often philosophical implications in the ways that discussions unfold. Hans-Georg Gadamer, in his engagement with Plato's work, has perhaps explored this implication of the dialogue form as much as anyone.[3] Gadamer was drawn to Plato's dialogues because he saw philosophical dialogue itself – the conversations we have with others about shared concerns – as fundamental to how we experience and develop understandings of the world we live in. In his readings of Plato, Gadamer rejects the search for an overall meaning or hidden doctrine. Rather, he pays close attention to the 'directions of questioning' between Socrates and his interlocutors (1985: 186). Similar to Gadamer's approach to Plato's dialogues, I have argued elsewhere that much of the philosophical import of the *Mahābhārata* is expressed through how dialogue unfolds throughout the text (Black 2021a: 10). In this chapter, I will not only look at the philosophical implications of a specific dialogue in the *Mahābhārata*, but I will also pay particular attention to how a woman's

---

[2] For further discussion, see Black (2021a), as well Matilal (2002) and Dalmiya and Mukherji (2018).
[3] For an excellent discussion of the dialogue form in philosophy throughout the Western tradition, see Hösle (2012).

voice is represented through dialogue, as well as what she says about dialogue itself.

Recovering the Voices of Women Philosophers

Many scholars have addressed the unique challenges in finding authentic voices of women philosophers from the ancient world. One of the major difficulties is that very few surviving texts are attributed to women. In the context of classical Mediterranean philosophy, Marguerite Deslauriers points out that works attributed to women often do not have 'independent evidence to establish the existence of the women in question' (2012: 343).[4] Another problem, also noted by Deslauriers, is that 'the most extensive evidence we have about women in ancient philosophy and the issues around women is found in men's philosophical treatises' (2012: 343).

Similar problems emerge when trying to find the voices of women philosophers in an ancient Indian context. The only text attributed to female authors from ancient India is the *Therigathā*. Although this attribution is not uncontested, the *Therigathā* nevertheless is widely regarded as the oldest extant book in the world composed entirely by women.[5] Even in cases where texts are attributed to male authors, there are many instances of women participating in philosophical discussions. The Upaniṣads, for example, which are often considered the first philosophical texts from India, include some notable women discussing philosophical issues.[6] Most famously, Gārgī, who appears in the *Bṛhadāraṇyaka Upaniṣad*, challenges the eminent brahmin Yājñavalkya in the court of King Janaka.[7] Gārgī does not win this debate, but she distinguishes herself from the other interlocutors by giving Yājñavalkya his strongest rebuke, after which she declares him the victor. The Upaniṣads also include Maitreyī, who is described as a knower of *brahman* (*Brahmavāœdinī*) (BU 4.5.1) and who engages in a conversation with her husband Yājñavalkya about the nature of the self (*ātman*) (BU 4.5.1–15).[8]

In addition to the Upaniṣads, the *Mahābhārata* also includes several women who make notable contributions to philosophical and religious

---

[4] See also the chapters in this volume about the Pythagorean women (Chapters 7 and 8).
[5] The *Therigathā* is a collection of poems composed by Buddhist nuns, which offers invaluable insights into the emancipatory potential of the Buddhist path for women. For an excellent translation of the *Therigathā*, see Charles Hallisey (2015).
[6] For brief introduction to the Upaniṣads, see Black (2015b).
[7] For further discussion of Gārgī, see Black (2007a: 150–55)
[8] For further discussion of Maitreyī, see Black (2007a: 162–67).

debates. Most famously, Draupadī, the major heroine of the text, makes *dharma*-based arguments to secure her own freedom after being staked by her husband in a dicing match. Other women who display their learning and knowledge in discussions about *dharma* and other central ideas include Śakuntalā, Sāvitrī, Gāndhārī, and Ulūpī. Although these and other women in the *Mahābhārata* have not always been recognised as philosophers, their knowledge and wisdom – particularly in relation to their male interlocutors – has been widely acknowledged. As Stephanie Jamison has noted: 'In story after story women see what needs to be done, take command, and order the bewildered, hand-wringing male participants into their supporting roles – and the enterprise fails only when one of these ninnies messes up his part of the woman's plan' (1996: 15).[9]

One of the challenges of assessing the philosophical views of these women in the *Mahābhārata*, including Sulabhā, is that we have no way of knowing whether their words are representative of the views of real women. To what extent can we interpret the words of female characters as expressing the philosophical views of women in a text likely composed by men? As is clear in the chapters throughout this book, this is a question facing scholars of women philosophers in many contexts from the ancient world. In the case of Sulabhā, since we lack conclusive arguments for or against her historicity, I find it more fruitful to focus on her philosophical arguments, what they contribute to our understanding of philosophy in the *Mahābhārata*, and why they are ascribed to a woman philosopher.

Because readers of this book are more likely to be familiar with ancient Greek philosophy than ancient Indian philosophy, it is worth noting some similarities and differences between Sulabhā in the *Mahābhārata* and Diotima in Plato's *Symposium*. Similar to Diotima, Sulabhā is a woman who offers a prominent argument in a text likely composed by men. An important difference, however, is that whereas we know that the *Symposium* was composed by Plato, the authorship of the *Mahābhārata* is a topic of considerable debate. The text itself attributes its authorship to the male sage Vyāsa, but most scholars today assume that many composers contributed to the redacted text, whether that took place over several centuries or by a committee over a shorter period of time. Considering the fact that we do not have any evidence about who might have contributed to authoring the text, I do not think we can discount the possibility

---

[9] For further discussion of Draupadī and other female characters in the *Mahābhārata*, see Falk (1977); Jamison (1996); Hiltebeitel (2000); Malinar (2007); Patton (2007); Dhand (2008); Black (2013, 2021a, and 2021b); and Chakravarti (2014).

that women participated in its composition, whether directly or indirectly.[10] Indeed, despite prohibitions against women learning sacred scriptures and receiving a formal education, many women depicted in the texts display their knowledge of traditional sources and reveal their educational backgrounds. In the same way that female characters, such as Gārgī in the Upaniṣads and Sulabhā in the *Mahābhārata*, appear in literary depictions of philosophical debates, there might have been women participating in the discussions about the redaction of the texts. In the case of Sulabhā, although we cannot assume that her words represent an authentic female voice, we cannot rule out that possibility either.

Nevertheless, like Diotima, we only know about Sulabhā as a literary character, as there is no external evidence indicating that her personage is based on a real woman. Indeed, the name 'Sulabhā' suggests that she is more allegorical than real. Arindam Chakravarti describes her name as ironic. Sulabhā, as he points out, means '"Easy-to-Get" because she remained so hard to get for Janaka, in every sense of "getting"' (2014: 246). Moreover, unlike Diotima, who appears in a work in which the historicity of most of the other characters – such as Socrates, Aristophanes, Agathon, and Alcibiades – is corroborated by other sources, there is no evidence for the historicity of most of the characters in the *Mahābhārata*. Rather than disqualify the *Mahābhārata* as a philosophically insignificant text, however, I think the lack of historical verifiability challenges us to consider whether historicity should be a criterion for philosophical merit. Just as we should take the arguments of all characters in the *Mahābhārata* seriously, regardless of not being able to establish their historical authenticity, so should we with Sulabhā.

A further parallel between Sulabhā and Diotima is that both characters seem to reveal their text's anxieties about the authority of the speech of women. Indeed, a striking similarity between them is that their voices are mediated by several male narrators within their respective texts. Diotima does not appear in the main episode of the *Symposium*, but rather her views are narrated by Socrates when he is delivering his speech at Agathon's house. Meanwhile, the account of the banquet itself is narrated by Apollodorus, who was not present but who had heard a first-hand description of the episode from Aristodemus, who was in attendance. Keeping in mind that Plato, as author of the text, is a narrator as well, then Diotima's

---

[10] A number of scholars have indicated the possibility of women contributing to the authorship of the *Mahābhārata*, in one way or another. See, for example, van Buitenen (1975: 183–85); Hiltebeitel (2001: 166–67); Mary Brockington (in Ram-Prasad 2018: 64 n. 18); and Black (2021a: 14).

views are mediated through the narration of four men. Intriguingly, Sulabhā's voice is also mediated through four male narrators. Her debate with King Janaka is narrated by Bhīṣma, whose dialogue with Yudhiṣṭhira is narrated by Vaiśaṃpāyana, whose dialogue with Janamejaya is narrated by Ugraśravas who tells Śaunaka. It is not entirely clear who narrates the Ugraśravas dialogue, but the *Mahābhārata* tells us that its author is Vyāsa.

Although it is certainly a coincidence that the voices of both Diotima and Sulabhā are filtered through exactly four male narrators, in both cases the multiple levels of narration bring up interesting issues related to the authority and veracity of the words of women. Modern historical sensibilities are likely to see the words of Diotima and Sulabhā as less authentically female because they are so heavily mediated through male narrators. However, once again, it is worth considering whether the demand for historicity is the most useful lens through which to make sense of Diotima's and Sulabhā's filtered words. We might entertain the possibility that the very need to have their views authenticated by male narrators indicates that their words and teachings were strongly associated with female perspectives.

Finally, while Diotima is somewhat of an anomaly in Plato's work, Sulabhā is one of many strong female characters who participate in philosophical dialogues in the *Mahābhārata*. Another compelling reason, then, for taking Sulabhā's characterisation as a woman seriously is because her views intersect with and amplify the views of several other female characters. As we will see, Sulabhā's arguments explicitly address issues related to her experiences as a woman, many of which overlap with the experiences of other women in the text. Although we cannot naïvely assume that the speech of female characters consists of the actual words of historical women, at the same time Sulabhā's arguments genuinely challenge and rethink the explicitly misogynistic views about women in other places in the text. Whether or not her character is based on a real person and whether or not her character was composed by a man, we will see that what she says offers a genuinely female perspective and has important implications for how we understand women philosophers in an Indian context.

The Sulabhā/Janaka debate (*Mahābhārata*, 12.308)

Now that we have addressed the issue of Sulabhā as a woman philosopher, let us look more closely at what she argues in her debate with Janaka and the philosophical contributions she makes to the *Mahābhārata* as a whole.

The debate between Sulabhā and Janaka appears in the *Mokṣa-dharma* section of the *Śānti Parvan*, which is the twelfth of the *Mahābhārata*'s eighteen books. It is narrated by the patriarch Bhīṣma to the recently crowned king Yudhiṣṭhira as part of the dharmic instructions to prepare him for assuming the throne. Although this is Sulabhā's only appearance in the *Mahābhārata*, Janaka – the legendary philosopher king from the late Brāhmaṇas and early Upaniṣads – features in several episodes, particularly in the *Śānti Parvan*.[11] Indeed, King Janaka is the character from the Upaniṣads who appears the most in the *Mahābhārata*. Like in the Upaniṣads, here he engages in a philosophical discussion about renunciation. But rather than the wise and approachable philosopher king of the Upaniṣads, here Janaka is represented as arrogant and petulant. Another significant difference from his portrayal in late Vedic literature, where he is depicted as a single individual who is king of Videha, is that in the *Mahābhārata* Janaka is the name of a number of different kings, all of whom are in one way or another related to Janaka of the *Bṛhadāraṇyaka Upaniṣad*, but many of whom have identities that seem to be distinct from him.[12]

At the beginning of her debate in the *Mahābhārata*, Sulabhā is a wandering ascetic who hears reports from other renouncers[13] that King Janaka has achieved *mokṣa* without giving up his kingdom. Doubtful of these claims, she uses her yogic powers to put on an immaculately beautiful body and travel to the court in the wink of an eye, to find out for herself about Janaka's claims to be enlightened (see below for more details about the special abilities afforded by *yoga*). When she arrives, after accepting the King's hospitality, she challenges him to a debate in front of the assembly. At this point, she uses her knowledge of *yoga* to inhabit his body, where she dwells for the remainder of the discussion.

Sulabhā on Rhetoric

As I have argued elsewhere (Black 2021a: 8–11, 17–21), the dialogue form of the *Mahābhārata* not only portrays philosophical discussions between interlocutors within the text but also provokes philosophical reflection by compelling its readers to contemplate its numerous moral dilemmas,

---

[11] For further discussion about the several episodes featuring Janaka, see Black (2022).
[12] For a discussion of Janaka across Hindu, Buddhist, and Jain literature, see Appleton (2017: 137–69).
[13] A renouncer is someone who has given up a life of marriage and children in favour of the solitary pursuit of enlightenment (*mokṣa*). See below for further discussion.

unresolved debates, and ambiguous arguments. Sulabhā makes an important contribution to this understanding of dialogue in the *Mahābhārata* by outlining how to engage in a philosophical conversation with someone who holds different views. Chakrabarti, who also discusses the dialogical features of the *Mahābhārata*, describes the Sulabhā/Janaka dialogue as 'the most philosophical of all the conversations reported in the text because it is designed to be self-reflexive – *a conversation about how to converse well* and how not to converse in public' (2014: 246). Although I hesitate to agree that it is the most philosophical of all the conversations in the *Mahābhārata*, it is nevertheless significant that in a text in which dialogue has such profound philosophical implications, Sulabhā is one of the few characters to theorise about dialogue itself.

Sulabhā's dialogue with Janaka is not presented as a back-and-forth exchange but rather as an argument and counterargument, with each interlocutor speaking just once. Janaka speaks first, posing a series of questions to Sulabhā about her social identity:

> Whose are you? And where are you from? ... I cannot get a clear sense of your learning, of your age, or of the ethnic group you were born in, so please convey answers to these matters in this assembly of the good. (12.308.20–21)[14]

Janaka returns to these questions throughout his argument, challenging Sulabhā's claim of achieving *mokṣa* by questioning her social identity in terms of class, family, and gender. As we will see, some of his accusations are explicitly sexist. In addition to challenging Sulabhā's ability to be enlightened, Janaka vehemently defends his own claims to have attained *mokṣa*.

Despite his positive portrayal in the Upaniṣads and other episodes in the *Mahābhārata*, here Bhīṣma – the narrator of this episode – portrays Janaka negatively. At the beginning of the dialogue, Janaka is referred to as *dharma-dhvaja*, which can mean 'hypocrite' or 'impostor' (12.308.4). Also, during his argument Janaka repeatedly insults Sulabhā, calling her a wicked woman and accusing her of using her yogic powers as a poison (12.308.65, 68). Moreover, after Janaka concludes his argument, Bhīṣma describes the king's statements as 'unpleasant' (*asukha*) and 'inappropriate' (*ayukta*) (12.308.76). It is also noteworthy that Janaka speaks first, because in many dialogical episodes in ancient Indian literature speaking first in a

---

[14] Translations are from Fitzgerald (2002). In some cases, I have slightly modified translations to leave key words, such as *mokṣa*, untranslated, or to convey a more literal rendering.

philosophical discussion can be an indicator that the speaker is too proud and/or has incomplete knowledge.[15]

Despite Janaka's aggressive tone and insulting words, Sulabhā begins her response by outlining the characteristics of a proper argument:

> King, a 'speech' is said to have an appropriate meaning, to be free of the eighteen faults that spoil words or thought, and to be endowed with the eighteen virtues; and a 'speech' has sophistication, careful discrimination, clear order, the presentation of a conclusion, and motivation – all five of these are aspects of the meaning to be conveyed. Listen to a careful description – in terms of sentences, words, and the meanings of words – of each one of these items, sophistication and the others, that occur over and over again. When there are several discrete things to be known, but the knowledge of them forms an undivided whole, the extraordinary understanding in that is 'sophistication'. When, in regard to whatever subject he has in mind, one weighs the good and bad points according to the divisions of the subject matter, that is 'careful discrimination'. The experts on speech say that speech is 'clearly ordered' when one considers what one wants to say with 'This should be said earlier,' and 'This should be said later'. (12.308.76–83)

Here, Sulabhā argues that words must be used precisely and that points must be ordered correctly for a speech to convey meaning. She then describes five aspects of speech: subtlety (*saukṣmya*), deliberation (*saṁkhyā*), clear order (*krama*), a conclusion (*nirṇaya*), and purpose (*saprayojana*), in each case giving an example to illustrate her point. Next, she explains how she will articulate her speech, promising not to say too much or too little, not to say anything off topic or untrue, adding that she will not be affected by her emotions: 'I shall say nothing whatsoever out of love, anger, fear, greed, desperation, vulgarity, shame, pity, or haughtiness' (12.308.90). She then talks about the interaction between speaker and hearer, explaining that when they agree, meaning arises; but when a speaker disrespects the hearer, then the speaker only speaks for his own sake, or the speech is simply useless for the other.

Beginning her rebuttal by outlining how to make a proper argument, Sulabhā brings attention to her own philosophical training, while characterising Janaka's entire case as unsophisticated and confused. Chakrabarti, who describes Sulabhā's discourse as 'a formal meta-discourse on the ethics of discourse' (2014: 262), draws some interesting parallels between the requisites of proper speech that she lists here and the rules of

---

[15] See Black (2015a).

debate as outlined in the *Nyāya Sūtra* (2014: 264–65).[16] In other words, Sulabhā's argument here resonates with practices that the Indian philosophical tradition adopted as formal rules for interlocutors to follow in public debates. One of Sulabhā's main points is that an argument should have a proper structure: 'The experts on speech say that speech is "clearly ordered" when one considers what one wants to say with "This should be said earlier", and "This should be said later"' (12.308.83).

The way that Sulabhā structures her own speech is to work from the general to the specific, from the impersonal to the personal. After introducing her rebuttal by instructing how to make an argument, she then responds to the king's questions about her identity. As we will see below, she first addresses Janaka's questions indirectly, by offering what we might characterise as a scientific or biological explanation of human identity. But gradually she builds towards her concluding remarks, when she reveals her family lineage, educational lineage, and her name. As Chakrabarti comments: Sulabhā 'structured her speech very cleverly, starting with a meta-discourse on discourse, and ending with a self-introduction' (2014: 246–47). By the end, she answers all of Janaka's questions, but by contextualising them in the process, she exposes them as indications of his ignorance. In contrast, both the way she argues and her arguments themselves demonstrate her enlightened status.

Despite adhering to her own guidelines for proper disputation, the agreement between the speakers – which Sulabhā claims constitutes meaning – never happens. Nonetheless, Sulabhā emerges victorious. This is indicated by the fact that she gets in the last word, which is often a marker of superiority in narrative accounts of debate. Also, Bhīṣma describes Janaka as silenced at the end. James Fitzgerald interprets this as another sign of Sulabhā's victory: 'As Janaka was reduced to silence by Sulabhā's rebuttal, we can safely conclude that the author of the text intended to proclaim Sulabhā's rebuttal an effective refutation of Janaka's claims' (2002: 642–43). Moreover, Bhīṣma portrays Sulabhā favourably, describing her as 'lovely' and her argument as 'even lovelier' (12.308.77). Chakrabarti sees Bhīṣma's words here as highlighting Janaka's inability to focus on her argument instead of her appearance: 'The text thus teases us to make sure we focus on her logic rather than on her looks, which is something that Janaka, the typical male philosopher, apparently has a hard time doing' (2014: 261).

---

[16] The Nyāya school of Indian philosophy is credited with formalising the rules of philosophical debate in ancient India. The *Nyāya Sūtra* was the Nyāya school's foundational text.

Although she wins her argument, Sulabhā's views remain in tension with the views of other speakers in other sections of the text, which support Janaka. Indeed, Janaka's lineage and philosophical perspective align him with a number of authoritative figures in the *Mahābhārata*. At the beginning of his argument, for example, he claims that his teacher is Pañcaśikha, who is from the same family lineage (*gotra*) as Parāśara. Interestingly, this would connect him to Vyāsa, the reputed author of the *Mahābhārata*, who is the son of Parāśara. As we will see in the next section, Janaka's argument, which is a defence of *karma-yoga*, resonates with Kṛṣṇa's teaching in the *Bhagavad Gītā*, which, in addition to being a well-known text independently, is a crucial episode within the *Mahābhārata*. Furthermore, Janaka's views are similar to those expressed by Bhīṣma, whose own stance throughout his post-war instruction to Yudhiṣṭhira – despite his apparent endorsement of Sulabhā's view when narrating this story – is more in line with the doctrine of *karma-yoga*. Taking all this into consideration, the text seems to endorse both arguments: within the context of the dialogue itself, Sulabhā is the clear winner of the debate; yet within the context of Bhīṣma's instruction to Yudhiṣṭhira, Janaka's views seem to be preferred.

Panning out further, when we consider the *Mahābhārata* as a whole, the views of Sulabhā and Janaka remain in unresolved tension with each other. In this way, the inconclusive dimension of this debate is in keeping with the *Mahābhārata*'s general tendency to put contrasting views into playful juxtaposition (see Black 2021a). In a text that is so thoroughly dialogical, one of Sulabhā's greatest contributions, then, is to offer one of the most explicit accounts of how to engage in dialogue with others. By doing so, she not only points towards an ethics of conversation but also demonstrates that how one makes an argument is part of what measures one's knowledge claims. As Sulabhā points out, Janaka's emotional and unstructured accusations are an indication that he is not enlightened. In contrast, Sulabhā's own speech – from her dispassionate delivery to the structure of her argument – is a demonstration of her enlightened status. In this way, Sulabhā, despite advocating non-attachment in human relationships, argues that how one engages with others is the true measure of whether one has achieved the highest knowledge.

Sulabhā on Renunciation

One of the major issues that is explored in the dialogue between Sulabhā and Janaka is the tension between householder and renunciate ideals.

These ideals are often understood in relation to the concepts of *pravṛtti* and *nivṛtti*. Broadly speaking, *pravṛtti* refers to the teachings that focus on *dharma*, morality, whereas *nivṛtti* refers to those teachings that focus on *mokṣa*, enlightenment. While *pravṛtti* centres on fulfilling one's duties and responsibilities according to caste, family, gender, stage in life, and other factors, *nivṛtti* focuses on severing one's ties to family and society to practise a contemplative life in pursuit of the ultimate goal of final release from the ongoing cycle of rebirth. The competing values of the householder and the renunciate had already been in tension with each other for centuries, but no text explores their relationship as extensively as the *Mahābhārata*.

Moreover, the *Mahābhārata* offers innovative doctrines that propose possible compromises between these ideals. Its great contribution to the *pravṛtti* ideal is the doctrine of *karma-yoga*, which brings the ascetic practices of mental discipline into the everyday life of the householder. The most famous articulation of the *karma-yoga* doctrine is Kṛṣṇa's teaching in the *Bhagavad Gītā*, when he reveals his cosmic form, as he urges Arjuna to fight a war against his own family members. In response to Arjuna's initial refusal to fight, Kṛṣṇa argues that he can avoid any negative *karma* if he fights disinterestedly, if he is not attached to the fruits of his actions. One of the implications of this teaching is that by disciplining one's own desires and emotions while performing one's daily tasks, even the householder can achieve the highest soteriological goals, ones that were otherwise confined to religious specialists. In this way, *karma-yoga* can be seen as part of what Arti Dhand describes as 'the *Mahābhārata*'s larger extension of religious franchise to embrace all people, to dislocate piety and virtue from being the exclusive preserve of the priestly class' (2018: 102).

Conversely, but in parallel with the ideal of *karma-yoga*, the *Mahābhārata* also offers the doctrine of *mokṣa-dharma*, a teaching that brings some aspects of the householder ideal to the life of a religious renouncer. In particular, *mokṣa-dharma* circumscribes the life of the renouncer within the realm of *dharma*, emphasising that even the solitary ascetic has duties and obligations towards others and that there are certain social practices expected of those who have achieved the highest knowledge.

The tension between *pravṛtti* and *nivṛtti* is a central concern of the debate between Sulabhā and Janaka. Janaka is clearly a proponent of *pravṛtti*, as his philosophical argument is that one can achieve enlightenment without renouncing the world. He claims to be beyond *karma*, because his knowledge keeps his actions from producing results, like a seed that has been roasted can no longer germinate (12.308.33). Janaka argues that *mokṣa* is not achieved by renouncing possessions but rather through knowledge that releases one's bonds with the world. As we can see, this argument is an articulation of the doctrine of *karma-yoga*.

In contrast, Sulabhā follows *nivṛtti* ideals, living a solitary and itinerant lifestyle. She is depicted as adept at *yoga* and as one who has attained *mokṣa*. An intriguing aspect of her encounter with Janaka is that she uses her knowledge of *yoga* to enter into the king's being (*sattva*) with her being (12.308.16). Sulabhā, thus, conducts her entire argument while dwelling within Janaka's body. As indicated by the *Yogasūtra* and other sources, the ability to inhabit another's body was widely accepted to be a power attained through the practice of *yoga*.[17] We can see, then, that an important implication of Sulabhā residing in Janaka's body is her demonstration of her yogic abilities.

Sulabhā rejects Janaka's arguments in favour of the view that one must live the life of a renouncer in order to achieve enlightenment. She brings attention to the various ways in which the life of a king is dependent upon those around him:

> The king is always dependent upon others, he himself attends to just a small part of things. How could the king be completely in control when making treaties and waging war? He is never completely in control, even when spending time in play with his wives. How could he be completely in control when he meets his councillors for advice. He is said to be in control when he commands others, but even there he is made to act without being in control, as he attends to this or that detail. (12.308.138–40)

Here, Sulabhā argues that Janaka cannot be free because of the many ways he, as king, is necessarily immersed in social relations as part of the day-to-day business of ruling his kingdom. Specifically, Sulabhā brings up war and sex as activities in which Janaka cannot maintain complete control over his own actions and emotions, not to mention the actions and emotions of others. Sulabhā then contrasts the king's presumption to control others through his royal commands, with the mundane reality of a king's life in which 'others are always telling him what to do' (12.308.142).

While rejecting the conceit of *karma-yoga*, that householders can achieve the religious ideals of *nivṛtti*, Sulabhā tacitly concedes that as a

---

[17] 'By loosening the cause of bondage, and by knowledge of the passageways of the mind, the mind can enter into the bodies of others' (3.38, translation Bryant). As White points out, many medieval texts also describe the technique for entering into a foreign body, including the *Yogavasiṣṭha*, Hemacandra, and *Yogaśāstra* (White 2009: 164).

renouncer she adheres to social conventions circumscribed by *dharma* (*mokṣa-dharma*): 'I hold firm to the practices of my own *dharma* (*sva-dharma*). I do not waver in my promises; I do not speak without careful examination' (12.308.185–86). In making these claims, Sulabhā acknowledges the social codes by which the life of a renouncer is regulated.

In addition to challenging Janaka, her interlocutor within this dialogue, Sulabhā's argument has important resonances with other sections of the *Mahābhārata*. Indeed, we might see Sulabhā's speech as one of the *Mahābhārata*'s most robust counterarguments to Kṛṣṇa's teaching in the *Bhagavad Gītā*. As noted above, Kṛṣṇa characterises *karma-yoga* as acting disinterestedly, or action without desire (*niṣkāma-karma*). Janaka's claim to have achieved *mokṣa* while retaining his position as king, as we have seen, is a reassertion of Kṛṣṇa's position. It is also worth mentioning that in the *Bhagavad Gītā* Kṛṣṇa refers to Janaka as an exemplar of *karma-yoga* (3.20). Sulabā's repudiation of *karma-yoga*, then, is not merely a dismissal of Janaka's arguments but is also, as Sutton describes it, 'a rejection of the *Gītā*'s notion of *niṣkāma-karma*' (1999: 59). As Sutton explains: 'For Sulabhā, the compromise offered by Janaka and the *Gītā* is trite and specious, at best an attempt to serve two masters, at worst, as clearly hinted at in this passage, a sop to the vanity of kings who wish to enjoy the delights of power and still claim superiority over members of ascetic orders' (1999: 61). When we see the tension between *pravṛtti* and *nivṛtti* as a dialectic that unfolds throughout the *Mahābhārata*, then we can appreciate Sulabhā as one of the most articulate and innovative advocates of the ideals and practices of renouncers.

Sulabhā on Gender

In addition to her contribution to debates about rhetoric and renunciation, Sulabhā makes original arguments about gender that have far-reaching implications on other sections of the *Mahābhārata*, as well as beyond the text. As we have seen, at the beginning of the episode Sulabhā decides to test the king's claim of achieving *mokṣa* by using her yogic powers to appear young and beautiful. As Bhīṣma describes it: 'By her yoga power she cast off her body and put on a flawlessly beautiful one' (12.308.10). We do not know what Sulabhā looks like before she changes her appearance, but presumably she transforms into a young, attractive woman as part of testing the king's claim to be detached from worldly pleasures.

This tactic seems to work, as throughout his argument Janaka is preoccupied with Sulabhā's identity as a woman. Indeed, his very first questions, as we have seen, are about her gender and social identity: 'Whose are you? And where are you from? ... I cannot get a clear sense of your learning, of your age, or of the ethnic group you were born in, so please convey answers to these matters in this assembly of the good' (12.308.20–21). As noted above, Janaka returns to these questions on several occasions, challenging Sulabhā's claim of achieving *mokṣa* by questioning her social identity in terms of gender, caste, and lineage. Although Janaka claims that he no longer sees things as pairs of opposites (12.308.31), much of his argument rests upon setting up binary oppositions between himself and Sulabhā, including brahmin/*kṣatriya* and householder/renunciate. Janaka focuses on the gender differences between Sulabhā and himself, raising doubts about her ability to attain *mokṣa*: 'Your delicacy and your form, your preeminent beauty and your youth – you have all of these and asceticism too? I wonder' (12.308.54). At the very end of his diatribe, he instructs Sulabhā that the power (*bala*) women have is their beauty, youth, and charm (12.308.73). If we were to take Janaka's view to its logical conclusion, not only is Sulabhā not enlightened, but she could not possibly be enlightened because she is a woman. Some of his accusations are explicitly misogynist: in addition to questioning how she can be an ascetic when she is so young and beautiful (12.308.54), he calls her 'wicked' (*duṣṭā*) (12.308.65). Here we see that Sulabhā not only encounters the gendered prejudices of her male interlocutor but also has to endure his sexist insults.

In particular, Janaka is preoccupied with the gender implications of both of them inhabiting the same body during their discussion. Janaka accuses Sulabhā of joining herself inappropriately with a man from a different social order, claiming that she has crossed distinctions of both caste and clan. Furthermore, Janaka argues that one who is unenlightened should not be joined with one who is enlightened and that Sulabhā should not give herself to another man if she already has a husband (12.308.62). In all of these accusations, Janaka suggests that there is a physical dimension to her inhabiting his body. Further on, he alludes to a sexual dynamic of their interaction, arguing that one who is a renouncer should not still love and comparing their encounter to a man and a woman who desire each other (12.308.69).

As we have seen, Sulabhā begins her rebuttal dispassionately, not responding to any of the king's accusations or insults directly but by outlining how to make a proper argument. Then, when she responds to Janaka's questions, Sulabhā refers to her identity from a radically different perspective. Rather than speak of herself in terms of social roles, she talks about herself from a psycho-physical point of view. Using what we might describe as biological terminology, she discusses twenty components that are responsible for the origination and passing away of beings, explaining that there is an unmanifest nature (*prakṛti*) that becomes manifest in these twenty components.[18] Within this scheme, the 'sex mark' that distinguishes 'female' from 'male' is just one component (12.308.118). As Chakravarthi Ram-Prasad explains: 'Sulabhā recognizes the morphological role of sex-properties that mark the developing human being, but gives it just one, contingent place in development' (2018: 83). Here we see that Sulabhā recognises a physical difference between men and women but does not characterise this difference as essential to one's overall identity.

More generally, Sulabhā argues that if Janaka were truly enlightened, he would not have been concerned about her social identity. In other words, Sulabhā is answering Janaka's initial question about who she is from the point of view of an enlightened person, explaining that her identity can only be discussed in terms of the combination of the twenty components, in the context of which anatomical differences are just one component within a complex matrix that characterises a human being.

She then summarises this discussion of the twenty components by making an analogy with fire:

> Just as fire comes to be from the combination of the sun, a crystal lens, and some twigs for tinder, so beings come to be from the combination of their components. (12.308.125)

At this point, Sulabhā poses a crucial question:

> Since you see yourself within yourself by means of yourself, why do you not, in exactly the same way, by means of yourself, see yourself in someone else? (12.308.126)

This question has generated considerable debate among scholars. Ruth Vanita interprets Sulabhā's question as making an argument for gender equality based on the doctrine of the universality of the self. According to Vanita, Sulabhā's point is that *ātman* 'is one and the same in all beings, regardless of the body's gender' (2003: 88). Fitzgerald, however, suggests that Sulabhā's words here do not seem to fit with other claims she makes. As he points out, taking her words here as an articulation of a monistic ontology 'clearly contradicts Sulabhā's later statement of the "singleness and separateness" of the soul (*jña*) at 308.176' (2002: 674).

---

[18] Many of these components feature in standard lists of the Sāṃkhya philosophical school. See Fitzgerald (2002: 643–46).

Taking Fitzgerald's suggestion into consideration, Ram-Prasad interprets Sulabhā's question as pointing out the inconsistency between Janaka's claim to enlightened status and the way that he treats others. In other words, Ram-Prasad takes Sulabhā's words as highlighting a contradiction between the king's words and actions but not as representing her own commitment to an ontology of the self. As he explains: Sulabhā's 'interest is not in the metaphysics, but in the psychological consequences that would result from a freedom that treated everyone as the same' (Ram-Prasad 2018: 85). Ram-Prasad further asserts that Sulabhā is 'altogether rejecting the doctrine that absolute freedom consists of the realization that one is fundamentally a neutral self (*ātman*)' (2018: 87).

Despite Fitzgerald's and Ram-Prasad's reservations, I have argued elsewhere that there are good reasons to take Sulabhā as positing a universal self that is beyond gender (Black 2021a: 140–41). As I point out, Sulabhā's use of the fire metaphor leading up to her question does imply some sense of an *ātman* behind the twenty components that constitute a human being. A few passages before asking Janaka this question, Sulabhā asks rhetorically: 'What is the connection between beings and the components that make them up?' (12.308.124). Then, in the fire analogy that immediately precedes her question, Sulabhā – as Fitzgerald points out – emphasises 'the theme of unifying a plurality (*samudaya*)' (2002: 674). With this in mind, it would make sense if she saw the twenty components as unified in the *ātman* in the same way that she saw the sun, a crystal lens, and twigs for tinder as unified in fire.

Although I stand by this argument, here I want to emphasise that, regardless of whether of we accept Vanita's or Ram-Prasad's interpretation of the ontological implications of Sulabhā's words, the fundamental point she makes is the same: that the gendered assumptions made by Janaka are an indication of his ignorance. In other words, regardless of her own ontological commitments, Sulabhā is clearly making the case that if Janaka were truly enlightened he would not make arguments based on gender distinctions, nor would he treat her the way that he does. In making this case, Sulabhā takes the innovative position that one's views on gender can serve as a litmus test of whether or not one has achieved *mokṣa*.

Furthermore, in response to Janaka's arguments that there is a physical dimension to inhabiting his body, Sulabhā maintains that her yogic powers afford her the ability to dwell inside him without touching him, and, consequently, that there is no actual mixing or merging going on:

> I am not touching you, king – not with my hands, nor my arms, nor my feet, nor my legs, nor any other parts of my body. (12.308.169)

Subsequently, she systematically challenges Janaka's arguments about her social identity: she claims she is not a Brahmin but a *kṣatriya*[19]; she is not unfaithful because she has no husband; she is the one who is enlightened because, if he were enlightened, she would not be able to inhabit his body; and finally, if Janaka were truly enlightened these class distinctions would not matter anyway. Sulabhā's inhabitation of Janaka's body, then, actively demonstrates her philosophical point – despite bodily appearances and social constructs, there is no ontological distinction between them.

Finally, when Sulabhā reveals her name, her family, and educational lineage – thus responding to the king's initial questions – she refers to herself as abiding by the *nivṛtti* ideals of a solitary, itinerant lifestyle:

> Since there was no husband suitable to me, I was trained in *mokṣa-dharma*, so, all alone, I live according to the hermit (*muni*) way of life. (12.308.184)

Here, Sulabhā portrays *mokṣa-dharma* as a way of life that is communicated as part of a tradition from teacher to student. Although it is pursued alone, it has implicit social practices and obligations associated with it. Moreover, by describing her renunciate lifestyle as the result of her not finding a suitable husband, Sulabhā characterises *mokṣa-dharma* as an option that could be available for women as an alternative to marriage. In this way, Sulabhā makes an important contribution to the *nivṛtti* ideal by presenting it as a way of life in which women can live independently, not to mention have the possibility of attaining the highest knowledge. Throughout both her arguments and her actions, then, Sulabhā articulates an understanding of enlightenment that is beyond the dualities of gender distinction and, therefore, as available for women as for men.

Conclusion

In this chapter, we have seen that Sulabhā makes innovative contributions to several philosophical discussions that reverberate throughout the *Mahābhārata*, as well as in other forums of ancient Indian philosophical discussion. Sulabhā offers an understanding of dialogue in which interlocutors are urged to engage respectfully with the views of others; she contributes to the *Mahābhārata*'s innovative doctrine of *mokṣa-dharma*

---

[19] This term, which is often translated as 'warrior', is better understood in this context as something like 'aristocrat' or 'member of the ruling class'.

by offering it as a superior alternative to *karma-yoga*; and she articulates an understanding of *mokṣa* that is beyond gender and available for women.

Although her historicity is doubtful, I have argued that we have much to gain by engaging with her arguments as a woman philosopher. Sulabhā is not a literary character who just happens to be female, as if what she argues, how she acts, and what she experiences has nothing to do with her gender. Rather, from the very beginning of her encounter, she confronts the gendered prejudices, words, and behaviour of her male interlocutor. Recognising her as a woman philosopher not only gives us a fuller appreciation of her own textual and cultural contexts but also has the potential to enrich philosophy today, as it challenges us to look at resonances between her arguments and current debates, particularly those within feminist philosophy. In this way, engaging with Sulabhā is not merely an attempt to add her to the philosophical canon but also to suggest that her arguments provide 'resources to address contemporary issues that feminist philosophers confront' (Schott 2006: 47).

In suggesting that Sulabhā might provide resources for feminist philosophers, I am not claiming that Sulabhā herself should be considered a feminist. One clear way that Sulabhā differs from many modern feminist thinkers is that she does not set out to make arguments in favour of gender equality. Sulabhā's initial reason for challenging Janaka seems to be for defending the superiority of the renunciate path, rather than anything having to do with gender. Despite her initial intentions, however, Sulabhā responds to the explicitly gendered abuse she endures by making arguments from a distinctly female perspective and explicitly interrogating traditional gender biases. In this way, her arguments are compatible with feminist concerns. Sulabhā not only refuses to be defined in terms of her relations to any man, but she demonstrates that she can achieve ultimate freedom completely on her own. Speaking from an enlightened perspective, she proclaims that distinctions based on gender are merely indications of an unenlightened point of view. Sulabhā makes a major contribution to Indian philosophy by portraying enlightenment as beyond the dualities of gender distinction and as available for women as for men.

CHAPTER 3

Women's Medical Knowledge in Antiquity
Beyond Midwifery

Sophia M. Connell

Introduction

This chapter will argue that women doctors participated in a philosophical tradition of thought in classical antiquity. One might wonder why in a volume on ancient women philosophers, there is a chapter on women doctors. The answer is that there was a significant and widely recognised overlap between medicine and philosophy in ancient Greece.[1] The fact that women had medical knowledge and expertise suggests that they were also involved in the philosophical aspects of the domain. This makes ancient medicine a particularly rich field to look for women doing philosophy.

Gathering evidence for women's medical and attendant philosophical expertise is challenging. There are two main difficulties: the lack of direct evidence and the fact that the sources that we do have are written by men. There are no extant writings by women doctors or scientists of this period; it is not clear that they ever wrote anything at all.[2] My proposed solution is to consider carefully the sources that we do have that hint at what women knew and theorised about; this is then, an 'argument from silence'. The second related strategy is to assess other doctors' and philosophers' views about women's knowledge in the field of medicine.[3]

In making this investigation, I propose to discover what I can about the nature and content of women's knowledge and theories to do with health and fertility. With respect to the nature of the knowledge, one must not assume that women practitioners were purely practically minded and that only male doctors had an intellectual perspective. There is evidence that

---

[1] The overlaps between medicine and philosophy in the period will be discussed in the third section.
[2] For a general account of the debate about women medical writers in the Roman period, see Flemming (2007).
[3] These two techniques are suggested by King (1998: 135). I expand the second one of 'what doctors say about women's knowledge' to include philosophers as well, particularly Plato and Aristotle.

both male and female doctors had aspects of theory as part of their practice and aspects that would seem to us more like nursing or attending to the sick.[4] The second part of the enquiry concerns what female doctors actually thought. A picture can be reconstructed of expertise not only about the female body and its functions and cycles but also a broader understanding of health, disease, fertility, and their relationship to nature. It is possible that women's expertise and knowledge was not confined to female health; there is evidence of a more general understanding of the nature of disease and how to mix and create medicines. Even within the confines of female medicine, it was only from a cosmological perspective that one could hope to make sense of 'what a woman is'.[5] And women's knowledge of the place of reproduction in nature related to the generation of male as well as female children.

Women as Doctors in Antiquity

The available evidence for female doctors in antiquity includes the Hippocratic treatises on women's diseases, which are among the oldest Greek prose writings we possess.[6] In these works, women doctors are sometimes present in the sick room and a feminine version of the word for doctor (*iatros*) – that is, *iatraousa* – is employed.[7] Some speculate that these are midwives (*maiai*). We learn more about this particular field of expertise from Plato, who has Socrates give an account of the skills of his own mother, Phaenarete.

> Midwives can bring on the pains of labour, and make them milder if they want to? And they can make women who are having a difficult labour give birth? And if they see fit to cause a miscarriage when the embryo is young, they do so? ... And have you also observed this characteristic of theirs: they are the cleverest of match-makers, in that there are no gaps in their wisdom as regards knowing which sort of woman should consort with which sort of man in order to produce the best possible children? (*Th.* 149c–d, trans. MacDowell)

---

[4] King (1998: 165).

[5] The medical texts of this period point out that medical knowledge, crucial for successful practice, involves knowing what a man is (e.g., *VM* 20, 1.620.7–8 L. = Loeb 1.52–3.8–10). For those practitioners that specialised in treating women, it would presumably require knowing what a woman is.

[6] Dean-Jones (1994: 26; 2018).

[7] *Iātros* and *iātreuousa* are spelled differently in the dialect used in the Hippocratic works on women's diseases. *Akestridas*, healers, is used for women assisting a birth in *Fleshes* 19 (8.614.11 L. = Loeb 8.164). The term is rare in the Hippocratic corpus but occurs in other literature, such as Sophocles *Oedipus at Colonus* 714.

This passage suggests that *maiai* had a broader basis of practice and theory than modern midwives, including administering drugs, causing abortions, and being knowledgeable about theories of reproduction to aid conception. Socrates' implication is that midwives do not just know how to bring about children but can produce the *best* children, suggesting a degree of knowledge and control over the general natural processes that underlie conception.

One piece of physical evidence that women took on the role of 'doctor' (and not just 'midwife') is a funerary monument from the fourth century that reads: 'Phanostrate, a midwife and doctor (*iatros*), lies here. She caused pain to none, all lamented her death.'[8] Striking here is the use of the masculine for doctor, *iatros*. While 'rational' medicine existed before the Hippocratic corpus, the extensive articulation of this outlook, which places emphasis on the authority of the disembodied 'doctor', can be seen as a transitional moment, where medicine asserts itself as an intellectual and philosophical subject.[9] This woman is clearly part of that movement. Furthermore, it seems unlikely that Phanostrate was the only female *iatros*; one surviving funerary monument indicates that there were many similar.[10] One can also note that the idea of the medical art aiming to 'cause pain to none' is found in one gynaecological work.[11]

> Do this gently and without violence in order to prevent anything from being unnaturally stretched and thereby provoking an inflammation. (*Superf.* 8, 8.480.16–18 L. = Loeb 9.324.5–7, trans. Potter)

That a woman doctor was remembered as 'causing pain to none' might indicate her own rational practice, based on the principle of helping nature gently along rather than more vigorous interventions.

Other evidence for ancient women doctors comes from Plato's *Republic* where Socrates argues that women can be rulers of the state. This is something that his audience finds hard to imagine; in order to make it more palatable, he has to begin with an acceptable female job. If a man and a woman can both be suited to be doctors, then they can also be suited to being cultured, warlike, and philosophical. Thus, they can both be rulers of the state. The audience readily accepts that women are already doctors (5.454d).[12]

---

[8] Lefkowitz and Fant (2005: 266–67). [9] Holmes (2013).
[10] By the Roman period, surviving monuments of this sort are more numerous (Lefkowitz and Fant 2005: 264–67).
[11] And in the *Epidemics*. See Totelin (2020). [12] On this passage, see Pomeroy (1978).

The Nature of Women's Medical Knowledge

There are at least two pieces of evidence that women had theoretical knowledge. The first is that they presented themselves as knowledgeable and the second is that they were treated as competitors by male theoretical doctors. The idea that male doctors in ancient Greece were the real purveyors of the medical art, whereas women doctors are folk healers, without any rational basis for their practice, relying on superstition or the mindless repetition of traditional cures is questionable.[13] Certain medical texts provide evidence of an awareness of the importance of presentation.[14] The performance of being a doctor with a cure would have been crucial: 'For some patients ... regain their health simply through their contentment with the goodness of the doctor' (*Praec.* 6, 9.258.11–13 L. = Loeb 1.318.15–18). It seems likely that both men and women doctors would have had to present themselves as knowledgeable in order to convince their clientele. This suggests that women would have been able to convince others of having a rational basis for treatment.[15] In the case of curing women of what ailed them because they are women, it would have been harder for male practitioners to convince women patients to trust their knowledge. The female practitioner would presumably add to her theory, the knowledge she has of her own bodily experiences. Plato uses this well-known fact in his discussion of female medical expertise in order to pronounce that: 'Human nature is too weak to acquire skill in matters of which is has no experience' (*Th.* 149c3).

While the profession of theoretical knowledge in the performance of medical practice does not definitely prove that women possessed such knowledge, the way in which their theories were taken seriously as rivals to male positions provides stronger evidence. One problem with using information about women doctors in ancient medical writings is that these women are presented in a negative light so as to convince the clientele of

---

[13] Lloyd posits that Hippocratic doctors writing about women's medicine desire 'to turn the practice of healing into a *technê*' (1983: 79), assuming that it was not already a *technê*, which in the case of the female medical tradition on which these women built, is unfounded. See Dean-Jones' idea that male 'scientific theories' replaced women's 'traditional therapies' (1994: 27). And Rousselle: 'Male doctors ... used logical reasoning to construct a male science of the female body, incorporating all the facts gathered patiently over the year by women who had built up an empirical science' (1988: 25).

[14] King (1998: ch. 2).

[15] 'In the ancient tradition words were very important; practitioners were expected to present their theories and explanations fluently ... when the client needed to be persuaded of the healer's skill' and 'taking the prescribed medication is less important than giving meaning to the patient's experience of illness' (King 1998: 154).

the male medical writers' own superior knowledge. In this context, we cannot trust accusations of quackery. For example, when the author of *Diseases of Women* 1 remarks that the medicines prescribed by women are 'irritating', this is in the context of them as competitors for the client's attention (*Mul.* 1.67, 8.140.15 L. = Loeb 11.146.9). In another case, male doctors pit themselves against women theorists on the relation between foetal health and the length of gestation. Women hold the view that stillbirths occur at eight months of gestation. One Hippocratic author questions the veracity of these reports.

> You should not distrust women about their giving birth, for they always say the same thing and they say what they know; they are not to be persuaded by either fact or argument to believe anything contrary to what they know is going on inside their own bodies. Although there may be some who wish to assert something different, in fact women who possess judgement and who furnish the most convincing arguments on this subject always say explicitly that they give birth in the seventh month, the eighth month, the ninth month, the tenth month, and the eleventh month, and that of these children, those born in the eighth month do not survive, whereas the others do. (*Oct.* 4, 7.440.13–42.4 L. = Loeb 9.80.21–82.6)

The passage might appear to begin disparagingly, suggesting a certain stubbornness in women who do not listen to fact or argument. However, it also indicates that these women 'know'. Although that knowledge might seem at first to be solely empirical, the passage ends by indicating that this is the basis for theory: 'women of judgement' convincingly argue for their position on the prospects of these children. The Hippocratic author proclaims, with some notable caution, that these women are wrong that only eight-month-old foetuses suffer because some on either side of the eighth month are also in danger. This doctor is quibbling the details but generally accepts the correctness of these women's theory.[16] That theory is of course wrong, but to conclude that male doctors construct rational theories and women do not is too hasty. Consider that in this same work, there is a theory that foetuses fight their way out of the womb rather than the women's body doing the work (*Oct.* 1, 7.436.8–14 L. = Loeb 9.76.15–78.3; *Nat. Puer.* 19, 7.506.3–12 L. = Loeb 10.80.26–82.8). On the basis of this view, it is recommended that women be strapped to beds and ladders and bounced up and down during a difficult labour (*Mul.* 1.68, 8.142.20–44.16 L. = Loeb

---

[16] For a fuller discussion, see Lloyd (1983: 76–78) and King (1998: ch. 2).

11.148.17–50.13; *Foet. Exsect.* 4, 8.514.14–16.9 L. = Loeb I9370–72).[17] Elsewhere, male doctors recommend tying up one or the other testis before sex in order to determine the sex of offspring (*Ep.* 6.4.21, 6.312.10–11 L. = Loeb 7.252). It is clear in these instances and others that the theories associated with what women say are often no more arbitrary or folklorish than any others we find in these ancient texts. There is no trustworthy testimony that women did not have a theory and practice just as viable as any others available at the time.

In fifth and fourth century Greece, medical knowledge was considered to require a theoretical basis. This could be articulated as knowing types rather than particulars – that is, types of people and types of illness – as well as discerning the underlying causes of or principles governing disease.[18] In *Metaphysics* 1.1, Aristotle distinguishes between experience and technical knowledge (*technê*) using a helpful medical example. Experience is judging what would benefit a particular person, such as Callias, who suffers from a disease; technical knowledge is to understand what benefits all persons of a certain type who suffers from certain sorts of disease (981a7–13). Women practitioners were called on to treat any number of different women and would have applied a general theory of what ails them. Thus, both male and female doctors, indeed anyone who treats a number of people, will have this technical knowledge.[19] When Aristotle distinguishes between practical (and technical) knowledge, under which medicine would fall, and theoretical understanding, he takes the latter to be necessary for the former.[20] He also explains that those with technical knowledge in general know the theory (*kata to logon*) and the causes (*tas aitias*; 981b5–6), and so they are also in possession of theoretical knowledge (*epistêmê*) (981b6–8). A key sign of this is the ability to teach others (981b8–10), which women practitioners would have done.[21]

Finding the philosophical content of the ideas that come from women doctors presents numerous challenges, some at the conceptual level and

---

[17] For an analysis of the passage, see Totelin (2009: 27). For fuller discussion, see Lloyd (1983: 80–81).

[18] *VM* 7, 9 (584.7–86.2 L.; 1.588.4–90.17 L.); Plato *Rep.* 3.408c6–e2; *Phaedrus* 270d7–71d7.

[19] While male doctors would sometimes treat women's ailments, there is less clear evidence of whether women doctors ever treated men. Even if they did not do so systematically, medicine required a theory of the body that applied to all people. Medical women were most often responsible for the treatment of both male and female children.

[20] On theoretical knowledge underpinning as necessary for ethical practice, see especially Henry and Nielsen (2015).

[21] There is no direct evidence about the training of medical women in ancient Greece, but we can infer from later history that midwifery was a skill passed from woman to woman.

others at the practical. Does the concept of philosophy include what doctors theorised about? If it can be seen that medicine includes philosophical ideas, is it also possible to discover that women doctors developed theories of this kind? Determining whether a doctor is also a philosopher requires an understanding of what is encompassed by 'philosophy'. The concept is hotly debated in fifth- and fourth-century Greece. While certain thinkers, such as Isocrates, argued that philosophy must be practical, and include the skills required for contemporary political life, Plato urged that philosophy is the pursuit of abstract truth about reality. Aristotle agreed but included natural knowledge: meteorology, botany, and zoology (*PA* 1.5; *Mete.* 1.1). He sees a significant overlap between medicine and philosophy, since both involve the study of nature (*Sens.* 1.436a17–b3, *Resp.* 21.480b21–30).[22]

Within the Hippocratic corpus, many writers make the discipline of medical expertise part of, or dependent upon, philosophy. Early philosophical speculation, of which we have only fragments, generally sets out an account of the nature and workings of the cosmos and of human beings as part of, or a reflection of, that cosmos. The Hippocratic works *Fleshes* and *Places in Man* are clearly part of a similar tradition. One of the most famous Hippocratic works, *On Ancient Medicine*, presents a challenge to this view by arguing that medicine ought to supplant philosophy as a way of understanding 'the nature of the human'. And yet, this author is clearly writing about natural philosophy too and discussing natural topics, such as what human beings are composed of and how bodies react to the environment. It is this sort of philosophy that one can find in the Hippocratic works and that lies behind much of rational medical practice. A medical practitioner will have a theory of health that presupposes an understanding of the nature of the cosmos.

Since there were women doctors, who worked almost exclusively with the bodies of female patients, it is reasonable to suppose that some, if not most, would have also had a particular understanding of the body and the cosmos into which that body fit. One possible objection is that what women practitioners thought about while practising healing arts could not be philosophical because it is not proclaimed in writing. We must first keep in mind that writing about medicine was only one small part of the discipline and practice in antiquity. While various ancient medical writers promote their 'books',[23] other thinkers, including some philosophers of the period, urge what seems somewhat obvious: that one cannot become a

---

[22] Bartoš (2021).
[23] *Dieb. Judic.* 1: 'A large part, I believe, of the medical art consists in being able to examine correctly its writing' (9.298.1–2 L. = Loeb 9.300.1–2).

doctor by reading about medicine.²⁴ That women doctors did not write about their theories does not mean that they did not have such theories.

And yet one still might attach importance to written articulation. While the Hippocratic author writes 'the nature of the body is the starting point of medical reasoning' (Φύσις δὲ τοῦ σώματος, ἀρχὴ τοῦ ἐν ἰητρικῇ λόγου, *Loc. Hom.* 2, 6.278.14 L. = Loeb 8.22.1–2), 'the doctor who is a philosopher is equal to a god' (ἰητρὸς γὰρ φιλόσοφος ἰσόθεος, *Decent.* 5, 9.232.10 L. = Loeb 2.286.4–5) and similarly abstract statements, it might be supposed that a women doctor who does not write down such thoughts cannot be thinking philosophically.²⁵ But if one thinks it possible that the male doctors who did not write (which must have been the majority of them) had a philosophical basis for their practice, then there is no good reason to exclude doctors of the other gender. We ought to be cautious about patrolling the borders of 'philosophy' too strictly since there is a continuing tendency to exclude marginalised groups from the discipline.²⁶

In any case, it ought to be accepted that theories and practices do not have to be written down in order to be philosophical.²⁷ There has been much recent progress towards making philosophical sense of oral traditions. The ethnophilosopher can discover rational ways of structuring individual and social life that counts as philosophical, even without written texts. This technique has been useful in helping to understand African philosophy.²⁸ When it comes to medico-philosophical theories of women in antiquity, we do not have anything that we can currently listen to.²⁹ It is clear, though, that an oral tradition existed and clues about its content can be found in the Hippocratic corpus and in works by Plato and Aristotle.

The Content of Women's Medical Knowledge

We have no guide written for women by women doctors who specialise in the knowledge of their ailments. This means that we have no direct

---

²⁴ Plato's *Phaedrus* 268c: 'They would say, I think, that that man is mad because he has heard somewhere from a book or happened to fall upon some remedies, and he thinks he has become a physician, understanding nothing of the art', cited in Totelin (2016: 246). See also Aristotle *EN* 10.9.1181b2–6.
²⁵ For Holmes, it is the act of fifth-century medical writing that produces the idea of the body as 'part of inquiry into nature' (2013: 450).
²⁶ On these difficulties for the modern concept of 'philosophy' as exclusionary and biased, see Dotson (2012)and Haslanger (2008).
²⁷ The life of Socrates is a case in point.   ²⁸ Outlaw (2017).
²⁹ There is scope to compare female medical practices in traditional cultures around the world today.

evidence of what exactly women knew or professed to know or theorised as the basis of their practice. The general technique in this section is to put forward a series of arguments from silence in order to conclude that certain parts of the information we find in works by men about women's medicine came from women. This knowledge falls into four key areas: (i) bodily experience, (ii) theories of the female body, (iii) pharmacology, and (iv) theories of reproduction.

The Bodily Experience of Women

Women hold ultimate knowledge of the frequency and duration of menstruation (*Mul.* 1.6, 8.298.2–4 L.; *Mul.* 2.24 (133 L.), 9.232.10 L.) and of various subjective perspectives, such as what it feels like to be pregnant and to experience female varieties of sexual desire or pleasure.[30] Male doctors could only ascertain such facts through 'question and answer' and interrogation (*Steril.* 1, 8.412.17 L. = Loeb 10.336.9, 338.7–8; *Mul* 1.6, 8.30.12–14 L. = Loeb 10.30.18.). It does not seem a stretch to think that there were certain women in the community who were known to have special knowledge of the collective experiences of women.

In the *Historia Animalium* 9(7), not a medical work but a collection of facts useful for the development of scientific explanations, Aristotle sets out a good deal of this sort of information including what period pains, premenstrual syndrome, conception, pregnancy, and labour pains feel like (*HA* 9(7).2.582a34, 582b10, 3.583a35, 4.584a2). He refers to women in the plural throughout; although this information could have come from women in his household, it is more likely to have come from women experts.[31] Some women are marked as authorities in the Hippocratic corpus, for example, with respect to the length of gestation (*Oct.* 4, 7.440.13–42.4 L.). In addition, 'women of experience' (*epistamenêsin*) can instruct about signs of pregnancy (*Carn.* 19, 8.610.15–16 L. = Loeb 8.160.19–21).[32]

---

[30] Dean-Jones (1994: 26–27; 1995). See also Aristotle *GA* 1.20.728a2–9, 2.4.739a37; *HA* 9 (7).4.585a11, 584a25ff, 585a17ff.
[31] Dean-Jones assumes that Aristotle 'would have had access to fewer women's bodies than the Hippocratics ... his wife, concubine, and slaves' (1994: 36). But it is much more likely that this information comes from women experts, probably women doctors and *maiai*. Aristotle's method in this treatise is to gather information from experts, such as herdsmen, fishermen, and beekeepers (Leunissen 2021).
[32] This could refer to any woman who has the experience of having been pregnant, for example, the courtesans discussed earlier, it seems more likely that this refers to those women who attended and advised them on reproduction.

The possibility that Aristotle is informed by women with expertise is strengthened when, immediately after this section, he gives several technical terms that he notes are 'what the women call' them – first of all, the amniotic fluid, which 'the women call the forerunner' (7.586a25), and then the excrement of newborns, which 'the women' call meconium (10.587a30). When he refers to information from 'the women', he implies that there are women experts who hold this sort of knowledge.

When it comes to women's own experiences, these are not mere firsthand accounts but theories based on shared information. Recall that Aristotle defines medicine as a *technê* in *Metaph*. I.1 on the basis of the ability to specify types of people who suffer from certain ailments; he further specifies that this knowledge counts as theoretical (or scientific) knowledge when the holders of it can teach another. The Hippocratic author of *On Fleshes*, in discussing signs of pregnancy, explicitly acknowledges his debt to the teachings of women, writing: 'It is to the extent that these women have *instructed* me that I know about these things' (ᾗ δέ μοι ἔδειξαν, κατὰ τοῦτο δὴ καὶ ἐπίσταμαι εἰδέναι, *Carn*. 19, 8.610.15–16 L.). In this, there is evidence that medical women had theories that they not only taught each other but that were also available to men who bothered to ask.

Theory of the Body

For the Hippocratic writers, male medicine is general medicine; it does not usually focus on the reproductive parts and functions of men.[33] But female medicine is almost exclusively focused on their reproductive functioning.[34] One must not imagine from this that the role of female medicine is being downplayed. The philosophically dense and complicated theories of how humans (and other animals) reproduce are firmly in the province of philosophy at this time.[35] It is the woman's body that supplies the young with what they are composed of, as this medical writer makes clear: 'So long as a human lives he manifestly has all these elements always in him; then he is born out of a human being [i.e. a woman] having all these elements' (*Nat. Hom.* 5, 6.42.19–44.2 L. = Loeb 6.14.15–17). One writer even proposes that after 'the divine', the nature of women is the most

---

[33] An exception would be *On the Nature of the Bones*, which describes how semen is produced in the marrow and carried from the head down the spinal column to the penis. See Craik (2015: 229).
[34] Dean-Jones (2018: 248, 252).
[35] This is very evident in Aristotle's dialectic with other philosophers and philosophical doctors in his *On the Generation of Animals*.

important topic to consider (*Nat. Mul.* 1, 7.312.1–2 L. = Loeb 10.192). When it comes to knowledge about women, male doctors were not the experts. For this author at least, women medics were in a privileged position, since they hold the key to the most important type of knowledge after the divine sort.

For Hippocratic medicine, the health of women is fundamentally different from that of men.[36] Male doctors are attempting to take over women's province. While it is tempting to suppose that women doctors are midwives who are only in charge of normal births while male doctors are brought in to deal with any complications, one must guard against this anachronism.[37] This is how modern medicine operates and is a legacy of a division that began in late antiquity and was later fiercely enforced.[38] But it is not a correct way to understand ancient practices. Women practitioners are noted to be present at quite a few of the male interventions, while male medical writers would have had access to births that did not require extraordinary measures.[39] Socrates says that medical women are able to deal with difficult births through to the end.[40] Aristotle states of the female doctor that she must 'not only be able to help over difficult births with her dexterity, but she must also be quick-witted in dealing with contingencies' (*HA* 9(7).9.587a10–12). In any case, there is no reason to assume that men had to have come up with some of the life-saving procedures detailed in the Hippocratic writings, in particular, the extraction of dead foetuses and the turning of babies being born in awkward positions.[41] Many of these techniques could well have been taken over from women doctors' practices, since women initially had the expertise involved through an oral tradition and their experience of assisting in birth. Indeed, this may be the reason why *On Diseases of Women* II makes clear that during a procedure in which two men are present, it is the woman doctor (*iatreousa*) that must remove the dead foetus and the placenta (*Mul.* 1.68, 8.144.22–24 L. = Loeb 11.150.21–23).

There is ample evidence in these Greek gynaecological works that male doctors are not entirely in control of any aspect of the care of women's

---

[36] Dean-Jones (1994: 33).   [37] Blundell (1995: 110).
[38] For a fuller account of this modern bias, see King (1998: ch. 9). Soranus strictly delimits the domain of the midwife (Temkin 1956: 5–6). By the mid-seventeenth century, a woman could be burned as a witch if she dared practice any medicine other than helping with birth (Donnison 1988: 17).
[39] E.g., *Mul.* 1.34 (8.78–82 L. = Loeb. 9.80–82); Aristotle *HA* 9(7).9. See Dean-Jones (1994: 212); King (1998: 180).
[40] Plato *Th.* 149a. See King (1998: 177).
[41] *Mul.* 1.68–70 (8.142–48 L. = Loeb. 9.148–54); *Superf.* 7 (8.480.3–12 L. = Loeb. 9.322), *Foet. Exsect.* 1 (8.512–14 L. = Loeb 9.368–70).

ailments or childbirth. Almost all references to examination of the cervix use feminine participles.[42] Although these Hippocratic works sometimes place the male doctor at centre stage, they also show that women were still partly in charge. Women themselves are said to know about their own bodies and to cooperate in or even initiate the administration of drugs and other treatments. The woman patient applies most of the medicines on her own, as instructed by the doctor. For example, 'have the patient draw their cervix aside with a finger' and 'have her remove the suppository' (*Mul.* 1.13, 8.52.1 L. = Loeb 9.52.18; *Mul.* 1.19, 8.58.13–14 L. = Loeb 9.60.21). While there is the speculation that a sense of impropriety was what led male doctors to insist that women inspect themselves, this is probably anachronistic; it was certainly a trend in the seventeenth and eighteenth centuries, but we have very little direct evidence of such qualms in antiquity.[43] Instead, we find that women's knowledge of their own bodies was respected by male doctors and even trumped their own level of expertise. In one case, the woman, after independent internal self-examination, discovers her own ailment and reports this to the doctor (*Mul.* 1.40, 8.96.16–98.5 L. = Loeb 11.100). There are various mentions of women doctors being present when the male doctor is attending to women.[44] At another point, the male medical writer recommends picking and choosing from the women doctors' medications:

> Try the medicines of the women and have the patient take the most appropriate one. (*Mul.* 2.4 (113 L.), 8.244.4–5 = Loeb 11.272.19–20)

Women's own knowledge and experience is evident in these works.

Given that male doctors are taking over the treatment and care of women's ailments, it is improbable that they came up with an entirely new set of theories of the female body distinct from those that were already formulated by women. Women preferred to be treated by female doctors.[45] In their attempt to attract women clients, male doctors had to present a medical theory that fell in line with women's views of their own

---

[42] E.g., *Mul.* 1.78 (8.188.17–18 L.); *Nat. Mul.* 32 (7.348.20–50.1 L.); *Mul.* 2.144 (8.318.1 L.); *Mul.* 1.37 (8.92.7 L.); *Mul.* 1.88 (8.212.11–12 L.); *Mul* 2.133 (8.290.3 L.); *Superf.* 35 (8.506.8–9 L.). See Totelin (2009: 248–57) for further references.

[43] On these more recent trends, see Doyle (2018: ch. 1). For speculation about ancient practices, see Dean-Jones (1994: 33–34), who concluded that despite one comment advising male doctors to act judiciously with women and girls, it was common for male doctors to treat female patients and so, in general, sexual impropriety was not a worry for them.

[44] 'The woman doctor (*iātreuousa*) should gently open the cervix' (*Mul.* 1.68, 8.144.22–24 L. = Loeb 11.150.18–19).

[45] King (1998: 169–70); Lloyd (1983: 79–80).

bodies, arguably held collectively.[46] Consider how the author of the Hippocratic work *On Diseases of Women* advises on women's ailments.

> Doctors may err in not inquiring carefully about a disease's cause, and in treating them like diseases in men: indeed, I have seen many women perish in such cases. Rather you must question a patient immediately and in detail about the cause; for there is a great difference in the treatment of women's diseases and those of men. (*Mul.* 1.62, 8.126.14–20 L. = Loeb 11.130.17–23)

The (trainee?) doctor is instructed here to ask the woman patient to supply the causes, rather than to try to discern these himself; knowledge of the basis for women's diseases is still considered to be a feminine area of expertise. Thus, the Hippocratic gynaecological works give us some clues to the views of women doctors and their patients about the rationale behind their treatments.[47] Many illnesses affecting the rest of the body are taken to be connected to the patient being a woman – through two key mechanisms: the need to purge blood from the body, on the one hand, and the motility of the uterus, on the other.[48] The general idea is that a woman's body retains excess blood that must be periodically voided. This blood can be used up on nourishing a foetus if she becomes pregnant and is converted into milk during lactation (*Nat. Puer.* 3–4, 7.474–76 L. = Loeb 10.36–42). The texture of the female body is much spongier and softer than the male one, which allows for the absorption of more fluid (*Mul.* 1.12–13, 8.48-52 L. = Loeb 11.48–54). To ensure health, the doctor must help the female body to discharge the right quality and quantity of blood; if retained, it can cause disease and pain. Thus, therapies concentrate on either bringing about regular menstruation or facilitating pregnancy, as pregnancy uses up the blood and anchors the uterus.[49] Signs of health for a woman include desire for and pleasure in sexual intercourse.[50]

---

[46] As Dean-Jones puts it: 'The treatment offered to women [by male doctors] ... must have been acceptable to them and have squared with their view of their own physiology' (1994: 27).
[47] 'The models of the female body in the Hippocratic Corpus are the product and the common property of society, women as well as men' (Dean-Jones 1994: 37).
[48] King (1998: 179).
[49] The needy womb can cause extreme physical and psychological illness according to *Virg.* 3 (8.468.9–17 L. = Loeb 11.50.6–7). Where such ideas originally came from is unknown. Emphasis on regulating menstrual cycles and keeping the uterus in place are available in the very earliest medical texts, such as the Kahun or el-Lahun gynaecological papyrus dating from 1800 BCE Egypt, during the reign of a female pharaoh, Sobekneferu (Smith 2011; Bose 2017). Ethnopharmacology tells us that in some contemporary African cultures, medicines, and techniques not dissimilar to those described in the Hippocratic treatises persist (Steenkamp 2003: 198).
[50] Thumiger (2017: 247–51).

Male medical authorities in antiquity may have somewhat adapted and changed women's theories or attempted to incorporate aspects of their own theories.[51] However, it is a fair assumption that the basic picture of how women's reproductive systems and interconnected body parts operate was already in place by the time male doctors began to encroach. In terms of the maintenance of health through regular menstruation, it is probably part of a women's collective experience to judge that healthy women tend to have regular periods.[52] Since only women have regular discharges of bloodlike fluid and also gestate and lactate, health was quite reasonably considered to require the regular flow of materials around the body.[53]

It may be that women were the first to think of the uterus as motile. Some recommended procedures are based on the view that the uterus is attracted to pleasant smells and retreats from the unpleasant.[54] In *HA* 10, using information from women, pseudo-Aristotle says that the uterus can be 'thirsty' (2.635a25). This idea of uterine agency could have been developed by male doctors,[55] but it is just as likely to have originated with women doctors to ground their practices. Indeed, the cervix can be felt to recede and move down, and this often coincides with certain parts of the menstruous cycle. Women also experienced uterine prolapse.[56] A theory of the uterus as sentient may strike us as unscientific, but for the ancients, it had a certain logic. Plato says that the uterus is like an animal, as is the penis, presumably because of its self-motion (*Tim.* 91a–c).

Some have felt that the theories about women's health found in the Hippocratic works reveal only male concerns, since they often focus on fertility and recommend sex and pregnancy as cures (*Mul.* 2.6, 10, 18, 19, 22, 24, 26). But it is very possible, indeed highly probable, that fertility

---

[51] *Places in Man* 1–2 explains the interconnection of all parts of the body similar to *Mul.* 2.29 (138 L.) (8.312.4–6 L. = Loeb 10.348.5–7): 'All of the parts [of the body] will be involved in the disease to a greater or less degree.' The importance of different complexions is part of the theory in *Aer.* and *VM* and is mentioned in *Nat. Mul.* 1, 2.312 L. = Loeb 10.192.

[52] In some pre-scientific cultures, such as the Rungus of Borneo, menses are viewed by women as fluids that need to be evacuated (Appell 1988). A recent study in the *BMJ* concludes that regular menstruation is indeed a sign of health (Wang et. al. 2020).

[53] King (1986: 60) also thinks it possible that women themselves held a model of the female body in which reproductive function and fluids could affect every other part.

[54] *Loc. Hom.* 47 (6.344–46 L. = Loeb 8.92–98); *Mul.* 2.22 (131 L.) (8.278–80 L. = Loeb 11.310–12); *Mul.* 1.13 (8.50–52 = Loeb 11.52–54).

[55] Manuli (1983) argues that the motile uterus is entirely a male construct designed to control women. It is also possible that women came up with this idea independently, developing many of the complex pharmacological procedures we find in the Hippocratic corpus.

[56] King suggests that this is the origin of the idea of a motile uterus (1985: n. 158). Cf. Dean-Jones (1994: 73).

was a top priority in the minds of women of this period. Women's province was the care of the home and family; producing healthy children would bring prestige and the sort of power accorded to women.[57] Within the Hippocratic texts, it is evident that women still held the main epistemic authority around these events as the author of *On Diseases of Women* remarks: 'It requires much attention and knowledge (*epistêmê*) to bring a child to term and provide for its nourishment in the uterus, and then to give birth to it' (*Mul.* 1.25, 8.68.15–17 L. = Loeb 11.70.24–26). Knowledge about giving birth to a child is something that only a woman could have.

Pharmacology

The Hippocratic writings on women contain more recipes than the entire rest of the corpus combined.[58] Much of the pharmaceutical practice, and the theory behind it, is thought to have come from women healers. These doctors must have been party to an extensive oral tradition.[59] There is a tendency to classify the administration of drugs as less scientific and more folklorish than other practices, such as dietetics (Hanson 1991). But there is no strong case for this. In fact, some of the medicines employed would have been effective, particularly as abortifacients, especially pennyroyal and hellebore.[60] Furthermore, pharmaceutical practices show aspects of rational engagement. What the recipes we find in the Hippocratic corpus lack is any detailed account of the instruments required and procedures to procure, prepare, and apply the medicine. A practitioner with knowledge of an underlying rationale for the use of certain medicines would have been able to take these very general recipes and adapt them, often finding similar substitutes for certain ingredients.[61] The use of *materia medica*, then, requires the mastery of complex theories of measurement, effective powers, and the results of their combinations under various conditions.[62] It may

---

[57] Lloyd (1983: 84); Dean-Jones (1992). [58] Dean-Jones (1994: 36); Totelin (2009, 2018).
[59] The Hippocratic gynaecological texts are compilations, which show signs of having been updated via written and oral traditions (Totelin 2009). There are many references to methods used by women themselves (Hanson 1991: 78).
[60] Riddle (1992) argued for the efficacy of many of the drugs, particularly abortifacients, used in the Hippocratic gynaecological treatises. King (1998) refutes his case. Totelin (2009) defends Riddle's general position, emphasising the continuity of many ingredients.
[61] This is convincingly argued in Totelin (2009).
[62] A work attributed to the Hellenistic Cleopatra provided complicated charts of relevant weights and measures, indicating an awareness of the importance of calibration in chemical compounds. See Pseudo-Galen, *De ponderibus et mensuris* 10, in Hultsch (1882: 233–39) and Totelin (2017).

well be that this theoretical knowledge was guarded by women who would have passed this on orally to each other. It seems likely that the lists found in the Hippocratic texts indicate that in the background are experienced women practitioners with such knowledge.[63]

In writing these ingredients down without enough instruction, the medical writer might be trying to take over this part of female medical expertise, but he is more likely to be showing off his knowledge – a knowledge gained from female practitioners and those they bought the ingredients from.[64] This display of prowess had potentially very dangerous consequences; many of the ingredients mentioned are highly toxic, particularly 'squirting cucumber' (*ecballium*). In very small quantities, it can have a beneficial effect, but if given without extreme care, this could well end the life of the woman. If too many women died under the 'care' of a male doctor from his ill mixing, this would only reinforce the need for a more experienced female mixer to intervene.

Knowledge of How Reproduction Works

It seems probable that women doctors entertained theories about how reproduction works, a matter of great importance to their patients. Compared with men, women were in a better position to judge some aspects of these processes, for they had their own and other women's direct experiences to draw on – experiences of sex and conception. It seems likely that female expertise included a store of information from the collective experience of women about how to aid (or prevent) procreation. The medical texts all agree, at least for humankind, that sex and male ejaculation are necessary for conception. Many also note the need for parallel female seed produced during sex (*Genit*. 4, 7.474–76 L. = Loeb 10.12–14; *Mul*. 1.7, 8.32 L. = Loeb 11.32–34; *Mul*. 1.10, 8.40–42 L. = Loeb 11.42; *Mul*. 1.24, 8.62–64 L. = Loeb 11.64–66). *Diseases of Women*, the text that we have already seen to contain so much information from women themselves, often mentions that in order for conception to occur women need to feel desire for and pleasure in sex (e.g., *Mul*. 1.7, 8.32 L. = Loeb 11.32–34; *Mul*. 1.10, 8.40–42 L. = Loeb 11.42; *Mul*. 1.12, 8.48–50 L. =Loeb 11.48–52). While this is untrue, it reveals an interest in female experience that is sometimes absent from more male-centred accounts. The theory that there are two parallel seeds, both released at sexual climax, shows awareness of female orgasm.

---

[63] Totelin (2009, 2016, 2018).   [64] See Totelin on 'root-cutters' and 'drug-sellers' (2018: 213).

This theory is not necessarily equalitarian, however. In the most comprehensive written account of it we possess, in a work entitled *Generation*, it is said that women always cease to feel pleasure as soon as men do. Here the perspective is a male one, making much use of the first-person plural. It is about what 'we' (as men) experience.[65]

> A man's seed falling into the uterus extinguishes a woman's warmth and pleasure. In fact, a woman's pleasure and warmth leap up at the moment the seed falls into her uterus, but then ceases. (*Genit.* 4, 7.474.24–76.1 L. = Loeb 10.12.15–17)[66]

Another medical text, the pseudo-Aristotelian *HA* 10.1–5, is more women-centred.[67] This author is careful to listen to women, noting their experiences of erotic dreams in particular (*HA* 10.2.634b28, 3.635a34). His own theory depends on this testimony, although he cannot help providing the caveat 'if the women are telling the truth' (*HA* 10.7.638a6), admitting that in fact women hold the upper hand and can choose to withhold or distort information about their bodies and experiences.

The resultant theory of generation is different from that found in *Generation* because it posits that women have their own independent sexual rhythm.

> For if it is true that the woman too contributes to the seed and the generation, plainly there is need of equal speed (*isodromêsai*) on both sides. Therefore, if he has completed quickly while she has hardly done so (for in most things women are slower), this is an impediment. (*HA* 10.5.636b15–17)

This theory is disputed by Aristotle in his *On the Generation of Animals*. The counter-theory also requires information from women about their own experiences, in this case, that they can become pregnant even when they feel no pleasure (*GA* 1.19.727b8–11, 2.4.739a29–33).[68]

At the same time, the nature of the female contribution was being debated, and these texts hint that women with expertise about

---

[65] One text recommends violent sex for the production of a male child (*Superf.* 31., 8.500.5–7 L. = Loeb 9.344.4–5). For use of the first-person plural to signal male solidarity, see Thumiger (2017: 236–37).

[66] The idea that women could not feel pleasure after the male had climaxed is a male-centred perspective. Another description of sex that leaves out the female experience can be found in Plato, who characterises desire for physical intercourse as 'giving birth in beauty', which brings to mind male ejaculation into an attractive partner but not the female experience of satisfying sex.

[67] Dean-Jones (2012) argues that the first five chapters of *HA* 10 ought to be called *On the Failure to Generation* (*Non Genit.*) and are 'embedded *endoxa*' that Aristotle copied out from a medical expert. As Dean-Jones notes, the work pays a 'great deal of attention to women's testimony about their sexual experience' (forthcoming).

[68] Connell (2016: 112–16).

reproduction had their own views.⁶⁹ It would be too simplistic to imagine that all women had the same theory of generation.⁷⁰ Some portions of the Hippocratic corpus reveal women's concentration on retaining male seed (*HA* 10.2; Cf. *Steril*. 1[214 L.], 8.408–10 L. = Loeb 10.330–32). As the author of *The Nature of the Child* says, this is the 'sort of thing women say to each other – that when a woman is going to conceive, the seed remains inside her and does not fall out' (*Nat. Puer.* 2 [13 L.], 7.490.5–7 L. = Loeb 10.34.19–22). While this is compatible with their contributing their own seed during sex, it does not require it, and some wise women, perhaps those Aristotle spoke to when composing the *GA*, may have had another way to understand what women contribute.

What they are likely to have agreed about, and which no right-minded scientist would deny, is that women provide a generative contribution. *HA* 10 tells the story of a woman who tries to prove this through a zoological experiment.

> There was once a woman who, capturing some singing grasshoppers while they were still young, kept them to see what would occur. And when they had grown, they became pregnant spontaneously. It is clear from these things that every female contributes to the embryo even if this is evident in only one type of animal. (*HA* 10.6.637b16–20)

Aristotle may have concluded that this theory is inductively invalid.⁷¹ He himself noted two species of fish where no male could be found but thought that there was not enough evidence to come to any conclusions about the possibility of parthenogenesis (*GA* 2.5.741a33–b2, 3.5.755b22, *HA* 5.11.538a20). In any case, this budding female natural scientist only hoped to show that the female animal contributes something toward generation. Parthenogenesis is an overdetermining case and may indicate a desire in this thinker to counterbalance the idea of the autogenetic male, which appears only in myth and never in nature.⁷²

---

⁶⁹ Rousselle's view that the account in the *HA* 10 was a theory held by women seems possible. She perhaps goes too far, however, in declaring that advances in science 'destroyed the traditional basis of reciprocal pleasure in heterosexual intercourse' (1988: 29).
⁷⁰ Rousselle assumes that the parallel seed theory found in some Hippocratic works is 'the theory held by women' (1988: 28).
⁷¹ Aristotle complains that Democritus makes a general conclusion about hybrids on the basis of only one sort, mules (*GA* 2.8.747a23–28). A similar complaint is also found at *GA* 3.5.756a4–6: 'Our friends base their study on a few instances and think the same holds good for all.' And again, later in the *GA* Democritus is accused of assigning 'a cause to apply generally although he has not undertaken an exhaustive investigation of the facts' (5.8.788b10–12). On the general complaint, see Lloyd (1987: 62).
⁷² For example, Zeus produces Athena without a woman (Homer, *Iliad* 5.880).

In the area of reproductive theory, both matchmaking and related time keeping were associated with women. Matchmaking in the ancient world was undertaken exclusively by women.[73] This explains why Socrates' attempt to say how he matches young interlocutors to sophists (*Th.* 151d) is so amusing: he is playing a feminine role, a source of great hilarity to the Greeks. Bio-medical authors seem to wish to share in knowledge about matching the right men to the right women in order to produce viable children (*Genit.* 7). For the author of *HA* 10, and his female influenced theory, fertility is lessened when the man and woman do not keep the same pace in love making and so do not ejaculate simultaneously (*HA* 10.6.363b7–9).[74] That male and female must be harmonious (*sunarmosthe*) fits other aspects of contemporaneous reproductive theory. Aristotle notes that 'it happens to many women and men that they cannot produce children in union with each other but can when apart from each other' – that is, with other partners (*HA* 9.6.585b9). For Aristotle, the combination of female menses and male semen must be correctly balanced or proportioned.[75]

Keeping track of time periods was another sort of knowledge assigned to women. There is a theory, based on several bone artifacts, that counting the days of the menstrual cycle sparked early human interest in abstract numbers and cosmic cycles.[76] This is highly speculative. Yet in the era we are examining not only did women count the timings of their 'monthlies' (*katameniai*), but they were also thereby (to the ancient mind) keeping track of the circular movements of at least one prime heavenly body, the moon. Aristotle links the moon's force on nature to menstruation (*GA* 4.2.767a2–9; Cf. *Oct.* 9, 7.446–52 L.); this is part of the more general effect that the heavenly bodies have on generation (*GA* 4.10.777b17–25). Women also measure the length of human gestation. As part of his philosophical science, Aristotle meticulously documents gestational periods in all animals (*HA* 6.18–31). In the case of humans, women hold the key to this knowledge. Aristotle readily accepts the women's theory of variable gestational periods, as mentioned above, and asserts it to be a special feature of humankind.[77]

---

[73] Noy (2013). [74] See also *Mul.* 1.17, Loeb 11.58–60.
[75] Aristotle says that 'proper blend' (*summetria*) 'is the reason why it happens that many couples fail to effect generation with one another, but if they change partners, they succeed' (*GA* 4.1.767a23–25). See also *GA* 1.23.723a27–31, 4.2.767a14–26. See Connell (2016: 71–76).
[76] The 40,000-year-old Lebombo bone, and a later artifact, show notches that add up to monthly periods of time. See Marshack (1972); Zaslavsky (1992); Darling (2004).
[77] *GA* 4.4.772b7–8. See Connell (2016: 85 n. 62).

In human affairs, then, time periods, measurements, and calculations of cycles in nature belong to the province of female expertise and can be joined to their knowledge of correct sexual mixing.[78] This may be part of the reason why Plato's rulers (*tois archousi*), who are eugenic matchmakers, combine the expertise of men and women in their ranks (*Rep.* 5.459e7–60a5). Matching the right men with the right women in 'marriages' is, for Plato, a case of timing.[79] If and when knowledge of the correct measurements of time periods for matching and mating people wanes, the whole civilisation suffers a decline.

> Not only for plants that grow from the earth but also for animals that live upon it there is a cycle of bearing and barrenness for soul and body as often as the revolutions of their orbs come full circle .... And when your guardians, missing this, bring together brides and bridegrooms unseasonably, the offspring will not be well-born or fortunate. (*Rep.* 8.546a2–d2)

Female expertise in measuring, mixing, and matchmaking continues to hold sway later on in antiquity, when treatises on alchemy and pharmacology are attributed to women.[80] In that context, women were taken to have the sort of knowledge required to transform through proper blending, which is likened to marriage and procreation.[81] While women doctors often focused on issues of particular importance to women, such as preparing medications that would be dangerous in the hands of others, they also speculated about matters of more general import, such as the cycles and timings of birth and death.

In conclusion, this chapter has shown how information from women doctors permeates male medical and biological writings and includes theoretical constructs. In a culture in which a woman's word was worth much less than that of a man, it is striking that on the subject of expertise about the body and nature's cycles, women had a certain authority. Given how ubiquitous women's health and reproduction were, women's philosophical contributions in this field of inquiry were arguably more widespread than in any other area of intellectual activity in antiquity.

---

[78] Female knowledge in this area would also include knowledge about the birth of male children and so is not confined entirely to the female sex.

[79] In Plato's *Symposium*, it is crucial that Diotima be a woman since among women lies the ultimate knowledge of physical pregnancy and birth and the cycles of the natural world more generally.

[80] The connection between sexual generation and metallurgy can already be found in Empedocles who likens the mixture of donkey and horse semen to a too dense mixture of bronze and tin (*GA* 2.8.747a34–b3).

[81] Berthelot (1888). One famous alchemist, Maria, spoke of the 'marriage' of metals (Plant 2004: 131–32; Patai 1982: 177–97). Another alchemist, called Cleopatra, employed reproductive metaphors to explain how materials transform (Lindsay 1970: 256). See Connell (2021).

CHAPTER 4

Ancient Women Epicureans and Their Anti-Hedonist Critics

Kelly Arenson

Introduction

Very little is known about ancient women Epicureans, and most of what we do know comes from sources who were hostile to Epicurean hedonism, such as Cicero and Plutarch. Some information is found in the doxography of Epicurus provided by Diogenes Laertius, who was not unsympathetic to Epicureanism, but Diogenes is at times a frustrating source since his habit was to report all manner of accounts on his subject rather than to determine their veracity. It was usually the case that ancient authors mentioned women Epicureans in order to embarrass the school by depicting its men as crude hedonists, who (so the slander goes) kept the women around for sexual gratification rather than intellectual stimulation.

It was not uncommon for ancient accounts of women philosophers to emphasise a woman's sexual status rather than her intellectual abilities or achievements, and such was certainly the case for ancient accounts of women Epicureans.[1] However, much of the misogyny directed at women Epicureans was noteworthy insofar as its main goal seems not to have been to undermine the women themselves (even if this was an inevitable consequence) but to reject the school's main ethical tenets; in other words, anti-hedonists used misogyny often as a tool for philosophical criticism. In addition, there is evidence that some critics and lampooners of Epicureanism believed that the women of the school had a negative effect on the quality of its intellectual activity: the women supposedly distracted the men, resulting in a philosophy that was less robust and coherent than it might have been in an all-male environment.

In what follows, I consider how accounts of Epicurean women were sexualised by critics who were intent on undermining hedonism, and I provide case studies of ancient Epicurean women, focusing especially

[1] Relevant here is Hawley (1994: 70–87).

on a *hetaira* (usually translated, controversially, as 'courtesan') known as Leontion and a woman named Themista. Since our extant accounts of Epicurean women are rather sparse, it is difficult to be choosy in our methods for evaluating the evidence. Since we know nothing about the philosophy of the Epicurean women – we have neither their own texts (if they wrote any) nor any accounts of their own philosophies – we cannot evaluate the intellectual quality of their contributions. Despite the scarcity of philosophical source material, there is still much to be gained by investigating the extant biographical accounts of Epicurean women: we stand to deepen our understanding of the place of women in the school, particularly our knowledge of how they were viewed by other members, as well as our understanding of the polemical tactics employed by ancient critics of Epicurean hedonism.

My strategy for engaging with the figures philosophically is multipronged. First, I attempt to separate the sexualised content from the intellectual content in polemical accounts of Epicurean women, and I consider how material from Epicureans themselves sheds light on the women's social status and philosophical roles in the school. This prong of my strategy operates under the assumption that the polemical accounts probably tend to exaggerate, or at the very least overemphasise, the extent to which the school's women and men desired, engaged in, or otherwise thought about sex. The goal here is to uncover as much as possible the bare 'data' regarding the women – evidence of their philosophical contributions, official relationships with others in the school (e.g., marriages), documented communication, etc. – while stripping away as much as possible any polemical chatter that may bias the data. This will be difficult given that so much of our information regarding the women comes from polemicists, but we will do well to consider why a critic is choosing to sexualise his account of Epicureanism: what is the critic's motivation for reporting the sexualised material, and is he targeting some aspect of the school's philosophy, the integrity of its members themselves, or some combination of these? Again, my underlying assumption will be that the sexualised content of the polemical reports needs to be separated from the 'data' because it is plausible that such reports distort the truth about who Epicurean women were and what their roles may have been in the school.

While the first prong of my strategy assumes that we need to view Epicurean women through a lens unclouded by anti-hedonism, the second prong operates under no such assumption: what if many, if not most, of the Epicurean women we know about were indeed prostitutes or *hetairai*, as many polemicists report, and what if the women did in fact have sexual relations, perhaps in their capacity as sex workers, with one or more members of the school? If this were true, how would it affect our understanding of the ways in which sex and women factored into Epicurean ethics? This formulation of my strategy relies on the view that it was not necessarily a problem for the women to be viewed both as intellectual contributors to the school and as sex objects. Indeed, we may do the women a disservice if we insist that chastity must have been a prerequisite for involvement in the school, as if there were something morally unsavoury about an intellectual woman engaging in sexual activity or attracting sexual attention. Nevertheless, given that philosophy and sexual promiscuity were often understood to be poor bedfellows in Epicurus' time, we need to envision how Epicureans might have responded to polemical charges that the presence of women in the school rendered its philosophy contemptible and its members disreputable.

Epicureanism and Its Critics

Epicureans were easy targets in antiquity because of their claim that the goal of life is pleasure, but this was frequently misunderstood – often wilfully, it seems – by their critics. Epicureans defined pleasure as the absence of pain in the body (*ataraxia*) and trouble in the soul (*aponia*), and they pursued a life focused on the fulfilment of natural and necessary desires, the enjoyment of friends, and a proper understanding of nature. In contrast to the Cyrenaics, another school of prominent ancient hedonists, whose goal was to achieve the most pleasure in the present moment,[2] Epicureans claimed that not all pleasures are choiceworthy all the time; although all pleasures are good in themselves, sometimes one should forgo a present enjoyment if doing so will bring oneself more pleasure later (*Ad Men.* 129). The Epicureans thought of their own philosophy as 'serious, restrained, and sober', to quote the Epicurean spokesperson Torquatus in Cicero's *De Finibus* (1.37).[3]

Around 307/6 BCE, Epicurus located his school – known as the 'Garden' because of its attached green space – outside the main gate of Athens, not far from Plato's Academy.[4] That Epicurus and many of his followers lived together in the Garden no doubt provided grist for the mill

---

[2] For more on women in the Cyrenaic school, see Katharine O'Reilly's chapter on Arete in this volume (Chapter 5).
[3] Translations in this chapter are mine except where otherwise noted.
[4] On the Epicureans' life in the Garden, see (Clay 2009: 9–28).

of his many critics, who imagined the place as a sort of hedonist frat house. And imagine they must have: unlike the Stoics and members of other Hellenistic schools, the Epicureans did not cultivate much of a public persona, preferring to keep to themselves in their Garden.[5] Social isolation was consistent with their goal of pursuing pleasure and avoiding pain: Epicurus writes in *Principal Doctrines* 14, 'the purest security comes from solitude and withdrawal from the many'. There are few extant, non-satirical accounts of the behaviour, dress, or physical appearance of the Epicureans, probably because they spent so much time out of the public eye.[6] There were ample statues of Epicurus in antiquity – which is how we know he had a beard and a long face – but these were often erected by his followers in private spaces such as villas, where the figures could be venerated by members of his school. As Caizzi notes: 'No living image of Epicurus as a person was presented day by day to the Athenians' eyes, and what came out of the school was just one word, "pleasure": something apparently very easy for everybody to understand and attack.'[7] If the facts about the Epicureans' lifestyle were not well known outside the school, critics' imaginations were free to concoct all sorts of salacious details about the habits of the Garden's resident hedonists.

According to Cicero, Epicurean habits are informed by Epicurean philosophy. In *De Finibus*, he claims that the Epicureans have no argument against the view that we should indulge in pleasure as much as possible. He accuses them of using philosophy as a justification for overindulgence – 'Epicurus appears to be looking for disciples, so that those who wish to be dissolute first become philosophers' – and quips that their work should be assessed by censors rather than philosophers (2.30). Much of Cicero's basis for this attack is a passage Diogenes Laertius attributes to Epicurus' lost text *On the Telos*. The fullest version of the passage is quoted by Cicero in the *Tusculan Disputations*: 'Indeed, I do not know how to understand the good, if you take away the pleasures that are experienced through taste, and the pleasures experienced in sex, and the sweet motions which are experienced by the ears through music and by the eyes through

---

[5] For more on the public image of Epicureans and Stoics, see Caizzi (1993: 303–29).

[6] See, e.g., *Vatican Sayings* 58: 'They must release themselves from the prison of common affairs and politics.' According to Diogenes Laertius (D.L. 10.119), Epicurus claimed in his lost text *On Life* that the sage will not take part in politics. (See also Cicero, *ad Atticum* 14.20). Diogenes also wrote that Epicurus 'was reasonable to such an excessive degree that he did not engage in politics' (D.L. 10.10). In the *Reply to Colotes*, Plutarch accuses the Epicureans of freeloading: they enjoy the advantages of living in society without 'paying their share', and they attempt to persuade others to avoid taking part in government and making public speeches (1127e).

[7] Caizzi (1993: 324).

forms, and the other pleasures which are generated in the whole person by any of the senses' (3.41).[8] In Cicero's mind, this passage shows that Epicurus has no idea what the highest good really is: on the one hand, it is sensory pleasures such as those from sex and taste, but on the other, it is the absence of pain. According to Cicero, Epicurus' philosophy is confusingly two-faced: it condones the pursuit of sensory pleasure to excess but also insists that the highest good is tranquillity and painlessness. In Cicero's eyes, Epicurean hedonism is not only immoral and therefore unsuitable for a virtuous Roman community, which should not be spending its time pursuing pleasure instead of virtue, but it is also logically flawed insofar as it equivocates about the meaning of 'pleasure' itself.

Prostitutes in the Garden?

Epicureans were easy targets not only because they were hedonists but also because they freely admitted women (and slaves) into their school. Ancient sources report the names of several women who philosophised in the Epicurean Garden, most while its founder was still alive. Among them were Batis, Leontion, Themista, Mammarion, Hedeia, Boidion, Erotion, Nikidion, and Demetria. Some of their names are so comical as to sound fake: in the modern parlance suggested by Nussbaum and Snyder,[9] Mammarion is 'Tits', Hedeia is 'Sweety' or 'Sweety-Pie' (Gordon argues for 'Pleasing' and claims that the name was not uncommon in Greek culture, yet Clay claims that the name suggests she was a prostitute),[10] Boidion is 'Ox-eyes' or 'Little Heifer', Erotion is 'Lovey', Nikidion is 'Little Victory', and Leontion is 'Little Lioness'. Both Nussbaum and Gordon consider that many of the names may indeed have been fake and that the only real women Epicureans were Leontion and Themista ('Righteous').[11] It is of course possible that many of the women never existed given that most of the extant references to them appear only in polemical works against Epicureanism, such as Plutarch's *Non Posse* (1089c, 1098b) and a work called *Delights* authored by Timocrates, a disgruntled Epicurean who supposedly left the school despite the fact that his brother Metrodorus was one of Epicurus' main disciples (D.L. 10.7).

---

[8] Nec equidem habeo, quod intellegam bonum illud, detrahens eas voluptates quae sapore percipiuntur, detrahens eas quae rebus percipiuntur veneriis, detrahens eas quae auditu e cantibus, detrahens eas etiam quae ex formis percipiuntur oculis suavis motiones, sive quae aliae voluptates in toto homine gignuntur quolibet sensu. Trans. Graver (2001), modified.
[9] Snyder (1989: 105).   [10] Clay (2009: 27); Gordon (2012: 101).
[11] Nussbaum (1986: 38 n. 10); Gordon (2004: 237).

However, as Gordon points out, the later Epicurean Philodemus of Gadara, from the first century BCE, mentions several of the women – Hedeia, Nikidion, Mammarion, and Demetria – which makes it less likely that all of them are pure fictions.[12]

In our extant evidence, the disgruntled Timocrates was the first to report that many Epicurean women were *hetairai* (D.L. 10.7), a position that modern historians have tended to describe as a high-class courtesan who was hired for companionship, entertainment, and usually sex. Ancient authors gave the impression that *hetairai* were something akin to prostitutes: Plutarch, for instance, remarks sarcastically that Epicurus settled himself in his Garden 'making babies with the *hetaira* from Cyzicus (παιδοποιούμενον ἐκ τῆς Κυζικηνῆς ἑταίρας)', who it has been suggested was Hedeia.[13] In their lexicon, Liddell and Scott specify that '*hetaira*' is opposed to both '*pornē*' (prostitute) and '*gametē*' (married woman, wife), indicating that *hetairai* belonged to a class of women who were unable to marry, perhaps because of lack of citizenship or lack of dowry. It has been thought that *hetairai* were educated, often foreign women who were expected to provide conversation, not just physical enjoyment, to male companions. *Hetairai* were known to have been well dressed and to have had control of their own money. Athenian men may have found *hetairai* to be more interesting than their wives, who were kept within the home and might therefore have been less cultured. It has been thought that many *hetairai* were former slaves from outside Athens, which meant they lacked many of the liberties of Athenian citizens. For instance, many scholars believe that a fourth-century BCE law prohibited non-citizens from marrying citizens, although scholarly interpretation of this law remains controversial.[14]

However, in recent years, scholars' description of *hetairai* as what amounts to high-class, non-citizen escorts has come under scrutiny, a fact which is important if we wish to consider Epicurean *hetairai* as more than mere sexual companions to Epicurus and his friends. Interestingly, one of the most famous *hetairai* of the ancient world, Aspasia, was an educated and cherished companion of the Athenian statesman Pericles, and she too was called a prostitute, perhaps, it has been suggested, in order to slander

---

[12] Gordon (2004: 238).
[13] *Non Posse* 1098b. For the reference to Hedeia, see Usener (1963: 416, col. 1) (listing for Polyaenus). There is no evidence that Epicurus himself had any children.
[14] The scholarly literature on the fourth-century BCE law supposedly prohibiting marriages between Athenian citizens and metics, cited at Demosthenes 59.16, is vast. For a recent rundown of the debate, see chapter 1 of Kennedy (2014).

Pericles.¹⁵ Kennedy has argued that the name '*hetaira*' originated in the late sixth and early fifth centuries BCE and designated women who were elite, educated, sometimes foreign and sometimes citizen, who participated in symposia and enjoyed luxurious lifestyles.¹⁶ These women were not necessarily prostitutes – many of them definitely were not, as proven by the fact that some were married to Athenian nobles. It is not until the fourth century BCE, she argues, that the behaviour exhibited by *hetairai* from the late sixth and early fifth centuries came to signify a woman who was not marriage material, and from then on *hetairai* and matrimony appear to have been sharply polarised, creating what Kennedy calls 'the wife-whore dichotomy'. Kennedy challenges the standard scholarly view that a woman who was a non-citizen or lacked a dowry in classical Athens must have been a sex worker: at the time, some women who were without dowries were indeed citizens, though many others were freed slaves or non-resident aliens. What such women had in common was not a career in the sex industry (since some were not working in such an industry at all) but their singlehood, which was forced on them because of their financial and/or political circumstances. Over time, the many different uses of the term '*hetaira*' were combined, most notably in the second and third centuries CE by the rhetoricians Alciphron and Athenaeus, leading to 'a confusion of the woman's behaviour (party going) and status (unmarriageable) with one potential occupation (sexual labour)'.¹⁷ If *hetairai* were not necessarily prostitutes or high-class escorts, this makes more sense of the fact that several of the Epicurean women, such as Leontion and Themista (who may or may not have been a *hetaira*), were in long-term, stable relationships with men of the school. Although we know that these women in particular were not Athenian citizens, nothing suggests that they were sex workers of any sort – either common or elite. The Epicurean women may have been labelled '*hetairai*' because they were engaged in behaviour that was unusual and possibly perceived as scandalous in their time, such as philosophising along with men.¹⁸ Or, they may have been guilty of the 'scandalous' behaviour of simply existing while poor and without male relatives.¹⁹

---

¹⁵ See Henry (1997). Plutarch describes Pericles as being weak and out of his mind for allowing himself to be manipulated by a prostitute (*Life of Pericles*, 24.1).
¹⁶ Kennedy (2015: 61–79).   ¹⁷ Kennedy (2015: 63).
¹⁸ There is also evidence that many Pythagorean women were described as prostitutes. See Dutsch (2020).
¹⁹ See Gordon (2012: 95); Kennedy (2015: 73).

The presence of women in the school factored significantly into ancient polemical accounts of Epicureanism. Cicero, one of the Epicureans' most ardent critics, chastises them for studying women instead of great men such as Solon and Lycurgus: he remarks in *De Finibus*, 'Would it not be better to talk of them than to devote countless volumes to Themista?' (2.68).[20] We unfortunately do not have much idea in what sense the Epicureans were in reality 'studying women' other than the little that is mentioned in the doxography: male Epicureans exchanged letters with women and in some cases dedicated works to them. In any case, Cicero clearly has no interest in discovering anything about the women who supposedly took up so much of the Epicureans' time; rather, he calls attention to the presence of women in the Garden merely to lampoon the school. We see something similar with Plutarch, who mentions Epicurean women in order to undercut Epicurus' claim that one should live outside the public eye. With tongue in cheek, Plutarch remarks in his polemical work *Live Unknown* that concealing oneself from others is indeed necessary if one wants to enjoy certain indiscretions: 'By all means, if I am to live with Hedeia the *hetaira* and spend my life with Leontion and "spit on what is fine" and put the good "in the flesh and in ticklings" – these goals require darkness, these goals require night, for forgetting and ignorance' (1129b).[21]

Ancient comic writers also had a hand in inventing scandalous stories about the women of the Garden. Alciphron, a second/third century CE rhetorician, wrote a fake letter from Leontion to her friend and fellow Athenian *hetaira* Lamia, in which Epicurus is depicted as a jealous lover, old and decrepit, who threatens to set his posse on Leontion if she continues to refuse to give up her lover, Timarchus of Cephisia.[22] 'Leontion' exclaims that this 'lice-ridden and sickly man ... is controlling me, criticising everything, suspecting everything, writing me incomprehensible letters and chasing me out of his garden'.[23] Perhaps the worst of the insults appears later in the letter, when 'Leontion' considers whether she should stay with Epicurus when 'he may even take what I have, and

---

[20] Nonne melius est de his aliquid quam tantis voluminibus de Themista loqui?
[21] Πάνυ μὲν οὖν, ἂν μεθ' Ἡδείας βιοῦν μέλλω τῆς ἑταίρας καὶ Λεοντίῳ συγκαταζῆν καὶ "τῷ καλῷ προσπτύειν" καὶ τἀγαθὸν "ἐν σαρκὶ καὶ γαργαλισμοῖς" τίθεσθαι· ταῦτα δεῖται σκότους τὰ τέλη, ταῦτα νυκτός, ἐπὶ ταῦτα τὴν λήθην καὶ τὴν ἄγνοιαν.
[22] *Epistles*, 4.17 [2.2] (trans. Granholm 2012).
[23] Alciphron, *Epistles* 4.17.2–4 [2.2]. οἷά με Ἐπίκουρος οὗτος διοικεῖ πάντα λοιδορῶν, πάντα ὑποπτεύων, ἐπιστολὰς ἀδιαλύτους μοι γράφων, ἐκδιώκων ἐκ τοῦ κήπου.

teach others'.[24] So not only is Epicurus a dirty old man, but he's also a plagiariser, borrowing philosophical doctrine from his *hetairai*.

In addition, Diogenes Laertius reports in the doxography of Epicurus that Diotimus, a Stoic from around 100 BCE, 'hostilely slandered [Epicurus] with the most cruel statements, producing fifty salacious letters as written by Epicurus' (D.L. 10.3).[25] The Greek rhetorician Athenaeus reports in his third-century CE work *Deipnosophistae* (*Dinner Sophists/ Experts*) that Diotimus was made to answer to Zeno the Epicurean for the forged books and was killed.[26] Nothing remains of Diotimus' fabricated letters, but, given Zeno's reaction to them and Diogenes Laertius' account, it would be surprising if they lacked salacious and embarrassing stories of the Epicureans' relations with the women of their school. Again, we have no reason to believe that ancient polemicists had any interest in describing the lives and accomplishments of the women themselves; the women were useful as mere tools for mocking Epicurean men, whose personal depravity served as evidence of the depravity of their philosophy.

But even if the critics were mistaken about the facts – perhaps the women were not high-class escorts, common prostitutes, or mere sexual distractions – we still find within the anti-hedonist polemic several significant details about the role of women in Epicurus' school. For starters, we learn from the critics that women were indeed members of the school, which is no small fact. In addition, we know that many of the women were very close to Epicurus and his main disciples – close enough to be given nicknames and special enough to have works dedicated to them. In addition, if many of the women were *hetairai* in the sense that Kennedy understands the term, they may very well have been educated and highly cultured. Perhaps this meant that the Epicureans were not terribly concerned about the social status of their fellows, which makes sense of the fact that they admitted slaves as well as women. One can speculate that what mattered more was that followers wholeheartedly committed to the school's lifestyle and were intellectually capable of mastering its philosophy. Even if critics believed that the presence of women in the school discredited Epicurean philosophy and tarnished the reputation of its practitioners, it is nevertheless the case that women took part in the life

---

[24] Alciphron, *Epistles* 4.17.20–21 [2.2]. λαβέτω καὶ ἃ ἔχω, διδασκέτω δ' ἄλλους.
[25] Διότιμος δ' ὁ Στωικὸς δυσμενῶς ἔχων πρὸς αὐτὸν πικρότατα αὐτὸν διαβέβληκεν, ἐπιστολὰς φέρων πεντήκοντα ἀσελγεῖς ὡς Ἐπικούρου.
[26] Athenaeus, *Deipnosophistae* 13.611b. Διότιμος δ' ὁ γράψας τὰ κατ' Ἐπικούρου βιβλία ὑπὸ Ζήνωνος τοῦ Ἐπικουρείου ἐξαιτηθεὶς ἀνηρέθη.

of the school, perhaps even as philosophers, as is suggested by other evidence that I turn to in what follows.

Women Epicureans: The 'Data'

What in fact do we know about Epicurean women? We have the most evidence concerning Leontion and Themista, much of it from polemical sources. Regarding Leontion (also known as Leontium), we have the following collection of facts from Diogenes Laertius, whose evidence comes from all manner of sources: she lived with one of Epicurus' brothers, whom hostile sources described as a pimp (προαγωγεύειν: one who prostitutes) (D.L. 10.4); she exchanged letters with Epicurus, who sometimes shared them with the rest of the school (D.L. 10.5); Epicurus' main disciple Metrodorus was supposedly quite fond of her and took her as his mistress (παλλακίς) (D.L. 10.6, 10.23). Plutarch wrote that Metrodorus and Leontion were actually married (*Non Posse* 1098b): the groom's mother and sister were said to be elated (ὑπερχαίρω) about the union. This bit of information is puzzling: it is unclear how they could have married given that Leontion was not a citizen, unless there were no laws prohibiting unions between citizens and aliens at the time. Diogenes reports that Epicurus joyously replied to her in a letter, 'O Lord Apollo, my dear little Leontion, we were filled with such loud applause when we read your little letter' (D.L. 10.5).[27] Philodemus too reports that Leontion wrote to Epicurus.[28] Athenaeus states that she had a daughter, Danae, who was also a *hetaira*, associated with Sophron, the governor of Ephesus in the middle of the third century BCE.[29] It is reported that Danae informed Sophron of a plot against his life by Laodice I, the former wife of the Hellenistic king Antiochus II. Upon learning that Danae had warned Sophron of the threat, Laodice supposedly threw Danae off a cliff.[30] In addition, Athenaeus reports that the third-century BCE poet Hermesianax of Colophon dedicated a three-book poem to Leontion, who was said to be his lover (ἐρώμενος).[31]

---

[27] ἔν τε ταῖς ἐπιστολαῖς πρὸς μὲν Λεόντιον Παιὰν ἄναξ, φίλον Λεοντάριον, οἵου κροτοθορύβου ἡμᾶς ἐνέπλησας ἀναγνόντας σου τὸ ἐπιστόλιον.
[28] Philodemus, *Herculanensium Voluminum quae supersunt. Collectio altera* (*VH2*) 1.119.
[29] Athenaeus, *Deipnosophistae* 13.593b.   [30] See Laale (2011: 129–30).
[31] Athenaeus, *Deipnosophistae* 13.597a. I think there is good reason to be suspicious of the veracity of these reports given that they are poorly documented (e.g., that concerning Danae) and/or come from comic sources (e.g., Athenaeus). I include the reports to show that many Epicurean women (and, evidently, their daughters) were depicted in antiquity as 'loose', even if this might not have been the case in reality.

Several sources report that Leontion practised philosophy. In *On the Nature of the Gods*, Cicero criticises Epicurus and his followers for letting women philosophise in the Garden, while at the same time Cicero compliments Leontion's facility with Attic Greek and notes that she authored a work against Theophrastus, the head of the Aristotelian school: 'Was it dreams like these that emboldened not only Epicurus and Metrodorus and Hermarchus to speak against Pythagoras, Plato and Empedocles, but even dared the little prostitute (*meretricula*) Leontium to write against Theophrastus? She is certainly skilled at Attic discourse, but nevertheless – so great was the licence in the Garden of Epicurus' (*De natura deorum* 1.93).[32] Pliny the Elder, in his *Natural Histories*, reports the same but does not name Leontion: 'I am truly not unaware that a woman no less wrote against Theophrastus, a man whose eloquence was so great that the name he acquired signified the divine, and from this was born the saying, "choosing a tree from which to hang" and that from this came the expression, "choosing one's tree for hanging oneself".'[33] The idea here is that in writing her refutation of Theophrastus, Leontion demonstrated her own lack of skill. Usener, in his compilation of Epicurean material, includes the work 'Against Theophrastus' among the books by Epicurus, which Gordon claims is an indication that Usener believed Leontion was not actually its author.[34] However, I think Usener's intention is not entirely clear: he does not explicitly doubt Leontion's authorship; includes the two known references to 'Against Theophrastus' (namely, those of Cicero and Pliny), both of which attribute the work to Leontion; and notes that Clitomachus the Carneadean 'followed the rumours of others' and attributed the books against Theophrastus to Leontion rather than to Epicurus.[35] Usener remarks elsewhere in his compilation that Leontion was thought to be the author of the work against Theophrastus owing to

---

[32] Istisne fidentes somniis non modo Epicurus et Metrodorus et Hermarchus contra Pythagoram Platonem Empedoclemque dixerunt, sed meretricula etiam Leontium contra Theophrastum scribere ausast—scito illa quidem sermone et Attico, sed tamen: tantum Epicuri hortus habuit licentiae.

[33] Book 1, Preface 29. Ceu vero nesciam adversus Theophrastum, hominem in eloquentia tantum ut nomen divinum inde invenerit, scripsisse etiam feminam, et proverbiam inde natum suspendio arborem eligendi.

[34] Usener (1963: 101–2); Gordon (2012: 76 n. 17).

[35] Usener 1963: 101: 'hinc colligas Clitomachum h.e. Carneaden aliorum famam secutum libros contra Theophrastum non Epicuro sed Leontio tribuisse'. When Usener says 'you may infer (*colligas*) . . .', he might mean that you would be wrong to do so (i.e., Clitomachus is mistaken in his attribution of the works to Leontion), but unfortunately it is not entirely clear.

her reputation as a learned woman.[36] Perhaps he means that she was mistakenly given credit for work that was not her own, but that would be odd given that he never claims that the several sources who attribute the work to her are mistaken. If Epicurus did put his name on a work written by Leontion, it strikes me as unlikely that Cicero, if he knew about it, would not have wasted an opportunity to point out another example of Epicurus' depravity. Pliny also mentions two paintings of Leontion, one of which may provide some proof that she philosophised. Pliny writes, 'Theodorus (or Theorus) painted "Epicurus' Leontion thinking" (*Leontium Epicuri cogitantem*)'.[37] Of the other painting, there is very little description: 'Aristides painted "Epicurus' Leontion (*Leontium Epicuri*)".'[38] Notice that Pliny says that she was Epicurus' when he might have said instead 'the Epicurean Leontion' or 'a follower of Epicurus'.

Further evidence that some Epicurean women may have occupied positions of prominence in the school is a Roman copy of a Greek statue depicting Leontion or perhaps Themista, which for many years was thought to depict St Hippolytus.[39] The figure wears a long tunic and is seated in a sort of throne, the bottom of which is decorated with the head and feet of a lion. Guarducci compared the statue, particularly the throne, to similar specimens in antiquity and discovered that leonine thrones of this sort were rather unusual in Imperial Rome and western ancient Greece, but several were found in Athens depicting Epicurus and some of his main disciples. For several reasons, Guarducci concluded that the statue bears the head of St. Hippolytus, which was added during restoration, and the body of a woman, who is very likely an Epicurean. Guarducci claims that the most likely candidate is Themista, but Frischer argued in the early 1980s that Guarducci exaggerated the significance of Themista in the school, and the figure most likely represents Leontion.[40] Frischer based this view on the fact that references to Leontion in ancient literature appear more frequently than do those to Themista and that it would make sense for a statue of Leontion to serve as the inspiration for later paintings of her, such as those noted by Pliny.[41] In any case, the point is that some women Epicureans – whether Themista, Leontion, or someone else – were prominent enough in the school to be immortalised in stone along with Epicurus and his other main people.

---

[36] 'Famosa erat ut docta mulier, adeo ut Epicuri aduersus Theophrastum libri ab ea scripti crederentur.' Usener (1963: 411).
[37] *Natural Histories* 35.144.   [38] *Natural Histories* 35.99.   [39] See Guarducci (1974: 163–90).
[40] Frischer (1982: 90).   [41] Frischer (1982: 90 n. 7).

Other evidence regarding Leontion is even more slanderous than that supplied by Cicero and Plutarch. Athenaeus has the character Myrtilus remark in the *Deipnosophistae*, 'Did not this same Epicurus take Leontion as his lover, who had become notorious for being a *hetaira*? When she began to philosophise she did not stop being a *hetaira*, but had sex with all the Epicureans in their gardens, even right in front of Epicurus, with the result that he fretted about her quite a bit, and wrote this in his *Letters to Hermarchus*' (13.588b).[42] Athenaeus depicts not only Leontion but all of Epicurus' followers in the Garden as the worst kinds of hedonists and perhaps in more ways than even Athenaeus realises: his point seems to be that Epicureans are indulging their excessive and baseless desires for sex, but notice that, were this true, they violate their own hedonism by causing themselves mental anguish by somehow 'fretting about' their relationships. Unfortunately, we cannot say for certain in what sense, if any, Epicureans were overly fixated on their lovers, but the fact remains that the passage from Athenaeus does add to the evidence that Leontion practised philosophy (φιλοσοφεῖν) in some way.

Boccaccio's fourteenth-century work *Concerning Famous Women* includes some choice jabs at Leontion, which were based on the writings of Latin authors and his own imagination. Boccaccio writes the following:

> If I am right, Leontium was a Greek woman who achieved fame perhaps in the time of Alexander the Great, king of Macedonia. If she had preserved her matronly honour, the glory attached to her name would have been much more radiant, for she had extraordinary intellectual powers. According to the testimony of ancient authors, Leontium so excelled in the study of literature that, prompted either by envy or feminine temerity, she dared to write an invective against Theophrastus, a famous philosopher of that period. I have not seen this work. But its fame has lasted throughout the centuries down to our own age: hence we cannot say that the work was a trifle or showed a lack of ability, although it is a clear sign of an envious disposition.[43]

---

[42] οὗτος οὖν ὁ Ἐπίκουρος οὐ Λεόντιον εἶχεν ἐρωμένην τὴν ἐπὶ ἑταιρείᾳ διαβόητον γενομένην; ἢ δὲ οὐδ' ὅτε φιλοσοφεῖν ἤρξατο ἐπαύσατο ἑταιροῦσα, πᾶσι δὲ τοῖς Ἐπικουρείοις συνῆν ἐν τοῖς κήποις, Ἐπικούρῳ δὲ καὶ ἀναφανδόν· ὥστ' ἐκεῖνον πολλὴν φροντίδα ποιούμενον αὐτῆς τοῦτ' ἐμφανίζειν διὰ τῶν πρὸς Ἕρμαρχον Ἐπιστολῶν.

[43] Trans. Brown (2001: 25). Leuntium, si satis bene arbitror, greca fuit mulier et forsan Alexandri magni, macedonici regis, evo conspicua. Cuius, si matronalem pudicitiam servasset, cum ingenii eius permaxime fuerint vires, longe fulgidior nominis fuisset gloria. Veterum enim testimonio tantum in studiis literarum valuit, ut aut invidia permota, aut muliebri temeritate inpulsa, in Theophrastum, celeberrimum ea tempestate phylosophum, scribere invehendo ausa sit: quid, ego non vidi. Sane postquam per tot secula in etatem usque nostram fama devenit, non minimum fuisse nec etiam parve facultatis inditium existimare possumus, esto invidi animi sit certissimum argumentum.

Like the account provided by Athenaeus, Boccaccio's treats Leontion's intellectual talent as a liability rather than an asset: given her intelligence, she should have been able to do something better with her life than prostitute herself to Epicurean men. It seems she cannot win no matter what: she is either unintelligent or too smart to be a consort to Epicureans. She fares no better in the rest of Boccaccio's account: 'Living in the brothels among pimps, vile adulterers, and whores, she was able to stain Philosophy, the teacher of truth, with ignominy in those disgraceful chambers, trample it with wanton feet, and plunge it into filthy sewers ....'[44] In Boccaccio's opinion, Leontion should have stayed away from philosophy altogether, no matter how proficient she may have been at it. Nevertheless, if we strip away the slanderous and prejudicial aspects of the account, we are left with more evidence that Leontion was indeed an Epicurean and an intellectual.

We know even less about the other Epicurean women than we do about Leontion. In addition to her and Themista, we have the names of several others, whom I mentioned earlier: Mammarion, Hedeia, Boidion, Erotion, Nikidion, and Demetria. Castner observes that it is possible that four of these women made dedications to certain healing gods.[45] The names Mammarion, Hedeia, Nikidion, and Boidion appear in ancient inscriptions recording the dedications, which may have been made before the women became members of the Epicurean school (if they are indeed the same women and not other, non-Epicurean women of the same names): it would have been unlikely for Epicureans to have paid much attention to any deity, owing to their view that the gods take no interest in human activity. In *Non Posse*, Plutarch mentions several of the women while he is in the process of ridiculing hedonists for requiring too many costly things to support their so-called philosophy, 'and not only this, but young and attractive women (γυναῖκας), like Leontion, Boidion, Hedeia, and Nikidion, who grazed (ἐνέμοντο) about the Garden'(1097d–e). Note Plutarch's phrasing: the women 'grazed',[46] an activity that is of course fitting for those named after heifers and other animals.

There are a few additional details regarding Themista. Among Epicurus' works listed in Diogenes Laertius' doxography, one was dedicated to her: a work called '*Neocles*', who was one of Epicurus' brothers (D.L. 10.28).

---

[44] Trans. Brown 2001: 253. Inter lenones impurosque mechos et scorta atque fornices versata, potuit magistram rerum phylosophiam inhonestis in cellulis et ignominiosis deturpare notis atque impudicis calcare vestigiis et cloacis immergere fetidis ....
[45] Castner (1982: 51–57).   [46] From νέμω, to pasture or graze.

Diogenes also reports that Themista was married to Leonteus, a disciple of Epicurus, a fact also reported by Clement of Alexandria.[47] She and Leonteus had a son, whom they named after the master himself (D.L. 10.26). At some point, Epicurus too may have been friendly with Themista, judging by a letter he wrote to her, as reported by Diogenes: 'To Themista, the wife of Leonteus, I am able to say that if you all invite me, I will be easily influenced to rush forth to wherever you and Themista should summon me' (D.L. 10.5).[48] In addition, Diogenes mentions her in his catalogue of prominent Epicureans: 'There is also Leonteus of Lampsacus, and his wife Themista, to whom Epicurus wrote letters (πρὸς ἣν καὶ γέγραφεν ὁ Ἐπίκουρος)' (D.L. 10.25). This passage is significant because it would be surprising for the wife of a distinguished member of any school to receive special mention unless she made some contributions to the school in her own right. It is also significant because Diogenes' syntax indicates that Epicurus sent his letters to *her* individually (πρὸς ἣν).

Clement also reports that Themista and several other women were intellectuals: 'Themista too, of Lampsacus, the daughter of Zoilus, the wife of Leonteus of Lampsacus, philosophised about Epicurean things, just as Myia the daughter of Theano the Pythagorean, and Arignote, who wrote the history of Dionysius.'[49] This may seem like praise, especially coming from Clement, who despises Epicureanism, but Gordon contends that Clement's phrasing is not necessarily complimentary: Themista is not described as a philosopher herself but as one who 'philosophised Epicurean things' (τὰ Ἐπικούρεια ἐφιλοσόφει), meaning that she might have been a student rather than a philosopher.[50] This might be plausible if there were some difference between *being* a philosopher and *studying* philosophy, but those are not necessarily mutually exclusive.[51] Even if the phrase in question is rendered as 'philosophised Epicurean things', it may nevertheless mean she was an Epicurean philosopher because she *lived* Epicurean philosophy – that is, she understood its doctrines and put them into practice in her daily life. Further evidence for the claim that Themista was something of an intellectual comes from Lactantius, an early Christian

---

[47] Clement of Alexandria, *Stromata* 4.19.
[48] πρὸς δὲ Θεμίσταν τὴν Λεοντέως γυναῖκα οἷός τε φησίν εἰμί, ἐὰν μὴ ὑμεῖς πρός με ἀφίκησθε, αὐτὸς τρικύλιστος, ὅπου ἂν ὑμεῖς καὶ Θεμίστα παρακαλῆτε, ὠθεῖσθαι.
[49] Clement of Alexandria, *Stromata* 4.19. ναὶ μὴν καὶ Θεμιστὼ ἡ Ζωΐλου ἡ Λαμψακηνὴ ἡ Λεοντέως γυνὴ τοῦ Λαμψακηνοῦ τὰ Ἐπικούρεια ἐφιλοσόφει καθάπερ Μυῖα ἡ Θεανοῦς θυγάτηρ τὰ Πυθαγόρεια.
[50] Gordon (2012: 78 n. 22, 89). [51] I thank Phillip Sidney Horkey for pointing this out to me.

from the third/fourth century CE, who writes in his *Divine Institutes* that although many philosophers, such as the Epicureans and Stoics, tried to introduce philosophy to the ignorant multitudes, those philosophers failed to include women, with one exception: 'In all of memory, no one ever taught any women besides Themista to philosophise.'[52] It is odd that he does not mention Leontion or any other women philosophers and perhaps odd too that Plutarch says not a word about Themista.

A more shadowy figure among ancient women intellectuals is Theophila, from the fourth-to-third centuries BCE. Martial, a Roman poet from the first century CE, describes her in an epigram to Canius Rufus, a poet and friend. Referring to a portrait of Theophila, who is described as the fiancé of Canius, Martial writes the following in Epigram 7.69:

> Canius, this is your promised bride, Theophila, whose mind is steeped in Cecropian riches. The Attic garden of the great ancient [Epicurus] could rightfully claim her, nor less would the Stoic throng wish her theirs. Whatever work you send forth through her ears will live; so unwomanlike is her taste, so uncommon. Your Pantaenis would scarcely claim to be her superior, well-known though she be to the Pierian choir. Sappho would love her and praise her verse-making. Theophila is more pure and Sappho was not more accomplished.[53]

Martial portrays her as chaste and rather masculine: she is unlike other women and also intelligent, traits that would seem worthy of praise. Yet Martial's tone is disapproving, as Swancutt points out: 'the whole is highly ironic, employing innuendo about Hellenic luxury to call Theophila's chastity into question'.[54] Swancutt comments further: 'She is a hellenized, masculine intellectual schooled in Sapphic licentiousness – not at all a good bride for poor Canius.'[55] Furthermore, if Theophila is indeed unscrupulous and unladylike, this reflects poorly on the philosophical schools that have attempted to recruit her. In the end, though, we do not know which school, if any, Theophila eventually settled on.

I cannot do full justice here to the question of what it meant for an Epicurean to philosophise, but I will suggest that women of the school

---

[52] Lactantius, *Divine Institutes* 3.25. Denique nullas umquam mulieres philosophari docuerunt praeter unam ex omni memoria Themisten.
[53] Haec est illa tibi promissa Theophila, Caius, cuis Cecropia pectora dote madent: hanc sibi iure petat magni senis Atticus hortus, nec minus esse suam Stoica turba velit. Vivet opus quodcumque per has emiseris aures; tam non femineum nec populare sapit. Non tua Pantaenis nimium se praeferat illi, Quamvis Pierio sit bene nota choro. Carmina fingentem Sappho laudabat amatrix: Castior haec, et non doctior illa fuit. Trans. D. R. Shackleton Bailey, revised by Swancutt (2006).
[54] Swancutt (2006: 42).   [55] Swancutt (2006: 43).

(as well as its men) were philosophising even if they were not authoring philosophical works or otherwise actively furthering the tradition; writing treatises was not the only way to earn one's credentials as an Epicurean philosopher. One of the main messages of Epicurus' *Letter to Menoeceus* is that being an Epicurean entails comprehending the key Epicurean doctrines concerning physics and ethics – especially those pertaining to the nature of death, pleasure, pain, and the gods – and living in accordance with such doctrines. Several times in the letter he exhorts Menoeceus to 'practise' (μελετάω) the Epicurean precepts in order to live 'as a god among men', perhaps indicating that one does philosophy by living philosophically, which entails acquiring true beliefs through study and then putting those beliefs into practice.[56] If Epicurean women were intelligent enough to master Epicurean principles – which is likely true of at least Leontion and Themista – and if they had an opportunity to 'practise' the Epicurean lifestyle, then I think it makes sense to say that they philosophised and were philosophers.

Epicurean Women as Philosophers and Sex Objects

By now I think we can see that most of the accounts of ancient Epicurean women follow a similar pattern: the authors aim to undermine and mock Epicurean hedonism by sexualising accounts of its practitioners. A common way that Epicurus' critics accomplished this was by ridiculing Epicurean women and sensationalising their interactions with the school's men. The accounts of Epicurean women were thus designed as ad hominem attacks on Epicurus and his main disciples, attacks that were ultimately aimed at undercutting Epicurean hedonism: pleasure should not be the goal of life because it leads to the licentiousness exhibited by its founder and his followers. Although ancient polemicists, such as Cicero and Plutarch, often provided accounts that were hostile, misleading, and incomplete, without them we would probably know nothing about any Epicurean woman. One might conclude, then, that we should be grateful for the critics, since some news of Epicurean women is arguably better than no news, even if the news was served up with a side of anti-hedonist misogyny. When the polemical ideology is stripped away as much as it can be, we are left with the 'data' confirming that women were members of the school and some were indeed intellectuals.

---

[56] See especially *Ad Men.* 122 and 135.

One way I have gone about attempting to separate fact from fiction in the critics' accounts is by determining what information about the women is corroborated by non-hostile sources, such as letters between Epicurean men and women and depictions of the women in ancient art. We get the sense from such sources that some women were highly respected by their fellow Epicureans – if this were not the case, presumably we would not find a statue of an Epicurean woman whose regal pose resembles that of the stone figures of her prominent Epicurean brethren – that some were quite close to or even in official relationships (e.g., marriage) with high-level members of the school (and so were not kept in secret, contra Plutarch's narrative), and that some of the women might have produced philosophical works, such as the piece against Theophrastus thought to have been penned by Leontion. The non-hostile sources seem to corroborate the 'data' from the critical accounts.

All of the above has been motivated by the assumption that the critics attempt to undermine Epicurean ethics by fabricating or distorting the dirty details of the amorous habits of Epicurus and his followers. I have contended that this critical tactic is motivated by anti-hedonist ideology; in other words, the attacks, even when ad hominem, originate mainly from differences of opinion about whether pleasure should be the goal of life. But it may also be the case that the critics are simply uncomfortable with the idea that a woman could be an intellectual, especially a supposedly promiscuous woman. And the critics might not be the only ones with this prejudice: their discomfort may be reflected in my own attempts to discount the racier bits of the polemicists' descriptions in order to further the conclusion that at least some of the women were respected and intelligent. But what if many of the women were indeed philosopher prostitutes? What if the school were something like a free-love community, a co-ed garden of swingers? If this were true, how would such a lifestyle have been consistent with Epicurean ethics, and what might have been the role of women in such an environment?

We should note that there is evidence that Epicureans did not disapprove of sex, and there is good reason to believe they would not have disapproved of its members having sex with each other. Epicureans categorise sex as a natural but unnecessary desire; it is compatible with living well as long as it does not disturb one's *ataraxia*.[57] Unlike, say, the pursuit of fame, sex itself is not inherently troublesome, but it might become undesirable under certain circumstances, such as if one obsesses about

---

[57] For more on sex, love, and the Epicurean taxonomy of desires, see Arenson (2016: 301–6).

procuring it, takes great risks to find or keep a partner, or neglects one's duties.[58] Lucretius actually recommends casual sex for those seeking physical pleasure without the emotional disturbance of love, which the Epicureans characterise as an unnatural desire, fuelled by false beliefs.[59] Since Epicureans think that they themselves have true beliefs about the causes of unhealthy desires and how to avoid them, they might say that a fellow Epicurean is a safer sexual partner than some random person: Epicurean partners will at least be more attuned to signs of obsessive attachment, which they will correctly see as a threat to their *ataraxia*. The members of the school might therefore have seen each other as useful, safe outlets for sexual desire, an attitude that may have accounted for their willingness to admit women: without the worry that sexual relationships would devolve into distracting obsessions, the Epicureans might not have seen any reason to turn a woman away. If she were having sex with, or even prostituting herself to, her male schoolmates, this need not have been inconsistent with Epicurean ethics or detrimental to her own intellectual pursuits or those of the men.

In the end, it does not seem to matter much whether the critics were right that Epicurean women were prostitutes and sex objects. Whether we separate the sexualised content from the 'data' and attempt to corroborate the latter with evidence from non-hostile sources or whether we simply acknowledge that the critics may have been right that the women were having regular sexual relations with other members of the school, we reach the conclusion that women were there in the Garden as intellectuals, mothers, friends, and lovers, roles that were not necessarily mutually exclusive.[60]

---

[58] See Metrodorus' letter to Pythocles (*Vatican Sayings* 51).   [59] *De Rerum Natura* 4.1063–72.
[60] For their comments on the various versions of this chapter, I would like to thank the participants of the Women Intellectuals in Antiquity Symposium, held at Oxford University in February 2020, the participants of the workshop for this volume, held online in March 2021, and especially Katharine O'Reilly and Caterina Pellò.

CHAPTER 5

Arete of Cyrene and the Role of Women in Philosophical Lineage
Katharine R. O'Reilly

Introduction

Arete of Cyrene (fl. 350 BCE) was daughter of the founder of the Cyrenaic school and mother to the figure who codified its principles, who was known as *mētrodidaktos* – 'mother-taught'. Her tomb was said to be inscribed with an epitaph declaring her the splendour of Greece with the beauty of Helen, the virtue of Thirma, the pen of Aristippus, the soul of Socrates, and the tongue of Homer. Her representation is consistently in relation to others. What can we learn from this about Arete as a figure in her own right? In this chapter, I explore what the depiction of Arete can tell us about the importance of women acting as links in an intellectual chain to maintain a philosophical lineage but to the detriment of revealing their unique philosophical contributions.

Ancient biographies are at pains to establish Arete as a reliable conduit through which the teachings of the Cyrenaics were transmitted between male members. However, doing so evidently did not require the preservation of her thought or writings. She is said to have had a thirty-five-year public teaching career, wrote forty books, headed the school after the death of her father, and passed her teachings on to her son, playing a crucial role in the philosophical lineage of the Cyrenaics. Yet none of her work is preserved. She directed a school. Yet, she is more often spoken of as daughter and mother to Cyrenaics than as a practising philosopher and teacher. Here I begin the assessment of the evidence with ancient biography and then consider the depiction of Arete in later sources, including a Socratic Epistle. I argue for three ways in which the role of Arete prompts us to question our understanding of ancient philosophical education and Cyrenaic commitments: first, in terms of the scope of philosophy and the inclusion of child-rearing and caring responsibilities within it; second, in terms of innovation and originality, as versus preservation, being the seat of philosophical value; and third, in terms of a perceived distinction between the object of philosophical transmission as formal theory versus lifestyle and performance. By gaining clarity on these issues, we are able to recognise Arete as a talented and esteemed teacher who significantly enhances and alters Cyrenaicism.

I follow this with methodological reflections on how we might access a figure like Arete given the state of the source materials and their exclusion of women. I argue that this task requires and licenses the adoption of three key methodological strategies, each related to an added open-mindedness to source material when it comes to the recovery of ancient women philosophers. In doing so, I speak to sceptical concerns about whether the project of reaching Arete as philosopher can get off the ground. I conclude by asking if contemporary treatments can do more than the impoverished historical record to reflect Arete's legacy as an intellectual and cultural icon in her own time.

Ancient Depictions of Arete

Arete of Cyrene was the daughter of Aristippus the Elder, who was a follower of Socrates and founder of the Cyrenaic school. Born in Cyrene, in modern day Libya, Arete may have remained there, at least until the death of her father (circa 355 BCE),[1] after which she is recorded as taking over as head of the school.[2] We will begin our exploration of Arete by considering her depiction in ancient biographies of her father.

---

[1] Lampe (2015: 17 n. 39). This is also suggested by Epistle 27, which I will discuss below. There is a question of whether she ever made it to Athens, or may have been stuck in Cyrene, and somewhat marginalised. See n. 2 for evidence of her presence in Athens.

[2] Boccaccio in Mozans (1913 198 n. 1). Mozans comments as follows:

> [Arete] is said to have publicly taught natural and moral philosophy in the schools and academies of Attica for thirty-five years, to have written forty books, and to have counted among her pupils one hundred and ten philosophers. She was so highly esteemed by her countrymen that they inscribed on her tomb an epitaph which declared that she was the splendour of Greece and possessed the beauty of Helen, the virtue of Thirma, the pen of Aristippus, the soul of Socrates and the tongue of Homer.

This passage is very problematic. Though cited as drawing on a work by the Renaissance Italian writer Boccaccio, it does not appear in any publication of his. There are a range of versions of the epitaph that come down to us. The reproductions seem to begin with Antonio de Guevara's *Reloj de príncipes, o libro aureo del emperador Marco Aurelio* (1529), a work that is prone to invention. This was translated into French, Italian, and English, and then Latin by J. Wanckel as *Horlogium Principum, sive de vita M. Aurelii Imperatoris* (1601). Book 2 Ch. 28 (early editions, 2.33 in Wanckel) is an essay on female learning: Non minus feminas quam viros sapientes (et eruditas) esse posse. Guevara, citing Boc(c)ac(c)io *De laudibus mulierum*, Book 2, credits Arete with 35 years' teaching in Athens, 110 philosopher pupils, and 40 books. He gives a long list of titles, including an Encomium of Socrates and a work on the prudence of ants, and quotes a version of the epitaph in

One of our principle sources for the Elder Aristippus is Diogenes Laertius' *Lives* (D.L.), which, in the biodoxographical style typical of the work, paints him as a sophist, arch-hedonist, and target of criticism and ridicule by many contemporaries (including Socrates and Xenophon).[3] He is said to have lived extravagantly yet at ease and to have been ever ready with a witty rejoinder in response to some snide remark from an intellectual rival.[4] Yet Diogenes' portrait softens when he describes Aristippus' relationship with his daughter:

> He gave his daughter Arete (τῇ θυγατρὶ Ἀρήτῃ) the very best advice, training her up (συνασκῶν) to despise excess. He was asked by some one in what way his son would be the better for being educated (παιδευθείς). He replied, 'If nothing more than this, at all events, when in the theatre he will not sit down like a stone upon a stone.' When some one brought his son as a pupil, he asked for a fee of 500 drachmae. The father objected, 'For that sum I can buy a slave.' 'Then do so,' was the reply, 'and you will have two.'[5]

Only the first line refers specifically to Arete, but the two anecdotes about Aristippus' attitude towards the education of children are clearly intended to shed further light on his role as father and teacher. They suggest that, for him, the value of one's children is closely tied to how well educated they are. We know that Arete, by contrast with the uneducated sons of others, was trained extensively by her father. There is an implicit contrast, then, between the well-trained daughter of Aristippus and the stone- and slave-like sons of others. Indeed, the suggestion is that her training is more than intellectual. Though subtle, the use of the verb *sunaskeō* (to join in practising), perhaps subtly contrasted with the *paideia* associated with males, suggests that Aristippus' means of educating his daughter also

---

prose. Later editions and translations set out to improve the style of the epitaph in various ways. Some turn it into verse (e.g., Thomas North) or elegiacs (Wanckel). Adding to this complexity is a further issue over the authority given for the information about Arete. Guevara cites Boccaccio but has previously mentioned a historian called Hiarchus, in connection not with Arete but with Plato's pupils 'Lasterma' and Axiothea. Tomaso Tomasi, in his *Idea del giardino del mondo* (1582), credits the information about Arete to 'un'historico greco per nome Hiarco', which is picked up by Petrus Colomesius in his *Observationes sacrae* of 1679, who is in turn reported by J. C. Wolf, in *Mulierum graecarum quae oratione prosa usae sunt fragmenta et elogia* (1739). This may all stem from D.L. 3.46 where Dicaearchus is credited with information about Axiothea, who is mentioned in the same bracket as Lastheneia. For my purposes, I do not require this passage to reflect an ancient source, since I am as much interested in how Arete was received in later history as antiquity. I am indebted to Lara Harwood-Ventura and Michael Trapp for their patient and expert assistance in tracking down earlier sources.

[3] D.L. 2.65–104. See especially 65–67. Hereafter I use the Hicks (1925/72) translation, with some amendments.
[4] D.L. 2.68–78.   [5] D.L. 2.72.

involved practical habituation to achieve the end of despising excess.⁶ The συν- prefix even subtly suggests that this is an activity pursued jointly. The analogy of uneducated sons as stones on stones suggests a kind of *stasis*, in contrast to the activity suggested by the practical aspect of Cyrenaic education and lifestyle. This adds to a picture in which Arete is joining her father in a lifestyle consistent with Cyrenaic beliefs, both living and studying alongside each other in close mentorship.

A bit further on in D.L. we find two anecdotes about Aristippus that imply that he is not generally interested in fathering and educating his offspring, suggesting that Arete was an exception:

> A courtesan having told him that she was with child by him, he replied, 'You are no more sure of this than if, after running through coarse rushes, you were to say you had been pricked by one in particular.' Someone accused him of exposing his son (τὸν υἱὸν) as if it was not his offspring. Whereupon he said 'Phlegm, too, and vermin we know to be of our own begetting, but for all that, because they are useless, we cast them as far from us as possible.'⁷

These anecdotes are taken as evidence that in addition to Arete, Aristippus also had a son, which, if accurate, raises the question of why he would not have been his choice to succeed him intellectually, as was the cultural norm in antiquity.⁸ The arrangement leaves open the possibility that Arete was the more intellectually gifted of the siblings, which licensed Aristippus' evident dismissal of the son. That said, it may have been the case that having trained one child was enough, and further offspring-pupils were not of interest to him. Further, the passage suggests that whether a child is legitimate or not may also be of importance; perhaps a son with a courtesan is considered dispensable. Nonetheless, Aristippus' comparison of his child to phlegm makes it clear that he places no value on hereditary ties alone.

The above section of D.L. also reports Aristippus having dismissed his son on the grounds that he thought him good for nothing (*akhreía*).⁹ Lampe suggests that in Greek popular morality the expectation of bestowing honour is fundamentally asymmetrical, with children being expected

---

⁶ Lampe (2015: 58–59) also speculates about this. On Aristippus the Elder's view of excess, see for instance D.L. 2.65.
⁷ D.L. 2.81.   ⁸ Aristippus' son is also invoked in *SSR* 4a. 135–36. See Lampe (2015: 17).
⁹ D.L. 2.81. As Lampe (2015: 104) notes, the longer version of this same anecdote in Gnom. Vat. 743 n. 25 = Cod. Vat. Gr. 1144 f. 216r makes it clear that it refers to a child who has grown up, rather than an infant.

to honour their parents but no expectation of the inverse.[10] He expands the idea from honour to care in general when he cites Plato's *Crito* for evidence that Aristippus is no more unfeeling about his son than we might think Socrates is towards his three sons.[11] Perhaps, then, we should not read too much into this anecdote. However, we need only think of *Meno* 93c6–e8, and the discussion of fathers who above all want to train their sons in virtue, to see that the picture is more complex.[12] While honour in particular, and care in general, may be expected to flow more from children to parents than vice versa, the desire to see one's offspring educated – in particular one's sons – is universal among the Greeks, according to Socrates. And for Aristotle, at least, the asymmetry of care and affection can go the other way, with parents loving and benefiting their children more than they are benefited by them (*EE* 7.8.1241a35–38).[13] So we should find Aristippus' willingness to cast his uneducated son aside like mere phlegm surprising, especially in contrast to his attitude towards Arete. The force with which he attributes value to the daughter and disvalue to the son is striking. Diogenes accentuates this point by positioning these anecdotes next to each other. This serves to heighten by contrast her use*ful*ness as a result of her education, training, and ability.[14] And importantly, it clarifies that her value is not tied to her heredity alone, since it is not the case that all of Aristippus' offspring share it, nor is it blocked by her gender.[15] Indeed, the sources' emphasis on Arete's success as evidence of Aristippus' own success as father-teacher might even suggest that part of *his* value stems from her.

The second time Arete is invoked in D.L. she is not named, but her role as teacher of her son, Aristippus the Younger, is made clear:

> There have been four men called Aristippus, (1) our present subject, (2) the author of a book about Arcadia, (3) the grandchild by a daughter of the first Aristippus, who was known as his mother's pupil (μητροδίδακτος).[16]

---

[10] Lampe (2015: 104). [11] See also *Phaedo* 116b4–5.
[12] See also the cautionary tale of Anytus, cf. Crito in *Euthydemus* 307a2.
[13] On which, see Connell (2019), especially section IV.
[14] Mann (1996: 108, n. 23) speculates about whether Aristippus the Elder's attitude towards courtesans, revealed in the biographical fragments, displays a propensity to see others in merely instrumental terms. There is then a question about the *type* of value he attributes to his daughter.
[15] Though outside the scope here, it would be interesting to reflect on whether there are aspects of Cyrenaic thought that license an indifference to gender uncommon in fourth-century BCE Greece. For instance, Aristippus the Elder displayed an apparent lack of shame about cross-dressing according to D.L. 2.78 and Sextus *PH* I.155.
[16] D.L. 2.83, and again at 86. In the latter passage, the philosophical lineage is made even more explicit. See also Strabo, *Geog.* 17.3.22.

Though unnamed, Arete's significance is made clear: she is the biological and intellectual link between the two named members of the school, the founder and his grandson, and this link bestows hereditary and philosophical legitimacy on the Younger and establishes continuity for the whole school. Indeed, her role is crucial in that it maintains the direct line of succession from Socrates down through to her son and his codification of the doctrines of the school.[17] Her role as philosophical teacher of her son, a highly unusual one for a woman at the time, is also testified in later sources.[18] This passage is followed by a list of books purportedly written by Aristippus the Elder, including one titled 'Letter to his daughter Arete' (Ἐπιστολὴ πρὸς Ἀρήτην τὴν θυγατέρα), which, like all of the Elder's writings, does not survive, though one of the Socratic Epistles discussed below takes up the same name.[19] Arete is named first 'disciple' (*diēkousen*) of her father in D.L.; but in the exegesis of the views of the Cyrenaics that follows, only those of the founder and of Hegesias, Anniceris and Theodorus are described.[20] This suggests a depiction of Arete and Aristippus the Younger as heirs of the Elder's thought, in contrast to the more thorough description of the other three who each modify the focus and arguments of the school and therefore require separate treatments.[21]

The inclusion of a daughter and mother in the line of mainstream Cyrenaics is strikingly unusual. Indeed, it is an arrangement unusual

---

[17] We might wonder if the choice of the name Arete is significant in this connection, too, since Socrates' mother was Phaenarete (*Theaetetus* 149a). Indeed, Socrates himself was taught by women (*Symposium* 201d), which may encourage the depiction of Aristippus the Younger as mother-taught. The name has other connotations, too, some of which we might think are problematic. There is the obvious connection to ἀρετή (virtue), whose more literal meaning ('she who is prayed for') might be in tension with Aristippus the Elder's attitude to prayer (on which see VS 743 n. 32 = SSR 4a.132; Clement *Strom.* 7.7.42.2–3 = SSR 4a.220; and Lampe [2015: 79 n. 63]). Then there are connotations of intellect and familial power with Arete of *Odyssey* 6.310, 7.46, 54, 66, 141, 233, and *Argonautica* 4.982–1170.

[18] See, for instance, Aelian, *De Natura Animalium* 3.40; Clement of Alexander *Stromates* 4.19.122.14; Eusebius of Caesarea, *Praeparatio Evangelica* 14.18.32.764a; Themistius *Orationes* 21. 244; Theodoret, *Therapeutike* xi, and in the *Suda*, s.v. 'Aristippus'. Aelian calls Arete '*adelphē*', usually 'sister' of Aristippus the Elder, but from the other evidence we should take this as 'kinswoman' and understand her as his daughter.

[19] D.L. 2.84. These titles may be spurious. For discussion of the debate concerning the authenticity of works attributed to Aristippus the Elder, see Mannebach (1961: 76–84); Lampe (2015: 17 n. 42, 58 n. 7).

[20] D.L. 2.85, 87-104. See also Strabo, *Geog.* 17.3.22, where Arete is described as having succeeded (*diedéxato*) her father. See Lampe (2015: 18) on ancient doxographies distinguishing two distinct lines of Cyrenaics: the mainstream one including Aristippus the Elder, Arete and her son, and divergent lines known for modifying the doctrine, including those of Hegesias, Anniceris, and Theodorus.

[21] See Warren (2009: 147) who argues that Diogenes omits the details of subjects he perceives not to have significantly added to or altered the doctrines of a school.

enough that the son carried evidence of it as his nickname at the time and thereafter.[22] What should we make of this? We might think the emphasis on this nickname is in part to distinguish the Younger Aristippus from the Elder. But there are any number of ways that could have been achieved, as we see in other examples of Classical name disambiguation. This tag is significant in that it emphasises the hereditary and intellectual chain stretching through three generations and – markedly – including a woman. It raises a question of how this line of hereditary succession, involving a woman as a teacher at its centre, might have been received in antiquity – both in Arete and her son's lifetimes and in later Classical reception.

We have little evidence on this question, but among what we do have is a report in Aelian, which connects Arete's teaching of her son to an ornithological comment by Aristotle:

> Many people sing the praises (ὑμνοῦσιν[23] οἱ πολλοί) of the son of Arete, the sister[24] of Aristippus, as being taught by his mother. Aristotle says that he has with his own eyes seen the young of the Nightingale being instructed by their mother how to sing. (Aelian, *De Natura Animalium* 3.40, trans. Scholfield [1959])

The passage from *Historia Animalium* that this refers to reads as follows:

> Of little birds, some sing a different note from the parent birds, if they have been removed from the nest and have heard other birds singing; and a mother-nightingale (ἡ ἀηδών) has been observed to give lessons in singing to a young bird, thus suggesting that language is not natural in the same way as voice but can be artificially trained. (*HA* 536b15–20, trans. Thompson in Barnes [1984])

Aelian's comment is evidently reporting approval of the arrangement of mother-teacher. The cross-reference to Aristotle may underline a sense of continuity: like the mother nightingale, Arete is teaching her son to speak 'the same language' as her and her father or, making literal the metaphor, to practice philosophy in the mainstream Cyrenaic vein.[25] There is an emphasis on Arete not just as a parent-teacher but as a *mother*-teacher. We might find Aelian's approval, and the fact that *mētrodidaktos* is not applied as a pejorative, quite surprising. Might the positive reception of this

---

[22] The sources use past tense when describing the ascription of this nickname, suggesting it was given to Aristippus the Younger in his lifetime and not attributed posthumously by biographers.

[23] The choice of *humneō* as a verb of praise creates a nice connection with the image of the nightingale singing.

[24] For which understand 'daughter'. See note 18.

[25] For a discussion of Aristotle on mothers educating their young in the animal kingdom, see Connell (2019: 9–12).

specific arrangement, in addition to highlighting its rarity, indicate that there is some advantage to Cyrenaic philosophy being transmitted from mother to son? The *mētrodidaktos* title suggests a reversion of gender roles and the revaluation of the role of mothers in early education. We might speculate that the early childhood caring responsibilities borne by mothers in ancient Greece would give them a unique position of influence on their children. A philosophy that is transmitted as much via a way of life as by doctrine would be especially well conveyed by a mother-teacher, if the maternal bond can be conceived of as a distinct means of very early pre-philosophical edification, which may then translate into an unique pedagogical relationship when the child is older.[26]

While our sources emphasise Arete's gender, and her role as a philosophical conduit between the Elder Aristippus and the Younger, she is also a philosopher in her own right. After all, she is said to have headed the Cyrenaics after her father's death, written her own books, and had her own students.[27] Yet, compared even to other ancient women, descriptions of her resist the attribution of philosophical independence, repeatedly figuring her importance solely in relation to her father and son.[28] Unlike other ancient women in similar positions in a philosophical lineage, she is described as a conduit for her father's teachings, rather than as generating her own, and as someone whose most impressive philosophical contributions are those formally made by her son.[29]

A rather different picture is preserved in an Italian renaissance work, which reports that Arete's tomb bore an epitaph calling her the splendour of Greece, possessing the beauty of Helen, the virtue of Thirma, the pen of Aristippus, the soul of Socrates, and the tongue of Homer.[30] This later depiction is representative of a contradiction we find in the way Arete is

---

[26] We might speculate that the Cyrenaics contribute something rather revisionary to a philosophical tradition of thinking about the importance of very early childhood experiences as they relate to one's philosophical and civic development, as discussed in Plato, *Laws* 765e, 788ff., 793e–94d and 797a–d; *Timaeus* 26b; *Republic* 2, 377b; and Aristotle, *Politics* 7.1336a–b, for instance.

[27] See note 18. For Arete heading the school, see also Strabo, *Geog.* 17.3.22.

[28] This is commonplace when it comes to the portrayal of ancient women philosophers. See Protasi (2020: 12).

[29] Compare for instance Hypatia, Sosipatra (on which see Jana Schultz (Chapter 10) in this volume), Theano or Asclepigenia.

[30] The epitaph read as follows, according to the problematic source cited in n. 2 (Boccaccio in Mozans [1913]):

> Nobilis hic Arete dormit, lux Helladis, ore
> Tyndaris at tibi par, Icarioti, fide.
> Patris Aristippi calamumque animamque dederunt,
> Socratis huic linguam Maeonidaeque Dii.

presented. On the one hand, it leaves her no independence. Setting the comments about her beauty and virtue aside, her writing, soul, and speech are all depicted as being that of another, and a man. In an attempt to honour her, the epitaph again disavows her of her sovereign place in the history of philosophy. On the other hand, the epitaph compares Arete to both female and male icons. The individual comparisons are gendered and problematic. But although the intellectual standard is male, taken together the comparison to all these well-known figures yields more than the individual analogies. Even Socrates does not have the tongue of Homer, after all. The representation suggests she is an all-rounder considered worthy of the esteem. If it accurately reports the inscription dedicated to her at the end of her lifetime, it is evidence in favour of her status and its recognition. Paired with facts about her students and her own education, the portrait is a remarkable one. As we will go on to see, there are some sources that suggest, if subtly, that there is more to Arete's portrayal than as a mere conduit. Before drawing conclusions about Arete's legacy, I now turn to her depiction in another problematic source: a spurious letter alleged to be written to her from her father.

Arete in Epistle 27

Among the Socratic Epistles, which are known to be spurious and to have been written much later than they purport, are five letters alleged to have been written by Aristippus the Elder and a further six of which he is the named recipient or the subject.[31] These letters belong to a set known to have been written before the fifth century CE and after the second century CE.[32] Malherbe places Epistle 27, addressed from Aristippus to Arete, and the only one of the set written in Attic, circa 200 CE.[33] Though spurious, it is relevant to this analysis because it demonstrates how Arete and her relationship to her father and her son are received and understood a few centuries after her death. Despite being temporally removed, it is in some ways the source that treats Arete most directly as a subject, since it depicts Aristippus answering her questions. Still, though, everything is communicated through 'the pen of Aristippus', as it were. This is notable since,

---

[31] See Malherbe (1977/2006). On the authorship of and language in the Epistles, see especially p. 30 n. 9, as well as Gaut (1998: 66–57); Lampe (2016: 207–8).

[32] Malherbe (1977/2006: 28). I use the page and line numbering from this edition to cite the Epistle.

[33] D.L. 2.84 includes, in the list of titles of dialogues authored by Aristippus the Elder, a *Letter to his daughter Arete* (Ἐπιστολὴ πρὸς Ἀρήτην τὴν θυγατέρα), a title by which the Epistle is presumably inspired.

being spurious, there is a deliberate decision to write in Aristippus' voice, yet to indirectly communicate Arete's questions.[34]

The letter purports to be in response to several letters received from Arete in which she complains of ill treatment by officials in Cyrene and of a husband who is shy and unable to handle her affairs. Aristippus then answers Arete about how she should regard the men he freed (*eleutheromenoi*), presumably referring to his followers, and suggests they are to be trusted because of their association with his way of life. This adds to a picture of her taking up his mantle, among his disciples. He describes her as possessing two gardens in Cyrene and a property in Berenice – enough by way of assets to live a luxurious life, he claims. Reporting that he has fallen ill and is unable to return to Cyrene, he implores her as follows:

> If, after I have departed this life, you wish to do my will, go to Athens, after you have given Aristippus the best possible education, and hold in the highest esteem Xanthippe and Myrto who often urged me to bring you to the mysteries. (283.3.28–32, trans. Malherbe)

He compares how Arete might live with Xanthippe and Myrto[35] to how he lived with Socrates, suggesting a philosophical lifestyle but one that is markedly among women.[36] That said, in the next lines Aristippus suggests as an alternative that Socrates' son Lamprocles could come to live with Arete in Cyrene and be raised no differently than her own child. We might wonder, given that her own son is also her student, if this suggests that she would educate the son of Socrates, which could imply a high regard for her as a teacher, and emphasises anew the interconnection between these two families. The next lines are telling:

> But above all I urge you to care for (ἐπιμελεῖσθαι) little Aristippus so that he may be worthy of us and of philosophy. That (ταύτην) is the real inheritance I leave for him . . . . (285.4.11–12, trans. Malherbe)

The intent here is uncertain: Aristippus urges his daughter above all (*pro pantos*) to care for her son so that he may be worthy of philosophy. There is a question of whether he means for her to teach the young boy philosophy

---

[34] It is also notable that Aristippus the Elder's son-in-law is not the target of any instructions. This might be explained by his shyness and political reluctance (282.27.1.5–6) yet might still suggest that Arete captured the attention of the sources who, given free hand, gave her this lead role in the Epistle.
[35] Xanthippe is Socrates' wife. Myrto is recorded as either a second wife, a common-law wife, or as living with Socrates. See D.L. 2.26; Plutarch *Aristides*, 27.3–4.
[36] One of whom is marked by having been excluded from philosophical conversation in *Phaedo* 60b6–9.

or if this first reference is to more basic child-rearing. The letter represents Aristippus' attitude towards his philosophically promising young grandson as in marked contrast to the dismissive attitude he evidently had for his own son. He seems to value philosophical promise regardless of gender, and displays confidence in Arete's ability to raise her son well.

Philosophy, perhaps transmitted via Arete, is then described as an inheritance from the Elder. This is ambiguous between the inheritance being the Elder's philosophy, passed via Arete to her son, or the education and care she can provide, where she herself is a valued asset and part of the bequest. We have grounds to resist the narrow reading, especially when combined with the *mētrodidaktos* tag: the scope of *tauten* could include philosophy and could also include acts of caring, parental bond, etc. This is both consistent with Cyrenaic lived philosophy and perhaps a challenge from this school to more narrow conceptions of philosophy, regarding its scope, and gendered ideas concerning who is best positioned to pass it on or teach it to the next generation. There is, at least, a Platonic tradition of depicting fathers as incapable of or too busy to teach their sons virtue.[37] Arete does what so many fathers could not, and this suggests something of a revisionary idea of what constitutes philosophical education.

The connection between grandfather and grandson is most prominent in the Epistle, which raises the question of what role Arete is represented as contributing and in what sense she is a conduit for her father's teaching. We find clues in the conclusion of the letter – a final injunction from father to daughter:

> But concerning philosophy (φιλοσοφίας) you have not written me that anyone has robbed you of it. So, my good woman, rejoice greatly in the wealth which you have accumulated and make your son, whom I would like to have as my own, its possessor. Since I shall die without enjoying him, I trust you will guide him (ἄξεις) on a course of life that is customary for good men (ανδρασιν). Farewell, and do not be distressed about us. (285.5.13–20, trans. Malherbe)

Again, we see the text pulling in opposite directions. Aristippus acknowledges Arete as someone who possesses philosophy and who can lead her son into the Cyrenaic way of life. Yet the emphasis is on philosophy or philosophical education as a possession – something one could be robbed of – once held by the father, being passed ultimately to his grandson. It is a life course customary for men (*andrasin*). There is a question of whether

---

[37] Cf. the texts in n. 12 and *Protagoras* 325aff.

the possession changes by way of the mother adding to or altering it – is it figured as being transmitted, unaltered, from man to man, or is the reference to the wealth Arete has accumulated (*ploutein plouton*) and her guidance suggestive of her adding something? 'Aristippus' subtly suggests, with the note that he would have liked to have had her son as his own, that a more direct transmission would have been preferable.

The conception of philosophy as an object to be transmitted clashes with philosophy conceived of as a way of life, the latter of which suggests something much less static and more influenced by the specific guide one has.[38] If what is passed on is in part a lifestyle, then it matters who you have as a direct role model, and, one might think, all aspects of their life matter, even including their gender. Further, we should not presume a conception of philosophy in which successful transmission *requires* addition or innovation. If Arete is depicted as a conduit between her father and her son, we should not assume that this counts against her. While later philosophy might privilege innovation and originality, there are ancient precedents for valuing preservation and conservatorship.[39] Indeed, we are not even safe to assume a sharp distinction between philosophical doctrine and performance when considering what is transmitted. Any tension we may perceive between Arete's importance and her role as a transmitter may be more reflective of the values of the author of the Epistle, or contemporary conceptions of philosophy, than it is of her reception in her own time and her role within the Cyrenaic school.

We need not take the letter to reflect historical facts to see its importance in terms of understanding the legacy of Arete. It emphasises earlier sources when it depicts her as a crucial link in the intellectual chain of Cyrenaicism and highlights questions of whether and how she is to be understood as a philosopher in her own right. Her opportunities to philosophise during her lifetime seem to vastly outweigh the credit she is given in most historical reception, and Epistle 27 underlines that delta. We might reflect on whether these sources nonetheless prompt us to consider other options for our contemporary reception of Arete.

---

[38] It is also very much at odds with how education is conventionally conceived of in Plato and Aristotle. A reader of Plato, for instance, would find the idea of a mere transmitter – where this is a kind of passing of the baton – very odd. There are versions of transmission, such as that in the Platonic tradition, which are positive and are not characterised by passivity or loss of agency (e.g., in the *Meno* and the *Gorgias*), sometimes following a parental model.

[39] Jana Schultz (Chapter 10) makes this point regarding late antique schools when she defends Hypatia's importance as a preserver of the legacy of Plato.

One way to escape a more limited view of Arete, short of finding some source that addresses her thought directly, is to speculate about what the role of a person who stands between the Younger and Elder Aristippus might be. The Elder is described by some as embodying a lived philosophy.[40] On one view, he is akin to a kind of performance artist.[41] Two generations down, the Younger is said to have been the one to formalise the school's doctrine for the first time, and there is not the same association with public acts demonstrating Cyrenaic principles in action.[42] What then is the role of the person who stands between performance artist and codifier? We might think that this person would have the important role of both transmitting *and translating* the values of the school. A passage from Eusebius[43] suggests that Arete taught her son to philosophise more theoretically (the term used is *lógous philosophías*), introducing him not only to the Cyrenaic art of living but also how to think systematically about it. Even if we cannot attribute codification to her, we may attribute to her the ability to teach her son how to codify, and that codification or formalisation is important. Paired with a holistic conception of Cyrenaic philosophical education, we have a means of substantiating Arete's philosophical contribution.

The evidence we have of the Elder Aristippus suggests that he resisted formalising the doctrines of the school in favour of imprecision.[44] The representations we have of Arete, on the other hand, suggest no such resistance and paint her as a dedicated intellectual, writer, and educator, quite opposed to her father the outspoken, rebellious wit. Her gender may contribute to this shift: we might think that women cannot do what

---

[40] See, for instance, Mann (1996: especially 1, 115–17, 119).

[41] Mann (1996: 119). Cf. Lampe (2016: 202–3).

[42] For evidence that Aristippus the Younger formalised Cyrenaic ethics see Eusebius *PE* 14.18.32.3 = SSR 4b.5, where Aristippus' loose way of speaking is contrasted with the grandson's formal theorising. This passage is also relevant to the question of what and how Arete taught her son:

> Among his other hearers was his own daughter Arete, who having borne a son named him Aristippus, and he from having been introduced by her to philosophical studies (λόγους φιλοσοφίας) was called his mother's pupil . . . . (Trans. Gifford [1903])

Eusebius' other uses of the phrase *lógous philosophías* (for instance, in *PE*, at 3.14.4.2, 3.14.9.1, 4.6.3.1, 4.8.4.2, 4.8.5.5, 4.9.7.9, 4.9.8.5, 4.22.15.7, 5.5.5.4, 5.5.7.2, 5.7.4.2, 6.Pref.3.6, 9.10.1.1, 11.1.1.1, 14.10.4.1, though cf. DE 3.6.39.8 and C.Hier 408.26) suggest that the term is being used to denote formal theories, where students can accept these *logoi*. In Plato *Symposium* 173c3, *lógous philosophías* are evidently verbal philosophical discourses. Eusebius seems to assume that Arete teaches something more formal.

[43] *PE* 14.18.32 = SSR 4b.5.

[44] *PE* 14.18.32 = SSR 4b.5. The caveat to this is the possibility that Aristippus wrote philosophical texts, which we could take as a kind of formalisation of his doctrine. See Lampe (2015: 17–18) for a summary of the evidence concerning whether we can attribute any texts to Aristippus the Elder.

Aristippus the Elder is said to have done in publicly performing his commitments.[45] With no access to brothels, public feasts, and other spaces her father is depicted as 'performing' in, the possibilities for women to be a Cyrenaic are limited and might come down to the transmission of doctrine.[46] This might help explain the shift between the Elder and Younger Aristippus in how Cyrenaic commitments are expressed. Somewhere between his early education and mature thought, the Younger Aristippus developed the ability and inclination to formalise the school's doctrines. We might think that alongside teaching her son forms of argument, logical principles, methods of expression, etc., Arete's influence extended to this inclination, too. If we can attribute to Arete an important role in codifying a way of life as a set of teachings and shifting the school towards new types of formal expression, her role looks even more obviously important and distinctive.

Of course, this is speculative, and in the next section I consider this and other methodological issues that this analysis raises.

Reaching Arete

This exploration has been disappointing in at least two ways. It has been more biographical than philosophical, focusing on texts that reveal details of Arete's life rather than her thought, her relations to her family members and fellow philosophers rather than how she conceives of these.[47] It has also been more indirect than direct: making use of reports and anecdotes that primarily concern Arete's father or son, rather than her. While I have attempted to focus as much as possible on Arete's *philosophical* life, this pursuit is frustrated by the lack of evidence. With none of her writings preserved, or even any writings that discuss her ideas directly, the case of Arete is particularly dire. Her philosophical credentials are well established by the evidence, yet the details of her work and thought appear quite deliberately left out of discussions that treat her father and her son, where a discussion of her work would fit quite naturally between them but is excluded.

In the face of this situation, the question is what to do, short of putting our hands up and abandoning the task. While acknowledging the frustration of the task, my answer here has been to use what sources we have,

---

[45] Hipparchia the Cynic being the exception that proves the rule, as it were.
[46] My thanks to Peter Adamson for this point.
[47] And even then, we should note how little biographical detail is preserved.

however unsatisfactory, to ask questions about Arete's role within the early Cyrenaics and how that role has been received by philosophers and biographers since. After all, though they minimise women like Arete, our sources do not leave them out altogether. The presence of even the limited coverage we have implies that they were there and had to be acknowledged, so we should acknowledge them as well. This requires adopting several methodological strategies, each related to interpretive generosity, which are worth calling attention to.

The first is the use of indirect sources. None of the sources for Arete are directly concerned with her, so our only evidence of her is indirect – often in biographies of her father. Indirect accounts are sometimes uncorroborated. This raises a cluster of questions: is her depiction more or less likely to be distorted if she is not the subject of a work? To what extent should we treat ancient biography as evidence of philosophical commitments? The first way in which I adopt a strategy of general interpretive generosity is to accept indirect evidence, even if cautiously, as evidence for the life and thought of Arete. This greater detachment is problematic, but no more problematic, we might think, than our access to certain Presocratic figures about whom we have only brief comments in texts that are not principally concerned with their thought or their lives.

One might raise an objection to my claim that Arete's thought has been deliberately excluded from these sources or that sexism has a role to play in the suppression of Arete's independent philosophical record. Perhaps the reason ancient biographies record her as a conduit is that *they* had no access to her philosophical ideas.[48] This would mean that her neglect is not due to her gender but rather because her writings had been lost by that time – a fate she would share with other Cyrenaic philosophers and other male philosophers more generally.[49] I propose two responses to this objection. The first is to admit that there may be suppression that took place earlier than some of the biographical sources, which might push the sexism claim back in time. This does not avoid the worry but rather shows that it may have been more long-standing. The second is to suggest that the way in which these sources treat Arete is still problematic, even if we assume that they have limited source material to work with. Her son's nickname, her epitaph, and other accounts we have considered demonstrate Arete's

---

[48] It is important to acknowledge that Diogenes is not generally reluctant to discuss women philosophers, since he dedicates a chapter to the life of Hipparchia. That he mentions others (e.g., Theano and Arete) only by name, despite acknowledging their philosophical abilities, suggests he had less evidence for them.

[49] My thanks to a reviewer for raising this objection.

importance at the time of her death, and the esteem granted to her in certain quarters, so it would not be fair to think that there was nothing worthwhile preserving. Rather, she is philosophically more important, as head of a school and a prolific author, than many ancient men who are not treated as conduits and whose gender is not emphasised. That said, I have suggested that some of the failure to highlight Arete's importance comes from later and contemporary biases towards philosophical innovation and novelty and that sources that emphasise her familial role may not share these. Nonetheless, the diminishment of her reputation that we find in indirect and biographical sources suggests a resistance to preserving or highlighting her independent intellectual life or lifestyle in favour of an emphasis on her role in legitimising her son (regarding whom these sources are also indirect).

As part of this strategy, I also treat biography as evidence for philosophy, by which I mean using ancient biography as indicative of the philosophical commitments of those they treat. This requires an interpretive generosity in general, and perhaps especially for sources like Diogenes Laertius, whose collections of anecdotes are vulnerable to objection on the grounds that they seem designed to entertain rather than inform and include stories whose historicity is questionable.[50] There is no *bios* of Arete, despite the notable inclusion of the life of Hipparchia, the female Cynic, and the anecdotes that mention Arete do so in order to promote a particular characterisation (perhaps even a caricature) of her father. Here I rely on scholars such as Momigliano (1971, 1993) and Mann (1996) who argue for the relevance of ancient biography to our understanding of the philosophy of their subjects. Mann suggests, of Diogenes' treatment of Aristippus in particular, that it is meant to depict not just a life, but a 'philosophical life', and that 'the life and the philosophy cannot really be separated'.[51] He argues that Diogenes' choice of anecdotes is part of an attempt to describe a philosophically informed lifestyle, rather than to engage in gossip.[52] This is particularly appropriate for early Cyrenaics, and Aristippus the Elder, as I have described him, whose way of life seems itself

---

[50] Despite his title (which promises the *bioi* and *gnômai* – lives and thoughts – of eminent philosophers), when referring to figures he perceives not to have added significantly to an existing school, Diogenes moves from the form of philosophical biography to *diadochê*: a form of successional list borrowed from Hellenistic scholarship (Warren 2009: 147). The list names philosophers chronologically, omitting further detail, and emphasises master–pupil relations. Diogenes prefers this form, Warren (2009: 136–39, 142 n. 38) suggests, when emphasising philosophical lineage over an individuals' ideas and theories. Diogenes' failure to engage with Arete, then, could reflect a view of her as failing to significantly modify Cyrenaic philosophy.
[51] Mann (1996: 99). [52] Mann (1996: 105).

to be informed by, and informative of, his philosophy. Where I make use of the close connection between this way of life and his means of raising and mentoring Arete, I rely on arguments like this to support Diogenes as a source that is of historic and philosophical importance for us.

The second, related methodological strategy I take here is to use one of the Socratic Epistles as a source, though again, as with Diogenes, not without reservation and caveats. I said above that Epistle 27 is relevant to this analysis, despite its spurious status, because it tells us something about the later antique reception of Arete and her role as daughter, mother, and teacher. Since my analysis concerns Arete's philosophical legacy, as well as her thought, the Epistle is a pertinent source. But it does not seem to be based on any direct knowledge of or even interest in the thought of Arete, and even where she is addressed, the letters Aristippus is purported to be responding to, written by her, are not quoted or described directly. She is very much in the background but only ever in the background. Where such a source might normally be disregarded, there is a special case to be made for its inclusion where our sources are so limited. And where our sources are so limited, there is a special case for making what we can of them nonetheless when they concern women philosophers. My second strategy, therefore, is a more general open-mindedness to source material when it comes to the recovery of ancient women philosophers, since we do not have the luxury of being picky, and we have good reason for doing all we can to recover them.[53] When it comes to ancient women, at least, using sources cautiously is preferable to discounting them.

The third methodological strategy I adopt is to accept the writings and thought of men as evidence for Arete. This is of course problematic. It leaves the work open to an objection such as that it really concerns men and possesses a mere veneer of being about a woman. Again, this is not a problem for Arete alone, but it is a problem, nonetheless. I acknowledge and share the concern about work that seeks to access the thought of women via the medium of men's writing. Nonetheless, when we face a choice between accessing the thought of a woman by this lesser means, or giving up on accessing her thought at all, my strategy is to use whatever means I can and accept that the result will never be fully satisfactory.

In the case of Arete, I have used the focus on her role within a philosophical lineage as a means of keeping attention on her while making

---

[53] Though I will not defend this here, this might include righting historic wrongs, correcting archetypes of philosophers to include women, and accurately reflecting the status of ancient women thinkers in their own lifetime.

use of material she is on the periphery of. I have also tried to say something about how her own philosophical thought and pedagogic expertise fits into that lineage. This is inevitably speculative. But I want to resist the sense that this is speculative in a problematic way and suggest instead that it involves the application of the principle of charity we frequently deploy for early figures where we lack direct sources, such as Thales, and without which our history of philosophy would be much less rich and interesting.

Waithe says 'we may speculate which parts of the Cyrenaic moral philosophy to attribute to the grandfather, which to Arete, his pupil, and which to the son who was, in turn, her pupil' (1987b: 198). But even this, we may think, is optimistic. It is very difficult to pull their contributions apart. By establishing Arete's unique role and positioning in the ancient accounts of early Cyrenaics, I have attempted to be more precise about what her role in the development of the school's doctrine could have been. And though disambiguating between the contributions of father, daughter, and grandson is still thorny, this analysis should prompt us to reflect on our reception of the school today. Here I have two minimal conclusions to draw. First, I suggest that whenever we are unable to pull the strands apart, we should at least acknowledge all three members of the hereditary dynasty, as we do in other traditions (Pyrrhonian, Stoic, Platonist, etc.). Second, when we discuss Arete, we ought to promote the idea that the most important and interesting thing about her is not her status as daughter of the Elder and mother of the Younger, or even that she is a woman, but that she is a Cyrenaic philosopher. Even with such limited material to work with, the specific focus on Arete is already in itself an improvement on the historical material. While we are limited by our sources, we can in this way do better than some of them by insisting on her inclusion, and the inclusion of and emphasis on her philosophical thought, in our account of the Cyrenaics. With this purview, we go some way towards reflecting her importance to the history of philosophy.[54]

---

[54] My thanks to audiences at the American Philosophical Association, the Institute of Classical Studies in London, the Collaborative Specialization in Ancient & Medieval Philosophy (CSAMP) Proseminar at the University of Toronto, the British Society for the History of Philosophy, the contributors to this volume, reviewers for the press, James Allen, Joachim Aufderheide, Rachel Barney, George Boys-Stones, Sophia Connell, Marguerite Deslauriers, Dorota Dutsch, Mehmet Erginel, Jessica Gelber, Lara Harwood-Ventura, Boris Hennig, Marta Jimenez, Jonathan Lavery, Mariska Leunissen, Fiona Leigh, M. M. McCabe, Peter Osario, John Partridge, Anne Sheppard, John Sellars, Shaul Tor, Michael Trapp, Máté Veres, Jennifer Whiting, Raphael Woolf, my co-editor Caterina Pellò, and the Footnotes Writing Circle for very valuable discussions of earlier drafts of this chapter.

CHAPTER 6

Women at the Crossroads
Life and Death for the Stoic Wife

Kate Meng Brassel[*]

The Stoics admitted women into the category of morally reasoning creature, attributed to women the same capacity for virtue as men, promoted companionate marriage, and even – at their edgiest – recommended women's equal education, observing that the division of labour between the sexes had more to do with convention than with nature. Stoicism's historically extraordinary views have motivated modern scholarly attempts to accommodate some aspects of the philosophy to a sort of proto-feminism. And a Stoic marriage remains from several angles an attractive partnership in a Greek and Roman landscape presenting few happier alternatives.[1]

Nevertheless, the Stoic woman as an object of enquiry remains difficult to recover substantively. The subject 'women *in* Stoicism' – which is to say women *from the perspective of* male Stoic writers – and 'Stoicism and feminism' are problems that have occupied a number of important scholars, including Elizabeth Asmis, Martha Nussbaum, Gretchen Reydams-Schils, and others, often via enquiries into marriage as a subset of Stoic community or family.[2] Much of this work has entailed the reconstruction of arguments from fragmentary evidence, in particular for the early Stoics. But even in the period of Stoicism for which we have a surfeit of written sources, the early Roman Empire, the Stoic woman's voice remains missing. While women appear in the copious writings of the philosopher and political advisor Seneca in a variety of literary positions, and while the reported 'sayings' of his contemporary the philosopher

---

[*] This chapter is dedicated to the memory of Ashley Ariel Simone, a philosopher. Thanks are owed to the editors, to Wolfgang Mann, Elizabeth Scharffenberger, and John Sellars for their comments, to James Ker for morale, and to the participants in the Women Intellectuals in Antiquity conference at Keble College, Oxford in 2020 for their insights.
[1] For a full treatment of a Stoic marriage, see Reydams-Schils (2005: 143–76).
[2] E.g., Motto (1972); Asmis (1996); Hill (2001); Nussbaum (2002); Reydams-Schils (2005); Gloyn (2017).

Musonius Rufus offer some surprisingly progressive ideas *about* women, it remains the case that we have no texts written by women Stoics. In consequence, as Asmis warns us, 'we cannot look directly at their self-image'.[3] This state of affairs is not surprising to any but the least jaded readers, given the histories of the pen and misogyny, and given the centrality of virtue – that is, manliness (*virtus*) – to Stoic ethics, in which the endurance required for a good life is exemplified by virile figures such as Hercules. But precisely because the Stoics apparently recognised that women have the same capacity for virtue as men, one might reasonably wonder where all the Stoic women are.[4] It is the very fact that Stoics argued in *theory* for a sort of women's equality – strikingly even for their participation in philosophy – that ought to make the absence of a Stoic women's record or some robust testimony to their philosophical activity at least somewhat surprising. Did the Stoics simply not practise what they preached? Why does the figure of the Stoic woman remain such a problem for a philosophy that is supposedly universal in its appeal to persons of all classes, in all situations, even and indeed especially, at the point of death?

In the absence of direct evidence, we must examine a confluence of indirect evidence to see what, if anything, may be gleaned about Stoic women. Several bodies of evidence provide routes into the problem: Stoic writings on marriage and family as constitutive of an ideal society; women addressees of Stoic writings; women 'exemplars' of behaviour to be imitated or avoided; and wives of Stoic men in the historiographical record who – though not often referred to as 'philosophers' themselves – might by the reports of their actions be said to have lived or died deliberately according to Stoic principles. This chapter will gesture to some of the most useful work on the above areas and then put forward a reading of a text from a rather different genre: tragedy. Can the space of drama allow us to imagine what we might find if we were to have more direct evidence of a woman at the crossroads of the most crucial questions – when to live and when to die? Can Megara, a woman who chooses death over a life she views as inconsistent with her values, help us to recover a Stoic

---

[3] Asmis (1996: 75).
[4] Manning (1973) argues that subordinating women cohered with Stoic principles, Hill (2001: 40) responds that the Stoics failed to realise their own potential, though their philosophy is 'at heart feminist'. Nussbaum (2002: 310–11) takes a different approach: feminist elements of Stoicism were meaningful but limited: for example, Musonius' lesson that women and men must be held to the same standard for sexual behaviour perpetuates the submission of women's behaviour to male scrutiny. Reydams-Schils (2005: 149) emphasises instead the progressiveness of such a precept in the historical context of a mostly male Roman audience.

womanhood that asks and answers the same questions as Stoic manliness? This chapter also probes the limits of understanding Megara as a Stoic exemplar. While she may elect to die in the manner of a virtuous Stoic philosopher, Megara *in fact* dies not as she chooses but at the hand of her husband, a casualty of domestic violence. Is Megara's volition permissible in Stoic drama precisely because myth and genre actually dictate her fate and shroud her quiet exemplarity in the spectacular disaster of her husband?

The Stoic Woman in Theory

Theorising the role of women in society was part of Stoicism since its very beginnings, though the extant evidence for the early period exists only in fragments and biographical accounts written centuries later. The founder of Stoicism, Zeno of Citium (fourth-third century BCE), discussed marriage in the context of his *Republic*, which outlined an ideal, radically reordered society. Zeno's revisions to conventional life included that – among the good and wise – men and women would dress alike and 'keep no part of the body entirely hidden'; women would be 'in common' to (wise) men, as partners both for sex and ethics, freeing the wise from sexual jealousy and enabling men to love all children as their own.[5] Zeno's formative closeness to his teacher, the Cynic Crates, and presumably thus the influence of *his* partner, the philosopher Hipparchia, may account for what may otherwise be thought of, as Asmis puts it, 'a Cynicizing aberration of the early Stoics'.[6] His successor as head of the Stoa, Cleanthes, evidently discussed the idea that women and men have the same virtue (*aretē*) – but we have only a title, no text.[7] The evidence for the next leading Stoic, Chrysippus, positions him closely alongside Zeno as regards women.[8] As utopian a place for women as the early Stoics may have theorised, it bears repeating that these are not women Stoics theorising their own role in society.

The early Stoics' views on women and marriage were probably originally closer to those of the anti-establishment Cynics but became increasingly entwined with social convention as the school gained traction and an

---

[5] D.L. 7.33 and 131. Asmis (1996: 90) argues that the language of being 'in common' with men means a virtue partnership in addition to the more readily available idea of sex partnership.
[6] Amis (1996: 68). I thank John Sellars for drawing my attention to this probable link.
[7] D.L. 7.175.   [8] D.L. 7.131.

appreciation for institutions.⁹ Nevertheless, by the first and second centuries CE, a Stoic marriage could still be thought of as remarkable because of the special dynamics between spouses, even if from the outside it might resemble other marriages. For this later period, there are three bodies of evidence principally used to understand Stoic views on women and marriage: the testimonia to Antipater (second century BCE); the collected sayings of Musonius Rufus (30–100? CE); and the extant excerpts of Hierocles (second century CE).¹⁰

A synoptic view of these three sources reveals an expansive theory along these lines: women are essential to the Stoic community of humankind, which begins with the relationship to the self, develops outwards to the spouse, to the children and enslaved members of the household, then to friends, citizens, and finally to all humankind. Marriage is, after the self, the first, elemental community (*koinōnia*), entered into for pursuing procreation and virtue, and cultivates like-mindedness (*homonoia*), a kindness (*eunoia*) not available elsewhere, and the mutual sharing of souls and bodies. In a Stoic household, life is a shared business: spouses are subject to the same standards for sexual fidelity and should practice exchanging typically gendered tasks. In this heteronormative and slave-owning model of partnership, women's relationships outside of those with her husband and children are not theorised, which means that female homosocial (to say nothing of the homoerotic) relationships that one might imagine to be philosophically helpful are excluded. But given the emphasis elsewhere on male homosocial relationships and the cultural misogyny (*misogunia*) that encouraged men to neglect their wives as ethical and intellectual partners, the Stoic idea that women not only *could* but *must* practise philosophy is extraordinary, as is the exhortation that men live philosophically *with* women as full partners (*sumbiōsis*). To this end, Musonius could even demand that a daughter be educated like a son, to learn not only household management but also philosophy and fighting in order to defend her children from attackers and herself from the sexual advances of a man who is not her husband, including (and even especially) a tyrant.¹¹ Again, with

---

⁹ Nussbaum (2002: 300–308) documents change over time via her useful assessment of Musonius' putative feminism against the backdrop of earlier Stoics.
¹⁰ Relevant passages attributed to Antipater of Tarsos were transmitted through the fifth-century Stobaeus' *Florilegium*, a teaching reference (= *SVF* 3.62 and 63). For a modern translation: Deming (2004: 221–29). Musonius is translated in Lutz (1947), but readers may wish to consult the translations of Nussbaum (2002). Relevant passages of Hierocles also come to us through Stobaeus, available with translation and commentary in Ramelli (2009).
¹¹ For this idealised picture, I omit internal discrepancies. For detailed evaluations of these and other sources, see Asmis (1996: 76–87) and Reydams-Schils (2005: 147–59).

sources so partial, we must exercise caution and remind ourselves that the Stoic woman's self-conception is not verifiably part of this theory.[12]

This rather rosy picture is often at odds with the presentation of women and womanliness by Seneca (1?–65 CE) and Epictetus (50?–135? CE), whose massive corpora often provide test sites for investigations of Roman Stoicism. These voluminous literatures display an extreme preference for masculinity, seeing femininity and 'effeminacy' as a threat. Moral courage is coded everywhere as manly. Before becoming generalised to mean 'bravery' and 'moral excellence', the Latin *virtus* first meant – and never stopped denoting – 'manliness'. In the Senecan corpus, 'womanly' (*muliebris* and other words) and 'manly' (*virilis*) are coded as negative and positive, respectively: moral failure, weakness, excessive grief, and rage are womanly while wisdom, endurance, and emotional control are manly.[13] While Seneca unequivocally states that women are equally endowed with the opportunity for virtue (*virtus*, *Marc.* 16.1), the 'manliness' (*virtus*) paradoxically available to women, Amanda Wilcox argues, does not actually undermine social norms. Rather, a woman is at her most 'virile' or virtuous when she acts according to Roman notions of women's duties.[14] Moreover, there is a way in which a woman's *virtus* depends on her rejection of qualities that are *muliebris*: acquiring virtue for the Stoic woman is therefore a process of sexual alienation.

Seneca's prose is often served up with a good sprinkling of misogyny: Women nowadays are sexually shameless (*Ben.* 3.16), decadent, luxurious; women's desire is unnatural, damnable (*Ep.* 95.20–21). Even Seneca's *On Marriage* (possible passages of which are only known to us through Jerome's fourth-century CE anti-marriage polemic *Against Jovinian*) is decidedly ambivalent: Liz Gloyn has shown that in addition to defining a good marriage as a joint pursuit of virtue, wholly appropriate to a Stoic *proficiens* (the philosopher in-progress), Seneca puts forward *pudicitia*

---

[12] The sayings of Musonius, leading Stoic of the first century, give us the most provocative insights on women in Stoicism and have attracted sustained discussion of Stoic feminism (Hill 2001; Nussbaum 2002) and marriage (Reydams-Schils 2005). The sayings were assembled from recollections, probably posthumously, and transmitted through Stobaeus and through Arrian's records of the diatribes of Epictetus. On the transmission, see Van Geytenbeek (1962: 7–12). Musonius proposed that women and men share the same moral capacities and need for philosophical training to withstand crisis. For Van Geytenbeek (1962: 51–52), the virtues are essentially the same but the spheres differ. For example, a woman's sense of justice is exhibited in her behaviour as wife and mother. Musonius manages both to maintain social norms and to reject the idea that male spheres and abilities are superior.
[13] For a detailed survey of Seneca's use of *muliebris* and related terms, see Mauch (1996: 26–44).
[14] Wilcox (2006).

(modesty or sexual restraint) as a form of *virtus* particular to women. In his depiction of bedtime reflection, as Gloyn points out, his wife is less a full partner than mercifully quiet confidante (*Ira* 3.36).[15] Similarly, as we shall see, Epictetus typically excludes women when delineating standards for behaviour and thought, a striking exclusion given that he presents his philosophy as applicable to a wide range of class-statuses.[16]

How do we account for this discrepancy between theory and rhetoric? Is our picture of a Stoicism that understands women as equal moral agents an illusion created by partial sources that dissipates when probed through the lens of ampler literatures?

The Stoic Woman in Story

Stoic discourse of the early Empire relied on anecdotes of exemplary behaviour to demonstrate principles in action: Socrates' courageous indifference in the face of death, for example, and Hercules' endurance through hardships. Women exemplars in the literature are more scarce. Musonius, for instance, refers to male figures from history and myth but does not supply us with female exemplars for courage (*andreia*) beyond the Amazons (those one-breasted, man-spurning warriors of myth), even when urging the equal education of sons and daughters so that all may be taught not to fear death.[17] The appeal to figures who live legendarily at the Eastern edges of the Greek-speaking world might strike one as lazy in

---

[15] See Torre (2000) for a comparison of the evidence from Jerome versus extant Senecan work. Gloyn (2017: 207–23) provides a useful history of attribution, text, and translation. From fragments likely to be genuine on a philological assessment, it is clear that Seneca thought *pudicitia* in women both extremely rare and also the appropriate route for women to pursue virtue. Gloyn (2017: 89–101).

[16] Epictetus' diatribes seek their overt audience in his students – young male elites of the Roman Empire – and thus address male character formation. As part of his general pattern of exclusion, Epictetus envisions marriage for the Cynic (as sort of stand-in for the committed, radical philosopher) as possible only in a community of the wise, where his wife (and in-laws) might be guaranteed to be similarly wise. Until such a utopia should emerge, however, the philosopher had better abstain from the time commitment of marriage and fatherhood (*Diss.* 3.22.67–70) – a sentiment perhaps suggestive of Epictetus' estimation of the likelihood of such a utopia comprising the wise of both sexes as envisioned by the early Stoics. It is important to note, however, that the content of Epictetus' diatribes is entirely mediated through his student Arrian, who published them. Epictetus himself may well have addressed a wider variety of philosophical problems than those presented in the diatribes as we have them, including the status of women in a pre-utopian society, to which his teacher Musonius applied himself. Indeed, it is peculiar that this striking aspect of Musonius' philosophy does not seem to surface in the much more copious literature of his pupil. I thank both Elizabeth Scharffenberger and John Sellars for pushing me to think more carefully on this point.

[17] Musonius 4.30. In 14, Alcestis is an example of love, not courage. Nussbaum (2002: 289) adds that Musonius also had the recent example of Boudicca.

light of a Roman history so grounded in women's interventions in crisis, such as the stories of Cloelia or Lucretia – not to mention the elder Arria, who lingered in recent memory as demonstrating fearlessness to her husband by preceding him in death, taking the blade and declaring, 'It does not hurt' (Plin. *Ep.* 3.16). As we will see, a rationally chosen death, or *voluntaria mors*, is an important problem for Stoicism, making Musonius' oversight even more conspicuous.

While Musonius' teachings survive in a comparatively small collection, the diatribes of his student Epictetus are copious. Epictetus' *exempla* range from myth to philosophy to contemporary politics – Odysseus, Hercules, Socrates, Diogenes, and everyday Romans populate the diatribes. Epictetus generally excludes female exemplarity: women are typically mentioned as proof of a man's moral failing (though he insists that a man's proper concern for his household is an important duty).[18] Examples of *voluntaria mors* abound in the diatribes, linked to manhood: an athlete requires medical castration; his philosophical brother warns that after such a procedure he could not then return to the gymnasium; the athlete refuses the treatment and dies in order to act in accordance with his character or ethical role (*prosōpon*) (*Diss.* 1.2.25–28). A philosopher is ordered to shave off his beard at pain of death; he refuses; to do so would be to abandon his *prosōpon* (1.2.29–30). These choices for death are motivated by the spectre of losing a highly gendered marker of the body – genitals and beard. There are vanishingly few, if any, women after whom one might model one's behaviour in the diatribes. To the contrary, Epictetus points out instead the incapacity (*adunamia*) of the generally admired Andromache in her famously complex conversation with her husband (3.22.108–9). Meanwhile, from the same court from which Epictetus, himself a freedman, drew many of his *exempla*, he omitted to draw Epicharis, the freedwoman who refused to bend to Nero's torturers and, even when her limbs were shattered, found a way to die rather than betray confidences to his agents.[19]

Seneca's engagement of women in his philosophical prose is more complex.[20] Two works, both consolatory dialogues, are dedicated to women addressees. *Consolatio ad Marciam* seeks to advise a mother grieving her son, while *Consolatio ad Helviam* seeks to advise his own mother

---

[18] Cf. *Diss.* 3.7.20–26.
[19] Her story is reported in both Tacitus, *Ann.* 15.51–57 and Cassius Dio 62.27.
[20] And the subject as a whole is well beyond the reach of the present chapter. For a systematic review of both negative and positive portrayals of women's moral competence in Seneca's prose, see Mauch (1997).

during his political banishment. Marcia and Helvia are clearly expected to be perfectly capable of philosophical learning and progress; but they are also clearly thought to be among the exceptional of their sex.²¹ These consolations deploy Stoic therapy through metaphor, precepts, and *exempla*, providing a greater density of female exemplars for admirable behaviour than elsewhere.²² Women are at their best in *Ad Marciam* when they grieve in such a way that does not distress other family members, especially male relations, or when they abandon their grief in favour of instead promoting the posthumous fame of a male relation they have lost.²³

At certain points in his consolation to Marcia, Seneca stops using both female exemplars and feminine vocatives, in favour of the male and masculine, to which his female 'interlocutor' objects. Seneca responds to 'her': 'In which city are we talking like this, good gods? The one in which Lucretia and Brutus overthrew a king who was oppressing the citizens of Rome: we are indebted to Brutus for liberty, to Lucretia for Brutus.'²⁴ Seneca's allusion Lucretia is abrupt – and omits her suicide, positioning her instead as a catalyst for Brutus' political achievement.²⁵ Seneca gestures to some generalised *virtus* that women may display but not to Lucretia's specific *voluntaria mors*. Seneca's oversight is the more conspicuous given Lucretia's awareness of her own exemplarity in Livy's canonical account: she declares that no woman would live unchaste relying on her example (*AUC* 1.58). Certainly, Lucretia's suicide cannot be considered off-topic, since the consolation begins with a reference to the suicide of Marcia's own father, facing trumped up charges from associates of the notorious Sejanus (*Marc.* 1.2).

The Significance of *voluntaria mors*

The eliding of Lucretia is all the more remarkable given the centrality of *voluntaria mors* as an index of Stoic virtue. Although Miriam Griffin has shown that the parameters within which the Stoics allowed for choosing death over life were strict,²⁶ the rhetorical prominence of a chosen death in the extant literature is a clear, even if rare, demonstration of virtue. The reverence of its exemplars indicate that if we were to find a fulsome example of a woman philosophically choosing death, we would at the

---

²¹ E.g., *Helv.* 16.1–5.   ²² See Shelton (1995) for Seneca's strategies of consolation.
²³ E.g., *Marc.* 4.1–2; 3.1.   ²⁴ *Marc.* 16.1: translation Hine (2014: 21).
²⁵ *Marc.* 16.2–5 for Lucretia, Cloelia, and the Cornelias.   ²⁶ Griffin (1976, 1986a, and 1986b).

same time find an example of a woman demonstrating the same virtue attributed to the greatest Stoic heroes.

The category of *voluntaria mors* included both suicide and martyrdom and was allowable insofar as the chosen death would be preferable to living in a way that would not conform to a person's values. A *voluntaria mors* for the Stoics was *not* a death of despair. On their view, a death of despair could not be truly *voluntary* because the feeling of despair itself, for Stoics, indicates confusion.[27] They could thus see the deaths of Cato the Younger (suicide) and Helvidius Priscus (execution) as morally similar.[28] I use the term *voluntaria mors* to accommodate the philosophical equivalence between the deaths that Hercules (suicide) and Megara (execution) consider in the Senecan drama under investigation in this chapter. For the Stoic, the extremity of moral deliberation when facing a tyrant makes such scenarios frequent sources for *exempla* of *virtus*, understanding what does or does not depend on us, what one's proper roles and duties are, and how that understanding is not merely theoretical but actionable. A person's attitudes towards life as a merely preferred indifferent and towards death as *not* an evil become exceptionally clear when facing the whims and compulsions of a tyrant.

For our purposes here, we can observe the following general features of the Stoic *voluntaria mors*: (A) Suicide or martyrdom is an available exit to the kind of life that is not preferable to death: the philosopher should judge for how long he may live properly, emphasising quality over quantity. If chosen, the exit must be a good one.[29] (B) Death may be *disallowed* when another equally virtuous path is available or when to die would be to fail in one's obligations to others.[30] (C) The desire for death as a general weariness of life is repudiated.[31] (D) Choosing death is only the correct option when in the service of preserving one's reason or dignity or not breaking faith with others.[32] Seneca writes that, in his youth, he opted *not* to die out of concern for his father, in spite of an intractable illness (*Ep.* 78.1–2). (E) An example of *voluntaria mors* is particularly useful to Stoic teaching when the moral actor has determined that death is preferable to compliance with a tyrant.[33] Epictetus tells of a condemned man twice stretching out his neck for the fatal blow from a henchman of Nero

---

[27] E.g., *Helv.* 10.8–11.
[28] See Mann (2015) on Cato and the importance of the *prosōpon* in the case study of Helvidius.
[29] Sen. *Ep.* 70.4 and 77.4.   [30] E.g., Epictetus, *Diss.* 1.1.27.
[31] Sen. *Ep.* 24.24–25; Epict. *Diss.* 1.9.12–17. Cf. Griffin (1986a: 71).   [32] Sen. *Ep.* 14.2.
[33] *SVF* 3.768.

(*Diss.* 1.1.18–20) and of another refusing, at risk of death, to degrade his character by going to Nero's festivals (1.2.12–18).

Seneca's enduring interest in suicide and death has deservedly attracted a great deal of critical interest that I will not seek to replicate here.[34] Suffice it to observe that he provides many examples of men facing death correctly and that he tells us that to face death incorrectly is to be *womanish*. Seneca condemns Maecenas' prayer to live as long as possible – including under compromised conditions – as 'that depravity of womanish song' and a marker of 'the most insane fear' (*timoris dementissimi*, *Ep.* 101.13).[35] That a morally cowardly attitude to death is *woman-like* – and *crazy* – in these letters will prove useful to understanding the role of Megara later on in this chapter. Elsewhere, Seneca outlines the proper attitude towards life: the wise will see clearly how, and how long, to live, providing a counterexample of a man facing death badly: Telesphorus of Rhodes has been caged like an animal by a tyrant. Clinging to hope, he refuses to starve himself to death as an act of defiance. Seneca disapproves Telesphorus' refusal to defy the tyrant in this way as extremely womanish (*effeminatissimam*) and a display of weakness (*Ep.* 70.5–7).

The frequent association of womanliness with cowardice, frailty, or insanity is tempered for some by Seneca's positive and even respectful depiction of Paulina, his wife, in particular. Letter 104 expresses the care between Seneca and Paulina, where the latter's concern prompts the former to take responsibility for his own health (*Ep.* 104.2–5). Mercedes Mauch has pointed out the Stoic bent of the husband's perseverance in life both as an obligation that arises specifically from the marriage covenant and as an obligation that is generalisable to others. For Mauch, Paulina's entire life – as narrated through her husband's prose – is made full and meaningful because of her philosophically inflected love for Seneca.[36] It is Paulina, moreover, for whom there is robust, if not unequivocal, evidence for a woman's *voluntaria mors*.

Roman historiography helps us to frame Seneca's discussion of his wife, while also introducing complicating factors. There are two relevant accounts of Seneca's death that include Paulina and her own near death. In Tacitus' narrative of the fall-out of the Pisonian conspiracy and Nero's

---

[34] The place of suicide in the Senecan corpus is complicated by his own eventual suicide. See Ker (2009) for the fullest treatment of the afterlife of Seneca's death. Critics have divided over whether Seneca is morbidly fixated on suicide or uses the problem as a way of clarifying what is important about life. For a sensitive assessment, see Busch (2009). Cf. Griffin (1976: 367–88).
[35] As often, there is overlap between misogynist and homophobic language.
[36] Mauch (1997: 67–70).

revenge, Seneca faces his imminent death unafraid and urges his distressed companions to recall the lessons of wisdom, to maintain reason in the face of threats (*Ann.* 15.62). He turns to Paulina, who reportedly wishes to die alongside him. Seneca – as he declares in direct speech – does not begrudge her this opportunity for *gloria* or the honour of a death (*mortis decus*) that she prefers to life, the status of *exemplum*, nor even a fame that would exceed his own (63). But from this moment of clarity, the narrative takes an obscure turn: weakening and fearing their inability to see each other's pain, Seneca persuades Paulina to remove to another room. In her absence, he summons secretaries, taking a final opportunity for his *eloquentia*. Once removed, she is involuntarily revived by Nero's agents (64).

An optimistic interpretation of the Tacitean narrative, such as that offered by Reydams-Schils, shows that Paulina's preference for death is philosophical, demonstrating her defiance of Nero and her *pudicitia* in not wishing to have another husband.[37] Indeed, on this interpretation, one hesitates even to name Seneca the philosopher and Paulina the wife or student; instead, on the basis of her choice, we might rather see Paulina as a philosopher married to another philosopher. But on a cynical reading of same passage, Paulina's exit from his performance of a Socratic death-scene merely eliminates Seneca's competition for the spotlight. Perhaps – as James Ker suggests – there proved to be an incompatibility between conjugal dying and Seneca's personal ambition as a philosopher.[38]

The truncated epitome of Cassius Dio's account (62.25) is tough, offering neither the ambiguity of Tacitus nor the possibility of Paulina's *gloria*. It was Seneca's wish that Paulina be killed alongside him – no wish of her own is indicated – and he who opened her veins. Instead of a philosopher, we have a victim of domestic violence perpetrated through, perhaps, philosophical delusion. Here we confront Tacitus' notorious ambivalence and subtle detraction with Dio's open hostility to Seneca. Historiography is not philosophy: it seems that two narratives, each with their own politics, emerged from those inner chambers. And even the more sympathetic version narratologically mutes Paulina's words while giving voice to Seneca's.

To hear a woman's voice on this matter, then, I suggest we turn to Stoic tragedy. Though it, too, is male-authored, I argue that recentring our interpretation of Seneca's *Hercules Furens* on the hero's wife Megara,

---

[37] Reydams-Schils (2005: 173–74) concedes that the positive display of *pudicitia* is 'blurred', noting the 'coinciding of philosophical norms with social exempla'.
[38] Ker (2009: 29).

allows us to perceive an important experiment with staging a woman defying a tyrant in her own words, at pain of death. *Hercules Furens* is attractive for three further reasons: (1) *Hercules Furens* has previously drawn attention for its hero's deliberation over suicide as a dramatisation of this fundamentally Stoic problem; (2) the wife's deliberating the same question in her own case has been largely overlooked and, when noticed, dismissed for ill-judged reasons; (3) Hercules' outsized importance in demonstrating *virtus* throughout antiquity means that any challenge to his status as ethical protagonist must be seriously examined and its consequences probed.[39]

The Stoic Woman in Tragedy

In the tragic imagination, the woman as moral deliberator moves from anecdote to centre stage. As both Shadi Bartsch and Nussbaum show us in their readings of Seneca's *Medea*, tragedy proves an important site for confronting and developing Stoic arguments about human emotions.[40] The tragedies are, to use A. J. Boyle's phrase, 'ideas made flesh'.[41] Moreover, in tragedies we see the Stoic philosopher stage *at length* women's voices in direct speech articulating a world abounding in moral crises. Among tragedies, *Hercules Furens* is significant because the Hercules myth had long been an important resource for philosophers seeking a moral exemplar. Prodicus' allegory of Hercules at the crossroads of virtue and vice, reported by both Xenophon (*Mem.* 2.1.21–34) and Cicero (*Off.* 1.118), testifies to this cross-cultural, eclectic appeal. In Senecan prose, Hercules exemplifies fortitude and self-sacrifice (*Ben.* 1.13.2; *Const.* 2.1) and, in Epictetus' diatribes, models knowing what does and does not 'depend on us' (*Diss.* 3.24.13–17). But it was Euripides who had 'initiated the most far-reaching re-evaluation of Herakles by internalizing his struggles and labors and viewing him in purely human terms'.[42] It is no surprise, then, that Seneca's own complicated intervention in the Hercules story should both follow and meaningfully depart from the paradigm set by the *Herakles* tragedy of Euripides.

Euripides' *Herakles* tragedy opens at Thebes: Herakles is absent, the stage dominated by the prayers and lamentations of his wife, Megara, and his aged father, Amphitryon. Lycus, the usurping tyrant, approaches. An *agōn* about the hero's worthiness unfolds between tyrant and father. Lycus,

---

[39] Galinsky (1972: 100ff). [40] Bartsch (2006: 230–81); Nussbaum (2009: 439–83).
[41] Boyle (1997: 32). [42] Galinsky (1972: 2).

intent on killing the family to secure his rule, leaves so they can prepare for death (327–35). Throughout the opening, Amphitryon tries to persuade his daughter-in-law that hope for a rescue by a returning Herakles still lingers, but Megara responds that hope is a sign of irrational attachment to life (90–94). Suddenly, Herakles returns triumphant. Humbled by the suffering before him, he rejects his status as victor, opting to defend his family (582). He kills Lycus. Madness (Lyssa) arrives on Hera's and Iris' orders and – after lamenting her target's innocence – drives Herakles insane, causing him to kill his wife and children. Awakening and discovering his deed, Herakles is about to turn his hand against himself, but he is persuaded to live on by Amphitryon, who begs him not to deprive him of his son. Theseus appears, offers refuge to the criminal at Athens, and the two heroes depart.

Seneca's *Hercules Furens*, too, opens at Thebes but is prefaced with a prologue of Juno accusing her stepson of working to disrupt the natural order. Next, the prayers and laments of Amphitryon and Megara give way to the entrance of Lycus. But where Euripides staged the *agōn* between tyrant and father, Seneca has his tyrant debate the wife – and in doing so makes room for Megara to be tested. The new Lycus offers her a scenario that requires moral reasoning: unlike his Euripidean forerunner, his preference is not to kill the queen and her children where compromise might be possible. He proposes reconciliation and marriage. She firmly prefers death. Again, Hercules returns in time to slay the tyrant and does. Again, he is overtaken by a madness, but the Senecan madness seems to come from within – there is no Lyssa to blame. He kills his family and awakes to confusion.

Morally problematic, less sympathetic than the Attic original, Seneca's hero is harder to pity. His insolence from the moment he appeared on stage has verged on the impious – reciting his own honours, ignoring his father's admonition to wash his hands before prayers (918–24). Upon his return, he does not acknowledge his wife, leaving it to his companion Theseus to comfort her (640). That Seneca does not eliminate the attempt to console Megara, but instead gives the part away, only emphasises the husband's failure. After Hercules emerges from his frenzy, he struggles with the decision of whether to end his life in shame for having murdered his family, but his deliberation over whether to commit suicide is substantially concerned with reputation: if he survives, his life will be that of a criminal; if he dies, that of a victim (1278).[43] He considers that since he is

---

[43] See Boyle (1997: 106–11 and 191).

well-known in the underworld, even there he would not escape infamy. Amphitryon threatens his own suicide if Hercules should go first, and so he finally relents to spare his own father the pain of losing a child. Hercules goes to Athens with Theseus.

Seneca's vaunting hero is not wholly undeserving of Juno's suspicion that he intends to disrupt the cosmos. Because of his doubly compromised moral position, the question of whether suicide is an acceptable solution for *this* Hercules is complicated even within the Stoic moral calculus, and the conclusion of the tragedy unsatisfying, even within its generic context. Understood as a re-visiting of Seneca's own decision against suicide in deference to his father, Hercules' decision conforms to Stoic filial duty.[44] Some have seen the drama as one about understanding what *virtus* is; some have suggested that Lycus is the ethical foil for Hercules – that the tyrant misunderstands what *virtus* is while the hero finally arrives at a proper understanding. Others have found that the conclusion presents the audience with the possibility of redemption – rare for the genre.[45] For our purposes, an assumption apparently underlying these readings, reasonable as they may be, is that the philosophical problems are staged through the male characters or that the foil for the male hero is the male villain.

Critics have generally missed the urgent moral deliberation over *voluntaria mors* that precedes Hercules'. Megara, his wife left behind at Thebes, perhaps forever, while Hercules pursues his labours, faces a tyrant offering a good deal: remarriage and restoration to her royal prerogatives. She would rather die. Seneca's divergences from his Euripidean model carefully cast Megara as a rigorous decision-maker, who chooses a death that accords with her values. By contrast, when it comes to his turn at a similar (though not identical) question of life and death, Hercules makes the opposite choice: after murdering his family, he is persuaded out of suicide. This woman's choice for *voluntaria mors* – a choice that her husband fails to make, even if for arguably appropriate reasons – is a major ethical experiment in female exemplarity that does not occur in Senecan prose. The radical and importantly *prior* choice of Megara is all the more striking given Hercules' own status as exemplar in the tradition.

Megara and the Tyrant

For his part, Clemens Zintzen noted the peculiarity of the encounter between Seneca's Lycus and Megara and suggested that the invention

[44] Motto and Clark (1981: 107). [45] Boyle (1997: 33).

was designed to display Stoic virtue in Megara – all the more so because no substantive plot change occurs as a result of their encounter.[46] But in his commentary on *Hercules Furens*, John Fitch dismisses Zintzen's suggestion, and it has not been generally taken up since in discussions of women or suicide in Stoicism. For Fitch, Megara's prayer exhibits 'near-*hysteria*' and the woman is reliant on Amphitryon to restrain her passion: 'it would be a distortion to see Megara in this scene as a Stoic heroine. She is in fact a *highly emotional* woman, and her defiance of Lycus is based on a passionate hatred of him'.[47] We shall see that what Fitch is observing is not the 'hysteria' of a *demens* woman, an interpretative mistake that Lycus also makes (429).

What such an interpretation fails to see is that there are no dramatic – or moral – stakes to Megara's choice if she fails to see what danger she is in. Megara indeed displays contradictions, but it is not Amphitryon who is required as a 'restraining influence'.[48] Megara pauses to revise her own feelings. After her first prayer, which engages in the language of disruption that generally characterises this tragedy (279–95), Megara stops herself from the wrong-headedness, saying 'But I'm speaking out of line (*nimium*), since I do not know my lot' (295–96).[49] Rather than a hysterical woman, Seneca stages a sole actor talking herself through her emotions and deliberating.

Megara privileges her sense of self and her proper role over life and material well-being, both Stoic indifferents, thus investing her later death with moral significance other than mere spectacular victimisation at the hands of her husband. She *chooses* to die rather than live under conditions that are unacceptable to her. Megara's eventual death is thus re-envisioned as a *voluntaria mors*. The fact that she ultimately meets her end in a manner that she does not foresee is immaterial from a Stoic perspective because the outcome does not depend on her. Her death is inevitable from the perspective of myth but voluntary from the perspective of Stoic ethics.

Prior to Lycus' entrance, Megara has arrived at acceptance, like the Euripidean Megara: if her husband is available in the upper world, let him come; if below, she will meet him there (304–8). Although Lycus mentions execution as the alternative to matrimony (351), the text makes it clear that Megara has not overheard him (354, 359). Seemingly full of

---

[46] Zintzen (1972: 173–76).   [47] Fitch (2009: 183–84), emphasis added.
[48] Fitch (2009: 183–84).
[49] To behave *nimium* is a quality of Hercules (186–87, 1226), but it is also a 'key word' throughout the drama for the entire family.

reconciliation, Lycus proposes that the union would be eminently practical: he needs her to legitimate his rule; she needs a husband in view of the fact that hers is missing in action; and if she could get past his slaughter of her family, she might find a worthy husband in Lycus (359–69) – who, though not one of the *nobiles*, likes to think of himself as a man of *clara virtus* (338–40).

Megara rejects Lycus' proposal with an appeal to her moral identity and family of origin.[50] The first word of her reply is an emphatic affirmation of her self: *Ego*.

> Egone ut parentis sanguine aspersam manum
> fratrumque gemina caede contingam?
> (*HF* 372–73)

'How could *I* take the hand sprinkled with my parent's blood and with the double slaughter of my brothers?'[51]

Her objection to the tyrant is the slaughter of her male kin. She continues, 'You have stolen my father, realm, brothers, hearth, homeland – what else is there?' And next, 'One thing alone remains for me, dearer than brother and parent, kingdom and hearth' (379–81). That one thing is not, as we might imagine, her husband. Rather, all that remains to her identity, once family and homeland have been stripped away, is her opposition to the tyrant (*odium tui*, 382).[52] Opposition to a tyrant is, as we have seen, a major justification for *voluntaria mors* for the Stoics. Lest there be any doubt as to how this confrontation should be construed, even Lycus calls himself a *tyrannus* (511). Megara does not first imagine her refusal within the framework of her marriage but rather within the set of relationships and obligations that would equally bind a heroic man.

Lycus asks what wedding arrangements he might make; Megara asks for her death or Lycus'. With some sophistical reasoning, he reminds her that part of life is to submit to authority outside her control and that this is the lesson she should draw from Hercules, alluding to the labours in service to Eurystheus (398). He says that she will be forced (*cogere*), to which she replies that someone who can be compelled to do something does not know how to die (*cogi qui potest nescit mori*, 426), sounding a great deal like

---

[50] Cf. Reydams-Schils (2005: 25–29) on the importance of pronouns and moral identity. Contrast Euripides' Megara declaring she will imitate her husband's *mimēma* (*Her.* 294).
[51] My translation.
[52] Similarly, Wray (2009: 253) shows that Seneca's Clytemnestra in her *agōn* adheres to her 'ethical self' (*Aga.* 306–7). Fitch (2009: 184) objects that Megara is spurred by passionate hatred. But *odium* of a tyrant forms part of a rational calculus.

an Epictetan exemplar. Megara's reply is philosophical in a robust sense: her language reflects the qualities of true freedom in Stoic literature *and* her moral reasoning undergirds her decision.[53] It is worth repeating: Megara – not Lycus – raises her death as an option in the Senecan encounter. He has presented himself as optimistic, pragmatic. It is she who turns his offer into an ethical crisis. She would rather follow her current husband to the grave (428–29).

Lycus' continued soliciting of Megara only demonstrates that her refusal reflects rational choice. The idea that Megara is hysterical is a misapprehension of Lycus, when he earlier supposed that if she were to refuse him it would be due to her being out of control (*impotenti . . . animo*, 350). Now, Lycus' accusation that Megara is crazy (*demens*, 429) only serves to ironise the fact that of the three figures whose moral faculties are at stake in this drama – tyrant, wife, hero – only hers is immoveable. The accusation *demens* also foreshadows her husband's real dementia that will soon direct the show: both she and the chorus will appeal to the murderous Hercules in his frenzy as *amens* (1021, 1033). As Lycus and Hercules both emerge as figures of moral confusion, Megara stands alone as a figure of moral clarity under pressure.

Her unwavering preference for death presents us with a model alongside which to measure Hercules' later belaboured deliberation, modifying and limiting any prior claim to *virtus* that he might have held. Megara demonstrates her philosophical mettle and capacity to perform the role of the *sapiens*. The manner of her death will not ultimately depend on her, but her act of volition does. Thus, Megara makes the unflinching choice to die and is ready to follow through on her word but for her husband's forceful intervention. Her lines throughout her encounters with Amphitryon and Lycus prove her philosophical countenance: Fortuna does not spare the virtuous (325–28); without hardships, there is no opportunity for virtue (433); it is virtuous to overcome what ordinary people fear (435).

But when Lycus raises the evergreen question of Hercules' paternity, Megara's moment is ruptured. Amphitryon intervenes: 'Pitiable spouse of Hercules the great, silence! It's my role (*partes meae*) to report Alcides' paternity and true origin' (439–41). Where Fitch interprets this intervention as Amphitryon's concern for Megara's delicate state along with his natural interest in the paternity question, I suggest that this reads rather like a fear of being upstaged. In view of his role as the agonist against Lycus

---

[53] Cf. Epictetus 4.1.1. See Mann (2006) on the general issue.

in the Euripidean drama, Amphitryon's interruption is as though a reminder of their proper *partes* in the earlier tragedy. In other words: stick to the script.

Megara speaks again only once Lycus threatens rape: 'But if she's unyielding in nuptials and refuses to be joined to me (*copulari*), even so I'll have noble offspring from her by force (*coacta*)' (493–94). In response, she summons dead ancestors, hoping to join them, again affirming her preference for death (495–500). Noticeably, she does not speak when her husband returns – and the Senecan Hercules takes little notice of her. Megara utters her last words when she is in his fatal clutches, begging him to *recognise* her (*agnosce Megaram*, 'Recognise Megara,' 1015–17). Significantly, she echoes Seneca's Medea's last words to *her* husband Jason as she kills their children and prepares to escape (*coniugem agnoscis tuam?*, 'Do you recognise your spouse?' *Med.* 1021). As much as mutuality may be theorised in Stoic marriage, in the 'idea made flesh', mutual recognition may be hard indeed to achieve.

Tragic Role Change

Tragic women, writes Nicole Loraux, 'are free enough to kill themselves, but they are not free enough to escape from the space to which they belong, and the remote sanctum where they meet their death is equally the symbol of their life . . .. The place where women kill themselves, to give it its name, is the marriage chamber, the *thalamos*'.[54] In view of this model, it is highly significant that Megara declares her fear of the marital bed (*thalamos tremesco*, 418) and that she declares her preference of death publicly, rather than by report. Megara seeks to remove herself from the tragic paradigm as the deaths she imagines for herself are virile, public, and political, rather than womanly, private, or personal: 'Let chains weigh down my body and slow death be drawn out even longer by starvation: there is not any force that will overpower my faith' (419–21) – deprivations and deaths that a man might suffer for political reasons.

The real change in Megara's conduct – from coherent moral agent to pleading wife – stages the tension between Megara-qua-Stoic and Megara-qua-tragic-wife. In (Attic) tragedy, Loraux has shown, suicide is not a heroic (i.e., manly) act but rather the death of a woman. The largely gendered patterns of ways of dying confirm that the tragic fantasy of a woman's death is that it is out of view, that the fantasy of a man's death is

[54] Loraux (1987: 23).

that it is on display. But Seneca's women may wield virile implements disallowed their Attic counterparts, as the Stoic tragedian departs from his models, reimagining women's deaths in 'masculine' terms.[55] Lauren Ginsberg has shown how Seneca innovatively recentred the Oedipus story in *Phoenissae* by focussing upon Jocasta, who exceeds her mythological context with rhetoric that positions her in the role of Roman *parens patriae*.[56] Phaedra kills herself with a sword in view of Theseus, whereas Euripides' Phaedra hangs herself within. But unlike Jocasta and Phaedra, who perceive themselves to have erred and punish themselves, Megara singularly is not complicit in the events that have resulted in moral crisis: she opts for death to *avoid* acting in a way that does not cohere with her identity and opposition to the tyrant. Hers is a death of resistance.[57]

I have suggested that Amphitryon fears being upstaged when he displaces Megara. That fear is paralleled by the risk of Hercules being upstaged as moral exemplar. The first silencing of Megara is by Amphitryon, a dislocated patriarch, who appropriates her position in the *agōn*. The second silencing of Megara is by Hercules, the repatriated patriarch, who appropriates her position as the figure of moral choice and *voluntaria mors*. Put another way: Megara's virile self-definition, her sense of her own heroic values and obligations, set her up for her murder at her husband's hands.

Why does Seneca stage the woman opting for *voluntaria mors* in tragedy while sometimes declining to treat such figures in prose addressing the same problems? The answer may be the imaginative space that tragedy allows – and the fate that myth dictates. For all her good Stoic reasoning, Megara ultimately perishes as a victim of domestic violence. While, as I have mentioned, this is immaterial from a Stoic perspective, it is not immaterial from a feminist one. The tragic assurance that she will die at her husband's hand (not her own, not the tyrant's) grants licence to the philosophical imagination. For she has not displaced the male exemplar or threatened his grimly starring role; her choice has been forgotten. It is precisely the fact that Megara is killed by her husband, that there is no material consequence to her moral deliberation, which allows for this

---

[55] Hecuba seeks a manly death of swords and missiles, to no avail (*Tro.* 1173–75).
[56] Ginsberg (2016).
[57] Compare Megara with Seneca's Andromache (*Tro.* 623–24; *HF* 414–15). In a moment analogous to the Megara-Lycus confrontation, Ulysses threatens 'You will be forced (*coacta*) to say what you refuse to confess willingly' (*Tro.* 573). Andromache responds 'That woman is safe who is able, who is obligated, who desires to die' (*Tro.* 574). Her declaration is similar to Megara's; but unlike Megara, her fear gives her away.

philosophical thought experiment – a woman vocalising her own radical choice – in tragic form.

To return to the question that originally motivated our enquiry into Megara's Stoic character: can the space of drama allow us to imagine what we might find if we were to have direct literary evidence from Stoic women? Put another way: does 'fiction' help us to understand the 'real' women philosophers whose words were not enshrined and passed down by 'the tradition'? I argue that investigating the direct-speech portrayal of Megara, the vocalisation of a woman's moral choice in a high-stakes dramatic context, helps us to *recognise* the women who are reported indirectly as 'wives' of Stoics or otherwise Stoic-adjacent as *themselves* philosophers. When we return to the historiographical, epistolary, and consolatory narratives reporting *exempla* and the lives of Stoic men, we can recognise figures such as the freedwoman Epicharis as living as Stoic philosophers: making their own moral choices in crisis, irrespective of the threat of compulsion.

CHAPTER 7

Pythagorean Women and the Domestic as a Philosophical Topic

Rosemary Twomey

Introduction

In ancient philosophy, primary source material written by women is hard to come by. While there were women in Plato's Academy and Epicurus' Garden, there are no extant writings by these women. Into this void falls a series of texts on moral instruction purportedly written by Pythagorean women during the Hellenistic period.[1] Whether these letters and treatises were really written by women is subject to controversy – about which more below – but the existence of documents even supposedly written by women demonstrates that they were thought to be able to exercise some moral authority. Yet, despite the relatively unique status of these texts as evidence of the intellectual influence of women, their philosophical value has been questioned. In this chapter, I discuss some of the later Pythagorean treatises and letters, and I argue that their content and methodology warrant their inclusion as contributions to the history of philosophy.[2] While their subject matter diverges from the standard philosophical topics of their time, they can be seen as complementary to other discussions of household management, like those found in Plato's *Republic* and *Laws*, Xenophon's *Oeconomicus*, and Aristotle's *Politics*. For example, in Aristotle's *Politics*, his remarks on household management assume the

---

[1] There are also writings purportedly by Pythagorean women on number and similar recognisably philosophical topics. In this chapter, I focus on the more challenging case for the philosophical value of the treatises and letters written on the topics of the running of the home and the care of one's husband and children.

[2] Following Salamon (2009), Dotson has argued that philosophy tends to employ a 'culture of justification' in that it '1) manifest[s] a value for exercises of legitimation, [and] 2) assume[s] the existence of commonly held, justifying norms that are 3) univocally relevant' (7) and that this has the effect of excluding 'incongruent' approaches that would diversify the field (2012). I agree that this is a legitimate concern for the field as a whole, but if (some of) the Pythagorean women's treatises or letters can be 'legitimated' then that should satisfy both those traditionalists who still buy into this culture of justification and those who do not.

standpoint of the master of the house and so he largely ignores issues that arise for female members of the household; but as we will see, women's responsibilities (such as they were) would also be essential to establishing stable households of the sort that raise good citizens and thereby compose successful cities.

My approach to these texts will require us to bracket our distaste with the limitations placed on women at the time and instead focus on how they worked within these limitations to contribute to the ethical development of their societies. To presuppose that 'real philosophy' must address our actions outside of the family unit amounts to the requirement that only the rare, outsider female of the ancient world was able to philosophise, and moreover, it leads to the expectation that were she to do so, she would speak in exactly the language that we are used to from her male counterparts. Such an approach artificially limits the opportunities that are opened up by diversifying the canon. Here we would like a diversity of approaches and interests as well as a diversity in the makeup of people contributing to the discipline. Indeed, these texts prompt us to consider how philosophy might have evolved differently (and might yet evolve differently) were these discussions to be taken seriously as contributions to the field.

Of course, I am not claiming that everything written about the internal running of a home would count as philosophy. Nor is it the case that the raising of children and support of one's spouse are inherently female interests, while public-facing action is masculine. Rather, I argue that both are of philosophical interest if we take one of the primary roles of ancient philosophy to be determining how to achieve *eudaimonia* and how to inculcate virtue as part of that effort. Moral and political philosophies aimed at *eudaimonia* are deficient to the extent that they do not substantively address the running of the home in its entirety. Finally, these texts can be used pedagogically to advance discussions of sexism in ancient Greece as well as in modern societies: we think it is clear that women are harmed insofar as they are marginalised and prevented from contributing to the public good, but part of what these texts show is that men are also harmed when they choose to limit their thinking only to how they engage with the wider public, since, as some of the texts below will argue, much of virtue is inculcated in domestic life.

In the first section of the chapter, I discuss the limiting factors that necessarily attend any effort to place women into ancient philosophy as well as the more specific complications that apply to the letters and treatises purportedly written by Pythagorean women. In the second section, we will look at some of the texts more closely and consider objections that have been raised to the idea that they make contributions to philosophy. I will argue that these objections presuppose a narrow conception of philosophy that is the result of the successful marginalising of these voices and that engagement with these texts leads to a fuller picture of human life than that offered by our canonical philosophers. The primary contrast here will be with Aristotle, who will be the subject of the third section.[3] In the third section, I will compare Aristotle's discussion of the household with those found in the texts discussed in the second section, arguing that both take the household to be relevant for similar reasons and that they employ a similar methodology. Each account is incomplete without the other. A full and happy human life encompasses both. In the fourth section, I will discuss how our conception of who matters shapes our conception of what matters (and vice versa).

Some Methodological Difficulties

Any discussion of ancient texts is inherently limited by the scarcity of source material, a difficulty that is especially acute in the case of women and other marginalised groups. In what follows, I will first outline the texts I rely on and then discuss the limitations of this method. We have no writings from Pythagoras (c. 570–490 BCE); our primary sources of doxographical information about him and his followers are the work of much later authors: Diogenes Laertius (c. 180–240 CE), Porphyry (c. 234–305 CE), and Iamblichus (c. 245–325 CE). The dating of the extant works purportedly by Pythagorean women is controversial, but they are usually dated to between the first century BCE and the first century CE.[4]

Diogenes tells us that Pythagoras got his ethical views from an otherwise unknown priestess named Themistoclea (8.8), and he also claims that Pythagoras' wife Theano left some written works (8.43).[5] According to Diogenes, Pythagoras left his writings to his daughter Damo, who refused

---

[3] To a lesser extent, I will also discuss Plato and Epicurus. Many interesting connections could also be drawn to Xenophon's *Oecomomicus*, but in the interests of space and given the goal of legitimating some of the treatises and letters as having philosophical content, I focus on canonical philosophers.
[4] For a recent discussion of the history of views about dating, see (Dutsch 2020: 5–11).
[5] Since these sources of biographical information on the historical Pythagoras are much later, their reliability is subject to debate. Indeed, already by Diogenes' time there is dispute as to whether Theano is Pythagoras' wife and the daughter of Brontinus or if she is rather the wife of Brontinus and merely a student of Pythagoras (8.42).

to sell them even as she underwent financial hardship (8.42).[6] Iamblichus gives us a list of 235 Pythagoreans, 17 of whom are women (Iambl. *VP* 267) – a disappointing percentage by today's standards, but there is no comparable evidence of percentages even this low among similar philosophical schools of the time. It can readily be seen why Pythagoras may have attracted a female following. Porphyry tells us that Pythagoras immediately impressed the officials in Croton when he arrived in approximately 530 BCE and was invited by the elders to give speeches to children and women (Porph. *VP* 18). Iamblichus gives us an account of the speech that he delivered, wherein he stresses the piety and virtue of his audience and tells them they should not be ashamed of sex (assuming it is with their husbands) (Iambl. *VP* 54–57).[7] Similarly, Diogenes tells us that Theano said a woman was pure immediately after sex with her husband but would never be pure after sex with anyone else and that she described her clothes as what makes her a woman, implying that there is no inherent difference between men and women (8.43).[8] It has also been suggested that a belief in metempsychosis would lead rather directly to the equality of the sexes as well as to a concern with the well-being of non-human animals (another alleged interest of the Pythagoreans).[9]

We find the earliest versions of some of the texts purportedly by Pythagorean women in collections by Stobaeus: *Eclogarum Physicarum* and *Florilegium* (fifth century CE). Gilles Ménage's *Historia Mulierum Philosopharum* (1690) is the earliest known work to call attention to women's contributions to philosophy, including the Pythagorean women. In modern times, Holger Thesleff released a collection of Hellenistic Pythagorean writings, including seventeen pieces purportedly written by ten women.[10] Mary Ellen Waithe also collects and discusses these texts in the first volume of her groundbreaking collection of the history of women in philosophy.[11] The first book-length treatment of Pythagorean

---

[6] Most now hold that Pythagoras left no writings, a view that was also common in Diogenes' time, but which he rejected (8.6).
[7] Porphyry and his original source Dicaearchus (350–285 BCE) also report a speech but don't elaborate on what was said, so it is certainly possible Iamblichus is confabulating its content. For more on the general role of women in Pythagorean societies, see Rowett (2014).
[8] On the other hand, Aristotle presents a Pythagorean list of opposites, where 'male' and 'female' are presented as opposed (*Met.* 986a22–b5), which at least one author proposes as responsible for 'the conception of women and men as significantly and intrinsically different' (Deslauriers 2012: 349). Moreover, other texts, including some written by Pythagorean women, do suggest some essential differences. Like any socially embedded tradition, particularly one that evolved over hundreds of years, there are significant differences of opinion. Still, it is interesting to find even one hinting at equality of the sexes.
[9] See Dutsch (2020: 20); Pellò (2018: 137–40). [10] Thesleff (1965). [11] Waithe (1987b).

women – including not just their philosophical contributions but also their way of life and other elements of their social environment – was published in 2013 by Sarah Pomeroy, who also has myriad essays and monographs that seek to elucidate the life of women in antiquity.[12] More recently, Dorota Dutsch has published *Pythagorean Women Philosophers*, a monograph that collects accounts of the roles and teachings of Pythagorean women from various authors, including Plato and the doxographers as well as the Hellenistic pseudonymous texts I will discuss below.[13]

It appears to be generally true of the time period that women rarely wrote treatises intended for public consumption: indeed, Pomeroy calls it an 'axiom of women's history' that 'women, in general, wrote shorter and fewer works and often kept them in private or published them only under a pseudonym' (2013: xxi).[14] These writings do not have the standard form of philosophical texts we are used to: they are generally addressed to specific problems and provide advice rather than a dispassionate collection of principles.[15] But, as we will see, many of the texts do not merely assert that this or that is to be done: they justify the advice by appeal to virtue.

We can safely assume that there were many more such writings that have not been discovered, many of which are lost to time. The further in the past one goes, the truer this is, and it would of course be especially true of women's contributions, which would not have been treated with the same level of respect and care as that of their male counterparts. Moreover, the oldest plausible dating of the texts in question is the fourth century BCE, centuries after Pythagoras flourished, and many are likely to be much later and seem to have been influenced by Platonism and other philosophical traditions. This has led scholars to describe them as pseudepigrapha.[16] Further concerns arise specifically when it comes to the texts written by

---

[12] Pomeroy (2013).   [13] Dutsch (2020).
[14] One notable exception is Ptolemaïs, who wrote a treatise on Pythagorean musical theory discussed by Porphyry. See Pomeroy (2013: 95–98).
[15] I refer here to how philosophical texts are composed in the modern era: there are countless examples of advice-giving philosophical texts in the ancient tradition, including letters like those written by Epicurus. This difference is also reflected in the orientation of philosophy over its history. Since Hadot (1987), it has been commonplace to note that much of ancient philosophy addresses how one should live. Though he traces the approach to Socrates, (i) Pythagoras' teachings fit the mould described by Hadot; and anyway (ii) all the letters and treatises by Pythagorean women are later than Socrates. I return to this below.
[16] A thorough discussion of early views on the matter can be found in Thesleff (1961: 30–41), though he subsequently changes his mind and dates them later. See also Huffman (2019b: §4.2); Huizenga (2013: 115–17). For a contrary view, asserting that though they are late and so influenced by other traditions, they are written sincerely and so do not deserve to be thought of as 'pseudepigrapha' and 'forgeries', see Kingsley (1995: 320–22) and Pomeroy (2013: 51). It is not important for the purposes of this chapter to establish whether the ideas reflected in the texts are written in a

women: some scholars are immediately sceptical of the idea that women would write to each other and find it more likely that they would have been written by men imitating women for the purposes of exercising persuasive power over their female relatives.[17] Sarah Pomeroy argues to the contrary that they are likely genuine and written by women, though she accepts the later datings, so she says that in cases of recognisable early Pythagorean names like Theano and Myia they are written by women named after their more famous counterparts. She notes that in the Hellenistic period to which the texts are dated, women were literate and contributed to other schools of philosophy. Moreover, there are references to women being involved in Pythagoreanism going back as far as the fourth century BCE in comedies by Cratinus and Alexis, and it is attested in the doxographical tradition, as discussed above.[18] Pomeroy also points to the example of Ptolemaïs, who wrote a treatise on musical theory cited by Porphyry, and she says that the fact Porphyry does not even point out she is a woman suggests that she was not entirely unique.[19] Finally, although she acknowledges that the content of the texts generally supports the status quo and so represents male interests, she does not take this as a sure sign they were written by men since 'it would be unreasonable to expect the Neopythagorean women to write like modern feminists'.[20]

Certainly, it is not possible to settle the issue decisively. However, the arguments against female authorship often rely on presuppositions about women that are commonplace but are not wholly supported by the historical record of the time. As Pomeroy notes, women could have written these texts, and it would not be surprising to find them advocating for rather traditional values. Consider, too, the audience for these treatises and letters. It is clear the intended audience is women, who were expected to

---

misleading way to suggest an earlier date than their actual composition. What is at issue here is whether they have philosophical value and should therefore be addressed alongside more canonical works. For more discussion of the options (and with a judgement ultimately in favour of the view that they are eponymous), see Waithe (1987b: 59–73) and Pomeroy (2013: 49–53). For an argument in favour of their being pseudepigrapha, see Dutsch 2020: 5–11.

[17] Cole (1981: 229); Deslauriers (2012: 343–44). There is precedent for men to write under women's names, see Lefkowitz and Fant (2005: 163).
[18] Dutsch discusses texts from Empedocles and Antisthenes that also, she takes it, suggest that Pythagoras was interested in the female perspective, albeit for different reasons (2020: 22–25). Though it is clear there were Pythagorean women, this doesn't particularly help us authenticate any particular text, since if women were already associated with Pythagoreanism, that would make it easier for men to pretend to be women effectively.
[19] Pomeroy (2013: 51).
[20] Pomeroy (2013: 51). I return to this point below in my discussion of Deslauriers' criticism of the letters.

entertain the texts and hopefully even find the reasoning persuasive. Thus, if the content of these texts can be called philosophical (about which more below), then that will suffice to show that women engaged with philosophy at least as far back as the datings of the earliest texts (and presumably long before that, but here we face the standard complications around preservation and retention of ancient texts, compounded by the marginalised status of women's contributions more generally). So even if we find ourselves sceptical about the female authorship of the treatises, the existence of these texts is still a testament to the philosophical acuity of women – as readers, if not as authors.

The Texts and Some Criticisms

As far back as Iamblichus, we find differing interpretations of the main aims of Pythagoras and the Pythagorean school: are Pythagoreans trying to offer a cosmology grounded in mathematics – as Aristotle would have it – or is Pythagoreanism more rooted in religious instruction and moral development?[21] The Hellenistic Pythagorean texts discussed in this chapter fit in the latter category: they advise their reader on topics of feminine virtue and on one's relationship with her husband and her children. But while some of the advice to be discussed below is unique to women, much of the overall philosophy is not gender specific. The strict rules for initiation into Pythagoreanism were the same for men and for women, and Pythagoras required monogamy from both husbands and wives (Iamb. *VP* 132). Moreover, as Pomeroy notes, the comprehensiveness of the rules that Pythagoreans were subject to – covering areas from diet, clothing, makeup, and jewellery to childrearing – would make it difficult to adhere to them without the support of other members of the household.[22]

The ideal household that the texts describe is what we would now consider a traditional one: the focus is on pleasing one's husband through moderation, simplicity, self-restraint, piety, and the like. When advice along these lines is offered from women to women, contemporary readers are likely to find themselves underwhelmed. For these reasons, Marguerite Deslauriers questions the status of these works:

---

[21] *Met.* 985b22–86b2, though note that Aristotle here refers to the 'so-called Pythagoreans' (*hoi kaloumenoi Pythagoreioi*), thereby implicitly distancing the doctrines he discusses from the historical figure of Pythagoras. For more on these two pictures, see Lloyd (2014: 32–34).
[22] Pomeroy (2013: 11); Dutsch (2020: 31, 34).

Do the sort of texts in which women are exhorted to dress modestly and practice chastity amount to contributions to moral philosophy? I am going to stipulate here that they do not, and that I am treating as philosophical only those texts that center on issues that other ancient philosophers would have considered philosophical (this spans a broad range, including logic, natural philosophy, moral philosophy, and metaphysics). On this basis, work in music theory and in gynaecology count as philosophical, but moral platitudes do not.[23]

Deslauriers seems to conceive of the project in her essay as one in the sociology of philosophy: much of the evidence she brings to bear addresses factors that would keep women from being recognised as contributors to philosophy at the time – things like the literacy of women and their ability to engage in activities outside of the home. If the question we are asking is whether some women should have been recognised as philosophers by their peers in antiquity, then we can look at whether they wrote on things that were topics of conversation in the philosophy of their own time. But this is not the only form the question of whether there were philosophical women in antiquity can take. We can also ask whether there are women who wrote on things that – though not considered philosophical at the time – nonetheless have philosophical value.[24] Deslauriers quotes John Rist, who observes that participating in philosophy in a typical way would take a woman far outside of her traditional role: 'the mere act of being a philosopher would involve abandoning the traditional pursuits of women and entering into debate with men' (Deslauriers 2012: 344, quoting Rist 1965: 220). Those women who choose a more traditional life will not be writing texts much less engaging with the philosophical vogues of the day, so by Deslauriers' definition they will be incapable of contributing to philosophy.

It is a side effect of this conception, moreover, that any ancient women who can be considered philosophers will have to engage with the domain as shaped by male interests and male perspectives. Such a figure will be unlikely to be a revolutionary, if it is a condition of being a philosopher that one engage with canonical topics (even if those topics are somewhat different than what we would consider philosophical today, as the gynaecological example is presumably meant to illustrate). To tie the conception of a philosophical text to its mainstream acceptability is to hamstring the

---

[23] Deslauriers (2012: 344).
[24] Deslauriers seems more open to a positive answer to the second kind of question since she later says about some of the letters that 'it is not that these works are devoid of philosophical claims, but rather that insofar as they involve philosophical claims, they do so only to uphold the subject position of women without critical analysis' (2012: 346).

effort of diversifying from the start. While it is nice to find marginalised voices that represent mainstream views to add to syllabi, to truly diversify the discipline we should be open to a broadening of what is to count as philosophy, and we should most expect to see this broader conception taken up by those voices that are most marginalised in their own time.

But while I have concerns about the stipulative definition that Deslauriers offers, even by its lights much of the content of these texts can count as philosophical. For they do discuss an issue that 'ancient philosophers would have considered philosophical', viz. the household. In the next section we will look at Aristotle's discussions of the household, and I will argue that they suffer from being too narrow and that they can be fleshed out by being supplemented with this material.[25] Here we consider some of the texts themselves.

Take, for instance, Perictione's treatise *On the Harmonious Woman*.[26] She takes up a major theme of Pythagoreanism – namely, harmony – and she argues that the harmonious women must have wisdom (*phronêsis*) and self-control (*sôphrosynê*):[27]

> We must deem the harmonious woman to be one who is well endowed with wisdom (*phronêsis*) and self-restraint (*sôphrosynê*). For her soul must be very wise when it comes to virtue so that she will be just and courageous (*andrêiê*) while being sensible and beautified with self-sufficiency, despising empty opinion (*kenên doxên*) . . . . Surely, by controlling her desire (*epithumia*) and passion (*thumos*), a woman becomes devout and harmonious, resulting in her not becoming a prey to impious love affairs. Rather, she will be full of love for her husband and children and her entire household. For all those women who have a desire for extramarital relations (*allotriôn lecheôn*, lit., alien beds) themselves become enemies (*polemiai*) of all the freedmen and domestics in the house . . . . For from all these activities comes the ruination that jointly afflicts the woman as well as her husband.[28]

---

[25] Of course, what one wants is for both aspects of the household – leadership and support – to be the role of both the husband and the wife, whereas at best what we get when we bring these texts together is lessons for the husband/master of the house, on the one hand, and the wife/supporter, on the other. In the concluding section, I will touch on how the sexism evident in both Classical philosophy and in these letters might be addressed in the pedagogical context.

[26] Thesleff claims there are at least two authors named Perictione. Perictione I is earlier – fourth to third century BCE – and she writes mostly in Ionic Greek. Perictione II, on the other hand, writes in the Doric style, and is dated to the third to second century BCE (1961: 17, 29, 77, 87). He later changes his view (Thesleff 1971). Waithe (1987b) and Pomeroy (2013) follow Thesleff (1961)'s dating. Dutsch (2020) follows the emended dating.

[27] For more on the centrality of harmony to Pythagoreanism, see Andrew Barker (2014).

[28] Thesleff (1965: 142.12–43.9), trans. Levin in Pomeroy (1975). Pomeroy claims that *sôphrosynê* was originally a distinctly feminine virtue that Pythagoreans and Socratics extended to include men (2013: 71).

Here the author is not satisfied just to offer moral platitudes (to use Deslauriers' phrase) but is instead compelled to justify her assertions by providing evidence. The harmonious woman must be wise in the area of virtue, and this seems to be true in at least three ways. First, if she is wise, she will be just and courageous, which implies that wisdom is sufficient for virtue.[29] Second, wisdom will free her from being controlled by others (besides her husband, one assumes): she will not need to rely on the wisdom of others and so will be self-sufficient. Third, as a wise person she will see through the empty opinions of others and so will not be influenced by them. While this text is addressed to women, it seems the same points could be made for the value of wisdom in a man, viz. that it inculcates virtue and self-sufficiency, even if the way these virtues manifest might have been thought to differ. The harmonious woman must also be self-restrained, and this the author takes to be equivalent to a prohibition on extramarital relations. But while it may seem obvious that having extramarital relations will undermine harmony, Perictione again provides an argument: it is not merely that it will lead to conflict but that she will literally make herself an enemy of the members of the household by choosing instead to go to the bed of another. The process of becoming an enemy (*allotriôsis*) is the opposite of *oikeôsis*. If she is an enemy at war with the family then she is not a proper member of it: extramarital relations (on the part of the woman) are inconsistent with the existence of the household unit.

Pythagoreans also valued simplicity and understatement, a commitment Perictione affirms a few lines later (Thesleff 1965: 143.9–28).

> With regard to the sustenance and natural requirements of the body, it must be provided with a proper measure of clothing, bathing, anointing, hair-setting, and all those items of gold and precious stones that are used for adornment. For women who eat and drink all sorts of extravagant dishes and dress themselves sumptuously, wearing things that women are given to wearing, are decked out for seduction into all manner of vice, not only the bed but also the commission of other wrongful deeds .... To be consumers of goods from far-off lands or of items that cost a great amount of money or are highly esteemed is manifestly no small vice .... For the body desires merely not to be cold or, for the sake of appearances, naked; but it needs nothing else .... Therefore, a woman will neither cover herself with gold or the stone of India or of any other place, nor will she braid her hair with

---

[29] Notice also that Perictione explicitly says a woman should be courageous, a virtue that is often reserved for men. Indeed, the word for courage, *andreia*, comes from the word for man as opposed to woman (*anêr*).

artful device; nor will she anoint herself with Arabian perfume; nor will she put white makeup on her face or rouge her cheeks or darken her brows and lashes or artfully dye her greying hair; nor will she bathe a lot. For by pursuing these things a woman seeks to make a spectacle (*thêêtêra*) of female incontinence (*akrasiês gunaikêiês*). The beauty that comes from wisdom and not from these things brings pleasure to women who are well born.[30]

As attested in later texts, modesty is a general commitment of the Pythagoreans, but it is here addressed to women in particular.[31] Women should have a 'proper measure' of the necessities: they should not eat or drink excessively and should dress moderately. Again, the author does not rest on mere assertion and instead provides argument. Fancy dress attracts men and might lead to indiscretion, which above we saw to be destructive to harmony. Moreover, such items are expensive and unnecessary. But Perictione also appeals to a very general principle in defence of her position. The body, she says, desires only to be clothed and free of the cold. Any more specific desires for fancy or expensive clothing do not originate with the body and so are signs of disorder in the soul. The claim that the body itself has desires (albeit limited ones) could be fruitfully contrasted with Plato's view in *Phaedo* that it is not the body but the soul that desires: while some pleasures are 'concerned with service of the body' (*peri to sôma therapeias*), it is the soul that either desires those pleasures or – in the case of the philosopher – does not (64d).[32] Perhaps there is an Epicurean influence here: Epicurus describes flesh as crying out not to be hungry, thirsty, or cold (*VS* 33).[33] Perictione continues, 'by pursuing these things a woman seeks to make a spectacle'. Since the author accepts the principle that the body only seeks to be clothed and warm, she concludes that any other goods one seeks, one seeks not out of need but for attention. The question remains whether this attention will be positive or negative: while 'spectacle' suggests negative attention, the Greek *thêêtêra* carries no such implication. The final sentence of the quoted passage – 'the beauty that comes from wisdom and not from these things brings pleasure to women who are well born' – implies that seeking attention for anything besides one's wisdom and the goods that wisdom brings is incontinent,

---

[30] Thesleff (1965:143.9–28).
[31] For modesty as a commitment of the Pythagoreans, see, for instance, *Golden Verses* 34–38; Iambl. *VP* 20.
[32] See also *Alcibiades* 129–30, where Socrates identifies the person with the soul and compares the body to inanimate tools used by craftspeople.
[33] Also note that the Pythagorean woman despises 'empty opinion', which could be an allusion to Epicurus' classification of some desires as based on empty opinion. Thanks to David Konstan for calling my attention to the possible Epicurean elements of the letter.

and we see that reflected in the sentence before: the woman so-adorned does not merely make a spectacle of herself but of her incontinence.

Exhortations like these fit squarely in the tradition of ancient philosophy when it is understood as grounded in determining how one ought to live.[34] According to this interpretation, much of post-Socratic ancient philosophy is focused on value theory. What ought to matter to us and how much? As rational beings, we should not blindly or unreflectively structure our desires but should instead engage in a conscious and intentional effort to get things right. We see Perictione doing just that in this treatise. When Plato, Aristotle, and the Stoics raise such questions, they do so from the standpoint of free men engaged in public activity, and as such the desires to be interrogated vary, but for a woman living a largely private life, dress and sexual mores loom large.

Sexual indiscretion is also the topic of Theano's letter to Nicostrate, but here the indiscretion is committed by the husband.[35] The author's advice is conciliatory but is again rooted in claims about what is good for the household:

> For the moral excellence (*aretê*) of the wife is not surveillance of her husband but companionable accommodation (*sumperiphora*); it is in the spirit of accommodation to bear his folly. If he associates with the courtesan with a view towards pleasure, he associates with his wife with a view towards the beneficial (*sumpheron*). It is beneficial not to compound evils with evils and not to augment folly with folly.[36]

Here the author exploits a connection between the wife's role as a companion to the husband and her aim as seeking to benefit her husband and the household. The author goes on to claim that since the courtesan excites pleasure in the man, her allure will only last as long as he is impassioned (Thesleff 1965: 199.8–11).

> Recognize the fact that he goes to the courtesan in order to be frivolous, but that he abides with you in order to share a common life (*sumbiôsonta pareinai*); that he loves you on the basis of good judgment (*kata gnômên*), but her on the basis of passion (*tô pathei*). The moment for this is brief. It almost coincides with its own satisfaction.

This argument turns on the conception of pleasure as a *pathos* (and accordingly temporary), while, on the other hand, determining what is beneficial requires judgement. Moreover, determining what is beneficial

---

[34] See, for instance, Hadot (1987); Cooper (2012).   [35] Thesleff (1965: 198–200).
[36] Thesleff (1965: 198.35–99.3), trans. Harper in Waithe (1987b).

requires a full conception of what is valuable in life and how one can best acquire those goods. Here it is suggested that ignoring your husband's passions will ultimately be for the best, for they are short-lived.[37]

A text purportedly by Aesara is even clearer about the importance of a harmonious household for a good life, and for a just city:[38]

> Human nature seems to me to provide a standard of law and justice both for the home and for the city. By following the tracks within himself whoever seeks will make a discovery: law is in him and justice, which is the orderly arrangement (*diakosmasis*) of the soul. Being threefold, it is organised in accordance with triple functions: that which effects judgment and thoughtfulness (*phronasin*) is [the mind], that which effects strength and ability is [high spirit], and all that effects love and kindliness is desire (*epithumia*). These are all so disposed relatively to one other, that the best part is in command, the most inferior is governed, and the one in between holds a middle place; it both governs and is governed. The god thus contrived these things according to principle in both the outline and completion of the human dwelling place (*tô anthrôpinô skaneôs*), because he intended man alone to become a recipient of law and justice, and none other of mortal animals.[39]

This provides an interesting counterpoint to Plato's arguments in *Republic*. Whereas Plato wants to disband the household in the guardian class in order to combat social divisions, Aesara sees the same natural order in the household as Plato finds in the city and in the individual soul.

---

[37] For a counterpoint to the view that *pathê* cannot be usefully leveraged in the quest to figure out what is beneficial, one could contrast Aristotle's views on moral development. According to Aristotle's picture of moral development, as described especially in *Nicomachean Ethics* 2.3, pleasure as a *pathos* is essential to moral development and precedes (and determines) what arguments one will respond to regarding what is good or beneficial for us. It is for this reason that we need a proper upbringing before we begin studying ethics. Finding pleasure in what one ought not to feel pleasure in will develop a bad character but, correspondingly, learning through habituation from a young age to take pleasure in what one ought to is what allows us to become virtuous and to judge what is truly beneficial.

[38] Thesleff (1965: 48–50). Thesleff conjectures the author is actually a male, Aresas of Lucania, on the basis of two emendations, but he later changed his mind, and most subsequent interpreters do not follow him; see Pomeroy (2013: 99) for references and Dutsch (2020: 123 n. 27) for a perspective more sympathetic to Thesleff's earlier view.

[39] Thesleff (1965: 48.22–49.11), trans. Harper in Waithe (1987b). Waithe takes this letter to be proto-feminist: 'If we assume, as did the Pythagoreans, that women bore the responsibility for creating harmony and justice in the home … then so-called "women's work" was the moral equivalent of "men's work". This is because justice in both arenas has the same natural foundation in the nature of the human soul. Just, harmonious cities require their component parts, households, also to be just and harmonious' (Waithe 1987b: 25).

Aesara goes on to observe that the unity of the parts comes precisely from their diversity: the parts of the soul, and of the city and household, must be different but complementary (Thesleff 1965: 49.11–21).

> A composite unity of association could not come about from a single thing, nor indeed from several which are all alike . . . . Nor could such a unity come from several dissimilar things at random, but rather, from parts formed in accordance with the completion and organization and fitting together of the entire composite whole. Not only is the soul composed from several dissimilar parts, these being fashioned in conformity with the whole and complete, but in addition these are not arranged haphazardly and at random, but in accordance with rational attention.

When Plato introduces the parts of soul, his analytical test for parthood looks for conflict, for he says where there is conflict there must be two different parts (*Rep.* 436b–c). This approach leads him to focus on cases where the parts are in disagreement and so not unified, but Aesara here calls attention to a feature of the unified soul: if it is to be well-ordered there must be a diversity of roles. This diversity does not require disagreement per se, but emphasising it does call attention to the importance not just of agreement among the parts but also to the fact that the different parts perform different roles.[40]

Much more can be said about the philosophical content of these and other texts, but my goal in this section has been to show that they present arguments that have as their goal the establishment of households that can best ground happy human lives. If Plato thinks we can do without households – and Aristotle, as we will see in the next section, only considers the household from the standpoint of the master of the house – then, according to these texts, they are missing aspects of life that have much influence over the development and maintenance of character in members of the household. According to the interpretation of ancient philosophy as a way of life, it can be argued that the pseudepigraphic works by women are a corrective for an overly myopic view of what matters. They can improve and contribute to the debate even if we think a full, careful, and idealised discussion of the household would lead to a less divided conception of the roles of husband and wife than we find in these letters.

---

[40] This is not to say that Plato is unaware of the importance of complementarity in the soul: his definition of justice as each part doing its own work relies on such a conception, and he does stress the importance of diversity in role in the analogous case of the city. Even so, his proof for there being different parts is rooted in the possibility of disagreement and conflict, and, as such, the examples at the end of *Rep.* 4 focus on the harms of divisiveness and the benefits of unity, not on the complementary nature of the parts.

Aristotle's Household

Like Aesara, Aristotle thinks of the household as composed of diverse parts, but unlike her, he takes this to show that the household (and the city) is not a true unity. In his discussion of Plato's proposal in the *Republic* to raise children in common, Aristotle highlights what he calls Socrates' 'assumption that it is best for a city-state to be as far as possible all one unit' (1261a15–16, cf. *Rep.* 462a). He claims that taking that assumption to its logical conclusion would destroy the *polis* (1261a16–22):

> And yet it is evident that the more of a unity a city-state becomes, the less of a city-state it will be. For a city-state naturally consists of a certain multitude; and as it becomes more of a unity, it will turn from a city-state into a household, and from a household into a human being .... Hence, even if someone could achieve this, it should not be done, since it will destroy the city-state.[41]

In Aesara, we find that the well-ordered whole cannot be understood apart from its rationally structured parts. Each has an essential role to play, and this is as true of the parts of the household as it is the parts of the city and in the individual soul. To focus on one part to the exclusion of the others is to give not just an incomplete account but an incorrect one. Aristotle's claim here that there is no unity in diversity points in a different direction: if the aspects of the city (and of the household) do not form a unity, then it would seem that they can be studied apart from each other, in which case some parts (viz. the female perspective) he might think to be of limited probative value. But for Aesara, in order to understand a city, you must study all of its proper and complementary parts, and the same is true of the household.

And indeed, this is what we find when we turn to Aristotle's remarks about the household, which focus exclusively on the husband/master's role. As is reflected by his discussion in Book 2, he views the city as a composite (*suntheton*) of disparate elements. Since he rejects the Socratic proposal to disband households, one of the elements of the city will be the household. Indeed, it is the first subject of discussion in *Politics*. Since the city is a composite, Aristotle says we must start by analysing the parts (1252a18–23). He next mentions two sorts of natural relationship: that

---

[41] Trans. Reeve (1998). Although Aristotle has mere diversity in number in mind here, in his very next sentence he points also to diversity in roles: 'A city-state consists not only of a number of people, but of people of different kinds, since a city-state does not come from people who are alike' (1261a22–24).

between a husband and a wife (which he says arises of necessity for procreation rather than by *prohairesis*, choice) and that between a master and a slave (1252a26–34). While he claims that these are two fundamentally different kinds of relationship (1252a34–b5), he does not make much of the distinction, instead collapsing it by observing that 'the first thing to emerge from these two communities is a household' (1252b9–10). It is immediately clear that his discussion of the household will assume the standpoint of the master of the house, for he goes on to illustrate his point by citing Hesiod: 'Hesiod is right when he said in his poem, "first and foremost: a house, a wife, and an ox for the plough"' (1252b10–12). When he gets around to the details about a page later, he describes the subject to be discussed not as the household (*oikon*) but as household management (*oikonomia*) (1253b1–2), and he takes the acquisition of wealth (a male enterprise at the time) to be an aspect of the subject (1253b12–13).

It is not hard to figure out why he has a blind spot for the role of the wife (and the slave): for him, the *polis* is primarily about exercising rule, not being subject to it. Later in Book 1, he says that while free men must take turns ruling over the city, they are naturally rulers (1259b4–10):

> In most cases of rule of a statesman, it is true, people take turns at ruling and being ruled, because they tend by nature to be on an equal footing and to differ in nothing. Nevertheless, whenever one person is ruling and another being ruled, the one ruling tries to distinguish himself in demeanour, title, or rank from the ruled.... Male is permanently related to female in this way.

In the *Eudemian Ethics* – where Aristotle describes man as not just a political animal but also a household-managing animal (*oikonomikon zôon*) (1242a23) – he describes a husband's friendship with his wife as based on utility, and in the *Nicomachean Ethics* we learn that utility friendships are more unstable and often derive from relationships among contraries (*EN* 1159b12–14). Thus, it seems that to learn more about the wife will tell us little about the husband who is the focus of Aristotle's theorising.

Despite all this, Aristotle himself seems to agree that a full account of the city-state will require a discussion of that role. At the end of *Politics* 1.1260b8–20, he says:

> As for man and woman, father and children, the virtue relevant to each of them, what is good in their relationship with one another and what is not good, and how to achieve the good and avoid the bad, it will be necessary to go through all these in connection with the constitutions. For every

household is part of a city-state, these are parts of a household, and the virtue of a part must be determined by looking to the virtue of the whole. Hence both women and children must be educated with an eye to the constitution, if indeed it makes any difference to the virtue of a city-state that its children be virtuous, and its women too. And it must make a difference, since half the free population are women, and from children come those who participate in the constitution.

Nonetheless, as Reeve observes in a footnote, 'No full discussion of these topics appears in the *Politics* as we have it' (1998: 24, n. 84).

In this section, we have seen that the household is an important subject for philosophical analysis in Aristotle. Similar observations could be made about Plato, especially in *Republic* 3–4 and *Laws* 3 and 6–8. But despite the fact that he seems to have recognised a lacuna, Aristotle's discussion of the household is a discussion of household management. He largely ignores the complementary roles of the other members of the household, focusing instead on the master of the house. The extant texts purportedly by Pythagorean women take up these neglected topics. *Contra* Deslauriers, the topic of these texts is recognisably philosophical, even if the angle they take on it is a neglected one. In fact, *especially* since the angle is neglected while the topic is philosophical, these texts have philosophical and pedagogical value.

Conclusion

Still, the texts leave much to be desired from a modern perspective. It seems that this is what troubles Deslauriers more than anything: in her essay she frequently notes that the contents support the status quo in a way that is harmful to women's interests. But the philosophy written by men at that time, and indeed throughout human history, has also often undermined women's interests, yet we still teach it in our philosophy courses. In our (necessarily selective) examination of the treatises and letters purportedly by Pythagorean women, we have seen that these texts often appeal to the very same virtues as those highlighted in ancient philosophy as written by men. However, it is often the case that the way the virtue is taken to manifest differs from its use in canonical philosophical texts because of the woman's role in the household and the male orientation of the canonical texts. In particular, the Pythagorean women's treatises and letters frequently turn to the topic of sexual mores. The often-abrupt shift and the tendency to focus on modesty and pleasing one's husband tend to distract us from the philosophical content of the letters, but they actually offer a powerful pedagogical tool. After all, it is not only these female-centred texts that shift from general considerations of value and virtue to topics of interest to a select audience: as we have seen with the example of Aristotle, he too moves from general considerations to a specific context, but his is the context of the 'ruler' of the house – and, further, man's public-facing role in the city. Why should these contexts be any riper for philosophical reflection than those in which women of the time found themselves? Here we can see how philosophy becomes the domain of men insofar as it comes to be taken as an assumption that only public-facing roles are up for philosophical consideration. Diversifying ancient philosophy requires that we challenge that assumption. Indeed, as we have seen, leaving out the perspective of female members leads to an incomplete account of the household.

Of course, this is not to say that we cannot wish that women of the time had more and varied socially respectable options in how they chose to manifest their virtue, and there is something decidedly disappointing about the abrupt transition from virtue to sexual mores. In a pedagogical context, a good teacher can probe that sense of disappointment and can use it to prompt discussions about the prospects of women even up to the present day. In what other directions would we have liked the letters to go, after their forceful openings and their appeals to universal virtues? And how much progress have we made since then?

Aristotle largely ignores the perspective of the wife because he thinks of her as only ruled and never a ruler. There are two ways we could respond: (1) we could challenge the premise that women are naturally submissive and meant to be ruled over; or (2) we can emphasise that everyone is ruled over sometimes and that as such much of what is important in life and in moral development is left out when we ignore issues that arise from that standpoint. These are not mutually exclusive options, so I hope in our rush to establish (1) we do not follow Aristotle in forgetting the importance of (2).[42]

---

[42] Thank you to the contributors to this volume, who read and commented on an earlier draft. Thanks especially to the editors, Katharine O'Reilly and Caterina Pellò, for their detailed comments and also to Sukaina Hirji, David Konstan, Marko Malink, Susan Sauvé Meyer, Phil Mitsis, Jessica Moss, John J. Mulhern, David Murphy, Debra Nails, Sarah Pomeroy, Maria Victoria Salazar, Iakovos Vasiliou, Denise Vigani, and Katja Vogt. This project was supported by grants from the Mellon Foundation, PSC-CUNY, and the CUNY Research Foundation.

CHAPTER 8

Perictione, Mother of Metaphysics
A New Philosophical Reading of On Wisdom

Giulia De Cesaris and Caterina Pellò[*]

This chapter focuses on *On Wisdom*, a metaphysical and epistemological treatise preserved in Stobaeus' *Anthology* and ascribed to a Pythagorean woman named Perictione.

In the two available fragments, Perictione makes two key statements: first, the purpose and function of a human being is the contemplation of the nature of all things. Second, wisdom is the highest-ranked human activity, for it enables us to grasp all kinds of things that are and brings us closer to the divine. This claim is supported by introducing a novel tripartition of theoretical sciences, where human wisdom is placed at the very top. *On Wisdom* is thus the first metaphysical and epistemological treatise ascribed to a female author in the ancient Greek philosophical tradition. As such, the treatise should receive more, and more thorough, attention.

The study of *On Wisdom* raises two main difficulties. First, the treatise belongs to a corpus of Hellenistic and post-Hellenistic texts written under the names of early Pythagorean philosophers. These writings are most likely apocryphal and aimed at portraying Pythagoras as a forerunner of Platonism and Aristotelianism. Specifically, the fact that *On Wisdom* is attributed to a woman philosopher bearing the same name as Plato's mother makes its authenticity dubious. Second, and most importantly, Perictione's *On Wisdom* shows substantial textual overlap with another pseudepigraphic text, also titled *On Wisdom*, but ascribed to the Pythagorean Archytas and preserved in Iamblichus' *Protrepticus*. Scholars

---

[*] Both authors contributed to the chapter at all stages. De Cesaris is primarily responsible for the commentary to Frs. 1 and 2.b and the conclusive remarks. Pellò is responsible for the introduction and the commentary to Fr. 2a. This study was initially presented at the Oxford 'Women Intellectuals in Antiquity' Symposium in collaboration with Phillip Horky. We are grateful to him and the conference participants for their feedback. We would also like to thank Dorota Dutsch, Constantinos Macris, Jan Opsomer, Katharine O'Reilly, Alessio Santoro, Angela Ulacco, and the contributors to this volume for their comments on an earlier draft.

have thus taken the two fragments quoted by Stobaeus in the fifth century to be part of ps-Archytas' text, rather than Perictione's.[1]

Our aim is to offer a philosophical reading of the arguments in *On Wisdom* and reclaim a place for Perictione in the history of Greek philosophy. We begin with some methodological considerations. First, we review the available evidence about Perictione, Plato's mother, to whom *On Wisdom* is ascribed. Then, we address the pseudonymity issue and the question of the relationship between this text and ps-Archytas'. While scholars have traditionally been halted by the issues of dating and attribution, we show how these barriers should not prevent us from engaging with the philosophical content of the text. The central section of the chapter is devoted to a close analysis of the surviving fragments of *On Wisdom*, with special focus on the triadic conception of theoretical sciences, which is unique to this treatise. In the conclusion, we advance a suggestion as to the originality of Perictione's *On Wisdom* in relation to ps-Archytas'.

Perictione and the Pythagorean Women

The available evidence for Perictione is limited. Except for Stobaeus, none of our sources identify Perictione as a Pythagorean. Her name is not listed among Pythagoras' disciples in Iamblichus' *Catalogue of the Pythagoreans* (*VP* 267)[2] and is only attested in Athens[3] in connection with Plato's mother.

The texts mentioning Perictione are twofold: some generally mention her as part of Plato's lineage, whereas others specifically focus on the event of Plato's conception.[4] The reports differ in detail. Yet they all agree in three respects: Perictione's husband Ariston once attempted to have intercourse with her but did not succeed due to Apollo's intervention; Perictione was a virgin; and, most importantly, Apollo was Plato's biological father.[5] Since Pythagoras was also believed to be the son of a virgin

---

[1] We refer to the author of the fragments quoted by Iamblichus as ps-Archytas to distinguish him from the fourth-century Pythagorean philosopher from Tarentum. By contrast, we refer to the author of the fragments quoted by Stobaeus as Perictione, although we do not take this to be the same person as Plato's mother.
[2] This, however, is also the case for other authors of the Pythagorean pseudepigrapha.
[3] See Macris (2012).
[4] All sources concerning Plato's divine birth are collected by Riginos (1976: 9–32).
[5] According to Origen (*Cels.* 6.8), the sexual intercourse between Apollo and Perictione was recounted by most Platonists in their biographies of Plato. The story most likely originated in Athens among

mother and Apollo,[6] these stories draw an initial connection between Perictione and Pythagoreanism. Attributing *On Wisdom* to Perictione, then, appears as a textual strategy to bridge the gap between Plato and the Pythagoreans. By picturing Plato as the son of a Pythagorean woman, the treatise establishes a direct biological connection between the two philosophical traditions.

Stobaeus attributes two texts to Perictione: *On the Harmonious Woman*, written in Ionic and focused on female virtues, and the Doric treatise *On Wisdom*.[7] The dating of these texts is debated, but the consensus view is that they were written between the first century BCE and the first century CE (Macris 2012). The Hellenistic and the Imperial Age are characterised by the production and circulation of a large collection of writings about metaphysics, logic, cosmology, ethics, and politics, authored under the pseudonyms of ancient Pythagorean philosophers.[8] Most importantly for the purpose of this chapter, this corpus includes ten letters and four treatises ascribed to Pythagorean women, the majority of which discuss women-related topics such as female virtues, married life, childrearing, home economics, and the role of women in society.[9] This raises a plethora of questions: are the texts truly written by women philosophers? In the case of Perictione, is the author named after Plato's mother or is (s)he using a pseudonym? If the latter, is the pay-off of writing under the authority of the mother of Plato greater than that of writing under the name of a woman philosopher?

Whether these texts were authored by women or rather by men using female pseudonyms is a point of controversy. Pomeroy, for example, suggests that, since the pseudepigrapha address an audience of women, they are more likely to be the work of female authors (2013: 49–53).[10]

Plato's immediate successors. Both Diogenes Laertius (3.2) and Jerome (*Adv. Iov.* 1.42) identify Speusippus as the earliest source.

[6] At least until Iamblichus, who rejects the accounts of Pythagoras' miraculous birth (*VP* 5–8).
[7] Because of the differences in style and content, some scholars attribute the texts to two different authors named Perictione (Waithe 1987b: 19–58; Pomeroy 2013: 49).
[8] Most scholars refer to these writings as Pseudopythagorean to highlight the discontinuities from the early Pythagorean tradition (e.g., Centrone 1990; Zhmud 2019). We follow Horky and refer to these writings as Pythagorean pseudepigrapha (2015: 21–22) to emphasise that they were not written by the named authors but leave open the question of their relationship with Pythagoreanism, a discussion of which is beyond the scope of this chapter.
[9] For a study of the Pythagorean women's letters, see Twomey in this volume (Chapter 7).
[10] Pomeroy identifies the authors as women named after or writing under the pseudonyms of their Pythagorean predecessors. By contrast, Waithe believes that the texts are eponymous – that is, written by the named author – and that the author of *On the Harmonious Woman* is in fact Plato's mother (1987b: 19–74). Female authorship is also defended by Wider (1986); Nails (1989: 291–97); Plant (2004: 68–91); and Montepaone (2011).

Conversely, Deslauriers argues that in antiquity it was customary for men to write under female pseudonyms with the aim of educating female pupils (2012: 343–45). Both arguments for and against the possibility of women authors rely on the claim that the Pythagorean women's texts are written for and about women. Some of these writings, however, do not focus on the female gender. For example, Aesara's *On Human Nature* proposes a new version of the Platonic tripartition of the soul and, as we shall see, Perictione's treatise discusses the value of wisdom in comparison with other theoretical sciences. These two texts challenge the assumption that in antiquity women were only reputed to be experts on the female gender, domestic virtues, and family life: the pseudepigrapha also ventured into epistemological and metaphysical speculations about the laws of the cosmos, the soul, and science.

So far, there is no conclusive case against or in favour of ascribing *On Wisdom* to a woman philosopher. The reader might then expect us to tackle the issue of the identity of its author. Our plan, however, is to take a different approach. Since the pseudonymity question is the issue most scholars tend to discuss and thus has been a great barrier to our engagement with the philosophical significance of the writings ascribed to the Pythagorean women, we shall leave this debate aside and open a route to the analysis of their arguments. Regardless of who the original author is, *On Wisdom* is the first text claiming to express the metaphysical and epistemological views of a woman. Our question is what these views are.

There is another, more challenging problem still left unsolved: the overlap between ps-Archytas' and Perictione's *On Wisdom*. Various options can be envisioned. First, Iamblichus and Stobaeus may be using two independent texts, one written under Archytas' name and the other under Perictione's. This seems unlikely given that portions of the texts are otherwise almost identical. Conversely, Stobaeus may quote excerpts from ps-Archytas' *On Wisdom* but attribute the text to Perictione. This, too, seems unlikely: the *Anthology* includes several quotations from ps-Archytas and it is unclear why Stobaeus would only question the authorship of *On Wisdom*. Alternatively, the text may have been ascribed to Perictione originally and then to Archytas in the *Protrepticus*. This is more likely, for ps-Archytas is credited with a larger number of pseudepigrapha, many of which are quoted by Iamblichus. Yet the direct link with Plato makes Perictione an equally effective pseudo-author. Finally, Iamblichus and Stobaeus might be reading the same anonymous treatise, which they ascribe to Archytas and Perictione, respectively. We shall return to this debate in the conclusion.

Overall, given the parallel with ps-Archytas, and since *On Wisdom* does not discuss women-related topics, neither scholars of Hellenistic Pythagoreanism nor scholars working on the Pythagorean women have taken the content of Perictione's treatise into serious consideration. Some scholars use the fragments to complement ps-Archytas' treatise (Horky 2015),[11] but none of them allows for the possibility that the text preserved by Stobaeus should be studied in its own right. Again, while we do not commit to saying that the author of *On Wisdom* was a woman, we suspect that the attribution to a female author is one of the reasons why its philosophical content was overlooked, and thus we propose to study it in more depth.

On Human Wisdom

To facilitate our analysis, we arrange the discussion of Perictione's *On Wisdom* into three thematic sections: an introductory section on Perictione's initial statements concerning wisdom (Fr. 1), a section focused on the relationship wisdom entertains with other sciences (Fr. 2a, 6–14), and a concluding section on the importance of attaining wisdom (Fr. 2b, 15–22). On Stobaeus' account, Perictione's *On Wisdom* begins as follows (Stobaeus 3.1.120, 146.2–5 Thesleff):[12]

Fr. 1: 1. Περικτιόνης Πυθαγορείας
2. Περὶ σοφίας.[13] Γέγονε δὲ καὶ συνέστα ὁ ἄνθρωπος ποττὸ θεωρῆσαι
3. τὸν λόγον τᾶς τῶ ὅλω[14] φύσιος· καὶ τᾶς σοφίας ἔργον ἐστὶν αὐτὸ τοῦτο
4. κτήσασθαι καὶ θεωρῆσαι τὰν τῶν ἐόντων φρόνασιν.

Perictione the Pythagorean, *On Wisdom*: The human has been born and is constituted for the purpose of contemplating the reason of the nature of the universe; and the function of wisdom is this very thing: to obtain and contemplate the intelligence of the things that are.[15]

---

[11] It should be noted that in our panel at the 'Women Intellectuals in Antiquity' Symposium, Horky argued for the original attribution of the text to Perictione.
[12] Although significantly revised, our translation of Perictione's fragment is indebted to Horky (2015).
[13] Stobaeus introduces Perictione's *On the Harmonious Woman* with a slightly different formulation: Περικτιόνης Πυθαγορείας ἐκ τοῦ Περὶ γυναικὸς ἁρμονίας ('Perictione the Pythagorean from *On the Harmonious Woman*', Stob. 4.28.19, 142.17–18 Thesleff). Since both formulations are interchangeably used by Stobaeus (see ps-Arch. *De Vir. Bon*, Fr. 9, Stob. 3.1.195, 13.13 Thesleff, and Fr. 12, Stob. 4.50.28, 14.18 Thesleff), this does not offer any conclusive insight about the texts. For a detailed study of Stobaeus' *lemmata* in the *Anthology*, see Piccione (1999). On Stobaeus' style, see Reydams-Schils (2011).
[14] τῶ ὅλω is suggested by Hense on the basis of Iamblichus' text, although Mss. MdABr report τῶν ὅλων, thus stressing the comprehensive totality of the *objects* in the world (Thesleff 1965: 146). The alternative option would not bring substantial changes to our interpretation.
[15] This is repeated almost verbatim in ps-Archytas' *On Wisdom* (Fr. 3, 44.17–20 Thesleff): καὶ τᾶς σοφίας ὧν ἔργον <κτᾶσθαι> καὶ θεωρὲν τὰν τῶν ἐόντων φρόνασιν.

Despite their conciseness, these opening lines of Fr. 1 provide us with a very meaningful beginning. Perictione's first statement is that the purpose of human beings is to contemplate the reason of the nature of the universe.

Line 2: Perictione employs two different verbs (γίγνομαι and συνίστημι) to describe the constitution of human beings and explain the relationship they have with their purpose. The employment of two verbs may be explained simply as a way to strengthen the importance of being directed towards their end for human beings. Yet not only is Perictione using two different verbs but also two tenses: a perfect (γέγονε) and an aorist (συνέστα). One way to do justice to this distinction is to understand the two verbs (and tenses) as stressing different aspects of how human beings receive and relate to their purpose. The end of human beings is both something naturally belonging to them (γίγνομαι) and that for which human beings are constructed (συνίστημι). If so, we may take the different tenses to strengthen these nuances:[16] the perfect expresses that this is the present end of the human being *qua* human being, whereas the aorist highlights how human beings were *structured* in view of such end and granted the capacities to fulfil it.

Speaking of humans as *constituted* conveys the idea of a cosmological dimension in which human beings, or at least their rational faculties, were put together by the gods or a demiurge.[17] This would then echo Aristotle's *Protrepticus*.

> Καλῶς ἄρα κατά γε τοῦτον τὸν λόγον Πυθαγόρας εἴρηκεν ὡς ἐπὶ τὸ γνῶναί τε καὶ θεωρῆσαι πᾶς ἄνθρωπος ὑπὸ τοῦ θεοῦ συνέστηκεν.
>
> Hence Pythagoras, according to this argument, was right to say that every human being has been constructed by the god for the sake of knowing and to contemplate.[18]

Aristotle ascribes to Pythagoras the claim that humans are crafted for the purpose of contemplating.[19] This offers a possible reason for linking *On Wisdom* to Perictione the Pythagorean (as well as Archytas): the author of this pseudepigraphic treatise could have taken the opportunity to expand

---

[16] This is also suggested by the connective particles δὲ καί.
[17] This is the case in ps-Archytas (*Wisdom* Fr. 2, 44.5–15 Thesleff).
[18] Ar. *Protr.*, in Iambl. *Protr.* 52.6–8 Pistelli. While we suspect that Aristotle's *Protrepticus* may help elucidate several issues raised by Perictione's (and ps-Archytas') *On Wisdom*, a thorough analysis of the interconnections between these works is beyond the scope of this chapter. All translations from Aristotle's *Protrepticus* are by Hutchinson and Johnson (2017).
[19] See also Ar. *Protr.*, in Iambl. *Protr.* 39.23–40.1 Pistelli: 'It is clear that the intelligent man will choose most of all to be intelligent (τὸ φρονεῖν); for this is the function (ἔργον) of that capacity. Hence it is evident that ... intelligence (φρόνησις) is the most superior good thing. So, one must not flee from philosophy, since philosophy is ... both a possession and a use of wisdom (**κτῆσίς** τε καὶ **χρῆσις** σοφίας)'.

on Pythagoras' quote, as reported and validated by Aristotle, and develop the Pythagorean views concerning the purpose of human beings and the role of wisdom.

Lines 2–3: Let us now turn to the proper object of contemplation: τὸν λόγον τᾶς τῶ ὅλω φύσιος, 'the reason of the nature of the whole'. Compared with the effectiveness of the opening line of the fragment, the statement concerning the object of the human end sounds a bit verbose. However, it may be that for Perictione these three aspects (λόγος, φύσις, τὸ ὅλον) are *all* of crucial importance for defining the purpose of human beings. The chain of genitives suggests the following: the universe in which we live must be considered as a complete whole (ὅλον), and it is only insofar as we consider the nature (φύσις) of the whole *qua* a comprehensive totality that we can contemplate its rationale (λόγος).[20] If so, the text appears to give prominence to the unity of the world in which we live[21] and to the way in which we are to approach its nature: when we consider the nature of the world as a whole, we are able to understand its rationale and contemplate it. This is our purpose as human beings, and we have been constituted so as to be able to fulfil it.

Lines 3–4: Wisdom is finally introduced. Rather than clarifying what wisdom (σοφία) is, Perictione introduces it by means of its function. Despite the absence of grammatical coordination between the two statements, the sudden introduction of the job (ἔργον) of wisdom suggests that Perictione is proposing some sort of functionalist argument about what humans (and wisdom) do.[22] Should the two statements be understood as a part of the same argument, we propose the following charitable reconstruction:

(i) Human beings have been born and are constituted to contemplate the rationale of the nature of the world.
(ii) [supplied] Human beings can attain wisdom.

---

[20] Note that the contemplation mentioned in the fragment is not of *things* directly but of their rationale (λόγος). We translate λόγος with 'reason', following Horky, given that we lack the broader context of Perictione's fragment. However, given the importance other pseudepigrapha grant to language, Perictione might be thinking of λόγος as the propositional articulation of a content. See ps-Arch. *Intell.* (Stob 1.41.5, 36.13–39.25 Thesleff); *Wisdom* Fr. 2 (44.8–13 Thesleff); *Univ. Log.* (especially 22.10–12 Thesleff).

[21] See Pl. *Grg.* 508a3–4, where some unnamed sages (οἱ σοφοί), arguably to be identified with Pythagoreans, refer to the whole of humans, heaven, earth, etc. as the universe (τὸ ὅλον τοῦτο ... κόσμον καλοῦσιν).

[22] Phintys, too, offers a functionalist argument (Dutsch 2020: 154–70).

(iii) The function of wisdom is:
(a) To obtain *and* (b) to contemplate the intelligence of the things that are.
That is, [supplied] Wisdom grants human beings an access to the intelligence (φρόνησις)[23] of the things that are and enables them to contemplate it.

Conclusion: [supplied] Human beings can fulfil their purpose (see [i]) by means of wisdom.[24]

We do not take this reconstruction to be conclusive, especially since some premises are implicit and it is not clear which premise is supposed to have more argumentative force. Depending on which claim one takes to be prior, the text offers two different arguments. If we take (ii) to have more argumentative strength, the passage recalls a weaker version of the function argument grounded in the biological capacities of the human being. Since human beings are equipped with the capacity to attain wisdom, and since the function of wisdom is to obtain and contemplate the intelligence of things, the human aim is to perform such a function to the maximum degree, by contemplating the whole of nature. However, given the order in which the claims are introduced, we find it more plausible that (i) should rule over (ii). On this reading, we have an argument that relies on the purpose of human beings: since human beings are constituted for the purpose of contemplating, they also have the capacities to accomplish it (i.e., they can attain wisdom).

What the function of wisdom precisely consists in is yet to be determined. Perictione uses two different verbs to illustrate this: κτήσασθαι and θεωρῆσαι. Contemplation holds a key role, as it serves both as the purpose of the human being and as the function of wisdom. Yet if we take Aristotle's *Protrepticus* to provide a fruitful background to this fragment, the two verbs are more than just an hendiadys. Aristotle distinguishes

---

[23] Note that φρόνησις here does not seem to mean 'practical wisdom', which is taken to be its standard translation in Aristotle. Rather, φρόνησις appears to denote some intellectual content about the things that are. This may well have a practical import, but insofar as humans are supposed to *contemplate* it, it is also theoretical. For a similar view concerning φρόνησις in Aristotle, see Broadie (2019: 296–97). For a parallel passage by Plato, see *Phd.* 65a9. In Aristotle's *Protrepticus*, φρόνησις is both theoretical ('Therefore one should say that this kind of knowledge (ταύτην τὴν ἐπιστήμην – i.e., φρόνησις) is an observational one (θεωρητικήν τινα)', Ar. *Protr.*, in Iambl. *Protr.*, 43.18–19 Pistelli) and what allows us to live happily ('Thus, if happiness is intelligence (φρόνησις), it is evident that living successfully would belong to the philosophers alone', Ar. *Protr.*, in Iambl. *Protr.*, 60.1–2 Pistelli). For a discussion of φρόνησις in the Pythagorean pseudepigrapha, see Centrone (1990: 160–61).

[24] Horky (2015: 38) offers a similar reconstruction for ps-Archytas' treatise.

between *possessing a capacity* and actually *exercising* such a capacity.[25] With this in mind, κτήσασθαι and θεωρῆσαι may express two different aspects of the function of wisdom: first, wisdom grants human beings *access* to the intelligence of the things that are by allowing us to acquire its content; second, by active contemplation (of the intelligence of the things that are) wisdom allows human beings to fulfil their aim and grasp the rationale (λόγος) of the nature of the whole/universe. The question is why Perictione differentiates the intelligence of the things that are from the λόγος of the universe. Our suggestion is that the two mainly differ in scope: our aim as human beings is the comprehensive and unitary contemplation of the rationale of the whole.

The second fragment clarifies what it means for wisdom to be set over what is (146.6–17 Thesleff):

Fr. 2a: 6. Ἐν ταὐτῷ. Γαμετρία
7. μὲν ὦν καὶ ἀριθμητικὰ καὶ τἆλλα τὰ θεωρητικὰ καὶ ἐπιστῆμαι καὶ περὶ
8. τῶν ἐόντων κατασχολέονται, ἁ δὲ σοφία περὶ πάντα τὰ γένη τῶν ἐόντων.
9. οὕτως γὰρ ἔχει σοφία περὶ πάντα τὰ ἐόντα, ὡς ὄψις περὶ πάντα τὰ
10. ὁρατὰ καὶ ἀκοὴ περὶ πάντα τὰ ἀκουστά. τὰ δὲ συμβεβακότα τοῖς
11. ἐοῖσιν ἃ μὲν καθόλω πᾶσι συμβέβακεν, ἃ δὲ πλείστοις αὐτῶν, ἃ δὲ
12. πᾳ[26] ἑνὶ ἑκάστῳ. τὰ μὲν ὦν καθόλω πᾶσι συμβεβακότα συνιδὲν καὶ
13. θεωρῆσαι τᾶς σοφίας οἰκῆον, τὰ δὲ τοῖς πλείστοις τᾶς περὶ φύσιν
14. ἐπιστήμας, τὰ δ' ἴδια καθ' ἕκαστον τᾶς περί τι ἀφωρισμένον ἐπιστάμας.
15. καὶ διὰ τοῦτο σοφία μὲν τὰς τῶν ἐόντων ἁπάντων ἀρχὰς ἀνευρίσκει,
16. φυσικὰ δὲ τὰς τῶν φύσει γιγνομένων, γαμετρία δὲ καὶ ἀριθμητικὰ καὶ
17. μουσικὰ τὰς περὶ τὸ ποσὸν καὶ τὸ ἐμμελές.

In the same work: Then, geometry, too, as well as arithmetic and the other theoretical activities (i.e., the sciences),[27] engage with the things that are, but wisdom engages with all the kinds of the things that are. For wisdom relates

---

[25] See Ar. *Protr.*, in Iambl. *Protr.* 56.19–21 Pistelli: 'The word "living" seems to mean two things, one with reference to a capacity and the other with reference to an activity, for we call all those animals 'seeing' who have sight and are naturally capable of seeing ... as well as those who are using the capacity and are casting their sight. And similarly, with knowing and cognising (τὸ ἐπίστασθαι καὶ τὸ γιγνώσκειν) we mean, in one case, using and observing (ἓν μὲν τὸ χρῆσθαι καὶ **θεωρεῖν**) and, in the other case, possessing the capacity and having the knowledge (ἓν δὲ τὸ **κεκτῆσθαι** τὴν δύναμιν καὶ τὴν ἐπιστήμην ἔχειν).' Note that the *use* of the capacity – that is, the actual activity – is grouped together with contemplation.

[26] As an alternative to πᾳ, the manuscripts also propose παρά or περὶ ἑνὶ ἑκάστῳ ('about each one thing'). This formulation is closer to καθ' ἕκαστον in Line 14. See n. 39.

[27] Horky's translation, which combines θεωρητικὰ καὶ ἐπιστῆμαι into 'theoretical sciences', may be justified if one reads ἐπιστημονικά with Schow (Thesleff 1965: 148), supposes haplography on the part of either Stobaeus or the copyist (καὶ αἱ ἐπιστῆμαι), or takes the καί as a doublet of θεωρητικαί. Our proposed translation aims to emphasise the introduction of ἐπιστήμη, science, as a technical term to designate what was previously described as theoretical activity.

to all things that are, just as sight relates to all things that are visible and hearing to all things that are hearable. Moreover, as to what pertains to the things that are, some pertain universally to all, some to most of them, and others in some way to each one thing. Thus, it belongs to wisdom to behold and contemplate what pertains universally to all things, whereas it belongs to natural science to contemplate what pertains to most things, and to the science concerning something determinate to contemplate the peculiar attributes of each thing. And therefore, wisdom retrieves the principles of the things that are altogether, whereas physics retrieves the principles of what comes to be by nature, and geometry, arithmetic, and music retrieve the principles concerning quantity and the harmonious.

From the previous fragment, we learn that the ultimate end of human beings is the contemplation of the λόγος of the nature of all things, and the function of wisdom is to enable this process. Three questions remain open: what is wisdom (σοφία) in the context of Perictione's treatise? What is the object of its contemplation? And what is the value of wisdom for humankind?

Fr. 2a can be organised into five subsections: (I) an introductory statement distinguishing wisdom from other sciences, (II) an argument by analogy, (III) a tripartition of things, (IV) a tripartition of sciences, and (V) a concluding statement connecting each science, including wisdom, to its objects. It should be noted that Fr. 2a is the only section of *On Wisdom* that does not overlap with ps-Archytas' treatise.

(I) Lines 6–8: The fragment opens with a list of disciplines, later identified as sciences, which all focus on the things that are. Wisdom, too, is set upon the things that are; but differently from other sciences, it focuses on 'all the kinds of things that are'. We take τὰ ἐόντα to indicate, generally, all that exists in the world. Perictione gives us two examples of disciplines set over what is, geometry and arithmetic, and then adds that the statement more generally applies to other theoretical, or contemplative, activities (τἄλλα τὰ θεωρητικά). From Lines 16–17, we gather that this group also includes natural sciences and music. In Section IV, the proper job of wisdom, physics, and mathematics is said to be the contemplation (θεωρῆσαι) of what is, which makes them all theoretical enterprises.

Next, Perictione introduces the notion of science, ἐπιστήμη. We take the καί to be explanatory,[28] thus introducing a new term that is more adequate than the previous for the purpose of the argument ('theoretical activities – i.e, the sciences').[29] The advantage of this interpretation is that

---

[28] See Humbert (1960: 412 nn. 724–25).
[29] There are at least two other ways to understand καὶ ἐπιστῆμαι. One option is to translate καί as 'and' – that is, as connecting two separate activities (theoretical and scientific) and bringing them to

it allows coextensive consideration of τὰ θεωρητικά and ἐπιστῆμαι: geometry, arithmetic, and other disciplines are all theoretical activities, better known as sciences. Furthermore, this reading suggests ἐπιστήμη is introduced by Perictione as a technical term for a contemplative activity.

(II) Lines 9–10: Wisdom is said to be different from other sciences because it considers all the kinds (γένη) of things that are. This is unpacked in two steps: an argument by analogy and a more complex argument organising the sciences into three different classes. First, Perictione compares wisdom to sight and hearing: just as sight is set upon everything visible and hearing is set upon everything hearable, the object of wisdom is everything that exists.[30] The suggestion is that sight concerns the visible kind – namely, all that is visible insofar as it can be seen[31] – whereas wisdom concerns the kinds of beings – namely, all that is insofar as it is.

(III) Lines 10–12: After stating what wisdom is about, Perictione distinguishes wisdom from other sciences, which also, to some extent, revolve around what is. The first step involves distinguishing three groups of objects: those that pertain to all things, those that pertain to most things, and those that pertain to each one thing in a particular way.

These objects are named τὰ συμβεβηκότα. In his philosophical lexicon, Aristotle introduces the term συμβεβηκός, accident, as that which applies to something by chance, neither necessarily nor regularly (Ar. *Met.* 5.30.1025a4–34).[32] A συμβεβηκός is an incidental and contingent property. Yet, although the Aristotelian undertones are palpable, both the

---

the same level. Yet this would suggest that geometry and mathematics are not sciences, while at lines 16–17 Perictione introduces a specific class of sciences later identified with mathematics and geometry. One could argue that Perictione distinguishes sciences *lato sensu*, which include all theoretical activities (i.e., geometry and mathematics) from sciences *strictu sensu* (i.e., physics). On this account, however, sciences would differ from τὰ θεωρητικά. Yet, at lines 12–14, both mathematics and physics are said to be contemplative. Another option is to take καί as pinning down and translate it as giving an example ('such as the sciences') or adding more specific details ('and particularly the sciences'). The absence of the article before ἐπιστῆμαι, however, suggests that this should not be taken as a stand-alone concept, which makes both readings harder to defend.

[30] Sight and hearing are recurring examples in function arguments (e.g., Pl. *Rep.* 1.352d–53b; Ar. *EN* 1.7.14–15.1098a7–17; Ar. *Protr.*, in Iambl. *Protr.* 43.27–44.26 Pistelli). For the employment of similar analogies in the Pythagorean pseudepigrapha, see Phint. *Moderation* (Stob. 4.23.61, 151.20–52.5 Thesleff). See also ps-Arch. *Wisdom*, where σοφία outclasses all other human activities in the same way as sight outclasses the other senses, for they have wider scopes (Fr. 1, 43.25–31 Thesleff), and where wisdom is set over all things that are just like sight is set over all things that are visible (Fr. 4, 44.25–26 Thesleff).

[31] While in the *De Anima* the object of sight is colour (2.6.418a12), in the *Protrepticus* it is the visible (τὰ ὁρατά, Iambl. *Protr.* 56.6 Pistelli).

[32] Aristotle also hints at a second sense of συμβεβηκός as *essential* property, what applies to something in virtue of its nature but is not part of its definition.

grammatical construction and the context of Fr. 2a suggest that τὰ συμβεβηκότα should not be read as a technical term.³³ First, Aristotle rarely uses συμβεβηκός with the dative unless it functions verbally: not 'the accident of' but 'what happens, pertains or applies to'.³⁴ Second, it is unclear why wisdom, the highest-ranked human activity, which is later said to bring humans closer to what is true and divine, should only focus on accidents, even if essential and applying to all things. Therefore, we propose to read τὰ συμβεβηκότα more loosely as 'that which pertains to'. The passage would then distinguish three classes of properties: those that pertain to all things universally, those that pertain to most things, and those that pertain to each one thing in some way.³⁵

(IV) Lines 12–14: The next section distinguishes three sciences and maps this epistemological tripartition onto the tripartition of objects from the previous lines. Perictione writes that it is fitting³⁶ for wisdom to behold and contemplate³⁷ what pertains to all things universally (τὰ καθόλω πᾶσι συμβεβακότα),³⁸ for natural sciences to contemplate what pertains to most things (τὰ δὲ τοῖς πλείστοις), and for the science concerning something determinate/defined (τι ἀφωρισμένον) to contemplate peculiar things that pertain (τὰ ἴδια συμβεβακότα) to each thing (καθ'ἕκαστον).³⁹ That the third group – namely, the particular sciences – includes geometry,

---

³³ *Pace* De Cesaris and Horky (2018: 28); and Ulacco (2016: 105, 143).
³⁴ For this alternative use in Aristotle, see *Met.* 5.6.1017a11, and *MA* 1.698a1–2.
³⁵ Note that if λόγος in Fr. 1 is to be interpreted with a propositional meaning, here Perictione may distinguish different forms of (categorial?) predication. Note also that the object Perictione assigns to wisdom (to behold and contemplate *what pertains to all things universally*) appears to contravene the requirements established in the *Metaphysics* (cf. *aporiai* nn. 3–4 in Book 3 and the related *aporiai* in Book 11), where Aristotle denies there can be a (demonstrative) science of all kinds, which deals with all attributes. We postpone a detailed analysis of this issue to another context.
³⁶ The adjective οἰκεῖος may also recall Aristotle's and Plato's function arguments (Pl. *Rep.* 1.353e; Ar. *EN* 1.7.15.1098a16–17). See also Phint. *Moderation* (152.15 Thesleff).
³⁷ As previously noted, the fact that their function is said to be the contemplation of what is explains why they are all classed as θεωρητικά, contemplative activities. Here Perictione does not seem to draw a distinction between the two verbs: rather than indicating two separate functions, συνιδεῖν and θεωρῆσαι reinforce the contemplative nature of the sciences.
³⁸ In Fr. 1, the object of wisdom was initially and generally identified as all things that are and then specifically linked to the rationale of the whole of nature.
³⁹ In this second tripartition, the third group – namely, those things that pertain to each one thing (ἑνὶ ἑκάστῳ) – is referred to as 'peculiar' (τὰ ἴδια συμβεβακότα). The fact that these apply to each one thing 'in some way (πᾳ)' may be explained as follows. With 'science concerning something determinate/defined', Perictione means any science that delimits its objects by means of (any of) their peculiar properties. In the example, geometry, arithmetic, and music study what pertains to their objects in a way that is peculiar to their quantitative (or well-proportioned) nature. This appears to be compatible with Aristotle's definition of ἴδιον in the *Topics* as what is counterpredicated with its subject, but not essential (1.8.103b7–10).

arithmetic, and harmonics, which focus on specific properties, is explained in the next lines of the fragment.

Again, the passage recalls Aristotle's own division of the different branches of learning in the *Metaphysics* (6.1.1025b3–26a32).[40] Aristotle organises theoretical sciences into three groups: first philosophy, then natural sciences and mathematics.[41] The first science concerns the being *qua* being (θεωρεῖ τὸ ὂν ᾗ ὄν, *Met.* 4.1.1003a21), natural sciences concern the class[42] of beings that are in motion and at rest, and mathematics concerns what is immutable but still inseparable from matter.[43] The object of the first science is also described as eternal, unmovable, separate from matter, and thus most honourable and divine, wherefore this first branch is named theology.[44]

The difference with Perictione's tripartition is that the highest-ranked activity is named wisdom (σοφία), rather than philosophy or theology.[45] Although σοφία is not explicitly said to be a science (ἐπιστήμη), Perictione's treatment of wisdom parallels that of physics, arithmetic, and music. The same criteria used to define and classify these sciences, namely their contemplative function and their objects, are used in relation to wisdom, which suggests that σοφία is here presented not as a virtue or an epistemic state but the first and highest science.[46]

(V) Lines 14–17: In the last lines, the tripartition is revised. Wisdom is said to retrieve[47] the principles (ἀρχαί) of the things that are, physics those of what comes to be in accordance with nature, and the third group of

---

[40] Besides the link to Aristotle, tripartitions are also a recurring theme in the Pythagorean pseudepigrapha (Centrone 2014: 333 n. 45). For a tripartition of virtues, see Phint. *Moderation* (152.5–18 Thesleff).

[41] See Ar. *Top.* 6.6.145a15–16; *Cael.* 3.1.298a27–32; *DA* 1.1.403a27–b2; *Met.* 11.7.1064a16–b3; *EN* 6.1.1139a26–28, 6.7.1141b29–32. Like Perictione, in the *Physics*, Aristotle includes harmonics, optics, and astronomy in the third group of theoretical sciences (2.1.192b8–94a8). The division is discussed further in Johnson (2015).

[42] The Greek term is γένος, which might be the reference behind Perictione's claim that wisdom relates to all the kinds (γένη) of things that are. Aristotle, too, debates whether first philosophy is about the being *universally* (καθόλου) or a specific kind (γένος), namely the highest kind of things.

[43] Like arithmetic and music in Perictione's Fr. 2a, these other sciences are said to 'divide off' some portion of being (ἀποτέμνω, *Met.* 4.1.1003b21–25).

[44] In Fr. 2b, Perictione also hints at the fact that the first science makes humans more divine.

[45] Note, however, that this is in line with Aristotle's description of σοφία in the *Metaphysics*, where wisdom is said to be the science of first causes and principles (1.1.982a21–b4). From Book 4, this becomes the science of the being *qua* being.

[46] Our interpretation differs from Horky's (2015: 34–35). Interpreting wisdom as a science clarifies why in Fr. 1 wisdom is said to have a function.

[47] The verb is ἀνευρίσκω, rediscover, which we take to be a reference to Plato's theory of knowledge as recollection. Noteworthy is that in ps-Archytas' *On Wisdom* Fr. 5 the wise is described with the Platonic image of a charioteer (44.31–45.4 Thesleff).

sciences enquire into principles of particular classes of beings, such as those having a magnitude, in the case of mathematics, and the harmonious, in the case of music. The latter clarifies what Perictione meant by 'sciences set over what is delimited' in the previous sentence. This second version of the tripartition of sciences brings Perictione closer to Aristotle. First, natural science is set over what changes and comes to be. Second, and most importantly, sciences are no longer only about τὰ συμβεβηκότα, what pertains to beings, but discover their principles (Ar. *Met.* 6.1.1025b5).[48]

Overall, in Fr. 2a Perictione clarifies what the object and the function of wisdom is by, first, comparing it with sight and highlighting that σοφία occupies itself with *all* the kinds of the things that are. Second, wisdom is connected to other theoretical sciences, which also contemplate beings. The difference is that σοφία concerns what pertains to all things, whereas natural sciences concern what pertains to most beings, and mathematics individual kinds of beings. The hierarchy of sciences explains why, in the closing lines of the fragment, wisdom is noted to be the highest form of learning (Stob. 3.1.121, 146.17–22 Thesleff).[49]

Fr. 2b: 17. Ὅστις ὦν ἀναλῦσαι
18. οἷός <τ'> ἐστὶ πάντα γένη ὑπὸ μίαν καὶ τὰν αὐτὰν ἀρχάν, καὶ πάλιν ἐκ
19. ταύτας συνθεῖναι καὶ ἀριθμάσασθαι,[50] οὗτος δοκεῖ[51] καὶ σοφώτατος εἶναι
20. καὶ ἀληθέστατος,[52] ἔτι δὲ καὶ καλὰν σκοπιὰν[53] ἀνευρηκέναι,[54] ἀφ' ἇς δυνατὸς
21. ἐσσεῖται τόν τε[55] θεὸν κατόψεσθαι καὶ πάντα τὰ ἐν τᾷ συστοιχίᾳ τε καὶ
22. τάξει τᾷ ἐκείνω κατακεχωρισμένα.

Therefore, whoever is able to resolve all kinds to one and the same principle and from this compose and enumerate them again, this person seems to be both wisest and truest. Moreover, this person has found a good lookout point, from which one will be able to behold the god as well as all things that have been placed in his column and order.

---

[48] On the search for principles in early Pythagoreanism, see Ar. *Met.* 1.5.985b23–26.
[49] For this reason, Horky suggests Fr. 2a should also be included in ps-Archytas' *On Wisdom* (2015: 33–36).
[50] In ps-Archytas' *On Wisdom* Fr. 5, we have **συν**αριθμήσασθαι, enumerate together.
[51] In ps-Archytas' *On Wisdom* Fr. 5, we find μοι ('it seems *to me*'). This stresses the protreptic nature of the fragment discussed by Horky (2015).
[52] See Euryph. *Life* (Stob. 4.39.17, 86.4 Thesleff); Ecph. *De regn.* (Fr. 2, Stob. 4.7.64, 79.14–80.1 Thesleff). In ps-Archytas' *On Wisdom* Fr. 5, the adjective is **παν**αληθέστατος, overall truest.
[53] See Pl. *Rep.* 4.445c4.
[54] A second reminder of Platonic epistemology. In ps-Archytas' *On Wisdom* Fr. 5, the verb is simply εὑρηκέναι.
[55] Among the few differences between ps-Archytas' Fr. 5 and Perictione's Fr. 2b is the use of τε. Ps-Archytas stresses the *continuum* of analysis and synthesis in the first part of the fragment (ὑπὸ μίαν **τε** καὶ τὰν αὐτὰν ἀρχάν καὶ πάλιν συνθεῖναι **τε** καὶ συναριθμήσασθαι), whereas Perictione stresses the *continuum* between the objects the wise beholds.

The conclusion of the argument contains a blend of Aristotelian and especially Platonic elements. Wisdom enables humans to contemplate the god. The tripartition of sciences from Fr. 2a clarifies why those who possess wisdom are said to be truest: they are closer to the truth because they contemplate all things. Specifically, Perictione deems to be wisest those who work their way back to the principle. This connects the two characterisations of wisdom in Fr. 2a as contemplating 'all the kinds of beings' and 'the principles of all things': wisdom studies the kinds (γένη) of things that are and then brings them back to their principle (ἀρχή).

The wise, then, follows a two-step method: reasoning back *to* the principle of all things (*analysis*)[56] and proceeding *from* the principle back to what is derived (*synthesis*) from them.[57] Notably, the wise are also able to enumerate things starting from the principle, which suggests that the knowledge of the universal includes knowledge of particulars.[58] The method of analysis and synthesis, then, has two consequences: first, it makes one wise and true; second, it enables the wise to behold[59] what is divine[60] and the like.[61]

Perictione's Originality and Contributions

In this final section, we outline the benefits of the study of Perictione's *On Wisdom* for the scholarship on the pseudepigrapha. Specifically, we envision the possibility that the text ascribed by Stobaeus to Perictione might preserve a more original version of the fragments paralleled by ps-Archytas' *On Wisdom* Frs. 2 and 5. Although some scholars suggest that Perictione's and ps-Archytas' *On Wisdom* should be treated separately,[62] no real effort

---

[56] On the method of analysis, see Ar. *Apr.* 1.37.47a4, 1.45.51a18, and *Apo.* 1.12.78a6–13. For the use of this method in ancient geometry and Plato's *Meno*, see Menn (2002).
[57] Ps-Archytas omits ἐκ ταύτας. Perictione's version makes the method of synthesis more explicit.
[58] See ps-Arch. *De Vir. Bon.* Fr. 11 (Stob. 3.3.65, 13.30–14.16 Thesleff) and the commentary by Centrone (1990: 171).
[59] Plato uses the verb καθοράω twice to describe the gods looking down on humans (*Pol.* 273d; *Phil.* 26b), which again suggests that the wise becomes similar to the divine.
[60] On the Platonic goal of 'becoming like god', see Sedley (1997).
[61] The verb χωρίζω is Aristotelian (*Top.* 1.18.108b8, 5.3.132a13). The term συστοιχία, column, is one of the few early Pythagorean elements in the treatise. See Aristotle's *Metaphysics*, where a group of fifth-century Pythagoreans organise the principles of all things 'into two columns' (1.5.986a22–b2). For further references to the pseudepigrapha, see Ulacco (2017: 27).
[62] See Thesleff (1965: 148); Des Places (1989: 54 n. 1).

has been put into determining what the differences between the texts imply for their textual transmission.[63]

In this final section, we briefly provide contextual evidence to show why a detailed assessment of Perictione's fragments is also valuable for a better assessment of ps-Archytas' *On Wisdom*. Let us consider the portion of text following the closing lines of Perictione's Fr. 2b, preserved by Iamblichus as the final lines of ps-Archytas' Fr. 5:

> ... καὶ ταύταν ἁρματήλατον[64] ὁδὸν ἐκπορισάμενος τῷ νόῳ κατ' εὐθεῖαν ὁρμαθῆμεν καὶ τελεοδρομᾶσαι τὰς ἀρχὰς τοῖς πέρασι συνάψαντα καὶ ἐπιγνόντα διότι ὁ θεὸς ἀρχά τε καὶ τέλος καὶ μέσον ἐστὶ πάντων τῶν κατὰ δίκαν τε καὶ τὸν ὀρθὸν λόγον περαινομένων.

> ... and[65] supplying this charioteer path[66] through intellect, this person will be able[67] to rush and complete the course straightaway by connecting the beginnings with the conclusions, and by recognising why the god is the beginning, end, and middle of all things that are accomplished according to justice and right proportion.[68]

Scholars who study Stobaeus' method of quotation in comparison with Iamblichus' generally agree on the reliability of the quotations preserved in the *Anthology*.[69] However, in the most extensive study of Iamblichus' style[70] in the *Protrepticus* (where ps-Archytas' fragments are preserved), Hutchinson and Johnson conclude that Iamblichus tends to quote Plato almost *verbatim* and that, even when found to abridge the text, he remains faithful to the original language and argument. Since ps-Archytas' Fr. 5 overlaps with Perictione's Fr. 2b with the addition of the four lines quoted above, the question of which version is more pristine arises.

---

[63] Romano, for example, expunges an ὤν from ps-Arch. *Wisdom* Fr. 2 based on Perictione's text (2006: 473 n. 27). However, no reason is given as to why we should rely on Stobaeus' version only in this case.
[64] The poetic style (Pl. *Phdr.* 246e–47a) may be an argument for the text's authenticity. See Centrone (2014: 320).
[65] The translation is indebted to Horky (2015: 38).
[66] Alternatively, 'il procure là *à son intellect* une voie carrossable' (Des Places 1989: 54). Horky does not translate τῷ νόῳ explicitly (2015: 36).
[67] See δυνατὸς ἐσσεῖται in Fr. 2b.
[68] The formula κατὰ τὸν ὀρθὸν λόγον is of Platonic-Academic inspiration. See Theag. *Virt*. Fr. 1 (Stob. 3.1.117, 191.15–21 Thesleff), where justice is defined as the right proportion of the parts of the soul. See also Centrone (1990: 225–26).
[69] See Huffman (2019a: 17), who agrees with Mansfeld and Runia (1997) that Stobaeus does not usually paraphrase nor abridge the text he quotes.
[70] See Hutchinson and Johnson (2005: 203–42).

It may well be that Stobaeus only selected a portion of text[71] (i.e., Perictione's Fr. 2a–b) from ps-Archytas' Fr. 5 and simply left out the rest of the quotation. However, we should note the following: first, Iamblichus customarily introduces the quotations by providing his own *incipit* and seals them with some re-workings of the text.[72] Second, the lines quoted above recall Plato's words in the *Laws*.[73] This could be a quotation already included in ps-Archytas' text.[74] However, the idea that the god possesses everything in itself, and hence is 'beginning and middle and end', is reiterated in many other passages of Iamblichus' corpus,[75] where it appears to convey a peculiarly Iamblichean view.[76] Finally, Iamblichus inserts an allusion to the charioteer at the end of the previous section of the *Protrepticus*, which he now reiterates. In light of the conspicuous number of elements matching Iamblichus' philosophy, the authenticity of these lines should be investigated in more detail, rather than taken at face value. Far from merely providing a fruitful parallel to compensate for the missing parts of ps-Archytas' *On Wisdom*, Perictione's fragments may offer a more faithful version of the original text. We leave this for future research to explore.

Overall, like the other pseudepigrapha, Perictione's *On Wisdom* appropriates Platonic and Aristotelian terminology and theories ascribing them to an allegedly Pythagorean author. Our goal has been to reconstruct Perictione's philosophical views by contextualising the arguments in *On Wisdom* within the Platonic and Peripatetic tradition. This philosophical analysis has revealed that the treatise urges its readers to pursue a life of

---

[71] On the hypothesis that Stobaeus is using Iamblichus' library, or inherited an almost identical library, see Macris (2002).
[72] See Hutchinson and Johnson (2005: 205).
[73] Pl. *Leges* 4.715e–16a: 'The god (θεός) who, as an ancient (arguably, Orphic) story tells, hold the beginning, the end, and the middle of all that is (ἀρχήν τε καὶ τελευτὴν καὶ μέσα τῶν ὄντων ἁπάντων), complete his circuit in accordance with nature in straight, steady course (εὐθείᾳ περαίνει κατὰ φύσιν περιπορευόμενος).'
[74] See Des Places (1989: 54); Horky (2015: 37 n. 34). The Doric words at the end (e.g., δίκαν) can be explained by Hutchinson and Johnson's note that Iamblichus' adaptations are often informed by the original context: 'Even when writing in his own voice, he borrowed a colourful word from the local environment, chameleon-wise' (2005: 207 n. 31).
[75] *De Myst.* 1.19.39, 1.19.53. See also ps-Iamb. *Theolog. Arithm.* 1.19, 3.7–9.
[76] According to Mesyatas (2012: 164–65), Iamblichus was inspired by the contradiction between the *Parmenides*, where the One is said not to have beginning, middle or end (137d), and the *Laws*, where God is called 'the beginning, middle and end of all beings' (4.715e–16a). Furthermore, Iamblichus conceives of mathematical sciences as the middle step of the elevating process (*DCMS* 54.8–10) and introduces ps-Archytas' fragments as the middle, or mixed, form of exhortation, namely that which illuminates the connection between the individual nature and the nature of the cosmos (Horky 2020).

wisdom and theoretical progress.[77] To this purpose, the tripartition of sciences is especially effective, for it shows how wisdom focuses on what pertains to all things universally and thus excels over all other disciplines. Wisdom is recognised as a science and placed at the top of the human theoretical enterprises. This, ultimately, is the treatise's contribution to the history of Greek philosophy. This makes Perictione an interlocutor in the ancient philosophical conversation and, as it were, the founding mother of ancient metaphysics and epistemology.

---

[77] On the protreptic features of ps-Archytas' *On Wisdom*, see Horky (2015).

CHAPTER 9

Not Veiled in Silence
The Case for Macrina

Anna B. Christensen

Introduction

In Gregory of Nyssa's dialogue, *On Soul and Resurrection* (*de Anima et Resurrectione*), Macrina, Gregory's sister, addresses two main questions. (1) What is the nature of the soul and its relation to the body? And (2) what happens at death, and do those who die survive? Her conversation involves striking similarities to Socrates' in Plato's *Phaedo*.[1] Both Macrina and Socrates are about to die, and both take the opportunity to philosophise about the soul and immortality. However, while Socrates' arguments are praised and commonly taught in classrooms around the world, Macrina's arguments are widely neglected. In this chapter, I argue that we should correct this oversight and pay more attention to Macrina as we include women in the philosophical canon of antiquity.

Two interrelated concerns complicate this project. First, Gregory's use of the dialogue form raises questions about the authenticity of Gregory's account, since it may indicate that he has copied Plato or used his sister as a convenient mouthpiece to support his arguments and avoid backlash. If so, his text would provide little real information about Macrina.[2] Similar concerns exist regarding Socrates in Plato's dialogues, but here the question has added urgency because of the second concern.[3] Little source material on ancient women intellectuals has survived. As Elizabeth Castelli remarks, looking for such information is like embarking on a 'treacherous and often disappointing search for buried treasure' (1986:

---

[1] Others noting this include Momigliano (1987: 208); Roth (1992: 21); Pelikan (1993: 8); Williams (1993: passim); Perioli (1997); Burrus (2000: 113); Smith (2004: 61); Drury (2005); and Muehlberger (2012: 277).
[2] Scholars doubting the authenticity of Macrina's portrayal include Sheather (1995: 33–35); Clark (1998: 27–31); Johnson (1998: 185); Burrus (2000, 2001); and Mcnary-Zak (2005: 7). I discuss their arguments below.
[3] See Press (2000). Does 'Socrates' in Plato's dialogues represent the historical Socrates, or is 'Socrates' merely 'Plato's mouthpiece'?

61). In Socrates' case, other substantial sources allow comparison to Plato's accounts, notably Xenophon's dialogues and the satirical Aristophanes' *The Clouds*. But in Macrina's case, all major sources are authored by her younger brother, including the dialogue, *Letter 19*, and the biography, *The Life of St. Macrina* (*Vita Sanctae Macrinae*, *VSM*), making it difficult to do more than speculate about the authenticity of Gregory's presentation.[4]

Despite these challenges, I argue that we have good reasons to think Gregory's portrayal of his sister's arguments is informative. Even if he does not record Macrina's deathbed speeches perfectly, he presents a reasonably accurate portrayal of her mannerisms, methods, and philosophical interests. As such, his dialogue provides a rare, lengthy, and illuminating glimpse into the activities of a woman philosopher in antiquity.[5]

In this chapter, I first summarise Macrina's life, emphasising aspects of her biography showing her commitment to philosophy. Next, I review her arguments in the dialogue to get a sense of her methods. Finally, I unpack objections against her philosophical authority and show how we can respond to them. I conclude that we should view and teach Macrina as a worthy philosopher in her own right. The evidence suggests she was not silent during her life. We should not allow her to remain silent in death (cf. *VSM* 1.5).[6]

Macrina's Life and Education

Macrina was born around 327 CE in Kabeira, a town in the Neocaesarean region of Pontus. As the firstborn of ten children in a prosperous Christian household, she had access to the finest educational resources available to young women in that era. Yet Gregory notes that she was taught by her pious mother, Emmelia, who had strict guidelines for Macrina's education. Emmelia wanted Macrina to be a proper Christian wife and mother and so excluded material she viewed as instilling habits detrimental to good ethics. She considered much Classical literature 'unsuitable' because of its violent and sexual content and insisted that her daughter should instead be educated in texts she deemed conducive to ethical development such as the *Wisdom of Solomon* (*VSM* 4.3–5).

---

[4] Other sources include some *Epigrams* by Gregory of Nazianzan. Macrina's brother, Basil, may implicitly refer to Macrina but never mentions her by name. See Silvas (2008).
[5] Scholars sympathetic to this interpretation include Pelikan (1993) and Smith (2000).
[6] Unless noted, references and translations of Gregory's texts use Silvas' edition (2008). Greek text uses corresponding passages in von Oehler's Greek/German edition (1858). Other notable English translations consulted while writing this chapter include Callahan's (1967) and Roth's (1993).

With this education, Macrina grew in wisdom as she reached adulthood. By age twelve, she could recite the Psalms perfectly, an ability that would have prepared her well for the ascetic religious life she eventually chose to pursue. However, this life was at first out of reach, since her parents betrothed her to a wealthy associate of her father's. Tragically, while she waited the required two years between her betrothal and marriage, her fiancé died. Although his death should have severed Macrina's obligation to him and allowed her father to espouse her to someone else, she refused a second betrothal. She argued that 'by nature, marriage is but once only, as there is one birth and one death' (*VSM* 6.2). She thought that marriage should only occur once. Betrothal, too, with its mutual promises of commitment, counted in her young mind as close enough to marriage that the distinction was inconsequential. Thus, being promised to a man should qualify as being married to him, and she ought to style herself as a widow (6.3).

This incident provides a fascinating possibility about Macrina's early commitment to the philosophical life.[7] At this time, women had little control over their lives and were largely subject to their menfolk: first their fathers, then their husbands, and eventually their sons. Macrina would have been expected to marry as her father required. However, social convention in fourth-century Pontus rejected digamy, the practice of marrying a second time. By styling herself as a widow, Macrina positioned herself as someone who had already been married and consequently should not marry again. In effect, she used the social convention against digamy to her advantage, taking the opportunity to devote herself to an alternative lifestyle of study and prayer. She clearly wanted to do more than merely follow social convention. Since conventional wisdom would not have recognised an unconsummated betrothal as 'marriage', it would have freed her for a second betrothal. Declaring that she was a widow thus allowed her outwardly to maintain social norms, even while unapologetically bending them to her will.[8]

---

[7] Pelikan argues that 'the philosophical life' means 'Christian asceticism' rather than 'technical Classical philosophy' for Macrina (1993: 9). But Pelikan's understanding does not fully capture Macrina's view. Macrina chose to live 'by herself' (μένειν ἐφ' ἑαυτῆς, *VSM* 6.1) a conventional phrase from the Hellenistic philosophical tradition that means to remain unmarried to pursue philosophy (Sheather 1995: 28; Silvas 2008: 115 n. 30). Many pagan philosophers sought communal life as part of their philosophical commitments, for example, the early Epicureans (Christensen 2020), since community increases potential to achieve higher ethical standards. One goal of Macrina's community was to increase members' ethical well-being (cf. Helleman 2001: 94).

[8] See Hotz (2001: 85); Silvas (2008: 115 n. 31).

Gregory notes that Macrina's early devotion to 'philosophy' soon attracted others to follow her example, including Emmelia, their brother, Basil, and several other siblings (7.5, 8.3). As her reputation grew, she would eventually establish a community of like-minded individuals at Annisa that expanded to welcome other members of her household, former slaves, and strangers from afar (cf. *Ep.* 19.7).[9] Macrina remained the head of the community in Annisa until her death, the occasion that prompted Gregory's writing *On Soul and Resurrection*.

The Texts

The events of *On Soul and Resurrection* require some context. During the summer of 379 CE, Gregory journeyed to visit his sister at Annisa. Their brother, Basil the Great, had died nearly nine months earlier, and Gregory remarks that he wished to see Macrina so he could mourn with her and be comforted by her (*de An. et Res.* Intr. 1). To his dismay, he arrived at Annisa to find her on her own deathbed, a discovery that precipitated the long discussions between them about death and resurrection detailed in the dialogue.

Gregory mentions his final meetings with Macrina three times in the years after her death.[10] He first records them in *Letter 19*, written in early to mid-380, less than a year afterwards. As expected in a letter-length text, *Letter 19* provides only a brief summary, noting his sister's abilities as a 'teacher of how to live' (τοῦ βίου διδάσκαλος, *Ep.* 19.6) and his own distress at her death (19.10).

He returns to the event in the *Vita Sanctae Macrinae* (*VSM*), written in late 381 or early 382. The text enlarges on *Letter 19*'s account, although not by much since Gregory claims the biography, too, is a letter (1.1). He adds a summary of Macrina's arguments, outlining her speeches that he unpacks more elaborately in the dialogue *On Soul and Resurrection* (*de An. et Res.*) shortly thereafter, likely between 383 and 385.

While both *Letter 19* and the *VSM* provide short accounts of Macrina's final conversations, the dialogue extends nearly seventy pages in length. It covers a period of two days. The only interlocutors are Macrina and Gregory, although a physician and 'many' other people were present (*de*

---

[9] Such growth was typical of early Christian ascetic communities. See Elm (1994).
[10] Silvas thinks three accounts exist because each is written for different purposes (2008: 154). Muehlberger argues that Gregory thought he needed more 'convincing' accounts of Macrina's character (2012: 284).

An. et Res. 2.6, 10.1). Gregory portrays himself as passionate, alternately grieving his sister's death and raging against the seeming futility of mortal life. Death frustrates him because it causes disturbance to 'see one who was so lately alive and vocal becoming all of a sudden bereft of breath and voice and movement' (Intr. 8). He adds a few lines later that he is particularly worried that there is 'nothing evident to rely on' (10) about death. Death worries him because it silences a living being and because no empirical evidence exists regarding what death is like for the dead or whether they survive. Since Macrina's death triggers his concerns, he seems specifically concerned that he will never see *her* again. In contrast, Macrina appears as a rational philosopher who quiets his passionate outbursts by arguing that death – including her own death – is nothing dreadful and that the dead will live again. As Gregory increasingly descends into grief, she takes charge of the conversation by gesturing him to silence (1.1) and continues to hold the upper hand throughout much of the dialogue. The text concludes before Macrina dies, leaving the reader to wonder how her arguments have affected him. However, the fact that Gregory becomes more philosophically active as the dialogue progresses might signal that her teachings help him regain control of his emotions. The *VSM* substantiates this suggestion when Gregory claims her example helps bring his 'soul back from the abyss' (29.1–2). To see how her arguments could be so effective, we must examine them in greater detail.

Macrina's Arguments

When Gregory summarises Macrina's arguments in the *VSM*, he prefaces his summary by claiming there is more to report than he had space to write.

> And if my narrative were not to expand to an unconscionable length I would recount everything in order, how exalted was her discourse as she philosophized to us on the soul and explained the cause of our life in the flesh, and why man was made, and how he became mortal, and whence came death, and what is the release from death back to life again. (*VSM* 20.5)

Macrina's arguments in *On Soul and Resurrection* correspond neatly to this summary, suggesting that part of the reason Gregory writes the dialogue is so that he may take the space to 'recount everything in order.' As the *VSM*'s summary suggests, Macrina elaborates her responses to two main questions in the dialogue: (1) What is the nature of the soul and its relation to the body? And (2) what happens at death, and do those who die survive?

Question 1: The Soul's Nature

Both Macrina and Gregory assume that living beings are composite identities consisting of a physical body and an animating soul. Gregory's initial worries provoke the first question: What is the nature of the soul and its relation to the body? He presents Epicurean arguments that death is annihilation, the complete destruction of the person, both body and soul. He fears that the soul, like the body, is material and will therefore decompose at death (1.4, 9). However, he does not think this argument necessitates the Epicurean conclusion that death is consequently nothing to fear (Epicurus *Ep. Men.* 124), since death may be dreadful precisely because it involves nothingness (*de An. et Res.* Intr. 10). Macrina replies that this conception of the soul is incorrect. The soul is not material but is immaterial, rational, and divine. Consequently, it is not subject to destruction like the body.

To make this case, she first argues against the Epicurean conception of the soul by a *reductio ad absurdum*. She says,

> For if these opponents think that if the soul is not connatural with the elements it therefore exists nowhere, let them teach first that the life in the flesh is also inanimate, since the body itself is nothing but a convergence of the elements, and then let them say that the soul is not in these either, giving life of itself to the compound. If, as they think, it is not possible for the soul even to exist after death, although the elements continue to exist, then our very life is shown by them to be nothing but a dead thing. But if on the other hand they do not doubt the soul's existence now in the body, how can they maintain that it vanishes when the body is dissolved into its elements? (1.19–20).

Macrina indicates that the Epicurean position is absurd because it disregards the visible evidence that the ensouled body is living – a position doubly incongruous since Epicureans believed that sense perceptions were truth-indicative. Here, the Greek helps her case, since the word translated 'inanimate' (ἄψυχον) literally means 'without soul'.[11] If the soul were made of similar material components to the body, then the ensouled body should be no more animate or alive than an unensouled body. This conclusion would be ridiculous, since the vast difference between a dead corpse and a living person is self-evident. Thus, the soul animating a body must be altogether distinct from the body's material nature.

---

[11] See Silvas' commentary (2008: 176 n. 10).

Next, she argues that the soul is rational and divine by appealing to the authority of an ancient philosophical tradition, in particular the Stoic notion of the microcosm and macrocosm, the little world of the individual human being and the larger world of the divinely operated universe. Regarding the microcosm of the individual human, she notes, 'That this rational animal, the human being, is the recipient of intelligence and understanding is attested even by those outside our doctrine' (3.16). She agrees with others that human beings have rational souls.[12] She then connects the soul's rationality to the macrocosm, claiming it is self-evident that the world is rationally and divinely ordered, with our individual human souls capable of reasoning about their place in the larger macrocosmic order. She maintains we can reason from the existence of created order to the existence of a creator (God), and the created order must reflect that creator (1.24–32).

She replies to an objection about how the material world, which is often corrupt, can provide accurate knowledge about what is perfect, divine, and pure – including knowledge of the soul (2.1). She responds that the soul itself is the source of information. 'Why the soul itself ... is a sufficient teacher of what is to be conceived about the soul .... The soul then is something immaterial and bodiless, active and moving in accord with its own nature, and giving evidence of its own movements through the organs of the body' (2.2). The soul, being rational, is most like the divine and therefore closest to truth. Since the individual soul resembles God, the soul giving life to the universe (2.41), it is able to provide the necessary knowledge as it animates the body and causes it to move through the physical world. However, she argues, the soul cannot be informative if it remains in the detrimental condition of being overly bound to the body. Since the soul is primarily 'rational', it must turn away from bodily concerns and associated passions like anger and grief, which distract it from pursuing truth. Such passions change the soul from being 'rational and godlike to the irrational and unthinking, being reduced to the level of an animal' (3.50). She later adds that we should 'as far as we can, separate and free ourselves from [bodily] inclination by a life of virtue' so that the soul's travel 'towards the Good may be light and unimpeded, with no burden of the body to drag it down' (7.5). For Macrina, pursuing the 'Good' involves the individual human soul becoming more like the divine

---

[12] Since 'our doctrine' refers to the Christian beliefs she and Gregory share, 'those outside our doctrine' must indicate some non-Christian philosophers share similar views, including the Stoics and Platonists.

soul, that is, like God, through virtuous living and eliminating bodily passions.[13] She notes that the divine nature transcends material creation and so does not permit the presence of passions such as anger and desire (3.11). Similarly, Macrina argues, the human soul should be altogether apart and distinct from the physical realm of the body (2.45), eliminating irrational passions to become more like the divine soul it emulates.

Thus, her response to Gregory's question is that the soul is not material by nature but is instead immaterial, rational, and akin to divinity. Indeed, it is so distinct from bodily elements that it even detaches from passionate emotions associated with the body (3.5–19).

Question 2: Death, Immortality, and Survival

Discovering the soul's nature was not sufficient to quell Gregory's fear that death will silence one who was lately alive, so Macrina must address another question: What happens at death, and do those who die survive?

Macrina identifies death as the separation of the body from the soul (2.3).[14] The body becomes a corpse, since the soul animating it has departed. She then expounds on the likeness she had already invoked between the individual human and divine souls. Since the human soul is supposed to be like God in its nature and rationality, Macrina asserts that it must emulate God in other ways. As God is immaterial and eternal, so is the human soul. It will therefore survive the body's destruction.[15]

It would be small comfort to indicate that the soul will survive if the dead person's identity is not preserved. Gregory frets that the soul will exist independently of the material body to which it was originally connected (2.51–52) or be reincarnated into another physical body (8.5). Neither option seems likely to preserve the person's original identity as a unique body-soul composite. Macrina responds that the soul will survive to be bodily resurrected in the future, thus preserving the person's identity. She says,

---

[13] Macrina's point that we should 'free ourselves' from bodily passions 'as far as we can' echoes Socrates' arguments that the philosopher will seek to separate her soul from her body while living by separating herself from bodily passions as much as possible (*Phd.* 67 a ff., 82c).

[14] Socrates also espouses this view (*Phd.* 67b).

[15] Again, this argument resonates with the *Phaedo*, especially the Argument from Affinity (78b–89b), where Socrates reasons that the soul's likeness to the forms proves its immortality. The difference comes from Macrina's inclusion of Christian theology and scriptures. On the role of scripture in Macrina's philosophical method, see Adamson (2022b).

> You will see this bodily covering which is now dissolved in death, woven again from the same elements, not according to its present dense and heavy texture, but with its fibre spun again into something more subtle and ethereal, so that you will not only have with you that which you love, but it will be restored to you with a brighter and more captivating beauty. (7.28)

The person who died will be raised from the dead and reembodied. She thinks this body will be made from the 'same elements', meaning that it will be constructed of the same material components from which it was originally constituted (cf. 8.8).

However, although the resurrected body will be numerically and constitutively identical to the original, it will be subtly different. Her spinning analogy explains this concept.[16] Spinners can use the same wool to construct a garment of mediocre or high quality depending on how coarsely or finely they spin threads from the wool. Similarly, the resurrected human body will be constituted of the same material elements that originally constituted it, only more finely spun to make the resulting resurrected body vastly superior – perfected, indestructible, and more beautiful than the original.

A reasonable question is how the resurrected person can be numerically identical with the person who once lived, especially since death involves decay where the bodily elements scatter across the universe.[17] Gregory raises the problem neatly with his image of a shipwreck. He says,

> Just as a sailor, when his vessel has broken up in a shipwreck, cannot float simultaneously on all the pieces of the boat which have been scattered this way and that over the surface of the sea, but surely seizes whatever comes to hand and leaves the rest to drift on the waves, in the same way the soul, which is by nature incapable of disintegrating alone with the dispersal of the elements, will, if it is reluctant to be parted from the body, surely cling to one of the elements and so be split off from the others. (2.51–52)

How, Gregory asks, can the soul be reunited with the whole body made of disparate parts, once the body has scattered over the universe? Wouldn't the soul be more likely to cling to one piece of the body like the sailor grasping a piece of flotsam?

Macrina responds, first, by noting that Gregory's argument has a latent assumption that the soul must be spatially present in the body. But, Macrina argues, intelligible natures (like the soul's) are not subject to the laws of spatial dimensionality. Since the soul is intelligible, it is simple and

---

[16] This analogy is fitting because she was adept at wool-working (*VSM* 5.1).
[17] Perioli (1997: 117–20); Drury (2005).

lacks spatial dimension and can therefore connect with those bodily elements with which it was originally united (2.58), even if these physical parts have been dissolved, scattered over the universe, or eaten by sharks and fishes. For this reason, the soul can reconstitute the bodily compound at the resurrection, recognising the same elements and rearranging them into their originally constituted whole.[18] She maintains,

> The soul therefore exists in those elements in which it once came into being, for there is no necessity tearing it away from its coherence with them. What cause for gloom is there, then, in this, if the visible is exchanged for that which is without visible form, and why does your mind bear such a grudge against death? (2.59)

Having no reason to assume that some necessity keeps the soul and the bodily elements apart after death, she thinks Gregory should not be worried about death.

Even so, Gregory's last words in the dialogue ask for further proof that the resurrection preserves one's identity. He says, 'We must therefore attend to the argument, that we may thoroughly secure the probability of the doctrine in every respect' (10.63).

Macrina's final argument grants that she may be unable to provide all he has asked. She begins, 'We may be unable to oppose your argument with matching rhetoric' (10.66). Her point is not that she lacks arguments but rather that she may not produce arguments in a satisfactory form. She explains that some secrets will not 'come to light until we are taught the mystery of the resurrection by the deed' (10.66). She cannot answer everything about the resurrection because she has not yet been resurrected. She elucidates further with another analogy. People who are awake only at night and hear about the sun may have some ideas about what the sun is; but until they have actually seen and experienced the sun first-hand, their understanding of the sun's nature will be grossly inadequate (10.67). Similarly, those who are living are like the people awake at night and have never seen the sun; they can talk about the resurrection, but until they have actually experienced it, they cannot fully grasp the thing itself. This response would be philosophically disappointing were it not that she continues by diagnosing the reason for this inability to understand the resurrection. Our embodied condition limits contact with the doctrine of resurrection (10.73–74). Living persons are bound by their bodies, which cause their souls to be mingled with blinding passions prohibiting them

---

[18] On this argument, see Perioli (1997).

from understanding complete truth. However, in death, they lose the connection between their souls and their bodies' corrupting passions, so their souls will pass to a 'spiritual condition free of passion' (10.99) and know what it is to experience resurrection.

Thus, Macrina answers that death is the separation of the soul from the body. It is this separation that frees the soul to be ready for resurrection. Resurrection itself will result in life everlasting for the person who died in a body made indestructible from its original, perfected material.

Macrina as Philosopher

Despite Gregory's portrayal of Macrina as a worthy philosopher, some scholars object that it involves literary invention and so provides scant information about her. In general, they raise two related concerns of authenticity. First, did Gregory accurately record her actual conversations? Doubt arises from suggestions that Gregory has used Macrina as a mouthpiece or merely copied content from Plato's *Phaedo*. Second, did Macrina really possess philosophical abilities that the dialogue accurately informs us about? Suggestions to the contrary arise from her childhood education and the circumstances of her final conversations. I discuss each of these concerns below.

Objection 1: The Mouthpiece Objection

Scholars who doubt the authenticity of Gregory's portrayal often object that, since Macrina did not author the dialogue herself, Gregory has merely used her as a convenient mouthpiece for his own views. They suggest two motives: either to use her reputation to support his arguments[19] or to use her femininity to avoid backlash for his unpopular ideas.[20]

According to the first motive, Gregory capitalises on her reputation by casually reminding the reader that he knew the holy, virtuous Macrina. So, when he mourns that after she dies no one will be able to expound on such difficult subjects as death and resurrection (*de An. et Res.* 10.1), he tacitly informs readers that he is now a trustworthy source for these subjects, since he knew and learned from her. Thus, he is free to present his own ideas through her mouth.

Some textual evidence supports this interpretation. When Macrina greets Gregory in the *VSM*, she attempts to bow from her bed (19.1–2),

---

[19] Mcnary-Zak (2005). [20] See Roth (1992: 20–30); Clark (1998); Burrus (2001: 112–22).

a gesture suggesting she recognises his authority as a bishop. A more evocative event occurs later. After Gregory complains about his life, noting that he had recently been exiled for his theological beliefs and was routinely exhausted by serving the churches, Macrina responds:

> [We] make it a special boast that we are well born and consider ourselves sprung of noble stock. Our father was highly esteemed in his day for his learning. Yet his reputation only extended as far as the law courts of the province .... But you are named in cities and peoples and provinces. Churches send you as ally and reformer and churches summon you. (23.4)

It is easy to interpret her response as enhancing Gregory's reputation even while it quietly informs the reader of their relationship. She mentions their father, thereby recalling that they are siblings. But she adds that their father's reputation pales in comparison to Gregory's own, which more conspicuously advises that Gregory is an impressive personage. If she was esteemed for her virtue and wisdom, then her words supporting Gregory's reputation and authority would have had great weight among ancient audiences, making them more receptive to Gregory's own message through her voice.

However, the objection that Gregory has used his sister to bolster his own reputation is prefaced on the unspoken assumption that Macrina in fact had that good reputation for him to use. He could only benefit from using her reputation for wisdom if she actually possessed that reputation in history. Nor could he have significantly altered his presentation of her from how her contemporaries remembered her. He wrote the dialogue approximately five years after Macrina's death and so wrote for an audience that could have known her by reputation, if not in person. An inaccurate portrayal of her philosophical prowess would have been noted by her community at Annisa and by Gregory's peers.

The other possible motive behind Gregory's use of Macrina is that he has appropriated Macrina's femininity to obscure his own views. Perhaps Macrina can get by with saying things about the body and passions that Gregory cannot because her womanhood provides a more appropriate vehicle for such discussions.[21] Moreover, in dealing with questions regarding the soul and the divine, Gregory sometimes dances with Origenist theological views that would be deemed unacceptable for him to hold as a

---

[21] Burrus argues that this results from 'a reflection of masculine erotics' where Gregory's philosophy borrows her femininity to 'ensure the success of its own procreative enterprise' (2001: 120). Similar arguments exist regarding Diotima in Plato's *Symposium*. See Halperin (1989).

bishop. Using Macrina would enable him to distance himself from those views.

Neither of these explanations has much merit. Since Socrates presents a respected counterexample of a man who discusses the body and passions (*Phd.* 64c–69a; *Phdr.* 254a–c), it is unlikely that Gregory would need to use a woman to tackle such subjects. Moreover, Macrina's status as a woman devoted to the ascetic, celibate life means that she is less identifiable with traditional gender norms of womanhood, that is, as a wife and mother. Gregory once even expresses doubt that she can really be called a 'woman' because she had 'so surpassed nature' (*VSM* 1.3).[22] Her self-declared status of widowhood sets her apart from traditional marriage and, although Gregory calls her 'mother', it is only in the metaphorical sense that her ideas have nurtured her community's well-being (28.5). So, her femininity is not 'typical', and anyway Gregory's absconding with it would be unnecessary.

J. Warren Smith notes further that the views Macrina expresses in *On Soul and Resurrection* are similar to views Gregory has no problem expressing in his own voice in his *On the Making of Man* (*De Hominis Opificio*, written c. 379, the year Macrina died). Moreover, Smith argues, the most Origenist ideas expressed in the dialogue come from Gregory's mouth rather than Macrina's.[23] Since Gregory has already exposed some Origenist tendencies, he would have little reason to use Macrina to hide his views.

Even if Smith is correct that Gregory would not need to obfuscate his views, someone might worry that Gregory merely uses Macrina to *repeat* his views. However, this idea also seems unlikely. Gregory remarks that he writes about Macrina so her voice will not be lost, and he grieves that no one will be left after her death who can teach about the soul and resurrection (*VSM* 1.5; *de An. et Res.* 10.1). Although Gregory tacitly informs readers that he can now tackle these subjects, the only proof he offers for his newfound ability is that he has learned about them from his older sister. Similarity between Macrina's views and Gregory's own could thus arise because Macrina, like many good teachers, has influenced her student's views.

In fact, examining the teacher–student relationship between Gregory and Macrina in the dialogue is enlightening. Gregory repeatedly emphasises Macrina's role as 'the teacher' (ἡ διδάσκαλος), a role that she fulfils as she educates Gregory throughout the dialogue. Gregory's other two texts

---

[22] On this contentious claim, see Castelli (1991); Burrus (2001); and Hotz (2001).
[23] For this argument, see Smith (2001: 63).

about Macrina confirm that role, with *Letter 19* referring to her as a 'teacher of how to live' (τοῦ βίου διδάσκαλος, *Ep.* 19.6) and the *VSM* repeatedly emphasising her teaching abilities. The *VSM* notes that she 'raised herself by philosophy to the highest summit of human virtue' (1.5) and then pulled others to that summit with her teachings (7.5, 8.3, 9.1, 13.1, 13.8, 14.1, 29.2).

Especially noteworthy is that Gregory's use of the title, διδάσκαλος, with twenty-two appearances in the dialogue and four in the *VSM*, far outnumbers appearances of other appellations Gregory uses, which include 'virgin' (παρθένος), 'father' (πατήρ), 'mother' (μήτηρ), 'counsellor of everything good' (ἀγαθοῦ παντὸς σύμβουλος), and 'leader' (ἡ καθηγουμένη). Although each title conveys Macrina's authority and influence, Gregory's repetition of 'teacher' emphasises her abilities as philosophical instructor. Thus, in the dialogue, Gregory can write that he was impressed by her arguments (3.51, 5.24) and conclude that others present during her final arguments were likewise enthralled (10.1). These are not words spoken of a mere mouthpiece but of someone to whom Gregory owes a great debt, such as any student owes a great teacher.

Objection 2: The Platonic Objection

The striking similarities of form and style between the dialogue and the Platonic dialogues might suggest that Gregory has modelled Macrina's activities on Plato's Socrates rather than on reality.[24] Macrina's imminent death and conversational topics identify her with Socrates at the *Phaedo*'s conclusion,[25] while her status as a woman compares well to Diotima in the *Symposium* (201d–12c).[26] Comparison with the *Phaedrus* is also possible when Macrina twice refers to Socrates' image of the soul as a charioteer striving to reach the Good (*Phdr.* 246a–64e; *de An. et Res.* 3.9, 3.47).

It is unclear how much weight we should give these similarities between Gregory's and Plato's dialogues. However, we should not let those similarities blind us to crucial differences. First, Gregory's dialogue is more directly transmitted to us. Gregory was actually present when Macrina died, and so would have had first-hand knowledge of Macrina's final speeches. In contrast, Plato's dialogues are often several times removed

---

[24] See Williams (1993); Clark (1998: 24); Burrus (2000); Smith (2004).
[25] Momigliano notes that Macrina 'is here Socrates to her brother' (1987), and several parallels between Socrates' and Macrina's arguments have already been indicated. See notes 569–71.
[26] See especially Burrus (2000).

from the event. Plato's recounting of Socrates' final speeches in the *Phaedo* is at least third hand, as Phaedo recollects Socrates' death to Echecrates (57a). Since Plato was ill when Socrates died (59a), he did not hear Socrates' deathbed arguments directly, and he never specifies his source.

Second, Gregory's dialogue more obviously suggests that two speakers' views are expressed, rather than one person's alone.[27] In Plato's dialogues, one primary speaker (e.g., Socrates, the Athenian Stranger, Eleatic Stranger) often presents the main arguments, while other interlocutors remain largely silent, occasionally providing insights or foils for the main speaker's view. But in Gregory's dialogue, both Macrina and Gregory are dynamically engaged, presenting their own arguments, replying to the other, and revising arguments in response.[28] Their different personalities shine through the dialogue. Gregory is passionate, while Macrina interrupts (1.5, 2.38), gestures to silence him (1.1), and groans at his ignorance (2.13). These personalities are similarly portrayed in the *VSM*, with Macrina refusing to give in to emotion (11.4–12.1, 24.3), while Gregory can barely cope with his emotions as her body is being prepared for burial (29.1).

A good example of the repartee between Macrina and Gregory happens in the dialogue at 3.33. After Macrina has argued that the passions disrupt a soul's ascent to the Good (3.30), Gregory objects that sometimes the passions are useful for attaining virtue (3.31–32). Desire, for instance, can attract one to the Good, while fear of losing the Good may enable one to hold fast to the Good. Macrina responds,

> It seems ... that I myself have occasioned this confusion in reasoning, by not making those distinctions in the argument of the case which would have imposed a certain logical order on our considerations. But now, as far as possible, some such order shall be devised for the investigation, so that by advancing logically in our considerations there may be no more room for such contradictions. (3.33)

Macrina's phrasing contains a conversational sense; she notes that she is to blame for Gregory's misapprehensions ('I myself have occasioned this confusion') and recognises why (by not making 'distinctions'). She proceeds to make those distinctions in the following paragraphs by clarifying that the passions are not wicked in themselves, but only in how they are used, becoming 'instruments of virtue or of vice according to the way we order our choice' (3.44). If reason remains in control of the human being,

---

[27] See Pelikan (1993: 9); Smith (2001: 61–62).   [28] See Smith (2001).

reason will direct the passions to reach the Good. It is only when reason gives up its position as head that the emotions become problematic, pulling the person whichever way they desire.

Although this explanation indeed overlaps Socrates' argument in the *Phaedrus*, the point I wish to note is how the exchange exhibits the conversational nature of the siblings' conversation. Gregory responds that her argument has progressed 'simply and spontaneously' (3.51), emphasising the extemporaneous nature of their discussion. While there are similarities between Gregory's and Plato's dialogues, Gregory's presentation of two views and his first-hand recounting – especially since it was witnessed by 'many' others who could have corrected inaccuracies (10.1) – underscores the possibility that Gregory records actual conversations rather than simply revises Plato's dialogues.[29] It must also be recognised that any similarities between Macrina's and Socrates' arguments need not arise because her character is copied. If (as Gregory indicates) she is truly a philosopher, she would have required familiarity with Socrates' arguments. Failing to reference them would be more seriously concerning, since it would imply that she lacked education.

Objection 3: The Education Objection

Some scholars interpret Macrina's religiously based early education as evidence that she could not have developed the philosophical knowledge 'Macrina' displays throughout the dialogue.[30] We have seen that she engages with Platonic, Epicurean, and Stoic arguments during the dialogue, an impossible feat if she never studied Classical moral philosophy. However, Macrina's early education does not necessitate her ignorance of Classical philosophy.[31]

First, Gregory's explanation of Macrina's education only explicitly excludes texts that Gregory says could 'teach a tender and impressionable nature either the tragic passions – those passions of women which gave the poets their starting points and themes, or the indecencies of comedy, or the causes of the miseries that befell Troy, which through their degrading tales concerning women tend to the corruption of character' (*VSM* 4.2). In other words, Macrina's early education only explicitly excluded Classical

---

[29] Whether these conversations occurred over the two-day period is another matter. See Objection 4.
[30] Johnson emphasises rejection of pagan studies as key to Macrina's importance (1998: 176–77).
[31] Other scholars suggest Macrina received a philosophical education, including Elm (1994: 42) and Beagon (1995: 171).

literature such as the tragedies and poetry, texts that notoriously prey upon the learner's emotions. The censorship in Macrina's education sounds much like the selective education Socrates recommends for young Guardians in the *Republic*'s Kallipolis 2.376c–3.417b). Just as the reason for Socrates' censorship was to form the souls of young people into good Guardians for the city, the goal of Macrina's education was to form her character. Additionally, Gregory's silence regarding philosophical texts such as Plato's dialogues in Macrina's education cannot alone be taken as proof that Macrina lacked education in moral philosophy. Since the criterion for inclusion in her education was that something should 'bear on the moral life' (*VSM* 4.3), many works of philosophy would have been suitable, including Plato's.[32]

Second, it is doubtful that Macrina lacked rhetorical knowledge of Classical texts given how she behaved in her family's life. Her contact with her father, who was a professional rhetorician, and with her brothers, who did receive a Classical education, would have ensured that she had some understanding of these subjects.[33] Macrina also had ever-increasing influence on her family as she grew older, even taking responsibility for educating her younger brothers after their father died. She could not have provided that education unless her own training had prepared her to do so. Moreover, Gregory recalls that she used her rhetorical skills to trounce their brother Basil after he returned home from school 'puffed up' with an inflated sense of his own abilities (*VSM* 8.2–3). Macrina's education must have allowed her to develop sufficient intellectual skills to defeat Basil, himself a master rhetorician.

Finally, Gregory only details Macrina's *early* education. Excluding a subject from an individual's early education does not necessitate that the same individual continues to be ignorant of that subject when she reaches maturity. Macrina's position as the head of the community at Annisa would have required her to be familiar with the philosophical and religious controversies of the time, many of which involved minutiae of theological and philosophical argumentation.[34] For these reasons, we can reasonably

---

[32] Macrina's siblings support this interpretation. Basil writes that Christians may use passages of Classical philosophy that do not contradict Christian Scripture (*On Reading Pagan Authors* in Migne PG 31, 569), and Gregory often uses Classical philosophy in his writings. See Pelikan (1993).

[33] Corrigan (cited in Hotz (2001: 90)) and Elm recognise this possibility (1994: 42).

[34] These controversies included the Donatist schism and the Arian controversy that would come to a head at the Council of Nicaea (and in which Gregory was very much involved) approximately one year after Macrina's death. It was common for heads of religious communities to correspond about

conclude that Macrina possessed the requisite philosophical background to discuss subjects like the soul and resurrection with Gregory.

Objection 4: The Deathbed Objection

A final objection concerns not merely whether Gregory recorded Macrina's deathbed conversations *accurately* but whether the conversations happened *at all*. As Anna Silvas says in her introduction to the text: 'It is doubtful that brother and sister conducted several hours of strenuous philosophical analyses with Macrina herself almost *in extremis*.'[35] How could a woman gasping out her final breaths be able to present such detailed and lengthy arguments that they continue for seventy pages?

There are two ways to respond to this objection. First, it is possible to respond that Gregory has recorded her deathbed conversations fairly accurately. All three of Gregory's sources corroborate that he was present when Macrina died. Crucially, when Gregory summarises the conversations in the *VSM*, he notes that he shortened his summary because he fears making the text too long to qualify as a letter (20.5). It is for this reason that he writes *On Soul and Resurrection* and perhaps for this reason that the dialogue is as long as it is, namely, because his final conversations with Macrina actually *were* long. He remarks later in the *VSM* that Macrina continued philosophising right until she died. 'For not even during her last breaths did she suffer any qualm at the prospect of her departure, or flinch at the separation from this life. No, right up to her last breath she philosophised with a lofty mind on the convictions she had formed from the beginning about the life here below' (24.3). This summary of Macrina's final hours, written within a year of her death, concurs with Gregory's account in the dialogue, where she philosophises until the final line.

Gregory could have kept a closely accurate recollection of Macrina's arguments, aided by taking notes during their conversation or shortly thereafter, and referring to them when writing the dialogue. The *VSM* records a large break in his visit while she prayed and he rested in a garden (21.1–22.1). This break would have permitted time to reflect on the conversation. The dialogue also indicates where Macrina pauses and Gregory 'recollects' her arguments (4.1, 6.9). In both places, the Greek

ongoing religious debates, partly so they may answer questions from community members. One reference exists that Macrina wrote such letters (see below).

[35] See Silvas (2008: 160).

verb translated 'to recollect' (συλλέγω) bears the sense of 'selecting and gathering up', which may suggest he is collecting his thoughts or jotting down notes to formalise later.[36] This evidence may allow for Gregory being able to provide a good account of the conversations.

However, since it is nevertheless unlikely that Gregory reports her final conversations verbatim, another possibility is worth briefly mentioning. In all three accounts, Gregory refers to Macrina as his beloved 'teacher' (διδάσκαλος) and indicates that her death troubles him because it deprives the world of her teachings about death and immortality (de An. et Res. 10.1; cf. VSM 28.1–2, Ep. 19.6). This evidence may substantiate the possibility that he is not merely presenting her final deathbed conversations but also referencing arguments she has made previously. The VSM shows that she faced death at least four times early in life, when fiancé (5.5), father (7.4), 'dearest' brother (11.2, 12.4), and mother died (15.1–5). Each time, she exhibits a rational demeanour (esp. 12.1–5), implying that she has already personally wrestled with the existential crisis regarding death that grips Gregory in the dialogue's opening scene. If so, she has likely not conceived the arguments in the dialogue only once and extemporaneously but rather is practised at making them. Perhaps then, instead of a verbatim account of a two-day visit, Gregory is providing arguments she was known for making throughout her life. This possibility would preserve the integrity of the dialogue as source material for Macrina. It even has the advantage that it nicely underscores why Gregory calls her 'teacher', since it would mean that Gregory's dialogue portrays her greatest contributions to philosophy rather than a mere two-day snapshot.

Conclusions from the Evidence

In the VSM, Gregory claims that he writes Macrina's biography so she would not be forgotten by being 'veiled in silence' (1.5) after death silenced her voice (27.1). But despite Gregory's efforts, Macrina has been veiled in silence, forgotten or hidden by scholars throughout the intervening centuries.

One tantalising reference that Macrina wrote texts that are now lost exists as a passing note in the fourteenth-century document 'Vatican gr. 578/II, folio 189'. The reference notes that the copyist chose to copy four letters from Theano but not the letters from 'holy Macrina' because the interval of time between Theano's and Macrina's writings was too

---

[36] See Silvas (2008: 197 n. 49).

long. The copyist apparently believes that copying both sets of letters in the same volume risks anachronism by juxtaposing documents from women philosophers who lived nearly ten centuries apart. This evidence suggests that Macrina's writings survived until at least the fourteenth century, when the copyist's choice ensured that her letters would not survive alongside those of Theano in his reproduction. Although the copyist may have had the best of intentions, his choice, along with choices made by countless other scholars and copyists throughout the sixteen centuries since Macrina's life, has ensured that Macrina's voice has rarely been heard.

We have seen several reasons to disprove the objections that Gregory merely uses her as a mouthpiece for his own purposes. But it is worth emphasising that Gregory did not need Macrina as a mouthpiece recounting a fictional conversation on the soul and resurrection. He would have had a readily available male interlocutor for such topics in their brother, Basil, who died nine months before Macrina. Even so, it is Macrina and not Basil who converses with Gregory. Recognising this detail further confirms Macrina's philosophical prowess, especially since the fourth century increasingly understood silence as a dominant virtue of the female sex.[37] But Macrina does not display this supposed 'virtue' in Gregory's writings. Instead, she appears vocally and actively engaged in philosophy, even going as far as to correct her brother's misconceptions.

Although little evidence beyond Gregory's writings exists about Macrina, this is not sufficient cause to assume that Gregory's writings are *uninformative* about her. Muehlberger (2012) contends that, once a story is told, it ceases to be 'merely a story' but becomes part of history. Recognising that Gregory took literary licence in telling Macrina's story cannot undercut that his dialogue is an 'interpretative device' to help us understand Macrina's life and contributions to philosophy. The most important point is that Gregory unveils Macrina as a vocal, engaged philosopher. He portrays a woman in antiquity who tackles some of the most important subjects in human life, including how to find meaning in the face of one's own mortality. Given her philosophical activity, Macrina should no longer be veiled in silence but should instead take her rightful place in the canon of antiquity.[38]

---

[37] On silence as a woman's virtue, see Sheather (2005). On the rising suspicion of women intellectuals in the fourth century in general, see Wolfskeel (1987); Elm (1994); Frank (2000).

[38] I thank Nicholas Baima, the editors and fellow contributors to this volume, and the attendees at the 'Libori Summer School 2019 on Teaching Women Philosophers' for their helpful comments.

CHAPTER 10

Women Philosophers and Ideals of Being a Woman in Neoplatonic Schools of Late Antiquity
The Examples of Sosipatra of Ephesus and Hypatia of Alexandria

Jana Schultz[*]

Introduction

In the Neoplatonic schools of late antiquity, women were involved on different levels, as teachers and students but also as wives and companions. Most prominent are Sosipatra of Ephesus and Hypatia of Alexandria who taught their own circles of students. When it comes to recovering and teaching the thoughts of these female Neoplatonists, we are confronted with the problem that none of their philosophical writings were passed down to us. In approaching their lives and thoughts, we depend on letters written to them and texts written about them.

In the available evidence, both philosophers appear to us as some kind of schism. On the one hand, we find Sosipatra and Hypatia the historical figures, to whom we have access through indirect sources. On the other hand, we find Sosipatra and Hypatia the literary characters, used by other authors to express their views of philosophical life in general and the ideal way of living as a woman in particular. My chapter aims at doing justice to both aspects, unpacking what the sources allow us to conclude regarding the content of the teachings of Sosipatra and Hypatia and discussing how both characters are used by other Neoplatonists to convey certain ideals of femaleness. This examination will be accompanied by short reflections on the nature of the sources in question, especially on the genre of late antique biography and the limitations this genre sets for the project of discovering historical truths.

[*] I owe thanks to Katharine O'Reilly and Caterina Pellò for their remarks and comments on earlier versions, which were crucial in helping the chapter take its current form, and to the participants of the *Philosophical Colloquium* at the Humboldt University Berlin. Finally, I thank the DFG (German Research Foundation) for funding the research for this chapter as part of the project *Die Frau und das Weibliche im Neuplatonismus* (GZ: WI 3873/4-1).

In what follows, I shall start, in the second section, with a brief introduction to Neoplatonic metaphysics, which provides the background for the presentation of the Neoplatonic ideals of femaleness and virtuous women in the third section. In the fourth and fifth sections, I shall then focus on Sosipatra and Hypatia respectively and discuss their philosophical theories, as well as the extent to which they epitomise the Neoplatonic models.

Neoplatonic Metaphysics: A Brief Introduction

Plotinus' metaphysical system is constituted by the three hypostases;[1] the One, the Intellect, and the Soul. The One is the first cause of all things that transcends being. The Intellect is the first entity proceeding from the One. It contains the Platonic Forms and thinks itself. The Soul proceeds from Intellect. It contains form-principles (λόγοι) as images of the Forms, which it unfolds discursively. The hypostasis Soul transcends bodies but causes the world soul and the particular souls, which descend into bodies.[2] Causation takes place through the double movement of procession and reversion. Procession is an emanation due to the overflowing perfection of the hypostasis. What emanates is indeterminate and must revert to its cause to receive determination, to become a specific entity. The Intellect turns towards the One, and the Soul contemplates Intellect. The late Neoplatonists adopt this basic structure but extend the system. A complete outline is beyond the scope of this introduction. I will therefore focus on the developments that are most important for my enquiry.

The late Neoplatonists introduce different intermediary entities between the One, the Intellect, and the Soul.[3] For example, they introduce a dyad between the One and the Intellect to fill the gap between the absolute simple One and the multiplicity of Intellect. They also divide the realm of Intellect, distinguishing between the object of contemplation (that is, being) and the thinking entity (intellect), and consider the object of intellection higher than the entity that contemplates. As the intermediate between intelligible being and intellect, they introduce what is simultaneously intelligible and intellective.

As this shows, the late Neoplatonists organise their metaphysical system in triadic structures. There is a monadic paternal cause (for example,

---

[1] From ὑφίστημι / ὑφίσταμαι. In metaphysics, ὑπόστασις means actual existence, reality, or substance.
[2] See *Ennead* V 1.
[3] For Proclus' metaphysics, see *The Elements of Theology*. For Damascius, see *On the First Principles*.

being), which contains the whole in a unified way, a maternal cause (the intelligible and simultaneously intellective), which incites the procession from the monad, and an offspring containing the whole in a multiplied way (the intellect).

The late Neoplatonists identify their metaphysical entities with gods and goddesses, integrating the Greek pantheon into their metaphysics. Examples of this are integrated in the next section.

Ideals of Femaleness and Being a Woman in Neoplatonic Schools of Late Antiquity

In this section, I will outline the ideals of femaleness and being a woman in the Neoplatonic tradition in order to better understand the literary descriptions of Sosipatra and Hypatia which I will examine in the fourth and fifth sections. I will focus on Proclus since his metaphysics provides us with good material to exemplify the Neoplatonic ideals of femaleness. However, the point I want to make is not that there was a direct influence between Proclus, on the one hand, and the biographical sources on Sosipatra and Hypatia, on the other hand. I want neither to state that Proclus somehow 'invented' the ideals, and that the writers of the biographies then adopted them, nor that Proclus took the ideals out of the biographical tradition.[4] My point is more general. I want to emphasise that there were three ideals of women effective in late Neoplatonism and that these ideals – even though we find them primarily in metaphysical writings – have influenced the way Neoplatonic women philosophers were presented in the biographical tradition.

In early Neoplatonism, the categories of 'maleness' and 'femaleness' play hardly any role in the conceptualisation of metaphysical realities. For Plotinus and Porphyry, the hypostasis Soul is genderless, and since all individual souls are potentially the hypostasis Soul,[5] they are also essentially genderless. Sex and gender come into play only when the soul takes on a body and starts living in a society that has certain expectations of men and women.

---

[4] Proclus never mentions Sosipatra and Hypatia, and thus we cannot know if their lives had influenced his idea of what it meant to be a female philosopher. It is striking that whenever Proclus refers to women philosophers, he refers to Diotima (*in Tim.* 3.281.20–27), or to the Pythagorean women (*in Rep.* 1.248.21–27), but not to the female Neoplatonists, although it is quite unlikely that he had never heard about Sosipatra and Hypatia. Not even his own teacher Asclepigenia is mentioned by him, but only by his student Marinus (*Procl.* 28.10–13).

[5] See *Enn.* 4.3.2.50–59, and also O'Brien (2016: 118).

Women Philosophers and Ideals of Being a Woman 193

As a consequence, according to Plotinus and Porphyry, there is no perfect way for women to *live as women*. Since the ideal way of living a human life consists in imitating the intelligible world, and since the intelligible world is without femaleness, a soul does best if it lives in accordance with its own genderless essence and not in accordance with the femaleness of its body:

> For we have been enchained by nature's chains with which she has surrounded us: the belly, the genitals, the throat, the other bodily members .... Therefore, do not be overly concerned about whether your body is male and female (μήτε οὖν εἰ ἄρρην εἶ μήτε εἰ θήλεια τὸ σῶμα πολυπραγμόνει); do not regard yourself as a woman, Marcella, for I did not devote myself to you as such. Flee from every effeminate element (θηλυνόμενον) of the soul as if you were clothed in a male body (ἄρρενος εἶχες τὸ σῶμα). (Porph. *Marc.* 33.6–16, trans. O'Brien Wicker[1987])

The late Neoplatonists, in contrast, conceive of crucial parts of the intelligible reality as gendered. In Proclus' system, maleness and femaleness proceed from the Living Being Itself, which belongs to the Intelligible Intellect (also called 'the third god'),[6] and is described as androgynous:

> And the third [intelligible] god is father and mother. Since if the Living Being Itself is in this god, the cause of maleness and femaleness must exist primarily there, for they [maleness and femaleness] belong to the living beings. (*Theol. Plat.* 4.81.20–23)

After the Living Being Itself, maleness and femaleness are differentiated. Therefore, from this level onwards most entities are not androgynous but either male or female. But what does it mean for a metaphysical entity to be male, female, or androgynous? Proclus and Damascius define these properties in relation to the fundamental principles of Limit and the Unlimited (understood as infinite power):

> For Power is also before the male and the female and it is in both and with both. Since Power extends to all beings and all being participates in Power, as the stranger from Elea says. For Power is everywhere, but the female participates to a greater degree in the peculiar nature of Power and the male participates to a greater degree in the unity according to Limit. (Procl. *Theol. Plat.* 4.91.21–26, for a similar definition in Damascius, see *in Phil.* 100.1–4)

Thus, Limit and the Unlimited exist purely only in their first manifestation. All beings that follow them participate in them to varying degrees. By

---

[6] The Intelligible Intellect has a triadic structure, and the Living Being Itself is the third part of this triad (Procl. *Theol. Plat.* 3.52–54).

participating in Limit to a high degree, entities receive what enables them to be paternal causes in procreation. As Limit provides stability, uniformity, and determination universally (Procl. *Theol. Plat.* 3.32.15–16), the paternal deities provide these features in the particular context of (metaphysical) procreation. By participating in the Unlimited to a high degree, entities receive what makes them maternal causes, providing to (metaphysical) procreation what the Unlimited provides universally, namely procession and multiplication (Procl. *Theol. Plat.* 3.32.17–19).[7] And we can speculate that androgynous deities are entities that participate in both principles in a balanced way.

What is important to notice is that although there are essential differences between male, female, and androgynous beings long before the corporal level, every being contains male and female elements, since every being must partake to some degree in Limit as well as in the Unlimited.

With Plotinus and Porphyry, the late Neoplatonists share the idea that humans should contemplate the intelligible reality to find a model for the perfection of their souls. However, according to them, the souls contemplating the intelligible realm are confronted with a reality in which gender is a crucial factor. Thus, they cannot advise women to simply transcend (their) gender and become psychologically genderless. Rather, the late Neoplatonists offer women three ideals that all derive from the intelligible reality.

The first ideal of femaleness is embodied by the maternal goddesses of the intelligible realm. These entities are distinguished by their generative and their intermediate (connective) nature.[8] The main function of the maternal goddesses is to incite (προκαλουμένη, Procl. *Theol. Plat.* 3.90.3–5) the procession from the father, whereby they multiply (πολλαπλασιάζουσα, Procl. *Inst.* 152.9–12) the powers that are unified in the paternal cause. By inciting the procession from the father perpetually, the maternal causes also establish a lasting bond between father and offspring and enable the offspring to revert to its cause (Procl. *in Cra.* 168.1–7).[9] Thus, one possible way for a woman to orientate herself to the intelligible world is to imitate the ideal of femaleness exemplified in the maternal goddesses, by choosing a life dedicated to the Unlimited and, in the case of humans, to sensible matters (Procl. *in Tim.* 3.338.2–6),

---

[7] See also Rosan (1949: 146); Kutash (2011: 178–80); and Schultz (2019b: 258–60).
[8] I argue for this thesis in detail in Schultz (2019b).
[9] Maternal causes are similarly described by Damascius (*in Parm.* 2.20.11–15).

including marriage and procreation.¹⁰ The contributions of paternal and maternal deities are not of the same value. While the activity of the paternal causes is unambiguously good, the activity of the maternal causes is somehow ambiguous. Kutash (2011: 59) shows that for Proclus 'the source of fecundity in the universe is also responsible for disorder' since by proceeding from their causes secondary entities become more particular and divided. That is why the manifestations of the Unlimited (mostly female entities) must be held in check by manifestations of Limit (mostly male entities):

> Even where gender had been divided, male and female of the same rank have the same tasks, it is accomplished in an initial way (πρώτως) by the male, and in a subordinate way (ὑφειμένως) by the female. (Procl, *in Tim.* 1.46.21–24, trans. Tarrant 2006)

Thus, women imitating the maternal goddesses will find themselves in an invaluable but subordinate position.

Second, Proclus' metaphysics integrates virgin goddesses, who are described as being detached from femaleness: Athena is characterised as 'unfemale (ἀθήλυντον)' (*in Rep.* 2.192, 18),¹¹ and Artemis as 'despising (μισῆσαι)' (*in Cra.* 179.6) the generative work of the maternal goddesses. These goddesses have distinctively male traits, namely they partake in Limit and act as unifying and determining causes (*in Cra.* 185.33–38).¹² And, surprisingly, the virgin goddesses appear to be even more characterised by Limit than the male goddesses of the same metaphysical level (*in Tim.* 1.166.5–10).¹³

Thus, the virgin goddesses offer women an alternative ideal to imitate, a life fully dedicated to what is due to Limit. In the case of the human soul, this is the contemplation of the intelligible realm (Procl. *in Tim.* 3.338.2–6). However, this kind of life involves a strong detachment from everything associated with femaleness, especially procreation – a much greater detachment from such matters than it is suggested for the average male – just as the virgin goddesses are also more detached from the Unlimited than the male (paternal) gods.

---

¹⁰ In the soul, Limit is manifested in the circuit of the Same and the Unlimited is manifested in the circuit of the Different (Procl, *in Tim.* 2.258, 11–14), which is responsible for grasping sensible entities (Procl. *in Tim.* 3.338, 2–6). See also Schultz (2019a).
¹¹ See also Iamblichus' *Thelougoumena Arithmeticae* 71.9.   ¹² See Schultz (2022).
¹³ Paternal causes must be open to the inciting activity of the maternal causes while the virgin goddesses can detach themselves from everything associated with the Unlimited.

Thus far, it seems as if – for the late Neoplatonists – women are in a position in which they can either connect positively to their femaleness by submitting to males or live a more independent life at the cost of detaching from what is female.[14]

However, a close examination of Proclus' metaphysics reveals a third model, the ideal of becoming androgynous. We can find an example of this ideal in Proclus' description of Diotima. As I have argued in a recent paper,[15] Diotima devotes herself to the contemplation of the intelligible realm – something associated with maleness. Yet nowhere does Proclus characterise her as un-female. On the contrary, he emphasises that her success is due to her unique understanding of and relationship to intermediate entities, especially the demonic realm, which is associated with femaleness due to its intermediary nature (*in Alc.* 68.4–7).

Diotima is presented as a person who does not cultivate one side of her soul – the male or the female – at the cost of the other, but who carefully counterbalances both parts and utilises them for her philosophical and religious progress. This ideal might be best described as becoming (or being) psychologically androgynous, for it combines both male and female traits in a balanced way. Only this third ideal allows women to cultivate their intellectual abilities and engage in philosophy while preserving their femaleness.

With these different ideals in mind, the examination will now turn to Sosipatra and Hypatia. What I hope to show is that the way different authors present Sosipatra and Hypatia is to some extent influenced by the ideals of being a woman outlined above. Thus, after analysing in detail what the sources tell us about these female philosophers, I will try to identify ways in which the different accounts of Sosipatra and Hypatia match one or more of the ideals.

Sosipatra of Ephesus

There is only one surviving source of evidence for Sosipatra of Ephesus, the *Lives of the Philosophers and Sophists* by Eunapius. Eunapius belonged to the circle of Iamblichus via a chain of successors: he studied under Chrysanthius who received his philosophical education from Iamblichus' student Aedesius. Sosipatra too belonged to this circle, for she married Eustathius, another student of Iamblichus, and established her own

---

[14] See also Damascius' description of the goddess Night (*in Parm.* 2.43.4).   [15] Schultz (2019c).

school in Pergamon where she taught the same group of students as Aedesius:[16]

> In her own home Sosipatra held a chair of philosophy that rivaled his, and after attending the lectures of Aedesius, the students would go to hear hers; and though there was none that did not greatly appreciate and admire the accurate learning (λόγοις ἀκρίβειαν) of Aedesius, they positively adored and revered the woman's inspired teaching (ἐνθουσιασμὸν). (6.9.2.1–6)[17]

Before going deeper into Eunapius' description of Sosipatra, I would like to take a brief look at the nature of our source.

Eunapius' work is a collective biography, which brings together several short biographies of philosophers and sophists of the fourth century. Collective biographies in late antiquity usually aim at giving an account of the holy life by portraying people who exemplify it.[18] This determines what information is provided concerning the historical Sosipatra.[19] Moreover, collective biographers who portray people as examples of one specific form of life tend to bypass differences between the lives and doctrines of various philosophers and aim to depict 'the philosopher' or 'the philosophical life' in general.[20]

Eunapius identifies the holy life with the life of the theurgist. He then assumes that a successful theurgist must also be a philosopher, since the appropriate practice of theurgic rituals depends on philosophical knowledge of the divine.[21] In most of his biographies, the focus is on the theurgic achievements of his subjects.[22] Thus, it is not surprising that his portrayal of Sosipatra is dedicated to her achievements as an outstanding theurgist.

Eunapius' description of her childhood focuses on her initiation into theurgy, which is reported to have happened thanks to two mysterious strangers (6.6.7.1–14.3), referred to as 'initiates in the lore called Chaldean' (6.7.5.6), who are not simply humans trained in theurgy but 'blessed spirits' (συμφανέστατα δαίμονας, 6.7.11.5). The exact content of their teachings remains secret but Eunapius reports on the effects of the initiation: Sosipatra had developed such clairvoyance and oracular speech

---

[16] See also Addey (2018b: 148–49).
[17] All translations of *Lives of the Philosophers and Sophists* are from Wilmer C. Wright.
[18] See Cox Miller (2000: 222–28) and Iles Johnstone (2016: 99–100). The holy life here means the life that connects the soul with the divine.
[19] See Cox Miller (1983: 6 and 45) and De Temmerman (2016: 13).
[20] See Cox Miller (2000: 228) and De Temmerman (2016: 22). [21] See also Penella (1990: 33).
[22] See 4.1.7.4–9.5 regarding Plotinus' biography, and 5.1.12–2.6.6 regarding Iamblichus' biography.

already at ten years old that her father 'was convinced that his daughter was a goddess' (6.7.5.3).

The account of Sosipatra's adult life is also centred around her achievements as a theurgist. Eunapius focuses on two aspects. First, he provides us with more examples of her clairvoyance and foreknowledge, namely that she revealed to her fiancé his future (6.8.3.4–6.3), that despite being absent she knew exactly how her student Maximus performed a ritual (6.9.7.1–4), and that she knew what happened to her kinsman Philometer who had an accident miles away (6.9.12.7–14.1). Second, Eunapius emphasises how Sosipatra's theurgic abilities enriched her teachings. He writes that her teachings were 'inspired (ἐνθουσιασμὸν)' (6.9.2.6) and that she gained knowledge from a divine source.[23] Besides this focus on Sosipatra's outstanding theurgic abilities, Eunapius' account provides us with further information about her philosophy. An important passage concerns her training after her Chaldean teachers left:

> And as she grew to the full measure of her youthful vigour, she had no other teachers, but ever on her lips were the works of the poets, philosophers, and orators; and those works that others comprehend but incompletely and dimly (μόλις ὑπῆρχε καὶ ἀμυδρῶς εἰδέναι), and then only by hard work and painful drudgery (τοῖς πεπονηκόσι καὶ τεταλαιπωρημένοι), she could expound with careless ease (ὀλιγωρίας ἔφραζε), serenely and painlessly, and with her light swift touch would make their meaning clear (εὐκόλως καὶ ἀλύπως εἰς τὸ σαφὲς ἐπιτρέχουσα). (6.8.2.1–9.8.2.6)

We cannot know whether Sosipatra really learned all this autodidactically, for a child being wise without going through a classical process of education is a common *topos* in late antique biographies dedicated to the holy life.[24] But what we can conclude is that she was seen by her contemporaries as a gifted teacher and commentator on the whole canon of philosophy and Greek *paídeia*. Unfortunately, however, Eunapius does not provide information about the content of Sosipatra's interpretations. Thus, we cannot know whether they contained original ideas (and if so, which ones). Two facts seem to speak in favour of Sosipatra's

---

[23] Surprisingly, Eunapius does not describe Sosipatra as actively engaging in rituals. The inspiration and clairvoyance just seems to come to her. This has been vividly discussed in scholarship. See Addey (2018b: 151–56), Denzey Lewis (2014: 276–77), and Iles Johnstone (2016: 113–14).

[24] There are two reasons for the prominence of this *topos*. First, a mysterious education was regarded as a sign of the divine nature of its recipient. See Tanaseanu-Döbler (2013: 130) and Iles Johnstone (2016: 108). Second, stability of character was regarded as a sign of goodness and holiness. That is why biographers tend to attribute to holy figures a permanent wisdom, rather than a wisdom received through a process of education. See Cox Miller (1983: 22 and 57).

interpretations containing original ideas, namely that Eunapius described her teaching as inspired – one might argue that it would be strange if the divine source had simply made her repeat what some other philosopher had said – and that he states that the students preferred her lectures to those of Aedesius (6.9.2.1–6).[25] It is also interesting that Eunapius describes Sosipatra's education as beginning with an initiation in divine things and then turning to philosophical discourses on various topics. This seems to suggest that she understood the philosophical and poetical tradition in the light of her religious knowledge, probably interpreting Plato as being in agreement with the *Chaldean Oracles*.[26]

There are two other passages on Sosipatra's philosophy. In one passage, she prompts her student Maximus to turn his soul to the intelligible (divine) world:

> 'Rise, my son. The gods love you if you raise your eyes to them (ἐὰν σὺ πρὸς ἐκείνους βλέπῃς) and do not lean towards earthly and perishable things (μὴ ῥέπῃς ἐπὶ τὰ γήϊνα καὶ ἐπίκηρα χρήματα).' (6.9.7.6–8.1)

The second passage is about a lecture Sosipatra held on the nature of the soul:

> The theme under discussion and their inquiry was concerning the soul. Several theories were propounded, and then Sosipatra began to speak, and gradually by her proofs disposed of their arguments (κατὰ μικρὸν ταῖς ἀποδείξεσι διαλύουσα τὰ προβαλλόμενα); then she fell to discoursing (ἐμπίπτουσα λόγον) on the descent of the soul (περὶ καθόδου ψυχῆς), and what part of it is subject to punishment (τί τὸ κολαζόμενον), what part immortal (τί τὸ ἀθάνατον), when in the midst of her bacchic and frenzied flow of speech (μεταξὺ τοῦ κορυβαντιασμοῦ καὶ τῆς ἐκβακχεύσεως) she became silent . . . . (6.9.11.3–12.6)

The suggestion is that she taught – like all Neoplatonists – that the soul had its origin in the intelligible realm and descended from there into the sensible world, that she held the soul to have parts and that one of these parts (reason) was considered immortal. This passage also reveals something about the way in which Sosipatra taught philosophy, for it shows

---

[25] However, these aspects of Eunapius' account can be explained differently. Iles Johnstone (2016: 108) suggests that Eunapius might have characterised Sosipatra's knowledge and teachings as divinely given because he wanted to provide Iamblichus' philosophy a divine justification and strengthen philosophy's connection with theurgy. Moreover, he might have described Sosipatra's lectures as preferable to Aedesius' simply because Aedesius is reputed to have mostly refrained from teaching theurgy and practising it publicly (6.1.4.6–6.1).

[26] See also Addey (2018a:428).

that she could easily switch between a dialectical mode of speaking, developing and refuting arguments, and an inspired mode of teaching.[27]

Let us now turn to the question of what model of womanhood Eunapius' portrayal of Sosipatra conveys. I will argue that Eunapius' Sosipatra exemplifies a person who harmonises the male and female elements in her soul and becomes (psychologically) androgynous. For Sosipatra is pictured as using the female powers of both generating and connecting (intermediating) but combines them with the male connoted powers of contemplating and ruling. As noted above, Eunapius uses Sosipatra, as well as other male philosophers, to exemplify the holy life as the life of the philosopher-theurgist. This shows that he does not consider philosophies through religion as something specifically female. On the contrary, this approach seems more appropriate for men, since Eunapius marks Sosipatra as an exception (6.6.6.1–3). Thus, in some way, Sosipatra is pictured as a woman who lives a life that is more suited for men, dedicated to the contemplation of the divine. Eunapius also reports that the Chaldeans promised that Sosipatra would have 'a mind not like a woman's or a mere human being's (οὐ κατὰ γυναῖκα καὶ ἄνθρωπον ἔσται μόνον)' (6.6.12.5).

Yet it is equally noteworthy that Eunapius does not describe Sosipatra as detached from what the late Neoplatonists connect with femaleness. She is presented as having much in common with the maternal goddesses, for she was a wife and mother and thus fulfilled her generative potential, and because she acted as a mediator. Due to the inspired nature of her teachings, Sosipatra acted analogously to the mediating activity of the maternal goddesses. For as the maternal goddesses provide their offspring intelligible nourishment from the paternal cause (Procl. *in Cra.* 168.1–7), Sosipatra handed over knowledge from a divine source to which her students had no direct access.

However, Eunapius emphasises that Sosipatra fulfilled these feminine functions in a self-determined way, using the male connoted power of ruling to order her own life. Sosipatra is in no need of male guidance and dominance. Already as a child, she gained independence from her father, for after her initiation he is reported to have 'permitted her to live as she pleased and did not interfere with any of her affairs' (6.8.1.3–4). In the arrangement of the marriage with Eustathius, she plays an active role

---

[27] It is important to notice that the Neoplatonists do not regard being inspired as being a passive mouthpiece of the gods. They understand inspiration as requiring a receptivity that the theurgist herself has to cultivate by acquiring the highest kinds of virtue. See Addey (2018b: 151).

(6.8.3.1–3). And when it comes to the education of her sons, she is not described as passing on the skills of her husband, but her own skills, which partly coincide with his and partly surpass them (6.6.5.1–6.1). Therefore, their son Antoninus is not pictured as the successor of his father but as the successor of both parents: 'But Antoninus was worthy of his parents (Ἀντωνῖνος δὲ ἦν ἄξιος τῶν πατέρων)' (6.9.15.3).

Thus, all in all, Eunapius characterises Sosipatra as a woman who neither neglects her femaleness nor lives exclusively according to what the late Neoplatonists conceptualise as female. Of the three Neoplatonic ideals of womanhood, Eunapius' Sosipatra can best be interpreted as exemplifying the androgynous.

Hypatia of Alexandria

We have several sources of evidence for Hypatia of Alexandria, but the most important ones for our examination are Damascius' *Life of Isidore* (*The Philosophical History*) and the letters her student Synesius wrote to her.[28] Damascius' *Life of Isidore* is – like Eunapius' *Life of the Philosophers and Sophists* – a collective biography aimed at depicting the holy life. However, Damascius' method differs from Eunapius': while Eunapius presents most of the thinkers as examples of the holy life, Damascius focuses on praising Isidore, presenting him as the ideal holy man whom no one else can rival. He therefore tends to downplay other philosophers. Regarding Synesius, it is important to notice that he used his collection of letters to present himself as the kind of philosopher who integrates various cultural heritages, especially Christianity, Neoplatonism, and Greek *paideia*.[29] All sources (except Synesius' letters)[30] place great emphasis on Hypatia's murder by Christian monks, which is connected to the power struggle between Alexandria's governor Orestes and its bishop Cyril. However, although most sources describe the murder in detail, the story of Hypatia's death is nowhere used to enlighten her philosophical teachings.

More informative are the accounts of her upbringing. Damascius tells us that Hypatia was taught by her father, the mathematician Theon, and that 'she was not content with the mathematical education her father gave her,

---

[28] Other sources for the life of Hypatia are Socrates of Constantinople's *Historia Ecclesiatica*, Cassiodor's *Historia Ecclesiastica*, John of Nikiu's *Chronicle*, Palladas' *Anthologia Platnania*; Philostorgios' *Historia Ecclesiastica*, Hesychius' *Onomatologus*, and Malalas' *Chronographia*.
[29] See Sogno and Watts (2018: 393).   [30] Synesius died before Hypatia.

but occupied herself with some distinction in the other branches of philosophy' (*Isid.* Fr. 102*, 3–4).³¹ Here, we see an important difference with Sosipatra. While Sosipatra was described as first gaining divine knowledge and then turning to philosophical discourse, Hypatia becomes a philosopher through a classical ascent, very similar to the one described in Plato's *Republic* (510b2–11e5). Thus, Sosipatra and Hypatia seem to represent alternative ways of becoming a philosopher, whereby Hypatia's education makes her example easier to follow. For while Sosipatra's knowledge is described as the result of a special grace of the gods, Hypatia's knowledge is the result of talent combined with a good – but not divine – education.

Despite acquiring philosophical knowledge on top of her mathematical education, Hypatia remained active as a mathematician.³² The only works by Hypatia we at least know by title are mathematical works, as noted by Hesychius (*Suda* 4.644.4–6). Hypatia also contributed to the third book of her father's commentary on Ptolemy's *Almagest*, and thus some of her mathematical knowledge is passed down to us in this form.³³ Regarding her teaching activity, Damascius portrays her as a gifted teacher of and commentator on the whole philosophical tradition: 'She progressed through town, publicly interpreting (ἐξηγεῖτο) the works of Plato, Aristotle or any other philosopher' (*Isid.* Fr. 102*.5–7).³⁴ We also learn that she used the method of dialectics (*Isid.* Fr. 104*.11). But again – as in the case of Sosipatra – the sources do not give information on whether Hypatia contributed original ideas to the interpretation of Plato and Aristotle.³⁵ Synesius presents Alexandria as replacing Athens as the 'haven of wisdom' thanks to Hypatia's school (*Ep.* 136.15–16), and this judgement might appear strange if one assumes that Hypatia has simply taught the interpretations of other philosophers. However, one must also consider first that originality was not such a central value in late antique schools as it

---

[31] All translations of the *Life of Isidore* are from Polymnia Athanassiadi. The fragments and lines are orientated on Clemens Zintzen's edition. The '*' indicates that it is likely, but not entirely sure, that the fragment belonged to the *Life of Isidore*.

[32] As Watts (2017: 35) argues, Hypatia's turn to philosophy means that she re-evaluated the relation between the two disciplines, coming to understand philosophy as leading to the highest reality, while Theon ascribed this role to mathematics.

[33] For Hypatia's mathematical achievements, see Deakin (2007: 87–101).

[34] Watts (2017: 40) takes 'or any other philosopher' to mean that the curriculum in Hypatia's school contains canonical texts of Aristotle and Plato and the interpretative tradition around them. As Dzielska (1995: 57) argues, the remark that Hypatia 'progressed through town' suggests that Hypatia was a public figure and gave public lectures.

[35] Gertz (2020: 145) argues that we can assume that Hypatia's interpretations include a harmonisation of Plato and Aristotle in accordance with interpretative traditions in Alexandria.

is in contemporary scholarship. Preserving the legacy of Plato was considered far more important. And second, one has to keep in mind that Synesius used his letters for self-presentation. The praise for Hypatia's school is also a recommendation of his own philosophy.

Besides her public teaching, Hypatia was engaged in Alexandrian politics. Damascius describes her as a counsellor for the people ruling Alexandria (*Isid.* Fr. 104*.13–15); and in *Letter* 81, Synesius asks her to use her influence to receive justice for two friends who lost their property (16–20). Her engagement points to an interest in ethics and political philosophy, but the sources do not give any details.

A highly debated question is what role theurgy plays in Hypatia's philosophy. While some interpreters regard her as critical towards or uninterested in theurgy,[36] others suggest that she considered theurgy crucial for philosophy.[37] There are two aspects of Damascius' portrayal that support the thesis that Hypatia was not much concerned with theurgy. First, Damascius states in one fragment that Hypatia is just a geometer and not a real philosopher (*Isid.* [Phot. *Bibl.* 242] 164.1–2). With this remark he might indicate that she falls short of being a real philosopher since she is not outstanding in theurgy (or engaged in it at all), for Damascius regards the ideal philosopher as someone who integrates philosophy and theurgy (*in Phd.* 1.138–44). Second, Damascius does not describe Hypatia as performing any forms of theurgy, although he is – like Eunapius – quite interested in the theurgic achievements of the people he portrays.[38]

Synesius' letters, however, refer to practices that suggest a shared interest in theurgy, such as divine inspiration and dream divination (*Ep.* 154.95–109), the making of a hydroscope (*Ep.* 15.1–11) and an astrolabe (*ad Pae.* 4.15–17), which might have been used for ritualistic purposes,[39] and the fact that Synesius praises Hypatia's 'oracular utterance (θεσπεσίας αὐδῆς)' (*Ep.* 5, 306, trans. Deakin), which might indicate that he regards her teachings as inspired.[40]

---

[36] See Dzielska (1995: 63); Deakin (2007: 84); Watts (2017: 43); and Gertz (2020: 142).
[37] See Cameron and Long (1993: 49–58), and Addey (2018a: 430–31).
[38] Other women are praised for their ritualistic achievements, like Anthusa (*Isid.* [Phot. *Bibl.* 242] 69.1–17) and an unnamed woman (*Isid.* [Phot. *Bibl.* 242] 191.1–4). Moreover, many of the male philosophers Damascius describes are distinguished by their theurgic abilities, such as Heraiscus (*Isid.* Fr. 174).
[39] However, Synesius does not state that these instruments are needed for rituals, and there are other possible uses. See Deakin (2007: 64–65, and 104–5).
[40] For all points, see Addey (2018a: 430–31).

Especially interesting is Synesius' *On Dreams*, which, according to *Letter* 154, he sent to Hypatia,[41] and in which he frequently refers to the *Chaldean Oracles* as an authority.[42] Here, Synesius values certain kinds of rituals that might be regarded as part of theurgy, while being critical of others.[43] He praises dream divination (131B1–3) and he refers to the common *sympátheia* (sympathy, corresponding affection) within the cosmos that can be used to establish some form of contact with the encosmic divine via rituals (132B9–D1). However, Synesius also distances himself from other rituals, namely those using cosmic objects to contact the divine transcending the cosmos (133A6–B4) and those aiming at acting forcibly towards the divine (145B3–7). This suggests that Hypatia and Synesius were in an ongoing dialogue on theurgy.[44]

Overall, our sources indicate that Hypatia was not altogether uninterested in theurgy. However, in contrast to Sosipatra, it is striking that almost no source describes Hypatia as a theurgist,[45] while all sources emphasise her philosophical, mathematical, and political achievements. Thus, it seems safe to conclude that theurgic rituals were not the heart of her philosophical teaching.

After this general picture of Hypatia's philosophy, let us now look at some more specific topics. In Damascius, there is just one passage that might give insight into the content of Hypatia's teaching – that is, the anecdote in which she cured a student of his love for her by throwing a napkin with menstrual blood and saying: 'This is what you are in love with, young man, and not a thing of beauty' (*Isid.* Fr. 102*.15–17).

As Cameron and Long (1993: 42–44) point out, the historicity of the anecdote is doubtful, for Damascius himself reports that there is another version of the story according to which Hypatia cured the student with music (*Isid.* Fr. 102*.12). However, I do not agree with Cameron and Long's interpretation that Damascius made up the anecdote to downplay Hypatia as a Cynic street philosopher. In contrast, I would argue that the anecdote fits quite well into a Neoplatonic context, due to its thematic connection to Plato's *Symposium* and the ascent from sensible to intelligible beauty.[46]

---

[41] For the question of whether it is justified to draw conclusions about Hypatia's philosophy from Synesius' works, see below.
[42] See Gertz (2014: 111–14 and 122–24).   [43] See Tanaseanu-Döbler (2012: 206–12).
[44] However, as Gertz (2020: 141) emphasises, being in discourse about the Chaldean Oracles and theurgy does not necessarily imply that one practices rituals.
[45] An exception is John of Nikiu's *Chronicle* (84.87–88).
[46] For the connection with Plato's *Symposium*, see also Dzielska (1995: 51).

If we read the anecdote in a Platonic context, it is striking that Hypatia does not interpret the situation in accordance with Plato's *Symposium* (201a4–11d1), saying that the young man loves something beautiful by loving her beautiful body but that he must learn to use this example of beauty to recall the true intelligible beauty. By contrast, Hypatia uses the situation to demonstrate that the body is an evil and that the soul should strive to separate itself from it.[47]

Thus, although I agree with Cameron and Long that the anecdote might not be historically true, I would argue that far from declassifying Hypatia as a Cynic street philosopher, the anecdote roots her within the Platonic tradition and thereby might reveal some information about Hypatia's attitude towards body and soul.

More hints at the content of Hypatia's philosophical interests might be found in Synesius' letters. Synesius presents himself as a student who adheres to the teachings received in Hypatia's school. Thus, it is not unreasonable to assume that his philosophy is close to Hypatia's.[48] However, for most philosophical topics in Synesius' letters to Hypatia – as imagination and dream divination (*Ep.* 154) and the role of fate in human life (*Ep.* 81) – we have no indication of whether they really aligned with Hypatia's interests. An exception is the *Dion*, a work in which Synesius argues in favour of integrating rhetoric and poetry into the philosophical life. In *Letter* 154, Synesius suggests that Hypatia approved the work for publication, which in turn might indicate that she agreed with its content or at least regarded it as philosophically interesting:

> Concerning all this I shall await your decision (ὑπὲρ δὴ τούτων ἁπάντων σε κρίνουσαν περιμενοῦμεν) .... If it [the *Dion*] does not seem to you worthy of Greek ears, if, like Aristotle, you prize truth more than friendship, a close and profound darkness will overshadow it, and mankind will never hear it mentioned. (90–98, trans. Deakin)[49]

Finally, let us turn to the question of what model of womanhood the portrayals of Hypatia convey. Regarding Synesius, it is important to notice that he does not take much interest in Hypatia's gender. In his letters, Hypatia's gender only becomes apparent when he directly addresses her, as, for example, in *Letter* 16:

---

[47] See also Dzielska (1995: 51) who argues that the anecdote shows 'Hypatia's repugnance toward the human body and sensuality'.
[48] For this methodological consideration, see also Deakin (2007: 78).
[49] As Petkas (2020: 17) points out, Synesius assigns Hypatia the role of the 'literary critic' and thereby places her in 'a prominent position, even a position of leadership, in an intellectual network'.

I am dictating this letter to you from my bed, but may you receive it in good health, mother, sister, teacher (μῆτερ καὶ ἀδελφὴ καὶ διδάσκαλε) and withal benefactress, and whatever is honoured in name and deed. (2–5, trans Deakin)

The fact that he calls Hypatia 'mother' does not indicate a special interest in her gender nor does it suggest that their relationship is affected by the fact that Hypatia is female and Synesius male, for it was quite common to refer to one's teachers as a parent.[50] Since Synesius does not address the issue of Hypatia's gender in his letters, one might speculate that he does not regard gender as being of much importance but encourages his readers not to put weight on the gender of the people with whom they interact but on their virtue and intellectual abilities. Damascius, in contrast, puts greater emphasis on Hypatia's gender. When contrasting Hypatia with Isidore, he mentions Hypatia's femininity as a disadvantage: 'Isidore and Hypatia were very different, not only as man differs from woman (οὐ μόνον οἷα γυναικὸς ἀνήρ), but as a true philosopher differs from a mathematician' (*Isid.* [Phot. *Bibl.* 242] 164). In other fragments (102*–4*), Damascius describes Hypatia as a philosopher as well as a mathematician, but that does not soften the impression that he uses Hypatia to show that femininity is an obstacle to the philosophical life. For he portrays Hypatia as a person who disconnects herself from femaleness.

When reconsidering the three ideals outlined in the second section above, we see that Damascius' Hypatia resembles the virgin goddesses in at least three aspects: She remains a virgin (*Isid.* Fr. 102*.9); she devotes her life to activities associated with maleness, namely philosophy, mathematics, and politics; and she shows a disdain of the procreative potential of the female body, as it is best shown in the above-mentioned anecdote in which she cures a student from loving her by arousing disgust for menstrual blood (*Isid.* Fr. 102*.13–16), the symbol of female procreative power.[51] In this way, Damascius' Hypatia contributes to the picture that a dedication to philosophy is best achieved if one's female aspects are set aside.

Thus, all in all, Synesius' and Damascius' Hypatia offer us two different pictures of what it means to be a female philosopher. Synesius provides us with a picture of Hypatia as a person for whom gender is not of much concern, while Damascius portrays her as a person who actively strives to

---

[50] See Harich-Schwarzbauer (2011: 76).
[51] See Deakin (2007: 63) who argues that due to the menstrual blood the anecdote connects Hypatia with the cult of Artemis.

live exclusively according to what the late Neoplatonists conceptualise as male. Of the three Neoplatonic ideals of womanhood, Damascius' Hypatia can be best interpreted as exemplifying the ideal of the virgin goddesses, while Synesius' Hypatia stands outside the three ideals.[52]

Final Remarks

We have seen that Sosipatra and Hypatia were influential figures in the Neoplatonic tradition. Both were gifted teachers and commentators who taught their own circle of students. Hypatia was also renowned for mathematical achievements while Sosipatra was regarded as an outstanding theurgist. Besides their direct contribution to the passing on of Neoplatonic philosophy, both became memorable characters in works written by other Neoplatonists. As literary characters, they were used to convey certain ideals of the philosophical life, especially of the philosophical life lived by a woman.

Sosipatra is pictured by Eunapius as a person who successfully combined the powers Neoplatonists connote as male and the powers Neoplatonists connote as female, unifying the contemplative life with the caring role of the mother and mediator. The example of Hypatia shows that one and the same character can be used by different authors to express different ideals. Synesius presents his relationship with Hypatia as one in which gender is not a determining factor, thus promoting the ideal of seeing each other primarily as (genderless) rational beings. Damascius, in contrast, uses Hypatia to show that femaleness is in tension with the philosophical life, and thus a woman can reach perfection in philosophy by focusing on the male (intellectual) parts of her soul.

Regarding the aim of the whole chapter, one might notice that a close examination of the sources has brought relatively limited insights into the philosophy of Sosipatra and Hypatia. That is partly due to the fact that we only have a few sources (letters and short biographical remarks) and partly due to the nature of the sources in question for whom transmitting philosophical thoughts is not the main concern. Thus, if we consider Sosipatra and Hypatia as historical figures, our ability to assess their contributions to Neoplatonic philosophy is limited.

---

[52] One might speculate why Synesius' and Damascius' portrayals of Hypatia differ in this way. One reason might be that Synesius was a Christian Neoplatonist and therefore might have felt closer to the Neoplatonism of Plotinus and Porphyry in which the traditional Greek deities do not play a major role. And as outlined above, Plotinus and Porphyry regard the metaphysical principles and the soul as genderless.

Nonetheless, if we consider Sosipatra and Hypatia as literary characters, the sources allow us to conclude what ideal of femaleness and being a woman they exemplified, which, in turn, helps us to understand the Neoplatonic concepts of gender and femaleness. However, the topic of Sosipatra and Hypatia as literary characters calls for further investigations that go beyond this chapter. In order to gain a deeper understanding of Sosipatra and Hypatia as literary characters, it would be especially interesting to examine them not only in relation to metaphysical ideals (as in this chapter) but also in relation to the descriptions of other (Neoplatonic) women in the biographical tradition. I leave this to future researchers to explore.

CHAPTER 11

Reappraising Ban Zhao
The Advent of Chinese Women Philosophers

Ann A. Pang-White

Introduction

A member of a family of accomplished scholar-officials during the Eastern Han dynasty (25–220 CE), Ban Zhao 班昭 (c. 45–117 CE) was the first woman historian and woman philosopher in ancient China with written works passed down to the contemporary world. The *Book of the Later Han* (*Houhanshu* 後漢書), an enormous dynastic history compiled by Fan Ye 范曄 (398–445 CE), describes her as '*bo xue gao cai* 博學高才 (an exceptionally gifted polymath)' and tells that she was summoned by Emperor He to complete the 'Treatise on Astronomy' and 'Eight Tables' at the imperial library after her eldest brother (the main official in charge of the *Book of the [Former] Han*, *Hanshu* 漢書) prematurely died. Fan Ye also mentioned that 'when the *Hanshu* was first completed, many scholars were unable to comprehend it. Ma Rong [a renowned scholar-official] from her county [and others] studied under her to receive instruction on how to read it'. Owing to her extensive learning and integrity, 'Emperor He often summoned Ban Zhao to tutor the empress and royal consorts and honoured her as "*Dagu* 大家" (great woman-teacher)'. After Emperor He passed away, Empress Deng became Empress Dowager and the regent of the state. During this period (106–21 CE), 'Ban Zhao participated in state affairs [as an advisor to the Empress Dowager]'.[1]

It should be noted that this is quite unusual in ancient China. Due to the enforced inner–outer, private–public, female–male distinction at the time, normally women were neither supposed to study subjects other than domestic matters nor were they permitted to engage in public roles outside of the household. In this context, as a rare woman public intellectual, Ban Zhao clearly broke with the prescribed gender roles. But she was also a

---

[1] See the *Book of Later Han*, vol. 84, 'Biographies of Exemplary Women'. Volume numbers may vary due to editions used, but section titles remain the same. For more information, see the bibliography.

follower of the ritual codes – she married young, was a mother of several children, and never remarried after becoming a young widow. Her personal life and writings exhibited an interesting contradiction between her independent spirit as a contrarian and a conformist compromise to constrictive social norms. Because of this, as to be discussed shortly, Ban Zhao – though revered for generations – was a controversial figure in the past one hundred years, both praised as an exemplary woman philosopher by scholars such as Robin Wang (2003: 177–78) and condemned as an accomplice to patriarchal oppression of women, for example, by the early twentieth century anarchist feminist writer, He Zhen (Liu et al. 2013: 145–46).

Among Ban Zhao's writings, she was best known for her didactic text, *Lessons for Women* (*Nüjie*, also known as *Admonitions for Daughters*). Dated around 100 CE, it was the earliest Chinese written work known to be authored by a woman solely intended for women's education. Before this work, no one had ever made as powerful an argument as hers in deconstructing popular opinion that excluded women from education purely based on their gender and sex. Ban Zhao advocated for the necessity of women's education by appealing to Confucian canonical texts such as the *Record of Rituals* (*Liji*) and the constitutive conditions for virtues. The *Lessons for Women* was widely studied since its publication. This work's long-lasting impact on Chinese philosophy of women is well attested by its inclusion in important anthologies in pre-modern China, including Tao Zongyi's *Compendium of Famous Writings* (*Shuofu*), Wang Xiang's *Four Books for Women* (*Nü shishu*), Chen Hongmou's *Remaining Instructions for Teaching Women* (*Jiaonü yigui*), and Chen Menglei's *Collection of Illustrations and Books from Antiquity to the Present* (*Gujin tushu jicheng*), among others (Pang-White 2018: 31). In addition to her *Lessons for Women*, Ban Zhao also composed numerous literary works including poetry and prose. Unfortunately, only a few of them have survived.

In a society such as pre-modern China, which traditionally divided the social-political space (especially the middle and upper classes) along strict gender lines (male: public/intellectual versus female: private/emotive), even when considering regional and epochal differences, it is not surprising that women's writings tended to be neglected, not preserved in major literary compendiums or published for circulation. Owing to limited available resources, coupled with Chinese philosophies' rejection of a rigid binary logic that separates philosophy from literature, speech from writing, this chapter will take an interdisciplinary postmodern approach to Ban Zhao. Postmodern thinkers such as Jacques Derrida and Hélène Cixous have often challenged the Western tradition's divide between philosophy and literature, reason and emotion, speech and writing, and its prejudicial prioritisation of the former over the latter.² To rectify this methodological bias and to resist the overly simplistic attempt to label Ban Zhao as antifeminist, I will situate her work in context and examine a wider range of her writings than is usually considered, including not only her *Lessons for Women* but also her poetry and memoranda. By analysing different types of her writings, we will be better positioned to reappraise her philosophical stance and her distinctive strategy to gender politics and the subversion of traditional gender norms.

Ban Zhao's *Lessons for Women*

Among Ban Zhao's writings, the *Lessons for Women* (*Nüjie* 女誡), comprising seven chapters, is her best-known work. It is the earliest Chinese work authored by a woman intended for women's education. Since its completion, her colleague and student Ma Rong – a Confucian scholar-official – immediately praised this work and asked his wife and daughter to study it.³ Although Ban Zhao stated in her preface that the *Lessons for Women* was intended to provide marriage advice to her daughters (and thus originally was not meant to be a public moral tract), this book became essential reading for women's learning for several unintended reasons.

First, since the full text was recorded in Ban Zhao's biography in the *Book of the Later Han*, a dynastic history of the Eastern Han dynasty, it was well preserved through the ages. Since history was a necessary subject of study for learned Confucian scholars – a tradition that began with the *Spring and Autumn Annals* (*Chunqiu*, one of the Confucian 'Five Classics'), Ban Zhao's *Lessons for Women* garnered the kind of attention that many women's writings did not have.

Second, this text pioneered a new genre in Chinese women's literary tradition – writing by women for women – particularly in didactic treatises authored by women intended for female readers. Thus, this text became a beacon for women authors and was well preserved in women's literary circles. For example, during the Tang dynasty (618–907 CE), both Madame Zheng's *Book of Filial Piety for Women* (Mann and Cheng 2001: 47–70) and Song sisters' *Analects for Women* cited Ban Zhao as their teacher-interlocutor and attributed certain views to Ban Zhao partly

---

² For more, see the last section of this chapter and Tong and Botts (2017: 250–44).
³ See the *Book of the Later Han*, vol. 84, 'Biographies of Exemplary Women'.

based on her *Lessons for Women* (Pang-White 2018: 69–118). In the Ming dynasty (1368–1644 CE), Empress Renxiaowen's *Teachings for the Inner Court* noted Ban Zhao's treatise as an essential primer in women's education (Pang-White 2018: 132). Towards the end of the Ming dynasty and the beginning of the Qing dynasty (1644–1911 CE), Madame Liu's (aka Chaste Widow Wang) *Short Records of Models for Women* praised Ban Zhao for her contribution to the *Book of the [Former] Han* and her *Lessons for Women* as an exemplary case of outstanding women who have both talent and virtue and as a real-life argument that debunks the patriarchal myth, 'without talent is a woman's virtue' (Pang-White 2018: 289). In 1908, Madame Shen-Zhang and her daughter-in-law Shen Zhukun provided commentary in vernacular Chinese for the *Four Books for Women*, which includes Ban Zhao's *Lessons for Women* (Pang-White 2018: xi–xii).

Third, many renowned Confucian male scholars (in addition to Ma Rong) also highly recommended Ban Zhao's *Lessons for Women*. For example, Zhu Xi (1130–1200 CE), the epitome of Song New-Confucianism, once was asked what books should be used for teaching women in addition to passages from the *Analects* and the *Classic of Filial Piety*. Zhu Xi replied that Ban Zhao's *Lessons for Women* was a good text.[4] Later, Tao Zongyi (1329–1410 CE) included the text in his *Compendium of Famous Writings*, Wang Xiang (c. sixteenth–seventeenth century) in his *Four Books for Women*, Chen Hongmou (1696–1711 CE) in his *Remaining Instructions for Teaching Women*, and Chen Menglei (1650–1741 CE) in his *Collection of Illustrations and Books from Antiquity to the Present*, among others (Pang-White 2018: 31).

Fourth, in 1580 Emperor Shenzong (r. 1573–1620) of the Ming dynasty issued an imperial edict. It commissioned a Confucian scholar-official to collect Ban Zhao's *Lessons for Women* and Empress Renxiaowen's *Teaching for the Inner Court* in one volume and to circulate it among the public as an exemplary text for women's education.

In this well-known work, Ban Zhao made several interesting arguments in advancing women's education and moral cultivation and in preventing domestic violence, as we shall see below. For example, in Chapter Two ('Husband and Wife'), she writes:

> The Way of husband and wife harmonizes and matches *yin* and *yang*. It teaches spiritual beings and manifests the great principle of Heaven and Earth and the important morals of human relations. Hence, the *Record of*

---

[4] See *Zhuzi yulei* 朱子語類 (*Classified Conversations of Zhu Xi*), vol. 7.

> *Rituals* honours the essential relation between men and women. The *Classic of Poetry* makes known the *Guanju* poem. Based on this, clearly the husband-wife relation ought not be taken lightly. (Pang-White 2018: 47)[5]

Owing to its symbolism of generative power, the *Record of Rituals* regards the marriage rite between husband and wife as the most important ritual and the foundation of all human relations.[6] For a meaningful spousal relationship, virtue is essential. Both husband and wife have the moral responsibility to cultivate it: 'If a husband is not virtuous, he will not be able to control his wife. If a wife is not virtuous, she will not be able to serve her husband .... Although the cases are two, their use is one' (Pang-White 2018: 47). To cultivate virtue, education is essential. For, knowledge is a prerequisite to practice – not knowing the good, one cannot practice the good. Ban Zhao, therefore, argues that excluding women from education is equivalent to excluding women from morality – a self-defeating practice. She contends:

> I find nowadays gentlemen-scholars only know that wives ought to be moderated by their husbands, and the authority and dignity of a husband ought to be properly established. For this reason, they instruct their sons and teach them canonical classics. They hardly realize that husbands ought to be served [by their wives], and ritual propriety and righteousness ought to exist. Yet only to educate men and not to educate women – are they not being partial in their treatment of the two sides? According to the *Record of Rituals*, at the age of eight, children should begin receiving instructions on the classics. At the age of fifteen, they should receive adult education. Why is [women's education] alone not following this as a principle? (Pang-White 2018: 47–48)

Women must be educated, she argues, both for their personal development and for the familial–social good. To exclude women from education not only is a self-contradictory practice to what the society desires but also goes against the instruction of Confucian canons, which these men so desperately seek to preserve. Before Ban Zhao, no one had made as powerful an argument as hers by tactically deploying the Confucian canon in refuting popular opinion that excluded women from education.

To prevent domestic abuse in a patriarchal society, in Chapter Three ('Respect and Compliance') Ban Zhao further assets that: 'For self-cultivation, nothing is more essential than developing respect' (Pang-White 2018: 50). While love and intimacy are certainly vital to the spousal relationship, yet without the restraint of respect, verbal dispute

---

[5] All English translations in this chapter are mine. For alternative translations, see, e.g., Idema and Grant (2004).
[6] See the *Jiaotesheng* and the *Hunyi* chapters.

often escalates and leads to physical violence. Thus, spouses must control their anger by exercising mutual respect. Husbands should exercise caution to avoid verbal abuse and physical beating of their wives, and wives too should refrain from provoking fights, if they both desire a happy marriage:

> If a wife does not moderate her affronts to her husband, scolding insults [from him] will ensue. If her husband's anger cannot be stopped, a whipping will surely follow. To be husband and wife relies on righteousness for harmonious intimacy, loving kindness for friendly union. If beating is enforced, where is righteousness? If scolding and insulting words are spoken, where is loving kindness? When loving kindness and righteousness are both deserted, husband and wife will part their ways. (Pang-White 2018: 51)

To encourage women's self-cultivation, in Chapter Four ('Women's Conduct') Ban Zhao clarifies the idea of 'four [womanly] conducts (*sixing* 四行)' – woman's virtue, woman's speech, woman's appearance, and woman's work – which first appeared in the *Record of Rituals* and the *Zhou Rituals*. To dispel superficial interpretations that could trap women in self-pity, Ban Zhao explains that women's virtue does not require spectacular brilliance but relies on integrity; beauty comes from within, not on fleeting physical allure that vanishes with age. She writes:

> Women have four areas of conduct: first, woman's virtue; second, woman's speech; third, woman's appearance; fourth, woman's work. Speaking about these four, woman's virtue requires neither unparalleled talent nor exceeding brilliance; woman's speech requires neither rhetorical eloquence nor sharp words; woman's appearance requires neither a beautiful nor a splendid look or form; woman's work demands no unsurpassable skills. Exhibit tranquility ... Safeguard integrity ... Guard one's action with a sense of shame .... This is what is meant by woman's virtue. Choose words [carefully] in speaking. Never utter slanderous words. Speak only when the time is right .... This is what is meant by woman's speech .... [K]eep one's clothing and accessories always fresh and clean. Bathe regularly and keep one's body from filth and disgrace. This is what is meant by woman's bearing. Concentrate on weaving and spinning .... Prepare wine and food neatly and orderly to offer to the guests. This is what is meant by woman's work. These four areas are matters of great integrity for women. No women should lack them. Yet to do them is quite easy. The key is to always keep them in mind .... [Confucius] had a saying: 'Is humaneness really so far away? If I desire humaneness, humaneness will surely come.'[7] This is what it means here. (Pang-White 2018: 54–55)

---

[7] See *Analects* 7.29

It is worth noting how Ban Zhao quotes Confucius and humaneness (*ren*, also known as human-heartedness) – a paramount Confucian virtue, typically accorded only to morally exemplary males (*junzi*) in the Confucian canon – to conclude her chapter on the achievability of the 'four womanly conducts'. Ban Zhao's intentional use of androcentric texts to deconstruct the patriarchal gender binary (both the use of *Analects* here on humaneness and her early use of the *Record of Rituals* on women's education) exhibits her great hope for women.

Despite the accolades it received, the *Lessons for Women*, nonetheless, encountered great hostility in the twentieth century. The most notable criticism is given by He Zhen (1884–c. 1920), an early twentieth-century Chinese feminist and anarchist writer. In her 'On the Revenge of Women', dated 1907, He Zhen labelled Ban Zhao 'an archtraitor to women' and 'a slave of men':

> By the time we come to the Eastern Han period, we encounter the case of Ban Zhao ... the teachings she promoted are particularly absurd. She opens her *Admonitions for Daughters* [aka *Lessons for Women*] by championing lowliness and weakness .... She also opines that if a wife fails to serve her husband, moral principles would falter ... that weakness is a woman's merit .... In spite of being a woman herself, Ban the traitor was seduced by the seditious teaching of the Confucian tradition. She hacked at her own kind and brought shame onto womanhood in its entirety. In being a slave of men, she was an archtraitor to women .... Ban the traitor actually said that 'it is proper for a husband to remarry, but a woman must by no means serve two men' .... I truly did not expect these words to have come from a woman's mouth, even less the fact that they would be eulogized in the ages that ensued. That the rights and power of women failed to develop can be attributed to the fact that women are well versed in Ban the traitor's book. (He in Liu et al. [2013: 145–46])

Is the *Lessons for Women* a poison to women as He Zhen and some Chinese intellectuals of the twentieth century have claimed? It is true that Ban Zhao opened her book with a chapter entitled 'The Lowly and the Weak' stating: 'These three responsibilities [being the lowly and the weak, being diligent, and continuing ancestral religious rites] depict the constant way of being a woman and the canonical teachings of the ritual law' (Pang-White 2018: 43). In Chapter Three 'Respect and Compliance', she wrote: 'Firmness is *yang*'s virtue; gentleness is *yin*'s distinction. A man is honoured for his strength; a woman is beautiful in virtue of her weakness' (Pang-White 2018: 50). And, in Chapter Five 'One-Mindedness', one reads: 'According to the [*Book of Ceremonial Rituals*], a husband has the ground of righteousness to remarry; however, no existing texts permit a wife to have a second marriage' (Pang-White 2018: 57).

These statements undoubtedly offend modern sensibility. Nonetheless, to claim Ban Zhao as 'an archtraitor to women', responsible for the failure of the women's rights movement, runs the risk of oversimplification and anachronistic prejudice. We must assess the *Lessons for Women* in its historical context and consider Ban Zhao's writings as a whole rather than proclaiming her philosophical outlook flawed simply based on one single work. We shall now turn to Ban Zhao's more adventurous, but lesser known, writings.

Ban Zhao's Poetry

Many of Ban Zhao's poems are lost. We are fortunate that her '*Dongzheng fu* 東征賦 (Rhapsody on a Journey to the East)' was preserved in its entirety in an early sixth-century anthology, *Wenxuan* 文選 (*Selections of Refined Literature*), one of the most important collections of poetry in Chinese literary studies.[8] From the first stanza, we learn that Ban Zhao composed this rhapsody in 113 CE when she was in her late sixties, travelling with her son to his new post in Chenliu, a few hundred miles eastbound from the capital Luoyang. Expressing her sadness in leaving their old home, she also reminded herself of their responsibility as governmental officials, commemorated past sages, and encouraged all to become morally exemplary persons despite life's uncertainty. The essential part of this rhapsody is translated as follows:

> In the seventh year of the Everlasting Beginning (*Yongchu* 永初),[9]
> I accompanied my son on an eastbound journey.
> . . .
> Leaving our old home behind,
> Heading toward a new place,
> My spirit was low, burdened by grief.
> . . .
> I poured myself a cup of wine to ease my nostalgia.
> With a long sigh, I tried to oppress my emotions and chastise myself.
> . . .
> How can I not do my very best accompanying my son and serving our country?
> I should join him and others,
> Accept what Heaven and destiny have in store for us.
> . . .
> Thereupon, I moved ahead gladly and continued our long journey.
> I let my eyes wander and my spirit roam.

---

[8] See *Wenxuan*, vol. 3.   [9] I.e., 113 CE during the first reigning period of Emperor An (r. 107–25).

...
We watched from afar the magnificent currents of the Yellow River and the Luo River,
Gazed at the nearby towering gates of Chenggao.
...
When we entered the outer city wall at Kuang borough's old site,
It made me reminisce about the distant past.
Recalling Confucius suffered hardship here.
During a time of decline and chaos,
The Way is abandoned,
Even the sage was threatened and in danger.
...
When we arrived at the borders of Changyuan,
I observed residents living in the fields,
Staring at the ruins of Pucheng,
...
Zilu's brave spirit came to my mind.
The people of Wei lauded his courage and righteousness,
Even today they still pay tribute to him.[10]
Quyuan was buried in the southeast part of this town long ago,
Yet people still come to show their reverence at his grave.[11]
Only great virtue is immortal!
Even after death the good name endures.
...
Know that our endowed nature rests in Heaven:
It relies on our own diligence to be near humaneness.
Aspire to lofty character,
Practice virtuous conduct.
Endeavour in loyalty and reciprocity,
Treat others with kindness.
...
May the many divinities be discerning:
Protect the virtuous and help the trustworthy.
Envoi:
The thoughts of morally exemplary men (*junzi*) necessarily manifest in their writings.[12]
...
My deceased father by his conduct has also composed a rhapsody.[13]

---

[10] Zilu, a student of Confucius, was killed when he refused to participate in a usurpation. He was once an official of Pucheng. When Ban Zhao saw Pucheng, she recalled Zilu's bravery.
[11] Quyuan 蘧瑗 (c. 585–484 BCE), well-known for his virtue and proposal to govern the state by humaneness, was a high-ranking official of Wei during the Spring and Autumn Period.
[12] '*Junzi* 君子' (literally, 'son of a ruler') takes on a moral connotation in Confucianism, often translated as 'gentleman' or 'morally exemplary man'.
[13] Ban Zhao's father composed '*Baizheng Fu* (Rhapsody on a Journey to the North)'.

> Although I am unintelligent, how do I dare not emulate him?[14]
> High or low ranks, riches or poverty, are not what one can control.
> Rectify one's person, realise the Way, and wait for the right timing.
> Long or short life pertains to fate: It's the same for both the foolish and the wise.
> Respectfully accept what fate has in store: auspiciousness or calamity.
> Be reverent and prudent without negligence.
> Think only of humility.
> Tranquil with few desires,
> Let's emulate Gong Chuo![15]

This rhapsody is rich in its overlaying of images and meanings. It first expresses Ban Zhao's weighty emotions – her reluctance in leaving their old home behind and moving to a distant place in her old age. A change of emotions from nostalgia to magnanimity took place and crystalized by a sequence of events. Her realisation that everyone has a responsibility to the advancement of social good brought her the first relief. With this realisation, the environs – the magnificent currents of merging rivers, the towering gates of mountains, the ruins of historical sites – all become places of her aspirations. What matters is a person's character, for 'Only great virtue is immortal! / Even after death the good name endures'. The past is past not as a bygone era. It has something to teach the living. Role models from the past (Confucius, Zilu, Quyuan, and Gong Chuo) still inspire us, so does her deceased father. She composed this rhapsody not only to record the physical journey but also to pay tribute to the past sages, to commemorate her father, and to articulate her aspiration to become a morally exemplary person. In her mind – contrary to the received opinion – *junzi* is not a gendered excellence limited to man. She, a woman, can aspire to it as well.

Two partially preserved rhapsodies, '*Zhenlü fu* 針縷賦 (Rhapsody on Needle and Thread)' and '*Daque fu* 大雀賦 (Rhapsody on Big Peacock)', can be found in the early seventh-century anthology, *Yiwen leiju* 藝文類聚 (*Collections of Literature by Categories*). The 'Rhapsody on Needle and Thread' (date unknown) is especially interesting because of her unique use of small sewing tools, essential to women's work but generally looked down upon by men, as metaphors of exemplary moral integrity and *junzi*:[16]

---

[14] In Chinese culture, a *junzi* often describes oneself as 'unintelligent' – humility is a key virtue in moral exemplariness. Confucianism also emphasises filial piety toward one's parents. Ban Zhao is doing both here.

[15] Meng Gong Chuo (sixth century BCE-?), a virtuous official in the State of Lu, was especially known for his temperance. Confucius advises his students to emulate him. See *Analects* 14.13.

[16] See *Yiwen leiju*, vol. 65.

Welded from the hardest essence of autumn metal,
Its shape is small and subtle, pointing and straight.
Its nature is to penetrate everywhere,
Yet it advances slowly.
With one single thread,
It reaches myriad things.
Only the traces of needle and thread,
Are indeed far-reaching, broad, and without a fixed origin.
It rejects the corrupt and repairs the mistakes.
Like a lamb with the whitest fleece,
It is not what bamboo baskets with small capacity can measure up to –
Even if their merits are engraved on stone and taken into the hall.

'People/men like bamboo baskets with small capacity' (*doushao zhiren* 斗筲之人) comes from the *Analects* 13.20, where Confucius use this metaphor to criticise small-minded governmental officials with little talents – they are the opposite of *junzi*. Ban Zhao's 'Rhapsody on Needle and Thread' taps into her experience as a woman and creatively reimagines sewing tools with new meaning. In her poetic observations that physical size amounts to nothing and that being recognised in the official hall is unimportant, she not only praises conscientious public servants banished by the court owing to their outspokenness (like a needle) but also brings to light the significance of women's work – although absent in the public eye, its lustre is not diminished. With the inversion of female imagery (not lowly and weak but powerful and strong) and poking fun at men who crave for grandiose public recognition but lack real content, this poem reveals the novel ways in which Ban Zhao is much more subtly subversive to gender norms than previous scholarship such as He Zhen (see above) has shown her to be.

Ban Zhao's Memoranda

Two of Ban Zhao's official memoranda are preserved in the *Book of the Later Han*. In the style of prose, these pieces provide us another standpoint to appreciate Ban Zhao's philosophical acumen. They are also immensely interesting in showing us how elite women in early second-century China participated in politics.

'Petition for a Replacement for My Elder Brother Chao (*Weixiong Chao qiudaishu* 為兄超求代疏)' is an official memorandum to Emperor He in support of her second elder brother's request (now at age seventy) to be relieved from his post at the Western border, where he had been stationed for thirty years, and be allowed to return home. The full text of Ban Zhao's petition, composed in 102 CE, is included in her brother's biography, following right after his own petition. Owing to its importance in illustrating Ban Zhao's unparalleled argumentative skills even surpassing his brother and her vast knowledge of the classics, the entire memorandum is translated below.

> My full elder brother, Chao, the guardian-general of the Western border and the Marquis Who Secured the Farthest Land, has been very fortunate to have received great rewards from Your Highness for his negligible merits. His rank is promoted to marquis, which brings him one thousand *dan* of rice annually.[17] The favour of Your Highness is beyond measure. It is truly not what an insignificant official should have received. When Chao first set out to his station in the Western border [in 73 CE], he was determined to sacrifice his life hoping to establish small merits for Your Highness. Soon after, he encountered the Chen Mu Uprising [in 75 CE]. All roads were cut off. Chao was stranded in this extremely dangerous region all by himself. He still managed to persuade all the states in the area to submit. Because their troops were in greater quantity, every time when an attack happened, Chao was always the first in the frontline. Although he was injured by the weapons, he never was afraid of death. Only because he relied on the protective spirit of Your Highness was he able to survive in the desert. Now, it has been thirty years. Although he and I are brother and sister, but having been separated for so long, we are unable to recognize each other. Those officers, who accompanied him to the Western border from the beginning, have all died. Chao is the oldest among them. Today he is seventy: old and ill, with not one single black hair on his head, his hands shaking, his sight blurry, and his hearing impaired. He can hardly walk without a cane. Although he desires to exert all his might to return Your Highness's favour, the old age has taken its toll on him – almost no teeth are left in his mouth.[18] It is the nature of the barbarians to rebel against authority and to bully the elderly. Chao would be entering his grave at any moment but for a long time no one replaces him. I am worried that this will give wicked people the thought and opportunity of sedition. Although the ministers and high-ranking officials in the imperial court consider all matters of the State, none has come up with a long-term plan. If some emergency suddenly happens at the border, and Chao's utmost efforts fail to follow his wish, the accomplishment of this country over many generations will be lost and the use of loyal officers' utmost effort will be abandoned. This would truly be a shame. Hence, Chao, from ten-thousand

---

[17] *Dan* 石 is a measuring unit in ancient China. One *dan* equals approximately 20 kg. Only highly ranked officials receive 1,000 *dan* of rice. The highest reward is 2,000 *dan*.

[18] '*Quan ma chi suo* 犬馬齒索' (dog and horse with hardly any teeth left) is a Chinese idiom indicating old age.

miles away, petitioned to return home and explained the urgency of the matter. He has been waiting anxiously for three years. Still, his petition has not yet been granted.

I have learned that the ancients joined the army at fifteen and returned home at sixty. There were also people who took time off and did not serve in office. Because Your Highness rules the world with utmost filialness, you have acquired delightful gratitude from all the nations. Your Highness does not even neglect minor officers from the smallest states, not to mention that Chao holds the rank of marquis. Therefore, I risk my life to beg Your Highness for mercy, to allow Chao to return home for his remaining years. If he is able to return alive and see Your Highness once again, it will not only free the country from having to worry about faraway regions and sudden emergencies at the Western border, but Chao will also receive grace from Your Highness akin to what is demonstrated by King Wen [of Zhou Dynasty] burying the bones of the slain and [Tian] Zifang [of the Warring States Period] showing mercy to an old steed. *The Classic of Poetry* says: 'The people are too tiresome. / They hope for some rest. / Care for the people in the capital. / Comfort people in all four directions.'[19] Chao once wrote me a final farewell letter fearing that we may never meet again. I am truly saddened by the fact that Chao spent his prime years in the desert out of loyalty and filialness to our country. Now that he is tired and old, he is going to die in the wilderness of a distant land. His situation truly deserves commiseration. If Chao is not rescued now, and he later encounters a sudden rebellion at the Western border, I hope Your Highness will exempt Chao's family from punishment as in the case of the mother of Zhao [Kuo] and Lady Wei, owing to their previous requests.[20] I am foolish and ignorant. Not understanding the great principles of state affairs, I have violated Your Highness's taboos. [Please forgive me.][21]

---

[19] See the Daya section, the Minlao poem.
[20] Zhao Kuo, arrogant and selfish, was a general of the state of Zhao during the Warring States Period (475–221 BCE). Before an impending war, his mother wrote a petition to the king, advising the king that her son should not be the general of the troops. The king would not listen. She said to the king: 'Your Majesty, if you insist on using Kuo but later he turns out to be unqualified, may his family and I be exempt from punishment?' The king agreed. Later, Zhao Kuo and his troops suffered a massive defeat. The king did not punish Kuo's family members because of the earlier warning. Lady Wei was a consort of Duke Huan of the State of Qi during the Spring and Autumn Period (770–476 BCE). One day Duke Huan and his ministers decided to attack Lady Wei's home state. When she heard the news, she took off her hairpin and accessories, bowed to the duke: 'I would like to ask for forgiveness and take the punishment for the State of Wei.' The duke replied: 'Nothing happened between I and the State of Wei, why do you ask for forgiveness?' Lady Wei replied that she heard the duke's plan to attack Wei and would take the punishment for Wei. Upon hearing this, the duke cancelled the attack. Both women were praised for their foresight. For the story of Zhao Kuo's mother, see Liu Xiang's (c. 77–6 BCE) *Biographies of Women*, vol. 3, ch. 15. For the story of Lady Wei, see vol. 2, ch. 2.
[21] See the *Book of the Later Han*, vol. 47, 'Biographies of Ban and Liang'.

After reading Ban Zhao's petition, Emperor He (r. 89–105 CE) was moved and permitted her brother to return home. Her brother finally arrived in the capital Luoyang in August 102 CE. One month later, he had passed away, at seventy-one.

Ban Zhao's memorandum is powerful in several ways. In a patriarchal society in first- and second-century imperial China, elite women in the aristocratic class and the royal court were prohibited from directly interfering with state affairs owing to previous political upheaval, a rigidified reading of the *Record of Rituals* and a hierarchical-essentialist interpretation of the *yin-yang* binary advocated by Dong Zhongshu (c. 179–104 BCE), a Confucian erudite and prime minister to Emperor Wu (r. 140–87 BCE) during the Western Han dynasty (206 BCE–8 CE). Dong invented a new brand of Confucianism known as 'Han Confucianism' and a correlative state cosmology that denigrated *yin*/women/ministers and honours *yang*/men/rulers. Women should concern themselves only with domestic matters (not state affairs), and rulers have absolute power over all their subjects. Her very act of writing the petition is defying gender norms and subverting the rule–subject power relation established by the state philosophy (Han Confucianism). Ban Zhao knows very well that she is tampering with political and gender taboos. One careless word and act could get the whole family clan killed rather than successfully rescuing her brother. Strategically, she therefore first expresses her gratitude to the emperor's favour, followed by highlighting her brother's decades of loyal service to the country in the desert. She then appeals to the emperor's sense by detailing her brother's fragile physical condition. To add weight to her argument, she also addresses the issue from the perspective of national security (again, violating the social taboo). To conclude her argument, she cites ancient military practice, the *Classic of Poetry* (one of the most revered Confucian classics), and several well-known virtuous figures from history, including two female figures (the mother of Zhao Kuo and Lady Wei). Her careful manoeuvring of gender politics and her insight successfully persuade the emperor and avoid a potential calamity. In writing this petition as a female subordinate to a male superior and citing female models who had wisely admonished the kings in the previous dynasties, she has cleverly undermined received gender norms by her very act of writing as well as the content of the letter.

Another official memorandum, 'Memorial to Empress Dowager Deng (*Shang Dengtaihou shu* 上鄧太后疏)', can be found in Ban Zhao's own biography in the *Book of Later Han*. It is a concrete example supporting the compilers' remarks that 'When Empress Dowager Deng was the regent of the imperial court, Ban Zhao participated in governmental matters. Owing to her diligence and hard work in serving the country, her son Cao Cheng was rewarded with the title "the Marquis of Inner Gate."'[22] The memorial was composed during the *Yongchu* era (sometime between 107 and 113 CE). At the time, Empress Dowager Deng's mother had passed away. The dowager's elder brother Deng Zhi, a powerful grand general, petitioned to retire from his official duty to observe the mourning rite. To maintain the balance of power, Empress Dowager Deng did not want to grant his request. She solicited Ban Zhao's opinion on this matter. Ban Zhao submitted this memorial, stating:

> In thinking that Your Majesty, Empress Dowager, embodies the splendour of abundant virtue, exemplifies the sagely rule of Yao and Shun, opens the doors in four directions to listen to opinions from all sides, adopts even the words of arrogant mad men, considers even the strategies offered by grass- and wood-cutters, and I, Zhao, am able to live under your sagely brilliance even with my foolish unrefined ability, how do I dare not to reveal my innermost thoughts so as to reply to even just one-ten-thousandth of Your Majesty's favour?[23] I have heard that humble yielding is the greatest virtue of all. Therefore, the ancient documents praised such virtue and spiritual beings gave their blessings for such actions. In the distant past, Bo Yi and Shu Qi left their kingdom [to yield the throne to each other], and all under heaven respected their lofty character. Taibo left the place Bin [to yield the throne to his young brother]; Confucius praises him for 'yielding [the kingdom] three times.'[24] This is why their virtue shines with brilliant light and their names endure in later generations. The *Analects* says: 'If one can use ritual and yielding to govern the country, what difficulty will there be in government?'[25] From this standpoint, clearly the effect of sincerity from recommending and yielding is far-reaching. Now Your Majesty's four brothers firmly abide by loyalty and filialness, requesting to retire from their office on their own accord. If Your Majesty refuses their request with the excuse that the frontiers are not yet settled, I am truly worried that if later a small error on their part occurs that overshadows their virtue today, they will never have the opportunity again to earn the good name of recommending and yielding. From what I can think of and what I see, I dare risk my life and offer my foolish opinion. I am fully aware that my words are unworthy of considering. But I offer them here to show my insignificant and yet the sincerest heart to Your Majesty.[26]

---

[22] The *Book of Later Han*, vol. 84, 'Biographies of Exemplary Women'.
[23] Readers may notice that confessing ignorance and foolishness is a trope Ban Zhao uses across her writings. This is owing to Confucian and Daoist emphasis on humility as a characteristic of genuine virtue.
[24] *Analects* 8.1.   [25] *Analects* 4.13.
[26] The *Book of Later Han*, vol. 84, 'Biographies of Exemplary Women'.

After reading Ban Zhao's memorandum, Empress Dowager Deng granted her brothers' request, and the brothers were able to return home to observe the mourning rite for their deceased mother.

Based on these two surviving official memoranda and Ban Zhao's biography in the *Book of Later Han*, we cannot but admire her independent mind, intelligence, strategic excellence, literary fineness, broad knowledge of the classics and history, and her bravery and integrity in offering contrary opinions to those held by the Emperor and Empress Dowager. Ban Zhao's action and her official memoranda (as well as Empress Dowager Deng's regency) – however rare they were in ancient China – demonstrated how these brave women by their actions challenged and subverted the binary opposition of the inner/domestic/female versus the outer/public/male that unfairly confine women to the domestic space and rob them of opportunities and personal development in public sphere.

Observations

As mentioned above, Ban Zhao lived during the time of a new form of Confucianism – Han Confucianism led by Dong Zhongshu – had arisen and dominated the political–intellectual atmosphere from 136 BCE to 220 CE. To serve the interest of the sovereign, Han Confucianism (the state philosophy of the Han dynasty) replaced early Confucianism's emphasis on reciprocal 'five human relations' (ruler *and* minister, father *and* son, husband *and* wife, older *and* younger, and friend *and* friend) with an autocratic 'three bonds' (the ruler *over* the minister, the father *over* the son, and the husband *over* the wife). It further enforced this political ideology by essentialising the originally mutually transformative *yin-yang* paradigm and by privileging *yang* over *yin*. The *yang* was equated with the Han dynasty, ruler, father, and husband. The *yin* was identified with the toppled former Qin dynasty, minister, son, and wife. In such an oppressive political, intellectual, and social climate, Ban Zhao wrote her *Lessons for Women* to give her daughters advice on how to navigate marital relationships. Speaking from her own experience, she confided in her *Preface*:

> At the age fourteen I was in charge of the work of dustpan and broom in the Cao family. Now, more than forty some years have passed; during these years, trembling with fear, I was constantly afraid that I may be dismissed or humiliated . . . . It, however, grieves me to see you, my daughters, who have just reached the age of marriage, to not have been gradually taught more nor have you learned proper rituals of being a married woman. I fear that you may lose face with other households and bring shame upon your family

clan. I am now seriously ill; my life is uncertain. As I think of you in such an [untrained] state, I am distraught by worries and frustration.

Her primary concern in this work, as an ill and aging mother, is how she may ensure her daughters' happiness after they become married. How do they thrive in a new unfamiliar environment? How does a wife maintain her dignity in an androcentric patriarchal society? The overarching language of the politicised Han Confucianism is '*yang* [= ruler/husband/father] the venerable, and *yin* [= minister/wife/son] the lowly.'[27] Thus, while acknowledging constrictive Han ritual norms on women, she took pains to argue for women's education and the four womanly conducts as an important means to maintain one's dignity in marriage. Ban Zhao wrote: 'A wife must seek to win her husband's heart. Nonetheless, to seek a husband's heart is not to rely on flattery and charm in a demeaning way in order to gain his affection. Such behaviour is not as good as if she is one-minded with solemn appearance' (Pang-White 2018: 57).[28] So too, in other chapters of this book, as mentioned earlier, she deployed the Confucian canon to combat gender prejudice (such as the physical beating of wives) and to encourage women to cultivate learning and virtue. Ban Zhao's language in her *Lessons for Women* is complex. She writes for women in social binds – more specifically for women born in the aristocratic families, whose burden to display unwavering loyalty to the throne far surpassed that of ordinary women, or they risked the slaying of their family clans. Thus, Ban Zhao writes in contradictions, in strategic indirectness – in what Hélène Cixous may call the non-linear language of love (Cixous 1976: 875–93) – to reveal the unthought new meaning of the canon that has long been ignored and to challenge the male narrative of Han Confucianism of her time. He Zhen's hostile assessment of Ban Zhao as 'an archtraitor to women' is too simplistic and overly hasty – it does not do justice to Ban Zhao's very subtle and careful strategic navigation of gender politics.

Beyond the *Lessons for Women*, Ban Zhao's other writings such as her poetry and official memoranda further demonstrate that Ban Zhao is hardly 'a slave of men' as He Zhen claims. In the *envoi* of the 'Rhapsody on a Journey to the East', her aspiration to be a morally exemplary person speaks to her vision that moral exemplariness transcend gender. In her

---

[27] Dong Zhongshu, *Chunqiu fanlu* 春秋繁露 (*Luxuriant Dew of the Spring and Autumn Annals*), chs. 43 and 53.
[28] This comment marks the difference between Ban Zhao's and Jean-Jacques Rousseau's standpoint on gendered nature and conduct in the *Emile*.

'Rhapsody on Needle and Thread', she purposefully used women's sewing tools and slow needlework, often looked down upon by men, to express moral integrity that all should aspire to. In the 'Memorial to Empress Dowager Deng', in advising Empress Dowager to grant Grand General Deng Zhi's request to retire from his official duties, Ban Zhao argued that 'humble yielding is the greatest virtue of all'. Clearly then, Ban Zhao did not believe that humble yielding is a gendered female virtue but a virtue that applies to all genders. Moreover, in 'Petition for a Replacement for My Elder Brother Chao', Ban Zhao risked her life to express her contrary opinion to the unreasonable demand of the emperor and high-ranking officials (all men!) – her act of bravery undoubtedly subverted gender-stereotyping of female submissiveness.

Although facing enormous constraints with very limited power in her hands in first- and second-century China, Ban Zhao did not project herself as a completely helpless victim, an oppressed object, the total other, who can only bury herself in grief. Although she compromised on certain constrictive norms on women, let us not forget what she had accomplished. She had negotiated unexplored space for women by her action as a public actor and by pioneering writing by women for women – a significant contribution to women's literary tradition. Hélène Cixous once wrote:

> Women must write herself: must write about women and bring women to writing, from which they have been driven away as violently as from their bodies . . . . Women must put herself into the text – as into the world and into history – by her own movement . . . . Not to strengthen their own narcissism or verify the solidity or weakness of the master, but to make the love better, to invent . . . . She gives that there may be life, thought, transformation. (Cixous 1976: 875–93)

A controversial figure by modern standards, Ban Zhao is a contradiction. But here also lies her greatness. She did not solve the gender problem; rather, she exposed it. She did not completely break away from binary thinking, but she questioned it in her action and writings. What she left with us is not a decisive solution but the *gestation* of a new thinking, a breaking-in of a new horizon, the precursor of a new history. Jacques Derrida once remarked:

> Here there is a sort of question, call it historical, of which we are only glimpsing today the *conception*, the *formation*, the *gestation*, *the labour*. I employ these words, I admit, with a glance toward the business of childbearing – but also with a glance toward those who, in a company from which I do not exclude myself, turn their eyes away in the face of the as yet unnameable which is proclaiming itself and which can do so, as is

necessary whenever a birth is in the offing, only under the species of the non-species, in the formless, mute, infant, and terrifying form of monstrosity. (Derrida in Macksey and Donato [1972: 265])

Not speaking in the language of rights that only becomes available in the West in modernity, Ban Zhao appears monstrous to He Zhen and others who have been influenced by the modern philosophy of rights. Yet, in our cross-epochal cross-cultural discourse on women philosophers, let us not forget those women pioneers, who were 'the as yet unnameable . . . under the species of the non-species, in the formless, mute, infant, and terrifying form of monstrosity', their struggles and triumphs.

CHAPTER 12

The Reception of Plato on Women
Proclus, Averroes, Marinella

Peter Adamson

As documented in the rest of this volume, ancient Platonism was distinguished by its inclusion of numerous women philosophers. This is perhaps to be explained in light of Platonic doctrines. For instance, Platonists at least sometimes hold that the contrast between male and female is only a feature of embodiment and does not apply to the true self (I will be returning to this idea below). Whatever the merit of such explanations, they should be considered only alongside the more obvious fact that Plato himself wrote the most famous and influential defence of philosophical training for women. This comes in the *Republic*, where he has Socrates argue that in the ideal city women would be part of the martial class of 'guardians' and participate in the communist arrangements of this class: private property is eliminated, and children are separated from their parents and raised by the whole community. Since philosophers are drawn from among the guardians, there will be philosopher queens as well as philosopher kings (*Rep.* 540c). Reactions to this part of the *Republic* begin already with Plato's student Aristotle and recur throughout pre-modern philosophy. The aim of this chapter is to study three unusually detailed engagements with Plato's proposals about women, drawn from three very different times and cultures: late ancient Athens, medieval Islamic Spain, and the Italian Renaissance.

I should however begin by explaining my choice of theme. This book is, after all, devoted to women philosophers in antiquity. Why then focus on responses to a book written by a man, albeit a man writing about women? First, because it will help us better to understand the context within which historical women philosophers worked. As we will see, such figures were invoked in defence of Plato's thesis, held up as a kind of empirical proof that women could do philosophy too. But misogyny and prejudice can be found even in male authors who agreed with Plato's proposals. These commentators issued caveats, for instance, that giving women a leading role in governance is a utopian idea and would be impractical in a more familiar political context. Tellingly, it is not until the final section of this chapter, when we reach the Renaissance, that we will see Plato's authority invoked in favour of genuine intellectual equality (or in fact, the superiority of women over men).

A second, more subtle rationale would be to point out that work on women philosophers in antiquity nearly *always* involves studying books written by men. With a few exceptions and possible exceptions, like the poems of Sappho and the letters ascribed to famous Pythagorean women,[1] the corpus on which we draw consists entirely of writings by men about women. Some of these women definitely existed (Hypatia, Augustine's mother Monica, Gregory of Nyssa's sister Macrina, etc.), some may or may not have existed (Diotima), and some are clearly fictional entities (Boethius' Lady Philosophy); but whatever the real historical basis of such presentations, the presentations themselves were composed by male authors. This is of course not to say that texts by men are useless as evidence for real women philosophers. But it is to say that there is no sharp contrast between studying ancient women philosophers and reading what ancient men said about women philosophers. To the contrary, these are usually just the same enterprise.

So it seems entirely appropriate that a book dedicated to this enterprise should include a discussion of the most famous of all classical texts about women in philosophy, which is of course the passage on women in the *Republic*. Happily, a survey of the reception of this passage will give us an opportunity to talk about a book that was after all written by a woman: the Renaissance proto-feminist, Lucrezia Marinella (d. 1653). My other two examples of philosophers who respond to Plato are Proclus (d. 485) and Ibn Rushd (often known by his Latinised name 'Averroes', d. 1198). One of my main contentions will be that these three figures anticipated points made in much more recent commentary literature, so I begin with a glance at modern-day interpretations.

Plato

The secondary literature on Plato's discussion of women in the *Republic* is, to put it mildly, ample. Restricting ourselves just to publications in English, there was a spate of articles on the topic in the 1970s, the most influential of which has been that of Julia Annas, who sought to pour cold

---

[1] See Pomeroy (2013) and the relevant chapters of the present volume.

water on the notion that Plato is a 'feminist'.² Subsequent contributions have adopted more or less forthright stances on that same question. Thus, Gregory Vlastos spoke up in favour of Plato's feminist credentials, while Morag Buchan's book-length investigation reached opposite conclusions.³ Obviously, this particular angle of approach to the *Republic* has been inspired by the political and cultural interests of our own age. It is no coincidence that the topic attracted significant interest during the 1970s, when feminism was on the rise.⁴ Yet, as I say, several key interpretive issues that recur over the last several decades of research on *Republic* V were already raised in pre-modern treatments of that same text.

A useful departure point is provided by Christine Garside Allen's distinction between what she calls the 'metaphysical' and 'pragmatic' aspects of Plato's argument.⁵ The former involves showing that if women and men have different natures, those differences are not relevant to the tasks of guardianship (*Rep.* 451d–56c). The latter involves arguing that it is in the best interests of the state to include women among the guardian class (456c–64b). Passages in the *Laws* spell out with particular clarity that it would be a waste of resources not to exploit talents found among women. At *Laws* 806c, for instance, we are told that excluding women from military service would mean 'leaving to the city only half of the happy life, instead of both halves (εὐδαίμονος ἥμισυ βίου καταλείπειν ἀντὶ διπλασίου τῇ πόλει)'. In studies from the 1970s, the metaphysical aspect of the argument was used to support a reading of Plato as being, to some degree, 'feminist'. Allen herself said that it led Plato to recommend education for women because it 'is crucial for the women themselves'.⁶ Likewise, Harry Lesser wrote that 'Plato's concern is precisely with the needs and capacities of the individual: he has a vision of a society in which each person leads the life for which he or she is best suited'.⁷ Somewhat later, Nicholas Smith expanded upon this point by setting it within Plato's broader metaphysics: we know from the *Republic* itself, in particular from the Myth of Er, that human souls can go from male to female bodies. It is because both men and women are 'sexless souls embodied' that 'Plato finds no difficulty in saying that just as a man can have the nature of a physician, so can a woman ... just as a man can be a lover of wisdom, so can a woman'.⁸ Smith drew a contrast here to Aristotle, for whom souls are

---

² Annas (1976). See also Dickason (1973–74); Pomeroy (1974); Allen (1975); Saxonhouse (1976), Okin (1977), Jacobs (1978).
³ Vlastos (1989); Buchan (1999).
⁴ For a later collection devoted to feminist approaches to Plato, see Tuana (1994).
⁵ Allen (1975: 135).   ⁶ Allen (1975: 136).   ⁷ Lesser (1979).   ⁸ Smith (1983: 472–73).

forms of bodies, which would explain why he 'offers a biological account of human reproduction that renders female psychology naturally and importantly different from that of males'.[9] But scholars do not agree on the implications of Plato's metaphysics for his views on women. Many point to the gendered metaphors he uses for the contrast between intelligible forms and matter, with the latter in particular seen as a feminine principle.[10] Embodiment is a bad thing in Platonist thought, and it is associated with the female, which is perhaps why 'woman's sexual, bodily nature is forgotten and she becomes almost irrelevant in Socrates' best city'.[11] Furthermore, while a passage on reincarnation at the end of the *Timaeus* does confirm that one soul can be first in a male, then a female, body, embodiment as a woman is there presented as the result of cowardice and injustice in a previous life (*Tim.* 90e). This is like a cosmic version of a proposal found in the *Laws*, whereby cowardly soldiers are made to live in disgraceful safety, like women do (944d–e). So even if women are not relevantly different by nature, they seem to be relevantly different by character: femaleness is an 'acquired condition',[12] so that women are really just 'lesser men'[13] and their souls are just 'inferior male souls'.[14]

As for the 'pragmatic' aspect of Plato's argument, this seems even less likely to support a feminist reading: notice that in the quotation from the *Laws* given above, it is the *city* that gets to have a happy life, not the women guardians (cf. *Rep.* 419b). Indeed, Annas' damning verdict is based on the 'pragmatic' considerations offered by Plato. 'The argument', she says, 'is not based on, and makes no reference to, women's desires or needs. Nothing at all is said about whether women's present roles frustrate them or whether they will lead more satisfying lives as Guardians than as housebound drudges'.[15] Likewise, Catherine Gardner sees Plato's arrangements as insufficiently radical, in that the 'patriarchal nuclear family' is retained but with women belonging to the state instead of specific men, because this will provide the 'dual benefit' of unity and controlled breeding (i.e., the matching of partners to produce the best offspring) among the

---

[9] Smith (1983: 477–78). For the role of biology in Plato's account, see also Dickason (1973–74); and for a more recent comparison between Plato and Aristotle on women, see Frede (2018).
[10] See, for instance, Buchan (1999: 45, 78).   [11] Saxonhouse (1976: 200).
[12] As nicely pointed out by Schultz (2019a: 888). Similarly, Brill (2015) suggests that gender precedes biological sex, since effeminate souls get female bodies (168), and that the male is the normative gender and is 'more quintessentially human' (171).
[13] Townshend (2017: 38).
[14] Buchan (1999: 44, cf. 36, 94). She goes so far as to say that 'no woman possesses' a philosophical soul, which may be an implication of the *Timaeus* but is flatly contradicted by the *Republic* (456a).
[15] Annas (1976: 311).

guardians.[16] Putting together this point with the inferiority of women admitted in this very part of the *Republic*, and confirmed in the *Timaeus* and elsewhere, Catherine McKeen argues that Plato's pragmatic argument does not guarantee that women would rule in the ideal city. Even if some women are more suited to rule than they are to do anything else, that does not mean that they would be better at ruling than the available men are.[17] While Plato himself apparently disagrees with that judgement, the point remains that a 'purely utilitarian' rationale, as Annas calls it,[18] will tend to ignore the interests of individual women and give them a chance at fulfilling their potential only if it suits the needs of the state. This is not the logic of feminism. Then too, even if individual women do incidentally wind up benefitting from Plato's proposals, this by-product will be enjoyed by only a happy few. There is no revision to the gender dynamics of the merchant and labouring classes, so that Plato's proposals only 'offer the opportunity to certain women who show a level of ability, a capacity for rational thought, a degree, in fact, of masculinity, to gain the status which should accompany these attributes'.[19] His political programme may be communist,[20] but it is also unhesitatingly elitist, something few modern-day readers (feminist or not) are liable to embrace.

Proclus

Pre-modern philosophers, you might think, must have read the *Republic*'s discussion of women very differently. Elitism was not going to be a problem, but any hint of 'feminism' certainly was. Far from chastising him for not going far enough in upholding the interests of women, Plato's exegetes had to excuse him for going as far as he did. This expectation is borne out by the most substantive late ancient reaction to the Platonic proposals, Proclus' two essays on the question in his so-called commentary on the *Republic*.[21] Yet we also find resonances between his treatment and

---

[16] Gardner (2000: 219–20).   [17] McKeen (2006: 536).   [18] Annas (1976: 315).
[19] Buchan (1999: 80).
[20] On the reading of Okin (1977), the point of the *Republic* V argument actually has nothing to do with giving women fulfilment but is intended to set up a situation in which family arrangements may be communal. Plato's aim is, in other words, not to promote women to a higher rank in society but to abolish the family.
[21] I say this because it is indeed a series of essays, presumably based on lectures, and does not have the format of his line-by-line commentaries on other dialogues like the *Timaeus*, *Parmenides*, and *Alcibiades*. For the text, see Kroll (1899), which I cite by page and line number in my own translations. For a French translation, see Festugière (1970). I am grateful to Dirk Baltzly for sharing with me a pre-publication of the forthcoming English translation of these two essays.

those just surveyed, beginning with the way Proclus divides his discussion in *Essay 8*. Taking his cue from Plato himself (*Rep.* 456c), he says that Plato offers different rationales for the *possibility* of legislating that women should be guardians and the *benefit* of doing so (238.16: ὅτι δυνατὰ νομοθετεῖ καὶ ὅτι ... ὠφέλιμα). This maps on directly to Allen's contrast between a 'metaphysical' and a 'pragmatic' argument, because the possibility thesis is established by the argument concerning the difference between male and female nature, while the benefit thesis is established by appealing to the interests of the state.

For Proclus, Platonic metaphysics supports the possibility of female guardians, whereas the Peripatetics 'tear apart the virtues (διασπῶσι τὰς ἀρετάς)' by assigning some to men and some to women (237.7–9: καθάπερ οἱ ἐκ τοῦ περιπάτου φασίν, cf. 252.24–25). Against this division of the virtues, Proclus substantiates the possibility thesis by referring to the single form in which all humans, regardless of gender, participate:

> 236.16–37.3: On these topics, it seems to me, Plato knew the truth and established it securely, laying it down that male and female are the same in respect of form, and determining that just as they have one form, so they have one virtue (καθάπερ τὸ εἶδος ἕν, καὶ τὴν ἀρετὴν μίαν ἔχειν διορίσας) .... It is those things that are different in form that differ also in their good, whereas to those things that are alike in form with respect to essence belongs virtue that is alike in form for them all (τῶν δὲ κατ' οὐσίαν ὁμοειδῶν καὶ τὴν ἀρετὴν ὁμοειδῆ πάντων ὑπάρχειν).

Proclus' argument gains some of its plausibility from the double meaning of the Greek word *eidos*, which is translated into English as either 'species' or 'form', depending on context.[22] His thought is that the *form* of a thing determines its virtue or good (*to eu*); since the male-female contrast is one drawn within a single *species*, men and women must have the same good. Further on, Proclus makes the same point by appealing to the concept of 'nature' and makes it explicit that a single nature is given to all humans by the divine craftsman whose work is described in the *Timaeus*:

> 237.28–38.1: Since, then, humans are all alike in form, and have the same perfections and natural activities, so too must they have the same natures (τελειότητας ἕξουσι τὰς αὐτὰς καὶ τὰς φυσικὰς ἐνεργείας, ὥσπερ καὶ τὰς φύσεις). 242.7–9: Thus, the nature of humans that has come to be from

---

[22] In fact, Festugière (1970) translates *eidos* here as 'espèce'. I should say that I am not accusing Proclus of an equivocation here: he would say that *eidos* as a species or class is unified by the participation of all its members in a transcendent *eidos* or form.

demiurgic creation is equivalent in respect of virtue (οὕτως ὁμαλὴ γέγονεν ἡ τῶν ἀνθρώπων φύσις πρὸς ἀρετὴν ἐκ τῆς δημιουργίας).

The idea of 'nature' helps to bridge the gap between mere class membership (which is all that is immediately implied by *eidos* in the sense of 'species') and the normative concepts of virtue and the good. For, as Proclus observes, 'in all cases we see that activities in accordance with nature follow upon the natures' (237.17–18), and each living thing 'partakes in a single idea by its nature (ὡς ἔχει μίαν ἰδέαν ἐκ τῆς φύσεως)' (237.21). The allusion to an 'idea' here, like the reference to demiurgic creation in the previous quotation, already situates the argument in Platonic metaphysics, but the wider philosophical context is still more explicit in *Essay 9*:

> 252.16–31: [Male and female] are the same in form and their virtue is the same, this on the basis of the principle (ἀξίωμα) that perfections are consonant with essences (ταῖς οὐσίαις ... συστοίχους), with the same belonging to the same. For it is the Intellect that gives the essences and the perfections to the forms. Inasmuch, then, as it gives essence, so it gives the perfection that corresponds to the essence.

If the natures of women and men are the same, so are their activities, and what it is to be a good woman is the same as what it is to be a good man: namely, to be a good *human* and participate as fully as possible in the 'idea' or 'form' of humanity bestowed by the Intellect. This leaves scope, Proclus hastens to add, for variations in 'intensity and laxity (ἐπίτασις καὶ ἄνεσις)' (237.26). Thus, all storks are clever (237.24), but some may be cleverer than others. With this point Proclus can accommodate Plato's admission that women are less excellent than men, without having to admit that women should pursue a different kind of excellence from men.

As I say, though, all this shows merely that it is *possible* for women to be guardians. In designing the ideal state, we do not legislate so as to realise every possibility but only those that are beneficial. So it must be shown why such legislation would be advantageous. At first glance, Proclus' remarks on this issue are grist to the mill of the anti-feminist reading given by Annas and others. He observes, in what looks like an echo of the above-cited passage from the *Laws* about making the city only half as happy as it could be, that 'the educating of women pays off more (λυσιτελέστερον) than educating only the men, for otherwise half the city will be uneducated' (247.5–7). In fact, women are in even more need of education because they are more prone to the influence of the passions (247.10). We want to avoid having uneducated citizens, at least among the guardian class, since if that class is entirely good it will be 'more in harmony with itself (ἑαυτῇ σύμφωνος)' than if some (the men) are good and some (the women) bad (247.14–15). All this makes it sound like women are educated solely for the sake of the city and its unity, not for their own good.

Plato's *Republic* does seem to say that the guardians' individual happiness may be sacrificed for the good of the city. That is suggested especially by the famous passage in which Socrates concedes that philosophers would prefer not to rule but says that they should rule anyway since they are the best qualified; besides, it is actually better for those who do not value political power to wield it. This sounds like bad news for the guardian-philosophers' individual interests, but 'it is not the law's concern to make any one class in the city outstandingly happy but to contrive to spread happiness throughout the city by bringing citizens into harmony with each other' (*Rep.* 519e).[23] As it turns out though, Proclus would deny that there is a conflict between the good of the philosophers and the good of the city. He would agree with aforementioned Harry Lesser, who says that when everyone in the city carries out their proper role, this 'has the consequence of benefiting both that person and the community ... [otherwise] the individual is robbed of fulfilment, and the community of the use of his talents'.[24]

For Proclus, similarly, both men and women guardians contribute to the unity and harmony of the city by being good and virtuous, and it is obviously in their individual interest to be good and virtuous. In this respect, he follows the lead of the earlier Theodore of Asine, whose interpretation is transmitted and discussed in Proclus' *Essay 9*.[25] For instance, one of Theodore's rationales for educating women is that if virtue were 'split up' and distributed in part to men, in part to women, then *everyone* would lack some virtues and be 'incomplete' (253.10). That is, even the men would lack those human virtues distinctive of women. Like Plato and Proclus, Theodore refers to the idea of realising the potential for virtue to an only 'half-complete (ἡμιτελές)' extent, but he refers this claim to each gender (*genos*), not the city. If we do not educate women then their class will be 'stunted (κολοβόν)' (253.9). On the other hand, Theodore has just said that without educating women, the *city* will be 'stunted' (253.6) by filling it with people who are not excellent (*spoudaios*) and also allowing children to be born from non-excellent parents, namely uneducated mothers. It is clear then that for Theodore, and for Proclus who evidently

---

[23] I here use the Grube/Reeve trans. from Cooper (1997).   [24] Lesser (1979: 116).
[25] For Theodore's interpretation and Proclus' use of it, see O'Meara (2003: 84) and Baltzly (2013).

accepts these arguments, the good of individual woman guardians, the good of women as a class, and the good of the city all stand or fall together.

With this line of thought Theodore and Proclus rebut in advance the concerns advanced by Annas and others who are troubled by the 'utilitarian' basis of Plato's proposals. Proclus also considers, and rejects, the claim that the misogynist account of reincarnation in the *Timaeus* undermines Plato's promotion of female education and virtue in the *Republic*. His first move is a striking one: he says that Timaeus, whom he takes to be a real historical figure steeped in Pythagorean philosophy, was well aware that there were actual women philosophers: 'Theano, Tymichas, and Diotima herself' (248.26–27). This striking invocation of the contributions of real (or supposedly real) women philosophers echoes what Theodore of Asine said in his defence of *Republic* V. He also mentioned Diotima as well as other figures like Helen of Troy as examples of virtuous women (255). While these passages are brief, they do show that our present-day concern with identifying real women sages was not unprecedented in antiquity. As I will mention below, it was a major theme of Renaissance European philosophy too.

In any case, Proclus' main response to the worry about the reincarnation passage in the *Timaeus* is that it supports, rather than casting doubt on, the argument of *Republic* V. This is for precisely the reason given in our own day by Smith, namely that sexual differentiation is due to embodiment, so that the souls of women and men are fundamentally the same:

> 249.15–21: If it is the same souls that come to be both men and women, taking their lives in exchange, and if the virtues belong to souls, not bodies, then by what device could it happen that their perfections are made different because of the bodies, rather than being the same because of the souls? This very evidence is sufficient to show that the virtues are common: the fact that the souls of both were common well before.

This, again, is not unlike what we can find in some modern interpreters, who see *Republic* V and the psychological theory of the *Timaeus* as being at least reconcilable, even as mutually supporting.[26] It must be said that Proclus' considered view on the gender of souls is more complicated than this, though. In his *Timaeus* commentary he says that, even though a given soul may be now in a man's body, now in a woman's, the soul also has a kind of 'gender' of its own depending on the divine principles with which it is individually coordinated. As Jana Schultz has pointed out, this should

---

[26] Harry and Polansky (2016).

not be taken to imply that some souls are intrinsically weak or corrupt: 'it would be absurd to state that a goddess is vicious and that she imparts this characteristic to those souls which follow her'.[27] Still, gods are superior to goddesses, because they are aligned with the cosmic principle of Limit rather than the Unlimited.[28] Likewise, the very best human souls are male ones. But that does not immediately undermine the proposals of *Republic* V either and could even give Proclus another reason to support them. After all, a male soul can be in a female body, and presumably at least some female guardians are in fact male souls that find themselves in the bodies of women this time around. It would clearly be wrongheaded to withhold an education in virtue from such persons or, for that matter, from excellent female souls who have a female body.

Or would it? After this spirited defence of the potential for female virtue and the importance of fulfilling that potential, we are apt to be disappointed by a passage in which Proclus pulls back from the practical consequences of his own arguments. Modern-day readers have often noted a disparity between the proposals of the *Laws* and the *Republic*: while both texts argue that women should receive military training, the *Laws* does not grant them the highest political offices. This did not escape Proclus' notice, and he tries to explain it as follows:

> 256.16–19: In the *Laws*, he considers people who have been living in other cities and who, even if they have remained uncorrupted, lack superlative natures (τὰς ἀκροτάτας φύσεις). By contrast here [in the *Republic*, the citizens] are sprung straight from the universe,[29] and then educated.

He goes on to say that the crucial difference between the ideal city of the *Republic* and the less-than-ideal city of the *Laws* is that in the latter there is private property, whereas property is abolished among the guardians of the *Republic*. Women's tendency to focus on the private sphere instead of the concerns of the whole city means that in a non-communist polity, they cannot be trusted with supreme authority, that is, 'rule over the whole (τὴν τῶν ὅλων ἀρχήν)' (257.4).

In these final lines of *Essay* 9, Proclus sounds not unlike Aristotle in the notorious passages of the *Politics* (I.13, 1260a) that assign to women authority in the private sphere of the household but not in civic life. Still, we should not leap to the conclusion that Proclus sides with Plato, when it comes to the fantasy scenario of a perfect city, but with Aristotle,

---

[27] Schultz (2019a: 889). The topic is also discussed in Dillon (1985) and Baltzly (2013).
[28] See on this topic Jana Schultz's chapter in the present volume (Chapter 10).
[29] I here borrow Baltzly's nice translation of φύντας εὐθὺς ἐκ τοῦ παντός.

when it comes to real life. As we have seen, he explicitly rejects the Peripatetic division of virtues into male and female. In fact, one could take Proclus' defence of both the possibility and desirability of Plato's proposals to be inspired in part by the need to respond to Aristotle's critique of those proposals. Aristotle denied both the possibility of Plato's scheme (ἀδύνατον, at *Politics* 1261a14) and the benefit of seeking maximal unity in the state: 'Even if it were possible to achieve this', he says, 'we shouldn't do so. For it would eliminate the city', given that the city is made up of different kinds of people (*Pol.* 1261a21–22). On the whole, then, Proclus clearly sides with Plato against Aristotle. Our next author, by contrast, will find a way to support the arguments of *Republic* V while adhering to his staunch Aristotelianism.

Ibn Rushd

Ibn Rushd, usually known in English by his Latinised name 'Averroes', was the greatest medieval commentator on Aristotle. After long study of the man's works, he came to believe that Aristotle was as close as any human to perfect intellectual fulfilment.[30] In light of this, it may seem inexplicable that Ibn Rushd would endorse a political programme that came in for such stern critique from Aristotle. In fact, though, the explanation is ready to hand: Ibn Rushd tells us himself that he was unable to find an Arabic translation of the *Politics*, so he would not have been aware of the criticisms of Plato in Book 2 of that work.[31] Ironically enough, it was to fill this gap in the Aristotelian corpus that Ibn Rushd elected to write an exegesis of Plato's *Republic* (4).[32] The resulting text survives only in a medieval Hebrew translation and was based not on Plato's *Republic* directly but rather on Galen's paraphrase of the dialogue.[33] Ibn Rushd more or less faithfully reports the contents of the *Republic* as accessible to him, in the style of his own paraphrases of Aristotelian works, which are sometimes called 'middle' commentaries.

---

[30] See Averroes' *Long Commentary on the De Anima* at Crawford (1953: 433). I take the reference from Taylor (2004).
[31] On the reception of the *Politics* more generally, see Pines (1975) and Syros (2008).
[32] I cite by page number from the English translation in Lerner (1974); and I also quote from this translation. For the Hebrew edition and an earlier translation, see Rosenthal (1969).
[33] This can in part be inferred from Ibn Rushd's own references to Galen as his source, at 63 and 147. It seems that there was no complete translation of the *Republic* into Arabic, though some passages were translated in full: see Reisman (2004).

At times, Ibn Rushd is at pains to say that he is only telling the reader what Plato said, the implication being that he may not accept the Platonic proposals. One notable case concerns the breeding practices recommended in *Republic* V (60).[34] Clearly, communal sharing of mates and raising of children was not an easy thing to endorse in medieval Islamic culture.[35] But when it comes to the idea that women should pursue the same virtuous activities as men in a well-run city, Ibn Rushd agrees with and even expands upon Plato. He offers an elaborate rationale for this thesis and for good measure complains that real-life cities are impoverished by failing to exploit the talents of women, treating them as if they were plants, good only for reproduction (59). This remark shows that Ibn Rushd finds Plato's ideas relevant to the imperfect, real-world communities known to him, whereas we saw Proclus suggesting that the *Republic* proposals are only an idealisation. By the same token, the passage could suggest that Ibn Rushd is a proponent of the 'utilitarian' or 'pragmatic' reading of Plato on women: their talents should be exploited in order to enrich the community. As with Proclus, though, this impression is misleading. In fact, Ibn Rushd draws on Aristotelian doctrines to argue that women must be allowed to pursue the same activities as men, so that they can achieve full happiness as individuals.

That one goal of his paraphrase commentary is to 'Aristotelianise' the *Republic* is clear from the very first lines, where Ibn Rushd says that he will be eliminating dialectical considerations so as to present only the demonstrative arguments that may be ascribed to Plato (3). In other words, he will present a version of Plato's ideas that is found only implicitly in the *Republic* but, that once made explicit, will rise to the standards of proof laid out in the *Posterior Analytics*. We can understand his treatment of the section on women in these terms. Ibn Rushd does repeat purely Platonic arguments, for instance, the comparison of men and women to male and female dogs, who perform the same task of guarding, even if the females are weaker (59).[36] But his main defence of women guardians rests on an idea borrowed from the *Nicomachean Ethics*: since women and men are of the same species,

---

[34] As pointed out by Belo (2009: 5).
[35] For information about the situation of women in Islam, see Roded (1999); Adamson (2016: ch. 60); and Howe (2020). An interesting study of the role of women as religious scholars is Sayeed (2013).
[36] As it happens, Proclus worries about the methodological status of this argument (240–41) and says that it is not a mere argument by analogy, as it may seem, but a demonstrative proof: if this is true of the inferior species of dogs, all the more must it hold of the superior species of humans, whose form should be even more unitary.

they share the same final end (57). So they must be allowed to pursue the same activities as the men, in order to achieve that end.

This makes it clear that, on Ibn Rushd's understanding, the arrangement whereby women engage in war and philosophy is not only, or even primarily, chosen for the sake of the city. Rather, it is for the sake of the development of individual citizens, in this case the female ones. He states clearly what Annas found missing in Plato: that women would 'lead more satisfying lives as Guardians than as house-bound drudges'. (Here 'satisfying' would mean not mere subjective contentment but the sort of genuine fulfilment or flourishing associated with Aristotelian *eudaimonia*.) Like Proclus and Theodore, Ibn Rushd furthermore offers empirical evidence to show that there really are individual women who can achieve full happiness, though compared to them he is vague on this score, alluding only to desert-dwelling warrior women. The implication, though, is stated clearly: 'Since some women are formed with eminence and a praiseworthy disposition, it is not impossible that there be philosophers and rulers among them' (58). To understand this more fully, we should look at passages in the commentary where Ibn Rushd explains why the city should be divided into classes. He seems to take the contrast between a dominant and less dominant group – 'the rulers' and 'the many' – as an inevitable feature of human communities (112). This is not only a description of how things go, but it is also how things *should* be, given the distribution of talent and natural aptitude among individuals:

> 6: Since it is impossible that the human perfections be attained other than in different individuals within a given population, the individuals of this species are all different in natural disposition corresponding to the difference in their perfections. For if each individual among them were potentially prepared for all human perfections, nature would have wrought something in vain; for it is absurd that there be something possible whose realisation is impossible. This matter has already been made clear in natural science.

As will have been suggested to him by his reading of the *Ethics* (e.g., 1180b25: 'it is by laws that we become good'), the purpose of political institutions is to put individual members of the society in a position to realise their potential, that is, to exploit their 'natural dispositions'. And it is a good thing that not everyone has the potential 'to be a warrior or an orator or a poet, let alone a philosopher', as he here adds. A variety of tasks must be performed in society, for which we need plenty of farmers, some warriors, and a precious few philosophers. Happily, natural aptitudes are distributed in the same proportion. While most humans will not attain the ultimate end of humankind, which is to achieve philosophical wisdom, it is important that each human can fulfil the potential they do have, however limited this may be. In fact, it may not be all that limited. Ibn Rushd says that it is possible for most people to achieve practical virtue through habituation (144) and that, in the Platonic ideal city, every single citizen will at least have the virtue of moderation (52), even if the virtues of courage and wisdom are especially appropriate to the guardian and philosopher classes, respectively. Still, there is no doubt that he embraces the frank elitism we found in Plato. As is clear from the above quotation, Ibn Rushd sees members of the various classes as being 'different in natural disposition', which gives them different final ends to pursue. His endorsement of the proposals about women in *Republic* V is the other side of this coin. It is precisely because such variation in natural aptitude is *absent* between men and women that the legislators should not assign to them different tasks, as they do to slaves,[37] labourers, merchants, warriors, and of course philosophers. Ibn Rushd too is a frank elitist, but he thinks that some members of the elite are women. When things go wrong and a city is run badly, the individual capacities of the citizens go unfulfilled. In the extreme case of a tyranny, only one person's 'end' is pursued, namely that of the tyrant himself. As Ibn Rushd says, this is diametrically opposed to the situation in the virtuous city, where 'it is intended that every one of the citizens receive as much of happiness as it is in their nature to achieve' (113). The plight of the slave-like victims of tyrannical rule is very much like the state of women in the cities criticised earlier by Ibn Rushd, where they are allowed to do nothing but reproduce and raise children.[38] In both cases, the oppression consists not in, say, a lack of freedom but the lack of opportunity to be trained in virtue and perform excellent activities up to the limit of one's capacity. This same sort of point is made in our third and final response to Plato, alongside a much less friendly attitude towards Aristotle.

Lucrezia Marinella

Marinella's treatise *On the Nobility and Excellence of Women, and the Defects and Vices of Men*, was published in 1600.[39] This work is simultaneously a contribution to two long-running Renaissance debates. First and

---

[37] He mentions explicitly that the *kallipolis* will have slaves, as at 53.
[38] It may not be a coincidence that the people of a tyranny 'are full of sighing, sorrow, and mourning' (141, cf. *Rep.* 578a) much as women are given to weeping (23, though the manuscripts here give different readings).
[39] I cite by page from the translation in Dunhill (1999), from which I quote with occasional modifications. I have consulted the original text in *La nobiltà et l'eccellenza delle donne co' difetti*

more obviously, the 'dispute over women' that stretches back to at least the turn of the fifteenth century, when Christine de Pizan attacked the French medieval poem *Romance of the Rose* for its misogyny, inspiring others to rise to its defence.[40] Similarly, Marinella is responding to a misogynist diatribe called *On the Defects of Women*, by Giuseppe Passi.[41] Marinella's contribution is one of several defences of women written in the period, with other outstanding female contributors to the genre including not only Pizan but also Moderata Fonte and Archangela Tarabotti.[42] Like these other authors, she reels off the names of outstanding women to show that excellence and virtue is to be found in both genders, in fact even more among women than men. Several of the names she mentions have links to Plato: Aspasia, Diotima, and 'Asfiotea' (presumably this is Axiothea of Phlius), whom she names as one of his disciples (84).

Second and less obviously, Marinella is expanding on the tradition of Renaissance polemic between defenders of Plato and defenders of Aristotle. While one can trace the roots of this dispute back to late antiquity,[43] the more proximate origin can be found in the late Byzantine and early Renaissance author George Gemistos Plethon. His *On Aristotle's Departures from Plato* touches on a wide range of philosophical topics, in each case saying that Aristotle would have done better to stay closer to the Platonic teachings.[44] In the early generations of Italian humanism, we find authors variously taking sides in the Plato vs. Aristotle debate – like George Trapezuntius, who wrote an attack on Plato – or arguing for the more traditional thesis of harmony between these two classical authorities, as did Cardinal Bessarion. In this debate among Italian humanists, issues of gender and sexuality came to the fore as they had not in Plethon. Trapezuntius accused Plato of debauchery, on the grounds of biographical reports about homosexual attractions and Plato's own erotic dialogues. A tacit response was given by Marsilio Ficino, who presented a desexualised understanding of 'Platonic love' in his dialogue-commentary

---

et mancamenti de gli huomini (Marinella 1621), this being the third printing after those in 1600 and 1601.
[40] See the texts collected in Hult (2010).
[41] Echoing the self-consciously ironic attitude that marked the original debate over the *Rose*, Passi answered Marinella's treatise by writing a work ascribing to men most of the vices he had blamed in women, calling it *The Monstrous Smithy of Men's Foul Deeds*.
[42] See further Chemello (1983); King (1991); Benson (1992); Panizza and Wood (2000); Kolsky (2001).
[43] Karamanolis (2006).
[44] Greek edition in Lagarde (1973), translation in Woodhouse (1986: 192–214). I have also suggested placing Marinella in the context of the Plato vs. Aristotle debate in Adamson (2022a: ch. 5). There, I also discuss earlier Byzantine and Arabic texts on the topic.

on the *Symposium*, a reading already anticipated by Bessarion in his defence of Plato.[45]

Marinella, by contrast, has no interest in harmonising the two classical authorities. She highlights the gender thematic of *Republic* V, instead of the erotic dialogues, precisely in order to cast Plato in a more favourable light than Aristotle. She is in fact caustic and relentless in her criticisms of Aristotle, who restricted women to the household because he was a 'fearful, tyrannical man (*huomo tiranno e pauroso*)' (79). She makes clear the connection between her own polemic and earlier attacks on Aristotle for his departures from Plato when she writes that he 'was led by scorn, hate, or envy (*ò sdegno, ò odio, ò invidia*) in many of his books, to vituperate and slander (*dir male*) the female sex, just as in many passages he reproved his master Plato' (40). By contrast, Plato argued for the emancipation of women, as in warfare (79), on the grounds that they are 'on the same level [as men] in valour and intelligence (*ingegno*)' (40).

Like Proclus, Marinella was a forerunner of the modern interpretations mentioned above, according to which the eminence of women is supported by 'metaphysical' and not just 'pragmatic' arguments, with Platonist metaphysics offering a better basis for gender equality than Aristotelian philosophy. Actually, her view is somewhat more nuanced than that. She suggests that Aristotelian doctrine *could* have been used to argue for a more favourable view of women. Thus, she alludes to Aristotle's theory of the virtues while extolling the excellence of women and points out that Aristotelian teleology is ill-fitting with the notion that women are imperfect by nature (68, 135). Aristotle persisted with misogyny at the cost of inconsistency with his own doctrines, then, something that can be explained only in terms of personal antagonism. Still, she finds in Platonism the strongest basis for asserting the equality and even superiority of women. Marinella notes that for Platonists, the outward beauty of a body is a sign of a beautiful soul within. For this idea she refers to the authority of Plotinus and Ficino. Ironically enough, she also cites the Aristotelian definition of soul as form of the body (57), precisely the idea that Smith connected to Aristotle's negative attitudes towards women. Since women are more physically attractive than men, they must have finer souls.

A more elaborate feminist argument proceeds from the Platonist premise that 'Ideas are the eternal exemplars and images of things'. Better,

---

[45] The work is translated in Jayne (1944). For the topic, see Reeser (2016); and for Ficino's position in the larger debate, see Monfasani (2002).

more beautiful things must have superior Ideas, as the Idea of a palace is better than that of a shack (her example). Marinella spells out the implications as follows:

> 53: Now, applying the example to my theme, I say that the Ideas of women are nobler than that of men. This is proven by their beauty and goodness, which is known to everybody. Not a philosopher nor a poet can be found who fails to attribute these [qualities] to them, rather than to men. I affirm, furthermore, that the Idea of a woman who is more graceful and adorned with beauty is more beautiful and nobler than that of a less beautiful and pleasing one, because Ideas exist of particular people (*d'alcuni particolari sono l'Idee*), as Marsilio Ficino and many holy teachers relate.

This argument is remarkable for its invocation of a rather technical, and much disputed, point of Platonist metaphysics, namely that there are Forms of individuals.[46] Since all people (or at least, all the philosophers and poets) agree that women are more virtuous and beautiful than men, individual women must have higher-ranking Forms than individual men do. A startling aspect of this proof is that it *denies* the principle that Proclus made a crucial premise in Plato's reasoning. For Proclus, women must have the same 'natural activities' as men because they share a nature, by virtue of participating in the *same* Form. For Marinella, instead, women have better natures than men, precisely because they do *not* participate in the same Forms but in better ones.

This line of argument is brilliant for its inversion of a sexist trope: that women are alluring on the outside but stunted or even repugnant within. But we must admit that it is questionable as an interpretation of Plato's own view – and not only because one would be hard pressed to find evidence in the dialogues that Plato posited Forms for individual humans. As we have seen, even the *Republic* admits that women are in fact generally inferior to men, and other Platonic works are still less favourable, with the *Timaeus* in particular claiming that female bodies are precisely the consequence of inner shortcomings. Marinella ignores this, contenting herself with the exaggerated claim that 'Plato praised women in a thousand places' (74). This is despite her evident familiarity with the relevant dialogues. She quotes from both the *Republic* and the *Laws* (79–80) and even refers to passages from less widely read dialogues like the *Cratylus* (49) and *Euthydemus* (90), referring to 297c, which compares the hydra to a female sophist. I take this to be a deliberate strategy on her part: Plato and

---

[46] A much-discussed problem in Plotinus: see, for example, Kalligas (1997).

Aristotle are presented respectively as a committed defender of women and an uncompromising misogynist, forcing the reader into a stark choice between the two main authorities of classical philosophy.

Conclusion

Throughout this chapter, I have tried to bring out the resonances between pre-modern interpretations of the *Republic* and those of more recent times. Unexpectedly, our three pre-modern exegetes seem to be more convinced than most contemporary readers that Plato can be read as a kind of 'feminist'. Especially striking is that Ibn Rushd and Marinella took inspiration from him in proposing reform of their own sexist societies and read him as valuing the individual fulfilment of at least elite women. But of course, neither they nor Proclus thought about Plato within the framework of feminism as we understand it. While their discussions do anticipate the modern scholarly debate on various points, they must also be understood within the different contexts that produced them. Much as Annas, Vlastos, and others brought the terms of the 1970s feminist movement to their reading of the *Republic*, Proclus approached it with the metaphysical and exegetical presuppositions of a late ancient Platonist. This meant assuming not only Neoplatonic metaphysical doctrines but also the exegetical principle that apparently contradictory passages in different dialogues – in this case the *Republic*, *Laws*, and *Timaeus* – can always be brought into harmony. Similarly, Averroes, as the Islamic world's greatest medieval expert on Aristotle, sought to clarify Plato's teachings by deploying Aristotelian terminology and concepts, like that of the 'final end'. Conversely, Marinella, as a Renaissance humanist, understood the *Republic* in light of lively debates over the relative merits of women and men, and of Plato and Aristotle, taking up the cause of the former over the latter. Should we then be sceptical of the interpretations offered by these pre-modern exegetes? E. R. Dodds once said, 'Arm yourself with a stout pair of blinkers and a sufficient but not excessive amount of scholarship, and by making a suitable selection of texts you can prove Plato to be almost anything that you want him to be.'[47] And certainly, one cannot absolve any of our three authors of the charge that they found in Plato what they wanted to find in him. Yet given the resonances between their interpretations and more recent readings of Plato, it seems fair to say that all three of them were latching on to genuine features of the text.

[47] Dodds (1945: 16).

Furthermore, while they were reading Plato in light of their own exegetical or polemical concerns, they were also updating him in light of new information. These authors took into account their own knowledge of emancipated and philosophically engaged women, women of the sort that have been discussed throughout this book. Thus, Averroes refers to warrior women outside the domestic sphere, while both Proclus and Marinella mention named women philosophers as evidence to support Plato's proposals. In this respect, our pre-modern witnesses testify that acknowledging the work of women philosophers has the power to change perceptions of women and of philosophy itself.[48]

---

[48] My thanks to the editors Caterina Pellò and Katharine O'Reilly (who brought to my attention the apposite passage just cited from Dodds) for their detailed comments on a previous version of this chapter.

References

Acker, C. 2002. *Femmes, fêtes et philosophie en Grèce ancienne*. Paris: Harmattan.
Adamson, P. 2016. *A History of Philosophy without Any Gaps: Philosophy in the Islamic World*. Oxford: Oxford University Press.
  2022a. *Don't Think for Yourself: Authority and Belief in Medieval Philosophy*. South Bend: Notre Dame University Press.
  2022b. 'Macrina's Method: Reason and Reasoning in Gregory of Nyssa's *On Soul and Resurrection*', in J. Schulz and J. Wilberding (eds.), *Women and the Female in Neoplatonism*. Leiden: Brill, pp. 255–75.
Addey, C. 2014. *Divination and Theurgy in Neoplatonism: Oracles of the Gods*. Farnham: Ashgate.
  2018a. 'Plato's Women Readers', in H. Tarrant et al. (eds.), *Brill's Companion to the Reception of Plato in Antiquity*. Leiden; Boston: Brill, pp. 411–32.
  2018b. 'Sosipatra: Prophetess, Philosopher and Theurgist: Reflections on Divination and Epistemology in Late Antiquity', in R. Evans (ed.), *Prophets and Profits: Ancient Divination and Its Reception*. London; New York: Routledge, pp. 144–62.
Aelian. 1959. *De Natura Animalium*, A. F. Scholfield (tr.). Loeb Classical Library 449. Cambridge, MA: Harvard University Press.
Allais, L. 2016. 'Problematizing Western Philosophy as One Part of Africanising the Curriculum', *South African Journal of Philosophy* 35(4): 537–45.
Allen, C. G. 1975. 'Plato on Women', *Feminist Studies* 2: 131–38.
Allen, R. E. (tr.). 1991. *Dialogues of Plato, ii: Symposium*. New Haven: Yale University Press.
Annas, J. 1976. 'Plato's *Republic* and Feminism', *Philosophy* 51: 307–21.
Antognazza, M. R. 2015. 'The Benefit to Philosophy of the Study of its History', *British Journal for the History of Philosophy* 23(1): 161–84.
Appell, L. 1988. 'Menstruation among the Rungus of Borneo: An Unmarked Category', in T. Buckley and P. Gottlieb (eds.), *Blood Magic: The Anthropology of Menstruation*. Berkeley: University of California Press.
Appleton, N. 2017. *Shared Characters in Jain, Buddhist and Hindu Narrative: Gods, Kings, and Other Heroes*. London: Routledge.
Arenson, K. 2016. 'Epicureans on Marriage as Sexual Therapy', *Polis* 33: 291–311.
Aristotle. 1942. *Generation of Animals*, A. L. Peck (tr.). London: William Heinemann.

1984. *Historia Animalium*, D'A. W. Thompson (tr.) in J. Barnes (ed.), *Complete Works of Aristotle*, vol. 1. Princeton: Princeton University Press.

1991. *History of Animals Books VII–X*, D. M. Balme (tr.). Cambridge, MA: Harvard University Press.

Armstrong, A. (tr.). 1984. *Plotinus in Seven Volumes*. Cambridge, MA: Harvard University Press.

Asmis, E. 1996. 'The Stoics on Women', in J. Ward (ed.), *Feminism and Ancient Philosophy*. New York: Routledge, pp. 68–92.

Athanassiadi, P. (ed. and tr.). 1999. *Damascius. The Philosophical History*. Athens: Apamea.

Baltzly, D. (tr.). 2009. *Proclus: Commentary on Plato's Timaeus. Vol. 4: Proclus on the World Soul*. Cambridge: Cambridge University Press.

2013. 'Proclus and Theodore of Asine on Female Philosopher-Rulers: Patriarchy, Metempsychosis and Women in the Neoplatonic Commentary Tradition', *Ancient Philosophy* 33: 403–24.

Ban, Z. 2013a. 'Memorial to Empress Dowager Deng', in Y. Fan et al. (eds.), *The Book of the Later Han (Houhanshu 後漢書)*, vol. 84. Reprinted with modern Chinese translation, introduction, notes, commentary in Wen Lianke et al. *Xinyi Houhanshu*. Taipei: Sanmin shuju.

2013b. 'Petition for a Replacement for My Elder Brother Chao' in Y. Fan et al. (eds.), *The Book of the Later Han (Houhanshu 後漢書)*, vol. 48. Reprinted with modern Chinese translation, introduction, notes, commentary in Wen Lianke et al. *Xinyi Houhanshu*. Taipei: Sanmin shuju.

2018. 'Lessons for Women', in A. A. Pang-White (tr. and ed.), *The Confucian Four Books for Women – A New Translation of the Nü Sishu and the Commentary of Wang Xiang*. New York: Oxford University Press, pp. 29–67.

2021a. 'Rhapsody on a Journey to the East', in T. Xiao (ed.), *Wenxuan 文選 (aka Zhaoming wenxuan 昭明文選)*, vol. 3. https://ctext.org/library.pl?if=en&res=91990.

2021b. 'Rhapsody on Needle and Thread', in X. Ouyang (ed.), *Yiwen leiju 藝文類聚*, vol. 65. https://ctext.org/library.pl?if=en&res=5982.

Barker, A. 2015. 'Pythagorean Harmonics', in C. A. Huffman (ed.), *A History of Pythagoreanism*. Cambridge: Cambridge University Press, pp. 185–203.

Bartoš, H. 2021. 'Aristotle's Biology and Early Medicine', in S. M. Connell (ed.), *The Cambridge Companion to Aristotle's Biology*. Cambridge: Cambridge University Press.

Bartsch, S. 2006. *The Mirror of the Self: Sexuality, Self-knowledge, and the Gaze in the Early Roman Empire*. Chicago: University of Chicago Press.

Bartsch, S., and Wray, D. (eds.). 2009. *Seneca and the Self*. Cambridge: Cambridge University Press.

Bar On, B.-A. 1994. *Engendering Origins*. Albany: State University of New York Press.

Beagon, P. M. 1995. 'The Cappadocian Fathers, Women and Ecclesiastical Politics', *Vigiliae Christianae* 49(2): 165–79.

Belo, C. 2009. 'Some Considerations on Averroes' Views Regarding Women and Their Role in Society', *Journal of Islamic Studies* 20: 1–20.

Benhabib, S. 1986/87. 'The Generalized and the Concrete Other: The Kohlberg-Gilligan Controversy and Feminist Theory', in S. Benhabib and D. Cornell (eds.), *Praxis International, Special Issue On Feminist Theory*, pp. 38–60; Reprinted in E. F. Kittay and D. Meyers (eds.). *Women and Moral Theory*. Totowa, NJ: Rowman and Littlefield, pp. 154–78.

Benson, P. J. 1992. *The Invention of the Renaissance Woman: The Challenge of Female Independence in the Literature and Thought of Italy and England*. University Park: Pennsylvania State University Press.

Bernasconi, R. 1997. 'Philosophy's Paradoxical Parochialism: The Reinvention of Philosophy as Greek,' in K. Ansell-Pearson, B. Parry, and J. Squires (eds.), *Cultural Readings of Imperialism*. London: Lawrence and Wishart, 212–26.

Berthelot, M. 1888. *Collection des Alchemistes Grecs*. Paris: George Steinheil.

Black, B. 2007a. *The Character of the Self in Ancient India: Priests, Kings, and Women in the Early Upaniṣads*. Albany: State University of New York Press.

  2007b. 'Eavesdropping on the Epic: Female Listeners in the *Mahābhārata*', in S. Brodbeck and B. Black (eds.), *Gender and Narrative in the Mahābhārata*. London: Routledge, pp. 53–78.

  2013. 'Draupadī in the *Mahābhārata*', *Religion Compass*, 7(5): 169–78.

  2015a. 'Dialogue and Difference: Encountering the Other in Indian Religious and Philosophical Sources', in B. Black and L. Patton (eds.), *Dialogue in Early South Asian Religions: Hindu, Buddhist, and Jain Traditions*. Farnham: Ashgate, pp. 243–57.

  2015b. 'The Upanishads', *The Internet Encyclopaedia of Philosophy*, ISSN 2161-0002. https://iep.utm.edu/.

  2017. 'The Upaniṣads and the *Mahābhārata*', in S. Cohen (ed.), *The Upaniṣads: A Complete Guide*. New York: Routledge, pp. 186–99.

  2021a. *In Dialogue with the Mahābhārata*. London: Routledge.

  2021b. 'Through the Eyes of Ulūpī: A Distinctive Snake Perspective in the *Mahābhārata*', *Journal of Hindu Studies* 15: 83–105.

  2022. 'Politics without Fear: King Janaka and Sovereignty in the *Mahābhārata*', *Religions* 13(10): 898. doi.org/10.3390/rel13100898.

Blackstone, K. R. 1998. *Women in the Footsteps of the Buddha*. New York: Routledge.

Blair, E. D. 2012. *Plato's Dialectic on Woman: Equal, Therefore Inferior*. New York: Routledge.

Blundell, S. 1995. *Women in Ancient Greece*. Cambridge, MA: Harvard University Press.

Bonelli, M. 2020. *Filosofe, Maestre e Imperatrici*. Rome: Edizioni di Storia e Letteratura.

Bose, C. K. 2017. 'The El-Lahun gynaecological papyrus', *Hektoen International: A Journal of Medical Humanities* 9(2). https://hekint.org/2017/01/27/the-el-lahun-gynecological-papyrus/.

Boyle, A. J. 1997. *Tragic Seneca: An Essay in the Theatrical Tradition*. New York: Routledge.

Bremmer, J. M. 1990. 'Adolescents, *Symposion*, and Pederasty', in O. Murray (ed.), *Sympotica*. Oxford: Oxford University Press, pp. 135–49.

Brill, S. 2015. 'Animality and Sexual Difference in the *Timaeus*', in J. Bell and M. Naas (eds.), *Plato's Animals: Gadflies, Horses, Swans, and Other Philosophical Beasts*. Bloomington: Indiana University Press, pp. 161–75.
Brill, S. and McKeen, C. Forthcoming. *The Routledge Handbook on Women and Ancient Greek Philosophy*. London: Routledge.
Broadie, S. 2019. 'Practical Truth in Aristotle', *Oxford Studies in Ancient Philosophy* 57: 249–72.
Brodbeck, S., and Black, B. 2007. *Gender and Narrative in the Mahābhārata*. London: Routledge.
Brown, V. (ed.). 2001. *Famous Women*. Cambridge, MA: Harvard University Press.
Brown, W. 1988. 'Supposing Truth Were a Woman: Plato's Subversion of Masculine Discourse', *Political Theory* 16: 594–616.
Buchan, M. 1999. *Women in Plato's Political Theory*. Houndmills: Palgrave Macmillan.
Burkert, W. 1992. *The Orientalising Revolution*. Cambridge, MA: Harvard University Press.
Burrus, V. 2000. *'Begotten, Not Made': Conceiving Manhood in Late Antiquity*. Redwood: Stanford University Press.
  2001. 'Is Macrina a Woman? Gregory of Nyssa's *Dialogue on the Soul and Resurrection*', in G. Ward (ed.), *The Companion to Postmodern Theology*. Oxford: Blackwell, pp. 249–64.
Bury, R. G. 1932. *The Symposium of Plato*. Edited with Introduction, Critical Notes and Commentary. 2nd ed. Cambridge: Heffer.
Busch, A. 2009. 'Dissolution of the Self in the Senecan Corpus', in S. Bartsch and D. Wray (eds.), *Seneca and the Self*. Cambridge: Cambridge University Press, pp. 255–82.
Buxton, R., and Whiting, L. 2020. *Philosopher Queens*. London: Unbound.
Caizzi, F. D. 1993. 'The Porch and the Garden: Early Hellenistic Images of the Philosophical Life', in A. Bulloch, E. Gruen, A. A. Long, and A. Stewart (eds.), *Images and Ideologies: Self-Definition in the Hellenistic World*. Berkeley: University of California Press, pp. 303–29.
Calame, C. 1999. *The Poetics of Eros in Ancient Greece*. Princeton University Press.
Callahan, V. W. (tr.) 1967. *The Fathers of the Church: St. Gregory of Nyssa Ascetical Works*. Washington, DC: The Catholic University of America Press.
Cameron, A., and Long, J. 1993. *Barbarians and Politics at the Court of Arcadius*. Oakland: University of California Press.
Cantor, L. 2022. 'Thales – the "First Philosopher"? A Troubled Chapter in the Historiography of Philosophy', *British Journal for the History of Philosophy*. DOI: 10.1080/09608788.2022.2029347.
Castelli, E. 1986. 'Virginity and Its Meaning for Women's Sexuality in Early Christianity', *Journal of Feminist Studies in Religion* 2(1): 61–88.
Castner, C. 1982. 'Epicurean *Hetairai* as Dedicants to Healing Deities?', *Greek, Roman, and Byzantine Studies* 23: 51–57.
Centrone, B. 1990. *Pseudopythagorica Ethica*. Naples: Bibliopolis.

2014. 'The Pseudo-Pythagorean Writings', in C. A. Huffman (ed.), *A History of Pythagoreanism*. Cambridge: Cambridge University Press, pp. 315–40.

Chakrabarti, A. 2014. 'Just Words: An Ethics of Conversation in the Mahābhārata', in A. Chakrabarti and S. Bandyopadhyay (eds.), *Mahābhārata Now: Narration, Aesthetics, Ethics*. New Delhi: Routledge, pp. 244–83.

Chakravarti, U. 2014. 'Who Speaks for Whom? The Queen, the Dāsī and Sexual Politics in the Sabhāparvan', in A. Chakrabarti and S. Bandyopadhyay (eds.), *Mahābhārata Now: Narration, Aesthetics, Ethics*. New Delhi: Routledge, pp. 132–52.

Chemello, A. 1983. 'La donna, il modello, l'immaginario: Moderata Fonte e Lucrezia Marinella', in M. Zancan (ed.), *Nel cerchio della luna: figure di donna in alcuni testi del XVI secolo*. Venice: Marsilio, pp. 59–170.

Chouinard, I., McConaughey, Z., Medeiros Ramos, A., and Noel, R. (eds.) 2021. *Women's Perspectives on Ancient and Medieval Philosophy*. New York: Springer.

Christensen, A. B. 2020. 'Epicureans on Friendship, Politics, and Community', in K. Arenson (ed.), *The Routledge Handbook of Hellenistic Philosophy*. New York: Routledge, pp. 307–18.

Cixous, H. 1976. 'The Laugh of the Medusa', *Signs: Journal of Women in Culture and Society* 1: 875–93.

Clark, E. A. 1998. 'The Lady Vanishes: Dilemmas of a Feminist Historian after the "Linguistic Turn"', *Church History*, 67(1), 1–31.

Clay, D. 2009. 'The Athenian Garden', in Warren, J. (ed.), *The Cambridge Companion to Epicureanism*. Cambridge: Cambridge University Press, pp. 9–28.

Cohen, S. 2008. *Text and Authority in the Older Upaniṣads*. Leiden: Brill.

2018. *The Upanishads*. London: Routledge.

Cole, S. 1981. 'Could Greek Women Read and Write?' *Women's Studies* 8: 129–55. Reprinted in H. Foley (ed.), *Reflections of Women in Antiquity*. London: Routledge, pp. 219–45.

Connell, S. M. 2016. *Aristotle on Female Animals: A Study of the Generation of Animals*. Cambridge: Cambridge University Press.

2019. 'Nurture and Parenting in Aristotelian Ethics', *Proceedings of the Aristotelian Society* 2: 119.

2021. 'Women in Science', in T. Whitmarsh (ed.), *Oxford Classical Dictionary*. Oxford: Oxford University Press. https://oxfordre.com/classics/display/10.1093/acrefore/9780199381135.001.0001/acrefore-978019 9381135-e-8584;jsessionid=6B7B03197DD49A5F6441B84586BD8D3B.

Cooper, J. M. (ed.) 1997. *Plato. Complete Works*. Indianapolis: Hackett.

2012. *Pursuits of Wisdom: Six Ways of Life in Ancient Philosophy from Socrates to Plotinus*. Princeton: Princeton University Press.

Cox Miller, P. 1983. *Biography in Late Antiquity: A Quest for the Holy Man*. Oakland: University of California Press.

2000. 'Strategies of Representation in Collective Biography: Constructing the Subject as Holy', in T. Hägg, P. Rousseau, and C. Høgel, (eds.), *Greek Biography and Panegyric in Late Antiquity*. Oakland: University of California Press, pp. 209–55.

Craik, E. 2015. *The Hippocratic Corpus: Content and Context*. London: Routledge.
Crawford, F. S. (ed.) 1953. *Averroes. Averrois Cordubensis Commentarium magnum in Aristotelis De anima libros*. Cambridge, MA: Mediaeval Academy of America.
Dalmiya, V. and Mukherji, G. 2018. 'Introduction: To Do', in S. C. Bhattacharya, V. Dalmiya, and G. Mukherji (eds.), *Exploring Agency in the Mahābhārata: Ethical and Political Dimensions of Dharma*. Abingdon: Routledge, pp. 1–27.
D'Angour, A. 2019. *Socrates in Love: The Making of a Philosopher*. Oxford: Oxford University Press.
Darling, D. 2004. *The Universal Book of Mathematics: From Abracadabra to Zeno's Paradoxes*. New York: Wiley.
Deakin, M. A. B. 2007. *Hypatia of Alexandria. Mathematician and Martyr*. Amherst, NY: Prometheus Books.
Dean-Jones, L. 1992. 'The Politics of Pleasure: Female Sexual Appetite in the Hippocratic Corpus', *Helios* 19: 72–91.
   1994. *Women's Bodies in Ancient Greek Science*. Oxford: Clarendon.
   1995. 'Autopsia, Historia, and What Women Know: The Authority of Women in Hippocratic Gynaecology', in D. Bates (ed.), *Knowledge and the Scholarly Medical Traditions*. Cambridge: Cambridge University Press, pp. 41–59.
   2012. 'Clinical Gynecology and Aristotle's Biology: The Composition of HA X', *Apeiron* 45: 180–99.
   2018. 'Female Patients,' in P. E. Pormann (ed.), *The Cambridge Companion to Hippocrates*. Cambridge: Cambridge University Press, pp. 246–62.
   Forthcoming. *Historia Animalium Book X: Aristotle Endoxon, Topos, and Dialectic On Failure to Reproduce*. Cambridge: Cambridge University Press.
de Beauvoir, S. 1949/1952. *The Second Sex*. Translated and edited by H. M. Parshley. New York: Knopf.
De Cesaris, G., and Horky, P. S. 2018. 'Hellenistic Pythagorean Epistemology', in F. Verde and M. Catapano (eds.), special issue of *Lexicon Philosophicum: Hellenistic Theories of Knowledge*: 221–62.
Deming, W. 2004. *Paul on Marriage and Celibacy: The Hellenistic Background of 1 Corinthians 7*. Grand Rapids: Wm. B. Eerdmans.
Denzey Lewis, N. 2014. 'Living Images of the Divine: Female Theurgists in Late Antiquity', in K. B. Stratton and D. S. Kalleres (eds.), *Daughters of Hecate: Women and Magic in the Ancient World*. Oxford: Oxford University Press, pp. 274–93.
Derrida, J. 1972. 'Structure, Sign, and Play in the Discourse of the Human Sciences', in R. Macksey and E. Donato (eds.), *The Structuralist Controversy: The Languages of Criticism and the Sciences of Man*. Baltimore: Johns Hopkins University Press, pp. 247–65.
Deslauriers, M. 2012. 'Women, Education, and Philosophy,' in S. L. James and S. Dillon (eds.), *A Companion to Women in the Ancient World*. Oxford: Blackwell, pp. 343–53.

Des Places, E. 1987. *Jamblique. Protreptique*. Paris: Les Belles Lettres.
De Temmerman, K. 2016. 'Ancient Biography and Formalities of Fiction,' in D. De Temmerman and D. Demoen (eds.), *Writing Biography in Greece and Rome: Narrative Technique and Fictionalization*. Cambridge: Cambridge University Press, pp. 2–36.
Dhand, A. 2007. 'Paradigms of the Good in the *Mahābhārata*: Śuka and Sulabhā in Quagmires of Ethics', in S. Brodbeck and B. Black (eds.), *Gender and Narrative in the Mahābhārata*. London: Routledge, pp. 258–78.
  2008. *Woman as Fire, Woman as Sage: Sexual Ideology in the Mahābhārata*. Albany: State University of New York Press.
  2018. '*Karmayoga* and the Vexed Moral Agent', in S. C. Bhattacharya, V. Dalmiya, and G. Mukherji (eds.), *Exploring Agency in the Mahābhārata: Ethical and Political Dimensions of Dharma*. Abingdon: Routledge, pp. 81–106.
Dickason, A. 1973–74. 'Anatomy and Destiny: The Role of Biology in Plato's View of Women', *Philosophical Forum* 5: 44–53.
Dillon, J. 1985. 'Female Principles in Platonism', *Itaca* 1, 107–23.
Diogenes Laertius. 1925/1972. *Lives of Eminent Philosophers* (D.L.) tr. R. D. Hicks. Cambridge, MA: Harvard University Press.
Dodds, E. R. 1945. 'Plato and the Irrational', *Journal of Hellenic Studies* 65: 16–25.
Donnison, D. 1988. *Midwives and Medical Men: A History of the Struggle for the Control of Childbirth*. New Barnet: Historical Publications.
Dotson, K. 2012. 'How Is This Paper Philosophy?', *Comparative Philosophy* 3(1): 3–29.
Dover, K. 1978. *Greek Homosexuality*. London: Duckworth.
  1980. *Plato: Symposium*. Cambridge: Cambridge University Press.
Doyle, N. 2018. *Maternal Bodies: Redefining Motherhood in Early America*. Chapel Hill: University of North Carolina Press.
Drury, J. L. 2005. 'Gregory of Nyssa's Dialogue with Macrina: The Compatibility of Resurrection of the Body and Immortality of the Soul', *Theology Today* 62(2): 210–22.
du Bois, P. 1988. *Sowing the Body: Psychoanalysis and Ancient Representations of Women*. Chicago: University of Chicago Press.
  1994. 'The Platonic Appropriation of Reproduction', in N. Tuana (ed.), *Feminist Interpretations of Plato*. University Park: Pennsylvania State University Press, pp. 139–57.
Dunhill, A. (tr.). 1999. *Lucrezia Marinella: The Nobility and the Excellence of Women and the Defects of Men*. Chicago: University of Chicago Press.
Dutsch, D. M. 2020. *Pythagorean Women Philosophers*. Oxford: Oxford University Press.
Dzielska, M. 1995. *Hypatia of Alexandria*, tr. F. Lyra. Cambridge, MA: Harvard University Press.
Elm, S. 1994. *'Virgins of God': The Making of Asceticism in Late Antiquity*. Oxford: Oxford University Press.
El Murr, D. 2020. 'Eristic, Antilogy, and the Equal Disposition of Men and Women (*Resp*. 5. 453b–454c)', *Classical Quarterly* 70(1): 85–100.

Eusebius of Caesarea. 1903. *Praeparatio Evangelica* (PE), tr. E. H. Gifford. Oxford: Typographeo Academico.

Evans, N. 2006. 'Diotima and Demeter as Mystagogues in Plato's *Symposium*', *Hypatia* 21(2): 1–27.

Falk, Nancy. 1977. 'Draupadī and the Dharma', in R. M. Gross (ed.), *Beyond Androcentrism: New Essays on Women and Religion*. Missoula: Scholars Press, pp. 89–114.

Fan, Y. et al. 范曄 (eds.). 2021. The *Book of the Later Han* (*Houhanshu* 後漢書), 120 or 130 vols. (depending on editions). https://en.wikipedia.org/wiki/Book_of_the_Later_Han, or https://ctext.org/hou-han-shu/zh. Reprinted with modern Chinese translation, introduction, notes, commentary in Wen Lianke et al. 2013. *Xinyi Houhanshu*. Taipei: Sanmin shuju.

Faucette, A. 2014. 'Fucking the Binary for Social Change: Our Radically Queer Agenda', *Counterpoints: The Gay Agenda: Claiming Space, Identity, Justice* 437: 73–88.

Festugière, A. J. (ed.) 1970. *Proclus: Commentaire sur la République*. Paris: Librairie Philosophique J. Vrin.

Fitch, J. G. 2009. *Seneca's Hercules Furens: A Critical Text with Introduction and Commentary*. Ithaca: Cornell University Press.

Fitzgerald, J. L. 2002. 'Nun Befuddles King, Shows Karmayoga Does Not Work: Sulabhā's Refutation of King Janaka at *MBh* 12.308', *Journal of Indian Philosophy* 30(6): 641–77.

Flemming, F. 2007. 'Women, Writing and Medicine in the Classical World', *Classical Quarterly* 5: 257–79.

Foucault, M. 1985. *A History of Sexuality: The Use of Pleasure*, vol 2. London: Penguin Books.

Frank, G. 2000. 'Macrina's Scar: Homeric Allusion and Heroic Identity in Gregory of Nyssa's *Life of Macrina*', *Journal of Early Christian Studies* 8(3): 511–30.

Frede, D. 1993. 'Out of the Cave: What Socrates Learnt from Diotima', in R. M. Rosen and J. Farrell (eds.), *Nomodeiktes: Greek Studies in Honour of Martin Ostwald*. Ann Arbor: University of Michigan Press, pp. 397–422.

   2018. 'Equal But Not Equal: Plato and Aristotle on Women as Citizens' in G. Santas and G. Anagnostopoulos (eds.), *Democracy, Justice, and Equality in Ancient Greece: Historical and Philosophical Perspectives*. Dordrecht: Springer, pp. 287–306.

Freeland, C. A. 1998. *Feminist Interpretations of Aristotle*. University Park: Pennsylvania State University Press.

Fricker, M., and J. Hornsby (eds.). 2000. *The Cambridge Companion to Feminism in Philosophy*. Cambridge: Cambridge University Press.

Frischer, B. 1982. *The Sculpted Word: Epicureanism and Philosophical Recruitment in Ancient Greece*. Berkeley: University of California Press.

Gadamer, H.-G. 1985. *Philosophical Apprenticeships*. Cambridge, MA: MIT Press.

Galinsky, K. 1972. *The Herakles Theme: The Adaptations of the Hero in Literature from Homer to the Twentieth Century*. Oxford: Blackwell.

Gardner, C. 2000. 'The Remnants of the Family: The Role of Women and Eugenics in *Republic* V', *History of Philosophy Quarterly* 17: 217–35.
Gaut, B. 1998. 'Just Joking: The Ethics and Aesthetics of Humour', *Philosophy and Literature* 22(1): 55–68.
Gertz, S. 2014. 'Dream Divination and the Neoplatonic Search for Salvation', in D. A. Russell and H.-G. Nesselrath (eds.), *On Prophecy, Dream and Human Imagination. Synesius, De insomniis.* Tübingen: Mohr Siebeck, pp. 111–24.
  2020. '"A Mere Geometer?" Hypatia in the Context of Alexandrian Neoplatonism', in D. L. Norman and A. Petkas (eds.), *Hypatia of Alexandria*. Tübingen: Mohr Siebeck, pp. 133–51.
Giannantoni, G. (ed.). 1990. *Socratis et Socraticorum Reliquiae (SSR)*. 4 vols. Naples: Bibliopolis.
Gilligan, C. 1982. *In A Different Voice: Psychological Theory and Women's Development*. Cambridge, MA: Harvard University Press.
Ginsberg, L. 2016. 'Jocasta's Catilinarian Oration (Sen. Phoen. 632–43)', *Classical Journal* 4: 483–94.
Gloyn, L. 2017. *The Ethics of the Family in Seneca*. Cambridge: Cambridge University Press.
Gordon, P. 2004. 'Remembering the Garden: The Trouble with Women in the School of Epicurus', in J. Fitzgerald, D. Obbink, and G. Holland (eds.), *Philodemus and the New Testament World*. Leiden: Brill, pp. 221–43.
  2012. *The Invention and Gendering of Epicurus*. Ann Arbor: University of Michigan Press.
Granholm, P. 2012. 'Alciphron: Letters of the Courtesans', unpublished PhD thesis, Uppsala University.
Grant, J. 1994. *Fundamental Feminism: Contesting the Core Concepts of Feminist Theory*. New York: Routledge.
Graver, M. 2001. *Cicero on the Emotions: Tusculan Disputations 3 and 4*. Chicago: University of Chicago Press.
Griffin, C. 2020. *Beyond Gender Binaries: An Intersectional Orientation to Communication and Identities*. Berkeley: University of California Press.
Griffin, M. 1976. *Seneca: A Philosopher in Politics*. Oxford: Clarendon Press.
  1986a. 'Philosophy, Cato, and Roman Suicide: I', *Greece & Rome* 33: 64–77.
  1986b. 'Philosophy, Cato, and Roman Suicide: II', *Greece & Rome* 33: 192–202.
Guarducci, M. 1974. 'La Statua di "Sant Ippolito" in Vaticano', *Rendiconti, Pontificia Accademia Romana di Archeologia* 47: 163–90.
Hadot, P. 1987. *Philosophy as a Way of Life*, A. Davidson (ed.) M. Chase (tr.). Malden: Blackwell.
Hallisey, C. 2015. *Therigatha: Poems of the First Buddhist Women*. Cambridge, MA: Harvard University Press.
Halperin, D. 1989. 'Why Is Diotima a Woman?', in D. Halperin (ed.), *One Hundred Years of Homosexuality*. New York: Routledge, pp. 113–53.
Hanson, A. 1991. 'Continuity and Change: Three Case Studies in Hippocratic Gynaecological Therapy and Theory', in S. Pomeroy (ed.), *Women's History*

and Ancient History. Chapel Hill: University of North Carolina Press, pp. 73–110.

Haraway, D. 1991. 'Situated Knowledges: The Science Question in Feminism and the Privilege of Partial Perspective', in D. Haraway, *Simians, Cyborgs, and Women: The Reinvention of Nature*. London; New York: Routledge, pp. 183–201.

Harich-Schwarzbauer, H. (ed. and tr.) 2011. *Hypatia. Die spätantiken Quellen*. Frankfurt: Peter Lang.

Harrison, V. S. 2012. *Eastern Philosophy: The Basics*. London: Routledge.

Harry, C., and Polansky, R. 2016. 'Plato on Women's Natural Ability: Revisiting *Republic* V and *Timaeus* 41e3–44d2 and 86b1–92c3', *Apeiron* 49: 261–80.

Haslanger, S. 2008. 'Changing the Ideology and Culture of Philosophy: Not by Reason (Alone)', *Hypatia* 23(2): 210–23.

Hawley, R. 1994. 'The Problem of Women Philosophers in Ancient Greece', in L. J. Archer, S. Fischler, and M. Wyke (eds.), *Women in Ancient Societies: An Illusion of the Night*. New York: Routledge, pp. 70–87.

He, Z. 2013. 'On the Revenge of Women', in L. Liu, R. Karl, and D. Ko (tr. and eds.), *The Birth of Chinese Feminism: Essential Texts in Transnational Theory*. New York: Columbia University Press, pp. 105–68.

Helleman, W. E. 2001. 'Cappadocian Macrina as Lady Wisdom', *Studia Patristica* 37: 86–102.

Henry, D., and Nielsen, K. 2015. 'Introduction', in *Bridging the Gap between Aristotle's Science and Ethics*. Cambridge: Cambridge University Press, pp. 1–26.

Henry, M. 1997. *Prisoner of History: Aspasia of Miletus and her Biographical Tradition*. Oxford: Oxford University Press.

Hill, L. 2001. 'The First Wave of Feminism: Were the Stoics Feminists?' *History of Political Thought* 22: 13–40.

Hiltebeitel, A. 2000. 'Draupadi's Question', in A. Hiltebeitel and K. Erndl (eds.), *Is the Goddess a Feminist? The Politics of South Asian Goddesses*. New York: New York University Press, pp. 113–22.

Hine, H. (tr.). 2014. 'Consolation to Marcia', in *Lucius Annaeus Seneca: Hardship & Happiness*. Chicago: University of Chicago Press.

Hippocrates. 2010–18. *Works, Volumes IX–XI*, tr. P. Potter. Cambridge, MA: Harvard University Press [Loeb].

Holmes, B. 2013. 'In Strange Lands. Disembodied Authority and the Role of the Physician in the Hippocratic Corpus and Beyond', in M. Asper (ed.), *Writing Science. Medical and Mathematical Authorship in Ancient Greece*. Berlin: De Gruyter, pp. 431–72.

Horky, P. S. 2015. 'Pseudo-Archytas' Protreptics? *On Wisdom* in its Contexts', in D. Nails and H. Tarrant (eds.), *Second Sailing*. Helsinki: Societas Scientiarum Fennica, pp. 21–40.

2020. 'Anonymus Iamblichi, *On Excellence* (*Peri Aretēs*): A Lost Defense of Democracy', in D. Wolfsdorf (ed.), *Early Greek Ethics*. Oxford: Oxford University Press, pp. 262–92.

Hösle, V. 2012. *The Philosophical Dialogue: A Poetics and Hermeneutics*, tr. Steven Rendall. South Bend: University of Notre Dame Press.
Hotz, K. G. 2001. 'Speaking Funk: Womanist Insights into the Lives of Syncletica and Macrina', in E. A. Holmes and W. Farley, (eds.), *Women, Writing, Theology: Transforming a Tradition of Exclusion*. Waco, TX: Baylor University Press, pp. 71–94.
Howard, V. R. 2019. *The Bloomsbury Research Handbook of Indian Philosophy and Gender*. New York: Bloomsbury.
Howe, J. 2020. *The Routledge Handbook of Islam and Gender*. London: Routledge.
Huffman, C.A. (ed.). 2014. *A History of Pythagoreanism*. Cambridge: Cambridge University Press.
  2019a. *Aristoxenus of Tarentum*. Cambridge University Press.
  2019b. 'Pythagoreanism', in E. N. Zalta (ed.), *The Stanford Encyclopaedia of Philosophy*. https://plato.stanford.edu/archives/fall2019/entries/pythagoreanism/.
Huizenga, A. 2013. *Moral Education for Women in the Pastoral and Pythagorean Letters*. Boston: Brill.
Hult, D. F. (tr.) 2010. *Debate of the Romance of the Rose*. Chicago: University of Chicago Press.
Hultsch, F. O. 1882. *Griechische und römische Metrologie*. Berlin: Weidmann.
Humbert, J. 1960. *Syntaxe Grecque*. Paris: Librairie C. Klincksieck.
Hutchinson, D. S., and Johnson, M. R. 2005. 'Authenticating Aristotle's *Protrepticus*', *Oxford Studies of Ancient Philosophy* 29: 193–293.
  2017. *Aristotle's Protrepticus*. Unpublished.
Hutton, S. 2019. 'Women, Philosophy, and the History of Philosophy', *British Journal for the History of Philosophy* 27(4): 684–701.
Idema, W., and Grant, B. (eds.) 2004. *The Red Brush: Writing Women of Imperial China*. Cambridge, MA: Harvard University Asia Centre.
Iles Johnstone, S. 2016. 'Sosipatra and the Theurgic Life: Eunapius *Vitae Sophistorum* 6.6.5–6.9.24', in J. Rüpke and W. Spickermann (eds.), *Reflections on Religious Individuality. Greco-Roman and Judaeo-Christian Texts and Practices*. Berlin: De Gruyter, pp. 99–117.
Irigaray, L. 1989. 'Sorcerer Love: A Reading of Plato's *Symposium*, Diotima's Speech', *Hypatia* 3(3): 32–44.
Jacobs, W. 1978. 'Plato on Emancipation and the Traditional Family', *Apeiron* 12: 29–31.
Jamison, S. 1996. *Sacrificed Wife, Sacrificer's Wife: Women, Ritual, and Hospitality in Ancient India*. Oxford: Oxford University Press.
Jayne, S. (tr.). 1944. *Marsilio Ficino's Commentary on Plato's Symposium*. Columbia: University of Missouri.
Johnson, M. P. 1998. 'Daughter, Sister, Philosopher, Angel: The Life and Influence of St. Macrina the Younger', *Diakonia* 31(3): 176–86.
Johnson, M. 2015. 'Aristotle's Architectonic Sciences', in D. Ebrey (ed.), *Theory and Practice in Aristotle's Natural Science*. Cambridge: Cambridge University Press, pp. 163–86.

Kalligas, P. 1997. 'Forms of Individuals in Plotinus: A Re-Examination', *Phronesis* 42: 206–27.
Karamanolis, G. 2006. *Plato and Aristotle in Agreement? Platonists on Aristotle from Antiochus to Porphyry*. Oxford: Clarendon Press.
Kennedy, R. F. 2014. *Immigrant Women in Athens: Gender, Ethnicity, and Citizenship in the Classical City*. New York: Routledge.
  2015. 'Elite Citizen Women and the Origins of the *Hetaira* in Classical Athens', *Helios* 42(1): 61–79.
Ker, J. 2009. *The Deaths of Seneca*. Oxford: Oxford University Press.
Kersey, E. M. 1989. *Women Philosophers: A Bio-critical Sourcebook*. New York: Greenwood Press.
King, H. 1985. 'From Parthenos to Gyne: the dynamics of category', unpublished PhD thesis, University of London.
  1986. 'Agnodike and the Profession of Medicine', *Proceedings of the Cambridge Philological Society* 32(212): 53–77.
  1998. *Hippocrates' Woman: Reading the Female Body in Ancient Greece*. London: Routledge.
King, M. L. 1991. *Women of the Renaissance*. Chicago: University of Chicago Press.
Kingsley, P. 1995. *Ancient Philosophy, Mystery, and Magic: Empedocles and Pythagorean Tradition*. Oxford: Oxford University Press.
Kittay E. F., and D. Meyers (eds.). 1987. *Women and Moral Theory*. Totowa, NJ: Rowman and Littlefield, pp. 154–78.
Kolsky, S. D. 2001. 'Moderata Fonte, Lucrezia Marinella, Giuseppe Passi: An Early Seventeenth-Century Feminist Controversy', *The Modern Language Review* 96: 973–89.
Kroll, W. (ed.). 1899. *Procli Diadochi in Platonis rem publicam commentarii*, vol.I. Leipzig: Nabu Press.
Kutash, E. 2011. *The Ten Gifts of the Demiurge. Proclus' Commentary on Plato's Timaeus*. Bristol: Classical Press.
Laale, H. W. 2011. *Ephesus (Ephesos): An Abbreviated History from Androclus to Constantine XI*. Bloomington, IN: Westbow.
Lagarde, B. 1973. 'Le *De differentiis* de Pléthon d'après l'autographe de la Marcienne'. *Byzantion* 43: 312–43.
Lampe, K. 2015. *The Birth of Hedonism: The Cyrenaic Philosophers and Pleasure as a Way of Life*. Princeton: Princeton University Press.
  2016. 'The Life of Aristippus in the Socratic Epistles: Three Interpretations', in J. Hanink and R. Fletcher (eds.), *Creative Lives in Classical Antiquity: Poets, Artists, and Biography*. Cambridge: Cambridge University Press, pp. 198–218.
Lefkowitz, M. R., and Fant, M. B. (eds.). 2005. *Women's Life in Greece and Rome: A Source Book in Translation*. Baltimore: Johns Hopkins University Press.
Leitao, D. D. 2012. *The Pregnant Male as Myth and Metaphor in Classical Greek Literature*. Cambridge: Cambridge University Press.

Lerner, R. (tr.) 1974. *Averroes on Plato's Republic*. Ithaca: Cornell University Press.
Lesser, H. 1979. 'Plato's Feminism'. *Philosophy* 54: 113–17.
Leunissen, M. 2021. 'Empiricism and Hearsay in Aristotle's Zoological Collection of Facts', in S. M. Connell (ed.), *The Cambridge Companion to Aristotle's Biology*. Cambridge: Cambridge University Press.
Liddell, H. G., Scott, R., and Jones, H. S. 1940. *A Greek-English Lexicon*. Oxford: Clarendon Press.
Lindquist, S. E. 2008. 'Gender at Janaka's Court', *Journal of Indian Philosophy* 36: 405–26.
Lindsay, J. 1970. *The Origins of Alchemy in Greco-Roman Egypt*. London: Muller.
Littré, E. 1839–61. *Oeuvres complètes d'Hippocrates*. Paris: J. B. Baillière [L.].
Liu, L., Karl, R., and Ko, D. (tr. and eds.) 2013. *The Birth of Chinese Feminism: Essential Texts in Transnational Theory*. New York: Columbia University Press
Lloyd, G. E. R. 1983. *Science, Folklore, and Ideology*. Cambridge: Cambridge University Press.
  1987. 'Empirical Research in Aristotle's Biology,' in A. Gotthelf and J. G. Lennox (eds.), *Philosophical Issues in Aristotle's Biology*. Cambridge: Cambridge University Press, pp. 53–64.
  2005. '"Philosophy": What Did the Greeks Invent and Is It Relevant to China?' *Extrême-orient, Extrême-occident* 27: 149–60.
  2014. 'Pythagoras', in C. A. Huffman (ed.), *A History of Pythagoreanism*. Cambridge: Cambridge University Press, pp. 24–45.
Loraux, N. 1987. *Tragic Ways of Killing a Woman*, tr. A. Forster. Cambridge, MA: Harvard University Press.
Lovibond, S. 2000. 'Feminism in Ancient Philosophy: The Feminist Stake in Greek Rationalism', in M. Fricker and J. Hornsby (eds.), *The Cambridge Companion to Feminism in Philosophy*. Cambridge: Cambridge University Press, pp. 10–28.
Lutz, C. 1947. 'Musonius Rufus: The Roman Socrates', *Yale Classical Studies* 10: 1–147.
MacIntyre, A. 1999. *Dependent Rational Animals: Why Human Beings Need the Virtues*. Chicago: University of Chicago Press.
Macksey, R., and Donato, E. (eds.) 1972. *The Structuralist Controversy: The Languages of Criticism and the Sciences of Man*. Baltimore: Johns Hopkins University Press.
Macris, C. 2002. 'Jamblique et la Littérature Pseudo-Pythagoricienne', in S. C. Mimouni (ed.), *Apocryphité*. Turnhout: Brepols, pp. 77–129.
  2012. 'Périctionè (d'Athènes?)', in R. Goulet (ed.), *Dictionnaire des Philosophes Antiques V*. Paris: CNRS, pp. 231–34.
Malherbe, A. J. (ed.). 1977/2006. *The Cynic Epistles: A Study Edition*. Missoula, MT: Scholars Press for the Society of Biblical Literature.
Malinar, A. 2007. 'Arguments of a Queen: Draupadī's View on Kingship', in S. Brodbeck and B. Black (eds.), *Gender and Narrative in the Mahābhārata*. London: Routledge, pp. 79–96.

Mann, S., and Cheng, Y. (eds.) 2001. *Under Confucian Eyes: Writings on Gender in Chinese History*. Berkeley; Los Angeles: University of California Press.
Mann, W.-R. 1996. 'The Life of Aristippus', in *Archiv für Geschichte der Philosophie* 78: 97–119.
  2006. 'Learning How to Die: Seneca's Use of *Aeneid* 4.653 at *Epistulae Morales* 12.9', in K. Volk and G. Williams (eds.), *Seeing Seneca Whole: Perspectives on Philosophy, Poetry and Politics*. Leiden: Brill, pp. 104–22.
  2015. '"You're Playing You Now": Helvidius Priscus as a Stoic Hero', in K. Volk and G. Williams (eds.), *Roman Reflections: Studies in Latin Philosophy*. Oxford: Oxford University Press, pp. 213–37.
Mannebach, E. 1961. *Aristippi et cyrenaicorum fragmenta*. Leiden: Brill.
Manning, C. E. 1973. 'Seneca and the Stoics on the Equality of the Sexes', *Mnemosyne* 26: 170–77.
Mansfeld, J., and Runia, D. 1997. *Aëtiana I*. Leiden: Brill.
Manuli, P. 1983. 'Donne masculine, femmine sterili, vergini perpetue: La ginecologia greca tra Ippocrate e Sorano', in S. Campese, P. Manuli, and G. Sissa (eds.), *Madre Materia*. Turin: Boringhieri, 149–204.
Marinella, L. 1600, 1601, 1621. *La nobilta et eccellenza delle donne co' difetti et mancamenti de gli huomini*. Venice: Presso Gio.
Marshack, A. 1972. *The Roots of Civilization: The Cognitive Beginning of Man's First Art, Symbol. and Notation*. New York: McGraw-Hill.
Matilal, B. K. 2002. 'Dharma and Rationality', in J. Ganeri (ed.), *Ethics and Epics: Philosophy, Culture, and Religion. The Collected Essays of Bimal Krishna Matilal*, vol. 2. New Delhi: Oxford University Press, pp. 79–96.
Mauch, M. 1997. *Senecas Frauenbild in den Philosophischen Schriften*. Frankfurt: P. Lang.
McKeen, C. 2006. 'Why Women Must Guard and Rule in Plato's *Kallipolis*', *Pacific Philosophical Quarterly* 87: 527–48.
McKirahan, R. D. 1994. *Philosophy before Socrates*. Indianapolis, IN: Hackett.
Mcnary-Zak, B. 2005. 'Gregory of Nyssa and His Sister Macrina: A Holy Alliance', *Cithara* 45(1): 3–12.
Ménage, G. 1984. *The History of Women Philosophers*. Lanham, MD: University Press of America.
Menn, S. 2002. 'Plato and the Method of Analysis', *Phronesis* 47: 193–223.
Mesytas, S. 2012. 'Iamblichus' Exegesis of Parmenides' Hypotheses and His Doctrine of Divine Henads', in E. Afonasin, J. Dillon, and J. Finamore (eds.), *Iamblichus and the Foundations of Late Platonism*. Leiden: Brill, pp. 151–76.
Momigliano, A. 1971. 'Second Thoughts on Greek Biography', *Mededelingen der Koninklijke Nederlandse Akademie van Wetenschappen, Afd. Letterkunde* 34 (7): 245–57.
  1987. *On Pagans, Jews, and Christians*. Middletown, CT: Wesleyan University Press.
  1993. *The Development of Greek Biography: Expanded Edition*. Cambridge, MA: Harvard University Press.

Monfasani, J. 2002. 'Marsilio Ficino and the Plato-Aristotle Controversy', in M. J. B. Allen and V. Rees (eds.), *Marsilio Ficino: His Theology, His Philosophy, His Legacy*. Leiden: Brill, pp. 179–202.
Montepaone, C. 2011. *Pitagoriche*. Bari: Edipuglia.
Motto, A. L. 1972. 'Seneca on Women's Liberation', *Classical World* 65: 155–57.
Motto, A. L., and Clark, J. R. 1981. '*Maxima Virtus* in Seneca's *Hercules Furens*', *Classical Philology* 76: 101–17.
Mozans, H. J. (J. A. Zahm). 1913. *Women of Science*. New York: Appleton.
Muehlberger, E. 2012. 'Salvage: Macrina and the Christian Project of Cultural Reclamation', *Church History*, 81(2): 273–97.
Nails, D. 1989. 'The Pythagorean Women Philosophers: Ethics of the Household', in K. J. Boudouris (ed.), *Ionian Philosophy*. Athens: International Association for Greek Philosophy, pp. 291–97.
Noy, D. 2013. 'Matchmaker', in R. S. Bagnall et al. (eds.), *The Encyclopaedia of Ancient History*. Oxford: Blackwell, 43–44.
Nussbaum, M. 1979. *The Fragility of Goodness*. Cambridge: Cambridge University Press.
  1986. 'Therapeutic Arguments: Epicurus and Aristotle', in M. Schofield and G. Striker (eds.), *The Norms of Nature: Studies in Hellenistic Ethics*. Cambridge: Cambridge University Press, pp. 31–74.
  2002. 'The Incomplete Feminism of Musonius Rufus: Platonist, Stoic, and Roman', in M. Nussbaum and J. Sihvola (eds.), *The Sleep of Reason: Erotic Experience and Sexual Ethics in Ancient Greece and Rome*. Chicago: University of Chicago Press: pp. 283–326.
  2009. *The Therapy of Desire: Theory and Practice in Hellenistic Ethics*. Princeton: Princeton University Press.
Nye, A. 1989. 'The Hidden Host: Irigaray and Diotima at Plato's Symposium' *Hypatia: French Feminist Philosophy* 3(3): 45–61.
  1990. 'The Subject of Love: Diotima and her Critics', *Journal of Value Inquiry* 24: 135–53.
O'Brien, C. 2016. 'Plotinus on the Soul's *logos* as the Structuring Principle of the World', in J. Halfwassen, T. Dangel, and C. O'Brien (eds.), *Seele und Materie im Neuplatonismus*. Heidelberg: Universitätsverlag Winter, pp. 105–35.
O'Brien Wicker, K. (tr.). 1987. *Porphyry. To Marcella*. Atlanta: Scholars Press.
Okin, S. 1977. 'Philosopher Queens and Private Wives: Plato on Women and the Family', *Philosophy and Public Affairs* 6: 345–69.
  1979. *Women in Western Political Thought*. Princeton: Princeton University Press.
  1989. *Justice, Labour and the Family*. Princeton: Princeton University Press.
Olson, G., Horn-Schott, M., Hartley, D., Schmidt, R. L. (eds.). 2019. *Beyond Gender: An Advanced Introduction to the Futures of Feminist and Sexuality Studies*. London: Routledge.
O'Meara, D. 2003. *Platonopolis. Platonic Political Philosophy in Late Antiquity*. Oxford: Oxford University Press.

Outlaw Jr., L. T. 2017. 'Africana Philosophy', in E. N. Zalta (ed.), *The Stanford Encyclopaedia of Philosophy*. https://plato.stanford.edu/archives/sum2017/entries/africana/.
Ouyang, X. 歐陽詢 (ed.). 2021. *Yiwen leiju* 藝文類聚, 100 vols. https://ctext.org/library.pl?if=en&res=5982.
Pang-White, A. A. 2016. *The Bloomsbury Research Handbook of Chinese Philosophy and Gender*. New York: Bloomsbury.
  (tr. and ed.). 2018. *The Confucian Four Books for Women: A New Translation of the Nü Sishu and the Commentary of Wang Xiang*. New York: Oxford University Press.
Panizza, L., and Wood, S. (eds.) 2000. *A History of Women's Writing in Italy*. Cambridge: Cambridge University Press.
Park, P. 2013. *Africa, Asia, and the History of Philosophy*. Albany: SUNY Press.
Patai, R. 1982. 'Maria the Jewess: Founding Mother of Alchemy', *Ambix* 29: 177–97.
Patton, L. 2007. 'How Do You Conduct Yourself? Gender and the Construction of a Dialogical Self in the *Mahābhārata*', in S. Brodbeck and B. Black (eds.), *Gender and Narrative in the Mahābhārata*. London: Routledge, pp. 97–109.
Pelikan, J. 1993. *Christianity and Classical Culture: The Metamorphosis of Natural Theology in the Christian Encounter with Hellenism*. New Haven: Yale University Press.
Pellò, C. 2018. 'Women in Early Pythagoreanism', unpublished PhD thesis, University of Cambridge.
Penella, R. J. 1990. *Greek Philosophers and Sophists in the Fourth Century A.D. Studies in Eunapius of Sardis*. Cairns: Francis Cairns.
Perioli, E. 1997. 'Gregory of Nyssa and the Neoplatonic Doctrine of the Soul', *Vigiliae Christianae* 51(2): 117–39.
Petkas, A. 2020. 'Hypatia and the Desert. A Late Antique Defense of Classicism', in D. L. Norman and A. Petkas. (eds.), *Hypatia of Alexandria*. Tübingen: Mohr Siebeck, pp. 7–29.
Piccione, R. M. 1999. 'Caratterizzazione di lemmi nell'*Anthologion* di Giovanni Stobeo. Questioni di metodo', *Rivista di Filologia e Istruzione Classica* 127: 139–75.
Pines, S. 1975. 'Aristotle's *Politics* in Arabic Philosophy', *Israel Oriental Studies* 5: 150–60.
Plant, I. M. 2004. *Women Writers in Ancient Greece and Rome: An Anthology*. Norman: University of Oklahoma Press.
Plass, P. 1978. 'Plato's Pregnant Lover', *Symbolae Osloenses* 53, 47–55.
Plato. 1973. *Theaetetus*, tr. J. MacDowell. Oxford: Oxford University Press.
Pomeroy, S. B. 1974. 'Feminism in Book V of Plato's Republic', *Apeiron* 8: 33–35.
  1975. *Goddesses, Whores, Wives, and Slaves*. New York: Schocken.
  1978. 'Plato and the Female Physician (*Republic* 454d2)', *American Journal of Philology* 99(4): 496–500.
  2013. *Pythagorean Women: Their History and Writings*. Baltimore, MD: Johns Hopkins University Press.

Press, G. A. (ed.). 2000. *Who Speaks for Plato?* Lanham, MD: Rowman & Littlefield.
Protasi, S. 2020. 'Teaching Ancient Women Philosophers: A Case Study', *Feminist Philosophy Quarterly* 6(3): 1–26.
Ramelli, I. 2009. *Hierocles the Stoic: Elements of Ethics, Fragments, and Excerpts*, tr. D. Konstan. Atlanta, GA: Society of Biblical Literature.
Ram-Prasad, C. 2018. *Human Being, Bodily Being: Phenomenology from Classical India*. Oxford: Oxford University Press.
Reeser, T. W. 2016. *Setting Plato Straight: Translating Ancient Sexuality in the Renaissance*. Chicago: University of Chicago Press.
Reeve, C. D. C. 1998. *Aristotle: Politics*. Indianapolis, IN: Hackett.
Reisman, D. C. 2004. 'Plato's *Republic* in Arabic: A Newly Discovered Passage', *Arabic Sciences and Philosophy* 14: 263–300.
Rettig, G. F. 1876. *Platons Symposion*. Halle: Buchhandlung des Waisenhauses.
Reydams-Schils, G. 2005. *The Roman Stoics: Self, Responsibility, and Affection*. Chicago: University of Chicago Press.
  (ed.). 2011. *Thinking through Excerpts*. Turnhout: Brepols.
Riddle, J. M. 1992. *Contraception and Abortion from the Ancient World to the Renaissance*. Cambridge, MA: Harvard University Press.
Riginos, A. S. 1976. *Platonica*. Leiden: Brill.
Rist, J. M. 1965. 'Hypatia', *Phoenix* 19(3): 214–25.
Roded, R. 1999. *Women in Islam and the Middle East: A Reader*. London: I. B. Tauris.
Romano, F. 2006. *Giamblico. Summa Pitagorica*. Milan: Bompiani.
Rosán, L. J. 1949. *The Philosophy of Proclus. The Final Phase of Ancient Thought*. New York: Cosmos.
Rosenthal, E. I. J. (ed. and tr.). 1969. *Averroes' Commentary on Plato's Republic*. Cambridge: Cambridge University Press.
Roth, C. P. 1992. 'Platonic and Pauline Elements in the Ascent of the Soul in Gregory of Nyssa's Dialogue *On the Soul and Resurrection*', *Vigiliae Christianae* 46: 20–30.
Roth, C. P. 1993. *On the Soul and Resurrection*. Crestwood, NY: St. Vladimir's Seminary.
Rousselle, A. 1988. *Porneia: On Desire and the Body in Antiquity*. Oxford: Blackwell.
Rowe, C. J. 1998. *Plato: Symposium*. Liverpool: Aris and Phillips.
Rowett, C. 2014. 'The Pythagorean Society and Politics', in C. A. Huffman (ed.), *A History of Pythagoreanism*. Cambridge: Cambridge University Press, pp. 112–30.
Ruddick, S. 1980. 'Maternal Thinking', *Feminist Studies* 6: 342–67.
Saffrey, H. D., and Westerink, L. G. (ed. and tr.). 1981. *Proclus. Théologie Platonicienne 4*. Paris: Les Belles Lettres.
Salamon, G. 2009. 'Justification and Queer Method, or Leaving Philosophy', *Hypatia*, 24(1): 225–30.
Saxonhouse, A. 1976. 'The Philosopher and the Female in the Political Thought of Plato', *Political Theory* 4: 195–212.

1984. 'Eros and the Female in Greek Political Thought: An Interpretation of the *Symposium*', *Political Theory* 12, 5–27.

1985. *Women in the History of Political Thought: Ancient Greece to Machiavelli*. New York: Praeger.

1992. *Fear of Diversity: The Birth of Political Science in Ancient Greek Thought*. Chicago: Chicago University Press.

Sayeed, A. 2013. *Women and the Transmission of Religious Knowledge in Islam*. Cambridge: Cambridge University Press.

Schott, R. M. 2006. 'Feminism and the History of Philosophy', in L. M. Alcoff and E. F. Kittay (eds.), *The Blackwell Guide to Feminist Philosophy*. Chichester: John Wiley & Sons, pp. 43–63.

Schultz, J. 2019a. 'Conceptualizing the 'Female' Soul – a Study in Plato and Proclus', *British Journal for the History of Philosophy* 27(5): 883–901.

2019b. 'Mütterliche Ursachen in Proklos' Metaphysik', *Philologus* 163(2): 250–73.

2019c. 'Die proklische Diotima. Philosophie, Religion und das Weibliche', *Bochumer Philosophisches Jahrbuch für Antike und Mittelalter* 22: 75–98.

2022. 'Beyond the Binary Distinction? Athena and Other Virgin Goddesses in Proclus' Metaphysics', in D. A. Layne and J. Elbert Decker (eds.), *Otherwise Than the Binary: New Feminist Readings of Ancient Philosophy and Culture*. New York: SUNY Press, 263–95.

Sedley, D. 1997. '"Becoming Like God" in the *Timaeus* and Aristotle', in T. Calvo and L. Brisson (eds.), *Interpreting the Timaeus-Critias*. Sankt Augustin: Academia Verlag, pp. 327–39.

Segonds, A. Ph. (ed. and tr.) 1985. *Proclus. Sur le Premier Alcibiade de Platon 1–2*. Paris: Les Belles Lettres.

Sheather, M. 1995. 'The Eulogies on Macrina and Gorgonia: Or, What Difference Did Christianity Make?', *Pacifica Theological Studies* 8: 22–39.

Sheffield, F. C. C. 2017. 'Eros and the Pursuit of Form', in P. Destrée and Z. Gianopoulou (eds.), *The Cambridge Companion to Plato's Symposium*. Cambridge: Cambridge University Press, pp. 125–42.

2021. 'Moral Motivation in Plato's Republic? *Philia* and Return to the Cave', *Oxford Studies in Ancient Philosophy*, 59: 79–105.

Shelton, J.-A. 1995. 'Persuasion and Paradigm in Seneca's *Consolatio ad Marciam* 1–6', *Classica et Mediaevalia* 46: 157–88.

Silvas, A. M. 2008. *Macrina the Younger: Philosopher of God*. Turnhout: Brepols.

Smith, J. W. 2000. 'Macrina, Tamer of Horses and Healer of Souls: Grief and the Therapy of Hope in Gregory of Nyssa's *De Anima et Resurrectione*', *Journal of Theological Studies* 52(1): 37–60.

2004. 'A Just and Reasonable Grief: The Death and Function of a Holy Woman in Gregory of Nyssa's Life of Macrina', *Journal of Early Christian Studies*. 12(1): 57–84.

Smith. L. 2011. 'The Kahun Gynaecological Papyrus: Ancient Egyptian Medicine', *BMJ Sexual and Reproductive Health* 37(1): 54–55.

Smith, N. D. 1983. 'Plato and Aristotle on the Nature of Women', *Journal of the History of Philosophy* 21: 467–78.
Snyder, J. 1989. *The Woman and the Lyre: Women Writers in Classical Greece and Rome*. Carbondale: Southern Illinois University Press.
Sogno, Ch., and Watts, E. J. 2018. 'Epistolography', in S. McGill and E. Watts (eds.), *A Companion to Late Antique Literature*. Hoboken, NJ: Wiley & Sons, pp. 389–400.
Spelman, E. 1982. 'Woman as Body: Ancient and Contemporary Views', *Feminist Studies*, 8(1): 109–31.
Steenkamp, V. 2003. 'Traditional Herbal Remedies Used by South African Women for Gynaecological Complaints', *Ethnopharmocology* 86(1): 97–108.
Sukthankar, V. S. et al. (eds.) 1933–66. *The Mahābhārata for the First Time Critically Edited*, 19 vols. Poona: Bhandarkar Oriental Research Institute.
Sullivan, B. 2016. 'An Overview of *Mahābhārata* Scholarship: A Perspective on the State of the Field', *Religion Compass* 10(7): 165–75.
Sutton, N. 1999. 'An Exposition of Early Sāṃkhya, A Rejection of the Bhagavad Gītā and a Critique of the Role of Women in Hindu Society: The Sulabhā-Janaka-Saṃvāda', *Annal of the Bhandarkar Oriental Research Institute* 80: 55–65.
Swancutt, D. 2006. 'Still before Sexuality: "Greek" Androgyny, the Roman Imperial Politics of Masculinity and the Roman Invention of the Tribas', in T. Penner and C. Vander Stichele (eds.), *Mapping Gender in Ancient Religious Discourses*. Leiden: Brill, pp. 11–61.
Syros, V. 2008. 'A Note on the Transmission of Aristotle's Political Ideas in Medieval Persia and Early-Modern India. Was There Any Arabic or Persian Translation of the Politics?', *Bulletin de Philosophie Médiévale* 50: 303–9.
Tanaseanu-Döbler, I. 2012. 'Synesios und die Theurgie', in H. Seng and L. M. Hoffmann (eds.), *Synesios von Kyrene. Politik – Literatur – Philosophie*. Turnhout: Brepols, pp. 201–31.
  2013. 'Sosipatra – Role Models for Pagan Divine Women in Late Antiquity', in M. Dzielska and K. Twardowska. (eds.), *Divine Men and Women in the History and Society of Late Hellenism*. Cracow: Jagiellonian University Press, pp. 123–49.
Tarrant, H. (tr.) 2006. *Proclus. Commentary on Plato's Timaeus. Vol. 1: Proclus on the Socratic State and Atlantis*. Cambridge: Cambridge University Press.
  2017. *Proclus. Commentary on Plato's Timaeus Vol. 6: Proclus on the Gods of Generation and the Creation of Humans*. Cambridge: Cambridge University Press.
Taylor, R. C. 2004. 'Improving on Nature's Exemplar: Averroes' Completion of Aristotle's Psychology of Intellect'. *Bulletin of the Institute of Classical Studies* 47: 107–30.
Temkin, O. 1956. *Soranus: Gynaecology*. Baltimore, MD: Johns Hopkins University Press.
Thesleff, H. 1961. *An Introduction to the Pythagorean Writings of the Hellenistic Period*. Åbo: Åbo Akademi.

1965. *The Pythagorean Texts of the Hellenistic Period*. Åbo: Åbo Akademi.

1971. 'On the Problem of Doric Pseudo-Pythagorica. An Alternative Theory of Date and Purpose', in K. von Friitz (ed.), *Pseudoepigraphia I. Pseudopythagorica. Lettres de Platon Litterature Pseudepigraphique Juive*, vol. 18. Vandouvres: Foundation Hardt, pp. 59–102.

Thumiger, C. 2017. *A History of the Mind and Mental Health in Classical Greek Medical Thought*. Cambridge: Cambridge University Press.

Tong, R., and Botts, T. F. (eds.). 2017. *Feminist Thought: A More Comprehensive Introduction*. 5th ed. New York: Westview.

Torre, C. 2000. *Il matrimonio del Sapiens: Ricerche sul de Matrimonio di Seneca*. Università di Genova, Facoltà di lettere, Dipartimento di archeologia, filologia classica e loro tradizioni.

Totelin, L. 2009. *Hippocratic Recipes: Oral and Written Transmission of Pharmacological Knowledge in Fifth and Fourth Century Greece*. Leiden: Brill.

2016. 'Technologies of Knowledge: Pharmacology, Botany, and Medical Recipes', *Oxford Handbook Online*. doi.org/10.1093/oxfordhb/9780199935390.013.94.

2017. 'The Third Way', in L. Lemhaus and M. Martelli (eds.), *Collecting Recipes: Byzantine and Jewish Pharmacology in Dialogue*. Berlin: De Gruyter, pp. 103–22.

2018. 'Therapeutics', in P. E. Pormann (ed.), *The Cambridge Companion to Hippocrates*. Cambridge: Cambridge University Press, pp. 200–16.

2020. 'Do No Harm: Phanostrate's Midwifery Practice', *Technai: An International Journal for Ancient Science and Technology* 11: 129–43.

Townshend, M. 2017. *The Woman Question in Plato's Republic*. Lanham, MD: Lexington Books.

Trott, A. M. 2019. *Aristotle on the Matter of Form*. Edinburgh: Edinburgh University Press.

Tuana, N. (ed.). 1994. *Feminist Interpretations of Plato*. University Park: Pennsylvania State University Press.

Tuana, N., and Cowling, W. 1994. 'The Presence and Absence of the Feminine in Plato's Philosophy', in N. Tuana (ed.), *Feminist Interpretations of Plato*. University Park: Pennsylvania State University Press, pp. 243–70.

Ulacco, A. 2016. 'The Appropriation of Aristotle in the Ps-Pythagorean Treatises', in A. Falcon (ed.), *Brill's Companion to the Reception of Aristotle in Antiquity*. Leiden: Brill, pp. 202–17.

2017. *Pseudopythagorica Dorica*. Berlin: De Gruyter.

Usener, H. 1963. *Epicurea*. Rome: L'Erma di Bretschneider.

van Buitenen, J. A. B. (tr.) 1975. *The Mahābhārata: 2. The Book of the Assembly Hall; 3. The Book of the Forest*. Chicago: University of Chicago Press.

Van Geytenbeek, A. C. 1962. *Musonius Rufus and Greek Diatribe*, tr. B. L. Hijmans. Assen: Van Gorcum & Co.

Vanita, R. 2003. 'The Self Is Not Gendered: Sulabhā's Debate with King Janaka', *National Women's Studies Association Journal* 15(2): 76–93.

Vlastos, G. 1989. 'Was Plato a Feminist?', *Times Literary Supplement*, March 17–23.

1994. 'Was Plato a Feminist?', in N. Tuana (ed.), *Feminist Interpretations of Plato*. University Park: Pennsylvania State University Press, pp. 11–25.
von Oehler, F. 1858. *Gregor von Nyssa*. Leipzig: Engelmann.
Waithe, M. E. 1987a. 'Diotima of Mantinea', in Waithe, M. E. (ed.), *A History of Women Philosophers*, vol. I, Dordrecht: Martinus Nijhoff, pp. 83–117.
  (ed.), 1987b. *A History of Women Philosophers Volume 1: 600 BC–500 AD*. Dordrecht: Martinus Nijhoff.
  2015. 'From Canon Fodder to Canon-Formation: How Do We Get There from Here?' *The Monist* 98: 21–33.
Wang, R. R. (ed.) 2003. *Images of Women in Chinese Thought and Culture*. Indianapolis, IN: Hackett.
Wang, Y. X. et al. 2020. 'Menstrual Cycle Regularity and Length across the Reproductive Lifespan and Risk of Premature Mortality: Prospective Cohort Study', *British Medical Journal* 371. 10.1136/bmj.m3464.
Ward, J. K. 1996. *Feminism and Ancient Philosophy*. New York: Routledge.
Wardy, R. 2002. 'The Unity of Opposites in Plato's *Symposium*', *Oxford Studies in Ancient Philosophy* 23, 1–61.
Warren, J. 2009. 'Diogenes Laërtius, Biographer of Philosophy', in J. König and T. J. G. Whitmarsh (eds.), *Ordering Knowledge in the Roman Empire*. Cambridge: Cambridge University Press, pp. 133–49.
Warren, K. J. 2009. *An Unconventional History of Western Philosophy: Conversations Between Men and Women Philosophers*. Lanham, MD: Rowman and Littlefield.
Watts, E. J. 2017. *Hypatia. The Life and Legend of an Ancient Philosopher*. Oxford: Oxford University Press.
Wawrytko, S. A. 2019. 'Women on Love: Idealisation in the Philosophies of Diotima and Murasaki Shikibu', *Philosophy East and West* 68(4): 1314–44.
Wender, D. 1973. 'Plato: Misogynist, Paedophile, Feminist', *Arethusa*, 6(1): 75–90.
West, M. L. 1971. *Early Greek Philosophy and the Orient*. Oxford: Clarendon Press.
Westerink, L. G. (ed. and tr.). 1959. *Damascius. Lectures on the Philebus, Wrongly Attributed to Olympiodorus*. Amsterdam: North-Holland.
  1977. *The Greek Commentaries on Plato's Phaedo. Vol. II Damascius*. Amsterdam: North-Holland.
Westerink, L. G., and Combès, J. (ed. and tr.). 1986–91. *Damascius. Traité des premiers principes 1–3*. Paris: Les Belles Lettres.
  2002–3. *Damascius. Commentaire du Parménide de Platon 1–4*. Paris: Les Belles Lettres.
White, D. G. 2009. *Sinister Yogis*. Chicago: University of Chicago Press.
Whitmarsh, T. (ed.). 2021. *Oxford Classical Dictionary*. Oxford: Oxford University Press.
Whitmarsh, T., and Thompson, S. 2013. *The Romance between Greece and the East*. Cambridge: Cambridge University Press.

Wider, K. 1986. 'Women Philosophers in the Ancient Greek World: Donning the Mantle', *Hypatia* 1: 21–62.
Wilcox, A. 2006. 'Exemplary Grief: Gender and Virtue in Seneca's Consolations to Women', *Helios* 33: 73–100.
Williams, R. 1993. 'Macrina's Deathbed Revisited: Gregory of Nyssa on Mind and Passion', in L. R. Wickham and C. P. Bammel (eds.), *Christian Faith and Greek Philosophy in Late Antiquity: Essays in Tribute to George Christopher Stead*. Leiden: E. J. Brill.
Winkler, J. J. 1990. 'Laying down the Law: The Oversight of Men's Sexual Behaviour in Classical Athens', in J. J Winkler (ed.). *The Constraints of Desire: the Anthropology of Sex and Gender in Ancient Greece, 45–70*. New York: Routledge.
Woodhouse, C. M. 1986. *George Gemistos Plethon: The Last of the Hellenes*. Oxford: Clarendon Press.
Wolfskeel, C. 1987. 'Makrina', in M. E. Waithe (ed.), *A History of Women Philosophers: Ancient Women Philosophers 600 B.C.–500 A.D.* New York: Springer, pp. 139–68.
Wray, D. 2009. 'Seneca and Tragedy's Reason', in S. Bartsch and D. Wray (eds.), *Seneca and the Self*. Cambridge: Cambridge University Press, pp. 237–54.
Wright, W. C. (ed. and tr.). 1922. *Philostratus and Eunapius. The Lives of the Sophists*. London: William Heinemann.
Xiao, T. 蕭統 (ed.). 2021. *Wenxuan* 文選 *(aka Zhaoming wenxuan* 昭明文選*)*, 60 vols. https://ctext.org/library.pl?if=en&res=91990.
Zaslavsky, C. 1992. 'Women as the First Mathematicians', *ISGE Newsletter: International Study Group on Ethnomathematics* 7(1). https://web.nmsu.edu/~pscott/isgem71.htm.
Zhmud, L. 2019. 'What Is Pythagorean in the Pseudo-Pythagorean Literature?', *Philologus* 163: 72–94.
Zhu, X. 1270. *Zhuzi yulei* 朱子語類 *(Classified Conversations of Zhu Xi)*, ed. Li Jingde 黎靖德, 140 vols. https://ctext.org/zhuzi-yulei/zh.
Zintzen, C. 1972. '*Alte Virtus Animosa Cadit*: Gedanken zur Darstellung des Tragischen in Senecas *Hercules Furens*', in E. Lefèvre (ed.), *Senecas Tragödien*. Darmstadt: Wissenschaftliche Buchgesellschaft, pp. 149–209.

Index

Aelian, 102
Aesara, 146, 147, 148, 155
anti-hedonism, 93
  misogyny, 77
  polemic, 78, 81, 84, 85, 93
Antipater, 117
Arete of Cyrene
  ancient depictions of, 96
  education, 98
  Epistle 27, 104–9, 112
  epitaph, 96, 103
  as intellectual conduit, 96, 101, 103, 106, 107
  as philosopher, 103, 113
  philosophical lineage, 101, 106
  as teacher, 96, 100, 101, 102, 105
Aristippus the Elder, 97
  founder of Cyrenaic School, 97
  'Letter to his daughter Arete', 101
  relationship with Arete, 98, 104
Aristippus the Younger, 100, 102
  formalisation of Cyrenaic ethics, 108, 109
  mētrodidaktos, 96, 102
Aristotle, 237
  Eudemian Ethics, 149
  Historia Animalium, 65, 102
  Metaphysics, 62, 164
  Nicomachean Ethics, 149, 239
  Politics, 134, 148, 149, 238
  Protrepticus, 157, 159
Aspasia, 22, 82, 242
Athenaeus, 85–86, 89
Averroes. *See* Ibn Rushd

Ban Zhao, 209–11
  four womanly conducts, 215, 225
  'Memorial to Empress Dowager Deng', 222, 226
  memoranda, 219, 224
  'Petition for a Replacement for My Elder Brother Chao', 219, 226
  philosophy. *See Lessons for Women*

  poetry, 216–19
  Rhapsody on a Journey to the East, 216
  Rhapsody on Needle and Thread, 218
  undermining gender norms, 209, 219, 222
Boccaccio, 89–90, 97

Chinese philosophy, 210
Chinese society (Ban Zhao era), 209, 210, 219, 222, 224
Cicero, 77, 80, 84, 87, 88
Confucianism, 210, 213, 215, 219, 222, 224, 225
Crates the Cynic, 116
Cyrenaicism, 79, 96, 106

Damascius *Life of Isidore*, 201, 203
Deslauriers, Marguerite, 40, 140, 150, 155
Diogenes Laertius, 77, 85, 86, 111, 136
  Lives, 98, 111
Diotima, 196, 236, 242
  gender, 22–28
  as philosopher, 23
  role at symposium, 25
  spoken by Socrates, 22
doctors, women as
  evidence for, 57, 58, 59
  female preference for, 68
  self-presentation, 60
  teaching, 62
Dong Zhongshu, 222, 224

Epictetus, 118, 119, 120, 125
Epicurean women, 81, 84
  evidence for, 78, 93
  as philosophers, 78, 91, 92
  sexual status, 77, 79, 83, 93
Epicureanism, 79, 93
  critics of, 77, 79–81
  pleasure, 79, 80
  prostitution, 81–86
  and slaves, 85

Epicurus, 77, 80, 84, 89, 144
  doxography, 77, 85, 90
  School of, *See* Garden, the
eros (*Symposium*)
  context, 23
  as intermediate between opposites, 32–33
  as non-binary facilitator, 21, 34
  physical vs theoretical, 25
  topic of, 25
  vocabulary of, 28
Eros' parentage, 31, 33
eudaimonia, 26–27, 36, 135, 240
Euripides *Herakles*, 125–26

Gadamer, Hans-Georg, 39
Garden, the, 79, 84, 87
Gregory of Nyssa
  dialogue form, 170
  Letter 19, 171, 173, 183
  The Life of St Macrina, 171, 173, 183
  Origenist views, 181

hedonism, 77, 79, 81
hetairai, 78, 82–83, 85
Hierocles, 117
Hipparchia the Cynic, 109, 116
household management
  Aristotle on, 134, 148–50
Hypatia of Alexandria, 201–7
  as literary character, 208
  as mathematician, 202
  menstrual blood anecdote, 204
  murder, 201
  as philosopher, 202
  and politics, 203
  sources, 201
  as teacher, 202
  as theurgist, 203
  upbringing, 201

Iamblichus, 137, 140, 153, 196
  Protrepticus, 155, 167
Ibn Rushd, 238–41
  on Aristotle, 238
  on class, 240
  exegesis of *Republic*, 238
  on women guardians, 239
  on women's talents, 239
Indian philosophy, 39
  dharma (morality), 39, 41, 49
  karma (causality), 39
  mokṣa (enlightenment), 39, 44, 49
  nivṛtti, 49
  pravṛtti, 49
  yoga (discipline), 39, 49–51

Janaka, 44, 45, 48
  misogyny, 52
junzi, 215, 217–19

Leontion, 81, 83, 84, 86–90
  Against Theophrastus, 87, 89
  and Metrodorus, 86
  paintings of, 88
  as philosopher, 87
  statue of, 88
Lessons for Women, 210, 211–16
  criticisms of, 215
  on domestic violence, 213
  four womanly conducts, 214
  as new genre, 211
  on spousal relations, 212
  use of androcentric texts, 215
  on virtue, 213
  on women's education, 211, 212, 225
Lucretius, 95

Macrina
  community at Annisa, 173, 181, 186
  death, immortality, and survival, 170, 177–80
  deathbed, 173
  feminity, 181
  life and education, 171–73
  nature of soul, 170, 175–77
  as philosopher, 174, 180
  as teacher, 182, 188
  reputation, 181
  soul/body relation, 170
Mahābhārata, 38, 40, 48
  authorship, 41
  dialogue form in, 39–40, 44–45
  as philosophical text, 38–39
Marinella, Lucrezia, 241–45
  Aristotle vs Plato, 242
  and 'dispute over women', 242
  On the Nobility and Excellence of Women, 241
Martial, 92
medical knowledge
  bodily experience, 60, 66
  childbirth, 61, 65, 67
  content of, 64
  fertility, 70
  matchmaking and timekeeping, 75
  menstruation, 65, 70, 75
  nature of, 57, 60–64
  and nature of cosmos, 63
  pharmacology, 68, 72
  pregnancy, 65
  reproduction, 58, 66, 72–76
  sexual experience (female), 72

theory of body, 66–71
writings on, 63
medicine
  Hippocratic treatises on, 58, 61, 63, 69
  overlap with philosophy, 62
  theory vs practice, 57, 61, 62
Megara, 115, 125, 127
  death of, 127
  and Lycus, 126
  as Stoic, 128, 130, 131
midwifery, 58
Musonius Rufus, 115, 117, 119

Neoplatonism
  androgyny, 193, 196
  Diotima, 196
  ideals of femaleness, 192–96
  maternal goddesses, 194, 200
  metaphysics, 191–92
  soul and gender, 192
  virgin goddesses, 195, 206

On Soul and Resurrection, 170, 173
  deathbed objection, 187–88
  education objection, 185–87
  mouthpiece objection, 180–83
  Platonic objection, 183–85
On Wisdom (Perictione), 152, 154
  attribution, 155
  constitution of human beings, 157
  contemplation, 152
  fragment analysis, 156–66
  function of wisdom, 156, 158
  initial statements, 156
  overlap with ps-Archytas, 155
  tripartition of theoretical sciences, 152, 163
  wisdom and other sciences, 162

paiderastia, 25–26
Perictione, 142
  on dress, 143
  evidence for, 153
  On the Harmonious Woman, 142, 154
  On Wisdom. See *On Wisdom* (Perictione)
  originality and contribution, 166–69
  and Pythagorean women, 153–56
  virtue and wisdom, 143
Plato, 229–32
  Crito, 100
  elitism, 232
  feminism, 230, 245
  gender in, 21, 23
  Laws, 134, 230, 237
  location of the female, 28, 30
  Meno, 23, 100

Phaedo, 144, 170, 180, 183
Phaedrus, 183
'pregnant in body', 27
procreation, 28, 30
Republic. See *Republic* (Plato)
Symposium, 21, 24, 183, 204
Timaeus, 233, 236
transmigration of souls, 230
Platonism, 228
  gender as feature of embodiment, 228
Pliny the Elder, 87, 88
Plotinus, 194
  causation, 191
  three hypostases, 191
Plutarch, 77, 81, 82, 84, 90
Pomeroy, Sarah, 138, 139, 154
Porphyry, 193, 194
Proclus, 192, 195, 232–38, 244
  city vs citizens, 234
  gender of souls, 236
  Limit and the Unlimited, 193, 237
  possibility/benefit theses, 233
ps-Archytas, 153, 166
Pythagoras and Pythagoreanism, 136, 140
Pythagorean texts, 134, 154
  content, 134
  Hellenistic dating of, 139
  methodology, 134
  as pedagogy, 135, 151
  as philosophy, 135, 140
  sexual mores, 142, 145, 150
Pythagorean women
  source material, 136

Republic (Plato), 27, 36, 59, 134, 146, 202, 228, 237
  modern interpretations, 232
  Philosopher Queens, 26, 228
  women as guardians, 228, 230

Seneca, 114, 118, 120
  Consolatio ad Marciam, 120
  Hercules Furens, 124–26
  Lucretia, 121
  misogyny, 118
  on death, 123
  On Marriage, 118
  and Paulina (wife), 123–24
Socrates, 25, 34, 58–59, 100–1, 170
Sosipatra of Ephesus, 196–201
  Eunapius *Lives*, 196
  as literary character, 208
  as philosopher, 198, 199

Sosipatra of Ephesus (cont.)
  as psychologically androgynous, 200
  as teacher, 196
  as theurgist, 197, 198
Stoic women
  evidence for, 115, 117
  as philosophers, 117, 133
  in story, 119–21
  in theory, 116–19
  in tragedy, 125–27, 131–33
Stoicism, 116
  evidence for, 115
  gender equality, 114
  marriage, 114, 116
  virtue, 115, 116, 118, 121, 127
Sulabha
  cf. Diotima, 43
  debate with Janaka, 43–44
  as feminist resource, 56
  on gender, 51–55
  historicity, 41
  as literary character, 42
  male-mediated voice of, 43
  as philosopher, 52–55, 56
  on renunciation, 48–51
  on rhetoric, 44–48
  on speech, 46
Synesius (letters), 201, 203, 205

Theano, 136–37, 145, 236
Themista, 81, 83, 88, 90–92
Theodore of Asine, 235–36
Theophila, 92
Theophrastus, 87
Therigathā, 40

Upanishads, 40, 44

value theory, 145
voluntaria mors, 120, 121–25
VSM *Vita Sanctae Macrinae. See under* Gregory
  of Nyssa

Xenophon
  Oeconomicus, 134

Zeno of Citium, 116
  Republic, 116

For EU product safety concerns, contact us at Calle de José Abascal, 56–1°, 28003 Madrid, Spain or eugpsr@cambridge.org.

www.ingramcontent.com/pod-product-compliance
Ingram Content Group UK Ltd.
Pitfield, Milton Keynes, MK11 3LW, UK
UKHW021901010326
468546UK00019B/828